DEVELOPMENTS IN

FAMILY THERAPY

DEVELOPMENTS IN FAMILY THERAPY

Theories and applications
since 1948

Sue Walrond-Skinner

ROUTLEDGE & KEGAN PAUL LIMITED
London, Boston and Henley

First published in 1981
by Routledge & Kegan Paul Ltd
39 Store Street,
London WC1E 7DD
9 Park Street,
Boston, Mass. 02108, USA and
Broadway House,
Newtown Road,
Henley-on-Thames,
Oxon RG9 1EN
Printed in Great Britain by
St Edmundsbury Press
Bury St Edmunds, Suffolk

British Library Cataloguing in Publication Data

Developments in family therapy.
  1. Family psychotherapy
  I. Walrond - Skinner, Sue
  616.89'156   RC488.5

ISBN 0-7100-0812-0

CONTENTS

CONTRIBUTORS

Arnon Bentovim
Consultant Child Psychiatrist, Department of Psychological Medicine, The Hospital for Sick Children, Great Ormond Street, London.

Dora Black
Consultant Child Psychiatrist, Edgware General Hospital and Honorary Consultant, The Hospital for Sick Children, Great Ormond Street, London.

John Bowlby
Honorary Consultant Psychiatrist, Department for Children and Parents, Tavistock Clinic, London.

Peter Bruggen
Consultant Psychiatrist, Adolescent Unit, Hill End Hospital, St Albans, Hertfordshire.

John Byng-Hall
Consultant Psychiatrist and Co-Chairman, Family Therapy Programme, Department of Children and Parents, Tavistock Clinic, London, and Institute of Family Therapy, London.

Christopher Dare
Consultant Psychiatrist, Children's Department, The Maudsley Hospital, London, and Institute of Family Therapy, London.

Graham Davies
Senior Registrar, Adolescent Unit, Hill End Hospital, St Albans, Hertfordshire.

Erica De'Ath
Administrator, Centre for Therapeutic Communication, London.

Gill Gorell Barnes
Senior Social Worker, Department of Children and Parents, Tavistock Clinic, London, and Institute of Family Therapy, London.

Warren Kinston
Consultant Psychiatrist, The Academic Department of Child Psychiatry, Institute of Child Health, University of London, and Department of Psychological Medicine, The Hospital for Sick Children, Great Ormond Street, London.

R.D. Laing
Psychiatrist, psychologist and writer

Bryan Lask
Consultant Psychiatrist, Department of Psychological Medicine, The Hospital for Sick Children, Great Ormond Street, London. Lecturer and Tutor in Family Therapy at the Institute of Family Therapy, London.

John R. Lickorish
Formerly Principal Clinical Psychologist, Institute of Family Psychiatry, Ipswich.

Stuart Lieberman
Consultant Psychiatrist, Department of Psychiatry, St George's Hospital Medical School, London.

Susan Lipshitz
Senior Clinical Psychologist, in private practice as a psychotherapist. Currently Research Officer at Bedford College, London.

H.G. Procter
Clinical Psychologist, The Day Hospital, Bridgwater, Somerset.

Anthony Ryle
Director, University Health Service, University of Sussex.

R.D. Scott
Consultant Psychiatrist, Psychiatric Unit, Barnet General Hospital, Hertfordshire.

A.C.R. Skynner
Senior Tutor in Psychotherapy, Institute of Psychiatry, London. Honorary Associate Consultant, The Maudsley Hospital, London and Institute of Family Therapy, London.

Sue Walrond-Skinner
Family Therapist and Lecturer in Social Work, University of Bristol.

ACKNOWLEDGMENTS

The editor and publishers are grateful to the following for permission to reproduce material which has previously been published: Plenum Publishing Corporation for chapter 1 (from 'Human Relations', vol. 2, no. 123, 1949, pp. 123-8); Patrick Seale Books Ltd for chapter 2 (published by the Association of Family Caseworkers and the Philadelphia Association, 1969); 'Journal of Child Psychology and Psychiatry' and Pergamon Press for chapter 3 (from vol. 10, 1969, pp. 81-106); 'Social Work Today' for chapter 4 (from vol. 4, no. 3, 1973, pp. 65-70); the British Psychological Society for chapter 5 (from 'British Journal of Medical Psychology', vol. 46, 1973, pp. 239-50); Pergamon Press for chapter 6 (from 'Journal of Child Psychology and Psychiatry', vol. 19, 1978, pp. 57-62); 'British Journal of Psychiatry' for chapter 7 (from vol. 131, November 1977, pp. 433-47); 'Family Process' for chapter 8 (from vol. 13, no. 4, 1974, pp. 443-59); the British Psychological Society for chapter 11 (from 'British Journal of Medical Psychology', vol. 46, 1973, pp. 45-55 and 57-67); Pergamon Press and 'Journal of Child Psychology and Psychiatry' for chapter 12 (from vol. 19, 1978, pp. 1-12 and 119-43); the British Psychological Society for chapter 13 (from 'British Journal of Medical Psychology', vol. 48 (1975), pp. 39-48 'Family Process' for chapter 14 (from vol. 14, no. 4, December 1975, pp. 535-58).

INTRODUCTION
Sue Walrond-Skinner

British writers on the family as the unit of treatment have
made an important contribution to the family therapy literature.
This book presents a selection of previously published and original
British papers which retain relevance and interest for family therapists in the 1980s. It is divided into three parts, covering theory,
application to specific clinical situations, and differential approaches
within the modality. The papers in part 3 and two of the papers in
part 2 were specially written for this book and thus reflect the most
recent thinking on the topics covered.

Family therapy in this country has moved a long way since its
beginnings, marked by Bowlby's early paper which appropriately
opens part 1. As is by now well known, this paper holds some claim
to have initiated the whole family therapy movement, since it was on
reading Bowlby's paper (and misunderstanding the extent to which
Bowlby was engaging in conjoint therapeutic work) that John Elder-
kin Bell embarked on his own formative contributions in America
(Bell, 1961). Almost nothing appeared in the British literature during the 1950s, and the early 1960s saw only rather tentative attempts
at conceptualising the leap from individual casework, counselling
and psychotherapy, to the treatment of the family system. It is
obvious, looking back, that much quiet experimentation was going
on within workers' own practices, some of which found its way into
the professional journals (Howells, 1962; Martin and Knight, 1962;
Elles, 1961 and 1962; Roberts, 1968; Robinson, 1968 and Chandler
et al., 1968).

Elsewhere (Walrond-Skinner, 1979), I have noted the enormously
influential 'scene setting' work of R.D. Laing and his colleagues
which was occurring during this time, and one of whose papers
provides the next landmark for us in this collection. These two contributions by Bowlby and Laing are of particular interest. They
display both the simplicity and profundity of the change of approach
required of all who embark on the treatment of the family group,
whatever our original training. The difficulty of embracing and
retaining an approach to the family as a system was experienced
powerfully in the 1960s, as Skynner (1979) has described in relation to the publication of the paper reprinted here, and a considerable amount of anxiety attended the open acknowledgment of involvement in conjoint family work. Skynner's paper shows how far family

1

therapy had developed by the late 1960s. But it was the 1970s which saw the real burgeoning of interest in Britain, with family therapy becoming a powerfully novel reorienting paradigm within the mental health and social care fields. Agencies began to set up specialist units; training courses were started; an Association for Family Therapy was formed, with its own Journal; and the publication of clinical and research material increased.

Yet in the midst of all this activity, the British approach, in contrast to family therapy practised in the USA, has needed less urgently to claim that family therapy has made all things new. It has been more mindful (though not, I would argue, mindful enough) of the subtle influences from many different fields that have been responsible for the development of the family therapy modality and more sure of its historical perspective. British writers such as Skynner (1976) have drawn together the complex web of theoretical influences that have fertilised and enriched the family therapy field, though the lack of a sociological perspective or of more than a sideways glance at the field of family studies and research is remarkable, as Reiger (1981) has pointed out. Some would criticise the bulk of British family therapy on the grounds that it has been too influenced by a psychoanalytic past and has thus been less able to affirm its unique character as a form of psychotherapy involving a discontinuous change to a systems perspective. It is certainly true that the seed of family therapy in Britain has been nurtured in some of the traditional strongholds of psychodynamic thinking; but writers in this country, as the contributions in this volume will demonstrate, are making strenuous efforts to integrate reflective, existential and psychodynamic ideas within a systemic approach to relationship difficulties. Family therapy also requires the powerful ideas stemming from communication theory to help sharpen its identity within the largely psychodynamically influenced sphere of psychotherapy as a whole, for if family therapy rests too easily within a psychodynamic framework, enjoying the respectability that this confers, the price may be an erosion of its interactional perspective. However, there are tremendous difficulties in reconciling an over-emphasis on 'technology', which the strategic approach increasingly involves, with a therapy that is morally robust and fully committed to the integrity of persons in relationship. Nor do we solve the problem by asserting that all therapies are manipulative and potentially abusing of the person. There are obvious social and political reasons why the sphere of therapy in America should currently be so pervaded by ideas of skill, directiveness, strategy, targets, problem-solving, brevity and the evaluation of results. Conditions existing within the social macro-system cannot but pervade the therapeutic field. Americans, in common with the West in general, are having to come to terms with the fact that not all problems appear to have solutions. The limits to the supply of energy and other natural resources, the intransigent problems of the economy, the baffling prospect of a continuously escalating arms race - all these issues and many more seem to compel both a frenetic search for solutions and a growing despair in case none is to be found. This kind of milieu is pervasive and it is not surprising that the com-

plexity of family problems appears as overwhelming to the therapist
as social and political problems do to the politician. Both can be
tempted to seek and promise short-term global solutions. But if life
is more of a mystery to be lived than a problem to be solved, we
only diminish our abilities as therapists to get alongside the experiences of our families with a view to helping them both to accept and
to change, if we ally ourselves unthinkingly with the political and
social imperatives of our time. Far from enabling us to be more
effective as therapists of the family system, the strategic approach
may, in the long term, endanger our ability to engage existentially
with the unique culture of each family we meet and may diminish the
stamina demanded of us in entering into the struggle against hope-
lessness and despair. This is why the strategic approach's emphasis
on behaviour change, without the steadying influence of other perspectives, may lead us along the dangerous path of vitiating the
moral commitment of the person of the therapist to the persons of
the family, for it puts us in danger of endlessly refining our technique while neglecting a broader understanding of the human condition. As Sander (1974) points out, 'Family therapy has demonstrated
as a modality that it too can achieve symptomatic improvement. But
to embrace behavioural change as a raison d'être of family therapy
will doom its further development' (pp. 467-8). Sander suggests
that, 'Perhaps when we develop our family theories further, we can
go beyond [these] quickie miraculous-sounding strategies' (p. 466),
and points out that 'the emphasis on behaviour change and symptom
removal restricts the potentiality of the family approach to that of
psychoanalysis in 1895, when it was a naive, simplistic and mech-
anistic approach' (p. 461). Viewed from a different perspective, it
may be that the therapist's task is to share 'his own transient
uncertainty' with the family, as Kempler puts it (quoted by De'Ath,
p. 327, this volume) rather than to formulate 'solutions' to 'problems'.

A further difficulty posed by the strategic school of family therapy
is that its followers seem to take an imperialist view of their particular method in relation to the modality as a whole. Writers such as
Haley, Watzlawick and Weakland strongly differentiate their approach
from others on the false assumption that it is more fundamentally
systems-based than other methods. In contrast, most of the contri-
butors to this volume would, I think, reject Mandanes and Haley's
assertion (1977) that 'a therapy based on psychodynamics has an
individual focus whether a person is seen alone or in a family
group' (p. 91). Whatever these writers may say, it is, I believe,
perfectly possible to treat the *family* as the patient and yet to focus
attention on the family's history, the family's interlocking developmental crises, and the shared unconscious myths and symbolic processes operating within the family group. (See Byng-Hall, 1973,
this volume.) Even the distinction between individually-based psychotherapy and family therapy - a fundamental point of agreement
among all family therapists - should not, as Dare in chapter 15
points out, result in the cavalier dismissal of essential therapeutic
insights.

Confusingly, however, the strategists appear at one and the same
time both to claim a monopoly over the systems concept and then to

discard its centrality. Haley (1980), for example, sets out the limitations of systems theory as he sees it, listing it as one of those unfortunate ideas that have handicapped therapists. Brilliant and imaginative as are the intervention strategies described, they frequently do not address themselves to the *system* of relationships. Thus, the varied and innovative techniques of the strategic approach, whilst being worthy of serious consideration by all family therapists, should not be elevated to the position of a rival theoretical superstructure whereby they discredit the cornerstone of family therapy itself. On this cornerstone rests the value that family therapy places on us as social beings, for in family therapy, the meaning of the 'other' becomes central not as a competitor with the 'self' but as a means towards its affirmation. Thus, we are only fully human when we are systemically bound up with each other. Family therapy as a modality is therefore a systems-based interactionally focused treatment, whether the method employed be psychoanalytic, experiential, structural or strategic. Its focus is always on the interpersonal experience of members of the natural social system, the family, whether the primary focus is on current behavioural interpersonal events or on past shared unconscious interpersonal material. It is the system, not the individual, that must be the target of the family therapist's intervention, whatever his orientation. Thus, the pages in this collection do not reflect the strategic school's contribution to family therapy, partly because of the reservations I have already expressed and partly because British family therapists have, on the whole, developed other approaches, and I felt that these offered a fairer reflection of the state of family therapy in Britain in the 1980s.

In the main, family therapy in Britain has been less preoccupied with differentiating schools and methods of approach and more interested in integrating the essential insights of several approaches into a more coherent whole. This refusal to enter into polemics (a notable and unfortunate exception being Treacher and Street, 1980) stems partly from the recognition that such a preoccupation may only arise from a need to cloak the indecent transparency of family therapy's basic insight, for our focus as family therapists is not on the intriguing issues of psychopathology as presented to a psychiatrist, a social worker or a clinical psychologist. It is instead, as Dare (1979) points out, often a rather unsophisticated, mundane affair:

> The topics that the therapist and family members grapple with are extremely mundane . . . the content of a family therapy session is concerned with the demonstration and acceptance of love and care, the management of household tasks, the reflection of the marital relationship onto the life and experience of the children, the impact of the conflicting demands of work and family life on the parents and the tension of the childhood lives of the parents and the continuing or absent contact with the family of their childhood. The topics are to do with the fact of family life, not the presence of a labelled disturbed family member. (pp. 1-2)

The papers presented in this book attempt to weld together ideas from the behavioural, psychodynamic and experiential spheres of interest. Inevitably, some excellent papers have been omitted and, of course, none has been included from the new Journal of Family Therapy since they are easily available to family therapists through the journal itself. Hopefully, this collection will go some way towards linking family therapy's past to its present in this country, and will point the way in turn towards the future.

REFERENCES

Bell, J.E. (1961), 'Family Group Therapy', Public Health monograph, 64, US Department of Health, Education and Welfare.
Chandler, E., Holden, H.M. and Robinson, M. (1968), Treatment of a Psychotic Family in a Family Psychiatry Setting, in 'Psychotherapy and Psychosomatics', vol. 16, pp. 339-47.
Dare, C. (1979), Editorial comment in 'Journal of Family Therapy', vol. 1, no. 1, pp. 1-5.
Elles, G. (1961), Collateral Treatment in a Family by Psychoanalytic Techniques, in 'British Journal of Psychiatric Social Work', vol. 6, no. 1, pp. 3-12.
Elles, G. (1962), Treatment of a Family Problem Linked with Psychopathic Illness, in 'Case Conference', vol. 9, pp. 91-6, 135-40 and 153-8.
Haley, J. (1980), 'Leaving Home: The Therapy of Disturbed Young People', New York: McGraw-Hill.
Howells, J. (1962), The Nuclear Family as the Functional Unit in Psychiatry, in 'Journal of Mental Science', vol. 108.
Mandanes, C. and Haley, J. (1977), Dimensions of Family Therapy, in 'Journal of Mental and Nervous Disease', vol. 165, no. 2, pp. 88-98.
Martin, F. and Knight, J. (1962), Joint Interviews as Part of Intake Procedure in a Child Psychiatric Clinic, in 'Journal of Child Psychology and Psychiatry', vol. 3, no. 1, pp. 17-24.
Reiger, S. (1981), Family Therapy's Missing $64 Question, *Why* the Plight of the Modern Family?, in 'Journal of Family Therapy', vol. 3
Roberts, M. (1968), Working with the Family Group in a Child Guidance Clinic, in 'British Journal of Psychiatric Social Work', vol. 9, no. 4, pp. 175-80.
Robinson, M. (1968), Family Based Therapy, in 'British Journal of Psychiatric Social Work', vol. 9, no. 4, pp. 188-93.
Sander, F. (1974), Freud's 'A Case of Successful Treatment by Hypnotism (1892-1893)': An Uncommon Therapy?, in 'Family Process', vol. 13, no. 4, pp. 461-8.
Skynner, A.C.R. (1979), Reflections on the Family Therapist as Scapegoat, in 'Journal of Family Therapy', vol. 1, no. 1, pp. 7-22.
Skynner, A.C.R. Reflections on the Family Therapist as Scapegoat, in 'Journal of Family Therapy', vol. 1, no. 1, pp. 7-22.
Treacher, A. and Street, E. (1980), Some Further Reflections on Family Therapists as Scapegoats - a Reply to Robin Skynner, in 'Journal of Family Therapy', vol. 2, no. 1, pp. 1-21.

Walrond-Skinner, S. (ed.) (1979), 'Introduction to Family and Marital Psychotherapy', Routledge & Kegan Paul, pp. 1-12.

Part 1

THEORY INTO PRACTICE

1 THE STUDY AND REDUCTION OF GROUP TENSIONS IN THE FAMILY*

John Bowlby

Child guidance workers all over the world have come to recognise more and more clearly that the overt problem which is brought to the clinic in the person of the child is not the real problem; the problem which as a rule we need to solve is the tension between all the different members of the family. Child guidance is thus concerned not with children but with the total family structure of the child who is brought for treatment. This outlook is especially helpful when we think of the family group as a structured group of a kind not dissimilar in its nature and dynamics from any other structured group, for instance a factory group. Many of the same principles of approach appear to apply. Those working in the field of industrial relations have often emphasised how much they have learnt from those of us working in clinics. We on the child guidance side now feel it is our turn to be grateful, because in the last two years we have learnt a great deal from the experience and methods of our industrially oriented colleagues.

In the case of both child guidance and industrial consultation, the problem which is brought, be it a child who bites his nails, or a difficulty in selecting foremen, is seen to be but a symptom of a more complex problem. In each case the problem is commonly found to involve many, even all, the people with whom the so-called patient comes into contact. With the child, the problem usually lies in the relationships between him and the members of his family. With the industrial worker, it lies in the relationships between all members of the factory, from management downwards. In each case our first task is to reorient those consulting us, in order to help them see the real problem, of which they themselves are probably a part, and to see the alleged problem in its true light as a symptom. Such reorientation is, of course, the traditional role of the physician who, consulted about headache or rash, is concerned to discover the disease process, in the knowledge that treatment of the symptom only is futile and perhaps dangerous.

It is notorious in child guidance work that one of our principal difficulties is that of obtaining parental co-operation in resolving the adverse family relations. A similar difficulty arises, often less obviously but no less really, in industrial work, where management may be very loath to continue co-operation when it realises that this may require extensive reconsideration of its relations with workers. Faced with a situation where the co-operation of key people is difficult to maintain, there is a temptation for the professional worker to solve the group problem by removing one or more of the individuals concerned. In industry, management may wish to sack the trouble-maker. A similar procedure in child guidance has been to take the child out of the home and put him elsewhere. Although occasionally unavoidable, this seems to me a policy of despair.

The procedure which we are using in the Tavistock - in child guidance, in adult patient groups, and in industrial work - is different. In all these situations where there is tension in a group of people, it is our aim to help them to live together and to resolve their tensions. We do this in the belief that the experience of understanding and working through these tensions is itself valuable as giving all members of the group insight into the nature of their difficulties, and insight also into techniques whereby similar problems can be overcome in future.

Procedures of this kind presuppose that members of the group have a need and a drive to live together in accord. One of the striking things which we meet with in child guidance work is the tremendously strong drive which exists in almost all parents and children to live together in greater harmony. We find that, though caught up in mutual jealousies and hostilities, none of them enjoys the situation, and all are desperately seeking for happier relations. Our task is thus one of promoting conditions in which the constructive forces latent in social groups can come into play. I liken it to the job of a surgeon: he does not mend bones - he tries to create conditions which permit bones to mend themselves. In group therapy, and in treating the tensions of groups, the aim should be to bring about those conditions which permit the group to heal itself.

Now, there are many ways of setting about this. The purpose of this paper is to indicate some of the methods which we are trying in the child guidance clinic at this time. I emphasise trying, as we certainly have not arrived at any clear conclusions. First, we do not nowadays undertake systematic, individual treatment of a case until we have made a contact with the father. To those of us who hitherto have not done this as a routine, the experience is a revelation. In the past many of us have tended to leave the father out until we have got into difficulties, and then have sought to bring him in. But by insisting that everyone relevant in the case should have an early opportunity of making his contribution, and of finding out whether he wants to collaborate with us, we find the way towards collaboration very much smoother. These first steps in a case are vital and repay very careful study, but I shall not say more about them here.

The clinical problems with which we are faced are, very often, those of families where there is a nagging mother, and a child who is rebelling: there is mutual irritation and jealousy and father is tending to take one side or the other, thereby making matters worse. In addition to individual interviewing, we have been attempting, experimentally, to deal with these tensions by bringing all parties

together in a long session and examining the problems from the
point of view of each.

AN ILLUSTRATIVE CASE

To illustrate this technique I will describe a case that I have been
treating for a long time now. When originally referred two and a
half years ago, Henry was aged 13, and was attending a grammar
school, for which he was well suited on grounds of intelligence.
However, his work was poor and he had a bad reputation for being
lazy, untidy, and unco-operative. His mother, a very unhappy
woman, was intensely bitter about him and poured forth complaints
about his behaviour at home. He was dirty, untidy, disobedient,
and cruel to his sister (five years younger than he), and for ever
meddling with the electricity or plumbing, so that either they had
no electric light or the house was flooded. The history showed that
there had been tension between this boy and his mother since his
early years, that it had become exacerbated after his sister's birth
and had festered on ever since.
   The nature of the problem and its origins were fairly clear. The
solution, however, was far from easy. The mother had no insight
into the part she was playing, and blamed the boy. The boy was
equally hostile and critical towards his mother, and had equally little
insight into his own contribution. Each wanted to get the clinic on
his side against the other. Because of this intense mutual suspicion,
and because I feared that I would not get the boy's co-operation if
his mother also came to the clinic, I decided (probably mistakenly)
to work alone with the boy, keeping in touch with the home and discussing the situation with the headmaster to see how far the boy
could be helped at school. Progress was imperceptible. School reports remained very bad and the tension situation at home acute,
as was shown by occasional interviews with father or mother. During
therapeutic sessions Henry was evasive, although, as time went on,
confidence in the therapist's good intentions increased. As might be
expected there was a very strong negative transference, and opposition to analytic work was as pronounced as was his opposition to
school work or helping in the home. (All these connections were, of
course, interpreted.) After two years of weekly treatment sessions,
very many of which were missed, I decided to confront the main
actors with the problem as I saw it. Thus, I planned a session in
which I could see father, mother and boy together. This proved a
very interesting and valuable session, and it is important to note
that it lasted two hours, since it would have been very little use
had it been limited to one.
   Most of the first hour was spent in each member of the family complaining how very unpleasant and difficult the others were. A great
deal of bitter feeling was expressed and, had we left off at that
point, the session would have been most unconstructive. During this
time I had spoken little, but during the second hour I began making
interpretations. I made it clear to them that I thought each one of

them was contributing to the problem, and described the techniques of hostility each used. I also traced out the history of the tension, starting, as I knew it had, in the boy's early years, and gave illustrations of the incidents which had occurred. I pointed out that the mother's treatment of the boy, especially her insistence on immediate obedience and her persistent nagging, had had a very adverse effect on Henry's behaviour, but I also stated that I felt sure that her mistaken treatment of Henry was the result of her own childhood, which I had little doubt had been unhappy. For nearly half an hour thereafter she told us, through her tears, about her childhood and of her very unhappy relation with her parents – this, remember, in front of her husband, who may have known, and her 15-year-old son, who undoubtedly knew little of it.

After ninety minutes the atmosphere had changed very greatly and all three were beginning to have sympathy for the situation of the other. It was at this point that the desire of each one of them to live together happily with the others began to come into the open – it was of course present from the beginning, for without it the session would have had no chance of success. However, in the final half-hour this need, which each one of them felt, to live more amicably with the others, manifested itself openly and each one of them realised that it was present in the others. A constructive discussion followed. We discussed Henry's irritating and self-frustrating behaviour at home and at school from the point of view of how best he could be helped to change, which he obviously wanted to do, and how nagging made him worse. We discussed his mother's nagging from the point of view of her anxiety and its relation to her childhood; father remarked that the neighbours had for long criticised them both for nagging the boy too much. We discussed father's educational ambitions for Henry and the bitterness his son's failure had induced in him. In this final half hour all three found themselves co-operating in an honest endeavour to find new techniques for living together, each realising that there was a common need to do so and that the ways they had set about it in the past had defeated their object. This proved the turning point in the case.

RELATION OF JOINT INTERVIEW TECHNIQUE TO OTHER THERAPEUTIC TECHNIQUES

Now this technique stems directly from techniques used by Bion[1] in adult group therapy and by members of the Tavistock Institute of Human Relations for dealing with tensions in social groups in industry.[2] It is a technique whereby the real tensions existing between individuals in the group are dealt with freely and openly in the group, much as, in an individual analysis, the tensions existing between different psychic systems within the individual are dealt with freely and openly with the analyst. At what point in handling a case the technique of joint interview is appropriate we do not yet know, though it appears that, before it can be used effectively some private contact must be made with each member separately.

Private interviews afterwards, to work through material raised, are
also essential. My next interview in the case described was with the
mother, to work through her childhood history and its reference to
the present, and to work through also her relation to myself. Though
she resented what she had felt to be my criticism of her treatment
of her son, she also remarked what a good thing it would have
been had her own parents had the benefits of clinical help. After a
joint session of the kind described, private interviews are very different from what they are before. In the first place, the attempt of
each party in the dispute to get the therapist on his side, and his
fear that another party has probably already succeeded in this, are
both much reduced. There has been a first hand demonstration of
neutrality. Second, each has had a demonstration of the existence
in the others of a desire to mend the relationship. The real situation, even if bad, is then found to be far less alarming and hopeless
than the fantasy each had had of it.

I wish to emphasise that, so far as its use at the Tavistock Clinic
is concerned, this technique is still in an experimental stage. Though
we rarely employ it more than once or twice in a particular case,
we are coming to use it almost as routine after the initial examination
and before treatment is inaugurated. A joint interview at this time is
valuable as being an opportunity for the workers to convey their
opinion of the problem to parents and child together, extending
help to all and blaming none. Though one such joint interview can
never effect entirely the reorientation required - phantasies and
misconceptions of many kinds will remain - experience suggests that
it sets a process of reorientation in train, which can be developed
later in private interviews. These private interviews are commonly
carried on by two professional workers, psychiatrist or psychotherapist with the child, psychiatric social worker with the mother.
When this is the plan, it is essential that both workers should participate in the joint interview, since strong emotional responses are
evoked, which cannot be dealt with later by a worker who was not
present. In particular it is essential for the psychiatric social
worker to be present at such a joint interview, since it will usually
be her task to continue work with the parents helping them to understand their part in the problem and the nature and origin of any
unfavourable attitudes they may have to the child.

When I first came to consider this technique, I felt not a little
apprehensive of the scenes in which I might get involved. How much
safer to keep the warring parties apart, to divide and conquer! But
the recognition of the basic fact that people really do want to live
happily together and that this drive is working for us gives confidence, much as a knowledge of the miraculous healing powers of the
body gives confidence to the surgeon. Even so, one cannot help
asking oneself whether it is a good thing for all these problems to
be discussed in front of the child. But, once again, the answer is
reassuring - in a fragmentary and recriminatory way they have already been discussed many times before. There is nothing new in
the material discussed - but the atmosphere in which it is discussed
is different and, one hopes, better. I have come, in fact, no longer

to be alarmed by the hideous scenes which may occasionally ensue in the use of this technique - the violent accusations, the cruel sarcasm, the vitriolic threats. The fact that these scenes occur in one's consulting room is most unpleasant, but we know that they have occurred before and that, if they occur in our consulting rooms, there is a chance that the parent may be helped towards a different view, and the child can observe that the therapist is, at least, not allying himself with his accuser. By focusing our work on the tension existing between the child patient and the members of his family group, we are adding to the child guidance techniques already in use - psychotherapy along analytic lines, therapeutic interviews with parents, remedial teaching and so on - and developing techniques which permit of the direct study and therapy of the tension within the group.

CIRCULAR REACTIONS IN FAMILY AND OTHER SOCIAL GROUPS

Moreover, it is not unimportant that the use of these techniques influences the social behaviour of others besides the child. In the case I have described it was not only Henry who was helped in his social relations, his father and mother were helped also. And just as Henry's relations at school have been materially better during the past months, so, I believe, have his father's in the factory and his mother's in her office. Thus, child guidance work may be expected to contribute towards more co-operative industrial relations, in the same way that social psychologists working in the industrial field may be expected to contribute towards better family relations, through their influence on industrial personnel who are also parents. Margaret Mead[3] has spoken of the vicious circle of insecure parents creating insecure children, who grow up to create an insecure society which in its turn creates more insecure parents. It is clear that there is much truth in this picture, yet it is only half the truth. The interconnections which Margaret Mead emphasises can lead to beneficent circles as well as vicious. Though tension and friction in industry will lead to irritable workers taking it out on their wives and children at home, happy and co-operative relations in the factory will lead to contented workers treating their wives and children kindly. Moreover, employees in a factory are likely, to a degree far greater than they realise, to model their behaviour towards their children on the pattern the management adopts towards them. Dictatorial and punishing management is likely to increase the dictatorial and punishing attitudes of the workers towards their children; equally, democratic and participatory behaviour by management will encourage such parental attitudes in their employees. In a similar way changes brought about within the family group may lead to children growing up to be individually either more anxious and difficult and likely to increase tension and friction at their work and in their homes, or also friendly and co-operative and thus able to adopt friendly give-and-take relations in their working and domestic lives. Such repercussions are obvious and will one day have to be

taken into account quantitatively when we assess the value of our
therapeutic techniques.

Techniques of changing key social relationships can thus have far-
reaching repercussions either for good or for evil, in the same way
that man's agricultural methods can greatly improve soil fertility or
finally destroy it. We see, furthermore, that to attain the end of a
secure, contented and co-operative community, in which parents
can give love and security to their children, enabling them to grow
up to be stable and contented people, able to sustain and further a
just and friendly society, no one point in the circle is more vital
than another. The vicious circle may be broken at any point, the
virtuous circle may be promoted at any point. We may thus review
our therapeutic resources - each designed for its particular task
and each originating to some extent independently of the others -
social therapy in industry, child guidance, marriage guidance,
group therapy of adults, psycho-analysis of key individuals, therapeutic transitional communities, and others - as specialised parts of
one great therapeutic endeavour: that of reducing tensions and of
fostering understanding co-operation within groups of human beings.

---

*Adapted from a paper read during a Specialist Meeting of the
International Congress on Mental Health, August 1948.

REFERENCES

1   W.R. Bion, Experiences in Groups, 'Human Relations', vol. I,
    no. 3, 1948; W.R. Bion and J. Rickman, Intra-group Tensions
    in Therapy: Their Study as a Task of the Group, 'Lancet',
    November 1943.
2   Elliott Jaques, Interpretive Group Discussion as a Method of
    Facilitating Social Change, 'Human Relations', vol. I, no. 4, 1948.
3   Margaret Mead, The Individual and Society, paper read at the
    International Congress on Mental Health, August 1948, published
    in the proceedings of the Congress.

2 INTERVENTION IN SOCIAL SITUATIONS

R. D. Laing

The common ground between social workers and psychiatrists is the study of and intervention in social situations.

Studying and intervening in social situations is not all that social workers or psychiatrists do, but it is something we are always doing, whatever else we do. When a doctor, in a purely medical capacity, diagnoses tonsillitis in a child, or cancer in an adult, and orders the child into hospital for tonsillectomy, or the parent into hospital for investigation and operation, he is clearly intervening in a social situation to which, however, he usually has neither the time, nor the interest, to give more than passing notice. We hope family practitioners realise, and often they do, that 'purely' medical decisions have massive reverberations in a whole network of people, with consequences to many other than the patient alone. But in a medical emergency the person's physical health is usually felt to take precedence over all else, and the social reverberations generated by the medical emergency and the medical steps taken to cope with it are, more often than not left to reverberate away.

The child goes into hospital, yet it is difficult to keep track of even the individual let alone the social consequences of such a momentous event. We should not require research workers to tell us that there must be profound repercussions in the family system when a child or a parent is hospitalised. Hardly any psychiatrists, and too few social workers, fully realise the extent of social resistances against admitting these social repercussions. Yet I would guess that they are always considerable, and may be both unrecognised and catastrophic.

For some years I have been directly concerned with the study of people in situations. Usually I am 'called in', to a 'situation' which has already been defined by the people in it, and possibly also by other agents of society, as one in which there is 'something the matter' with one person in the situation: the others do not know what to do about him or her: it is implied that if that one person were all right the situation would right itself. That is, I am called into a social crisis, defined as (regarded as due to, caused by, generated by, occasioned by, provoked by), a medical emergency.

There are many types of social crisis: when defined as a medical emergency, the view usually is that if the medical emergency is dealt with, that is, if the patient is treated adequately and recovers, then this will resolve the social crisis (provided this crisis has not generated another: e.g. an economic crisis). When a particular social situation is defined as a social crisis occasioned by a medical emergency, this definition is a call for a particular type of action: it is an unequivocal prescription to get one person right by 'treatment' and, if thought necessary, to give auxiliary help to the other members of the situation to cope with illness in the one person, and with its secondary social consequences. The definition of the situation and the call for action are two sides of the same coin. The unique rational strategy of intervention is prescribed in and through the definition of the situation.

Much of the area between social work, medicine and psychiatry concerns such situations: the family of a retarded child, families where there is a physical disability in one person. In many cases, we talk about a mental disability (excluding subnormality, and other clearly organic conditions) acute or chronic; we construe the situation in terms of the above schema, and act towards it in the particular way demanded by those terms.

Let us examine some of the practical consequences when this medical model of a social situation is adopted by a team working in the field of psychiatry. Social workers and psychiatrists have to be practical. We have hectic jobs: our theorising is often done in the midst of our activity, or in our spare time when we are not too exhausted. We often discover what we do after we have done it. An advantage of this is a certain empirical pragmatic approach. Disadvantages are that without time for critical reflection we may become dogmatic in theory, and keep repeating ourselves in practice. We may even keep repeating a story about what we repetitiously do which does not even match what we do: especially if we do not have sufficient time to scrutinise what we are actually doing. When what we think we do does not coincide with what we do do, we sink into assumptions which get pickled, as it were, into our attitudes and we may find ourselves (if we ever find ourselves again) so pickled, that we can no longer see what our assumptions are, nor that we are perpetuating practices we do not recognise. Another danger is that we let others do the theorising, while we do the work. None of us can afford to take on trust statements by people who think they can tell us what we are doing, or should be doing: people who do not actually do the practical work themselves, but who feel they are in a position to theorise about it. This is a very dangerous state of affairs, particularly in the relationship between social work and psychiatry.

My impression is that much social work theory is based upon, or heavily influenced by, a medical model derived from psychiatry that psychiatry has itself derived from general medicine: that this psychiatric medical model has been taken, up until very recently at least, on trust even by psychiatrists. This model is in my view treacherous. It is in essence antisocial. It helps us see what is going on about as much as dark glasses in an already darkened room.

I said that the most common way I have been called into a situation is when one person in the situation has come to be regarded by others as having 'something the matter with' him or her: usually, before I encounter the situation, 'expert' opinion has begun to see something 'mentally' the matter with one person in this situation. I will give you an example. You will understand it has to be curtailed and highly schematised.

THE CLARKS

A letter from a child guidance clinic asks me to give an opinion on a 14-year-old boy who had been given a diagnosis at the clinic of? incipient schizophrenia. He had been attending the clinic one afternoon each week for three months seeing a psychiatrist. His mother took him along to the clinic, and she has been having, once a fortnight, a talk with a psychiatric social worker. The boy has not improved; his behaviour at home and at school is deteriorating; his psychiatrist wonders why because he is mute with him most of the time and thinks he might be developing schizophrenia. If this were presumed to be the case, things could be done, such as hospitalization to a child psychiatric unit.

When I receive such a referral letter (leaving out any discussion of the paperwork which is a neglected story) I have to decide not only how to meet the person who is already the elected patient, but how to get the best glimpse in the shortest time of what is going on. This is already not what I have been asked, I was asked for a diagnosis. I have re-defined my task. This is legitimate. Our client does not always define his terms as we would. We should not ignore his terms, but we are not bound to adopt them as ours, even when the client is a psychiatrist.

I could have arranged for mother and boy to come to see me. I could have gone to the clinic to see the boy alone or in a joint consultation with the psychiatrist. I could have done a number of things. What I did was to write asking his mother to telephone me. Over the telephone a visit to their home was arranged with two social therapists, in the early evening, when as many members as possible of the family would be present. We spent about two and a half hours with the nuclear family: the boy's mother, two elder brothers (17 and 15), his younger sister (12) and his father. In this period we saw Mr and Mrs Clark with the children; David alone; Mr and Mrs Clark alone. I was shown around the house and given details of the eating and sleeping and other arrangements of the family.

To pick out one or two bits. We met first in the sitting room: mother, father, a brother of 17 years, a brother of 15 years, David aged 14 and sister aged 12. I asked Mrs Clark at one point:

'Who do your children take after?' Pointing to her eldest son, she said:

'Well, that's his father sitting there.'

'The second son does not take after anyone.'

'Sister takes after David. That's part of the trouble, she is beginning to take after David.'

'Who does David take after?'
'David takes after me.'
'What is the matter with David then?'
The matter with David (Mrs Clark rattles the list off) is that he is completely out of her control, he will not do what he is told, she can't get to the bottom of him, he stays out of the house, he won't tell her when he is coming back, he is not interested in reading or writing, and finally 'he's not worried'.

This in the first twenty minutes. Later she showed me around the house; where the boys slept, where the girl slept, where she and her husband slept and so on. As we stood on the upstairs landing while the rest of the family were downstairs. I asked her:

'How did all this really start?'
'Well, he stays out all the time, he won't tell me when he is coming back, he just won't do what I tell him - he defies me. One afternoon when he was supposed to come back to lunch at 1 o'clock and father was away and he hadn't come in by 2 o'clock - I said "you've got to come in for your meals and you are going to do what I tell you." He said, "No. I won't" and I said, "Yes, you will - If you don't do what I tell you I will send you away" - "Go ahead".'

She did not know what to do. Hardly knowing what she was doing she phoned the police and said in front of him: 'I have a boy here who is out of my control. I don't know what to do with him.' They said 'Wait a minute.' She waited and waited (for two minutes) and then they came back on the phone and told her to take him to her local child guidance clinic and gave her the address. This she did, and they have been going once a week to the local child guidance clinic since then, for the last three months. She feels bad about it now, but David will still not do as he is told and he still does not seem to be worried.

After seeing Mrs Clark, I had a chat with David, both of us standing by the window in the boys' bedroom. It was a man-to-man chat in which he told me what he was doing - he was out with the workmen, helping them on a building site. He wasn't particularly interested in reading or writing but he was very interested in working with things. At the child guidance clinic the only thing he enjoyed was drawing: they had his permission to use his paintings at an exhibition of the children's art (another example perhaps of psychotic art?). But he said the main reason for going to the child guidance clinic was a bad one because he got off school that afternoon: it did not pay because he had to make up on his lessons the following day. I asked if there was anything I could do for him. He asked me to arrange if possible for him not to go to the child guidance clinic. I said I would see what I could do.

In the last forty minutes of the two and a half hours, we met Mrs Clark and Mr Clark without the children.

Mrs Clark had said that David took after her in those respects that the trouble seemed to be about.

Who did *she* take after in that case? She said, right away. 'My father.'

'In that case David takes after his grandfather.' She had not

quite put it together like that, but with only a slight pause she
said:

'Oh yes, of course, that's what my mother is always saying!'

Mother is an only daughter. Father is the younger son of two
brothers; his father (David's father's father) died when father was
a boy. Father's mother is still alive. David's mother's father died
just before David was conceived. David's father developed a close
bond with his first son right away. They had another son. This was
all right with Mrs Clark, but not with her mother-in-law. She had
had two sons: her elder son had had two sons: now her second son
had two sons. She wanted a grand-daughter. So Mrs Clark got pregnant again, to give her mother-in-law a present of a grand-daughter
just after her father died. As it was she produced David, called
after her father. Finally they tried a fourth time, and, thank God
she had a girl this time, who was immediately annexed by Mr Clark's
mother.

Mrs Clark had taken after her father when she was David's age.
He was an easy going sort of chap, out of the house most of the
time, doing what he shouldn't (according to her mother). He would
never tell her what he was up to and who he was with, or why he
would come in late. He was not very interested in making money,
but made enough, and never learnt to read or write. Mrs Clark was
very fond of her dad and took after him, but her mother beat that
out of her and she became a good girl. Now she sees the same things
'coming out of' David. Her mother keeps on telling her that she
should have beaten it out of David as had been done with her. But
she couldn't bring herself to do so and now it is too late. She sometimes feels that she likes him very much and maybe there's nothing
the matter with him. She remembers what she felt like when she was
his age.

From the foregoing it might be difficult to see why David should
have begun to be seen as a possible schizophrenic. The 'schizophrenia' can be helped to come out more in the way the 'history'
is inflected, and with skilful use of appropriate psychiatric schizo-
phrenese. In class he was irritable, distractable and restless (these
are 'hypomanic' terms), but his mother's story that he was impossible,
that she could not do anything with him, invites the term 'negativism';
he did not speak to the psychiatrist ('mutism') he was cheerful when
everyone was very worried '(inappropriate affect'): these are more
schizophrenic terms. This is a game of earnest triviality. Such differential diagnosis of David is an elaborate diversion from the important issue: to diagnose (literally to see through) the social situation.

We can just glimpse in this family a drama perpetuated over three
generations - the players are two women and a man: first, mother,
daughter and father; second, mother, daughter and daughter's son.
Daughter's father dies - daughter conceives a son, to replace her
father. The play's the thing. The actors come and go. As they die,
others are born. The new born enters the part vacated by the newly
dead. The system perpetuates itself over generations; the young are
introduced to the parts that the dead once played. Hence, the drama
continues. The dramatic structure abides, subject to transformations,

whose laws we have not yet formulated and whose existence we have barely begun to fathom.

David is playing the part his grandfather once played. What will happen when he gets married? Marry his grandmother, produce his mother in his daughter, who will marry his father and produce him in his grandson? Who was his grandfather? His grandfather producing his grandson in himself? To talk in terms of identifications is misleading. It is shorthand for, *b* plays the part *a* once played: grandson plays the part his grandfather played. The actors are never the parts they play (in this sense), even though they themselves may confusedly 'identify' themselves with their parts. The above, which I present to you in a very schematic abstract form, is all based on a type of everyday data open to any social worker. It is based on the actual attributions made openly by people about people. It can be put on tape, reproduced, and studied completely objectively.

A very important area of the study of social situations is all that goes on beyond words: the way words are spoken (paralinguistics), the movements of people (kinesics). This data is equally objective, but at present not so easy to reproduce as words. So I have left it out. But none of this can be seen if one studies the situation in a fragmented way.

This case is typical – a psychiatrist had seen the boy: but no one else in the family. A p.s.w. had seen the mother, but not the boy or anyone else. The p.s.w. and psychiatrist had seen each other at case conferences. No one had seen anyone else: or looked at the setting: no one had seen his home, his school, the streets in which he played, or rather, worked. No one had reconstructed the situation. If we are not lulled by habit to regard this as normal practice, is it not an odd way to go about things? If one has 'a referral' say, from a hockey team, because the left back is not playing properly, one wouldn't think only of getting the left back around to one's office, taking a history and giving a Rorschach. At least I hope not. One would also go to see how the team plays hockey. One certainly would get nowhere if one had no idea of hockey, and what games within games can be played through it.

In our type of work no one knows in advance what the situation is. One has to discover it. When one element of the situation is a story told by some members of the situation about the situation to the effect that 'there is something the matter' with someone in the situation, this is already a tricky situation that merits careful investigation. They may be right. Someone may have pneumonia, a brain tumour, epilepsy, etc. It is for the doctor to diagnose and treat such a condition. They may be wrong. Many psychiatrists are still extraordinarily socially naive. Most psychiatrists have never seen a whole family together, and if they do, their medico-clinical model makes it more difficult for them, than for an intelligent layman, to see what is going on. When all the members of a situation start to define a situation as:

'What is the matter with us all' is that we have to cope with what is the matter with him (or her), we must, first of all, put this manoeuvre in brackets, in the situation as we see it. Whether or not there was anything the matter with an elected scapegoat to begin with, there will soon be if this process continues. It is one of the most ancient, well documented, pervasive social processes known. In this case my report was that there was as yet nothing seriously the matter with this boy, but there soon would be (poor prognosis), in that if everyone continued to treat him as they were doing, he would be 'schizophrenic' in six months' time. I suggested that no one should see the boy if he did not wish to see anyone, but that someone have sessions with Mrs Clark and her mother.

This situation is one of many which have the characteristic: 'no one in the situation knows what the situation is'. If one stays in such a situation just a little, say for ninety minutes, one gets more and more lost, confused, disorientated. People talk as though they know what is going on: we come to think they have no idea, nor have we. They act as if they understood each other, when we think no one does. Not all situations are like this, though this is an important class of situation. The example I just gave can be regarded as a subtype of this class; a situation presented as a non situation.

Consider the following situation:

Two parents are worried about their daughter of 16 because they think she has started to take drugs, is keeping bad company, and is not talking to them. They consult a clinic. A p.s.w. in the clinic takes a history from the parents. She consults the psychiatrist. In view of the history she has taken from the parents, an appointment is given to the girl to see the psychiatrist. She does not keep the appointment. She is given another. She turns up an hour late. The psychiatrist finds that her way of communicating to him is defective. He arranges to see the parents together. He tells them that his colleague, the p.s.w., has consulted with him, and he has now seen the girl and in his opinion she is seriously ill; she is likely to be psychotic in six months time unless she comes off drugs: she has no insight into the harm she is doing herself. His recommendation (since she is without insight, is unco-operative, shows no desire to come off drugs, have psychotherapy or give up her association with the bad company she is keeping) is that they should refer her to the children's department and ask that she be brought before a juvenile court as being beyond their care, protection and control.

The psychiatrist has not seen the parents with the girl. She had never heard of the fact that the parents had gone to the clinic until she got a letter from the psychiatrist 'giving' her an appointment. The p.s.w. has not seen the girl. No one has seen the whole family together, no one has ever dreamt of talking to her boyfriend, who comes around the house often. Might it not be civilised to talk the matter over with all concerned including the boyfriend before we start psychotherapising anyone (a form of violence under certain circumstances only more subtle than bringing in the police)? I cannot give details of this situation, but I can say that when it was eventually investigated as a situation, we found one 'real' issue to be between the girl's father and her boyfriend. They both 'smoked' less than average in their school. They were in fact, for their age,

'conservative': they took their stand on principle, as their parents
had done on other matters in their time.

THE SITUATION HAS TO BE DISCOVERED

No one in the situation may know what the situation is. We can never
assume that the people in the situation know what the situation is. A
corollary to this is: the situation has to be discovered. You may
think this is a banal proposition, but consider the implications. The
stories people tell (people here includes all people, parents, children,
fellow social workers, psychiatrists, ourselves) do not tell us simply
and unambiguously what the situation is. These stories are part of
the situation. There is no a priori reason to 'believe' a story, because
anyone tells us it, as is there any a priori reason to disbelieve a
story, because anyone tells us it. Something is not more likely to
be true, because we are told it. One may have good reason, after
putting it to the test, to trust certain people's stories. The stories
we are told and tell are always significant parts of the situation to
be discovered, but their truth value is often negligible.

This includes the stories that professional 'history' takers tell.
Imagine a psychiatric 'history' of Jesus. It is naive to think one dis-
covers a situation by taking a history from one or two parties in the
situation. But such a 'history of' the situation, is a sample of the
situation. What one does when 'taking a history' is not primarily to
discover history. One uncovers a story, that is, one person's way
of defining the situation: this way of defining the situation may be
an important part of the situation we are trying to discover and
define. Nor do dates make history. Dates are discontinuous points –
markers left behind by history: dates are made by history. During
our initial intervention in a situation, it may be very instructive to
hear the stories people tell. Psychiatrists are not experts in sorting
out these stories. They are experts in construing certain situations
in terms of a few standard psychiatric myths.

Everyone has their stories as to why and what is happening. Often
they agree – no more likely to be true thereby. There is no necessary
or constant relationship between what people do, what they think
they do, and what they say they are or have been doing.

When the situation has 'broken down' to the extent that an outside
agency is brought in to help, not only may the people in the situation
not themselves see what the situation is, but also, they may not see
that they do not see it. To realise this may be very frightening for
them, and is frightening enough for us, who are not 'in' it, in the
same way. If they can see they cannot see it, and begin to see it,
we sometimes hope that thereby they will be better able to cope
adequately themselves. But frequently, a contributing cause of the
breakdown of the situation, as well as an effect of the breakdown
(so it seems to us), is that the situation cannot itself be seen by
any of the people in it for what we think we can see it to be.

Any formulation of this type invites us to develop a social theory
of social ignorance and mystification. We must get ourselves off the

hook of applying theories of the 'unconscious' from the psychology
of one person to social situations, where such theory is not
applicable.

Our field of distinctive competence is the study and intervention
into relatively small (micro) social situations: in no social situations
can we assume that the participants know what the situation is; maybe some do - maybe they do not - we cannot take the definition of
the situation as given us by the members of the situation as more
than a story they tell, itself part of the situation we are to discover.
We have to discover what the situation is in the course of our intervention in the situation. One way to discover what a situation is,
(so obvious, and yet frequently not done), is to convene in the one
place, at the one time, the set of people we have good initial reason
to suppose comprise the key elements of the situation (almost always
we shall later discover other key members thereof).

We require to formulate the possible and the most appropriate
strategies of intervention in situations. Case work or psychotherapy
with one person is one strategy of intervention in that situation of
which that one person is a member.

We have hardly begun to list and to classify strategies of intervention, much less to think what may be best adapted to what situations. We have not even systematic typology of situations in the
first place, much less a classification of the ways one may intervene.

For instance: situations are presented to us, defined by the
people in them in the following ways:
1.   Something is the matter with someone.
2.   Nothing is the matter with anyone, but nothing's working
     properly.
3.   Something is the matter with everyone, according to everyone
     else.

In other situations we are called in where the people 'in' the situation, about which there is concern or complaints, say:
4.   Nothing is the matter either with us, or the situation (don't
     bother us, why are you interfering, everything is fine as far
     as we are concerned. But it might not be fine as far as the
     police are concerned or the neighbours).

By what criteria does who decide whose views are 'right'? Is this
an inappropriate question? If we are already embarked on the peril-
ous project of intervening somewhere, it is a different situation for
us, whether the people in the situation say that there's nothing the
matter with them or the situation, or that there is something the
matter with one or two persons in the situation, or that there is
nothing the matter with any of them, but the situation is a mess.
And so on.

I can do no more here and now, than allude to the major task of
finding adequate ways to formulate the problems implicit in the above.

Similarly, I can no more than allude to the whole subject of the
practical strategies of intervention open to us. Let me do so by way
of an example, intended to indicate that there may be many more
possible forms of intervention than we imagine.

This is a story told by Gregory Bateson about a situation in

Hawaii (unpublished. It is in his words.

In a family with ten children there was a little boy, the fifth or
sixth child who had a long delinquent history: he was in and out of
institutions; finally he landed in the hands of a particular psychiatric
casework agency (the Lilinokalani Trust) who are Hawaians themselves.

They have an occidental psychiatrist who works with them and a
young male social worker who went to see the mother of this boy,
the father being dead. The social worker discovered that this
history was related to a broken promise of the mother. When he
learnt this related to a broken promise the social worker wanted to
drop the case at once. Hallucinating schizophrenics are one thing
and everyone knows that this is psychiatry; but when you deal with
broken promises . . . The boy's behaviour seemed 'psychiatric'
but the broken promise seemed to be something else. You deal with
broken promises in Hawaii with ritual precautions. Something can rub
off on you, because every promise contains a curse. You can't get
a Hawaian to promise to come and do your gardening work on a
Saturday for this reason and in old Hawaii they did not make
promises. However, the mother had made a promise to her mother,
that is the grandmother of the patient, that she would never marry
a divorced man – grandma had married a divorced man and it had
turned out wrong and she had her daughter promise not to marry
one. Grandma died – the daughter married a divorced man, had ten
children, the middle one was now the patient.

It is interesting, Bateson says, that in general this broken up
culture remembers what is wrong and how you get into religious and
supernatural trouble but it can't remember the nature of the old
cultural remedies. Perhaps we are further 'gone' than that. We cannot even 'diagnose' what is the matter any more.

In old Hawaii the correct thing to do in the above circumstances
is to have a 'Ho'o Pono Pono'. This is a gathering of the entire
family which may comprise several households of married siblings and
offsprings. In this meeting each member is asked to voice everything
he has against every other member of the group. Having voiced
all the complaints he can think of against members of the group he
is asked by the meeting's chairman (who is usually a priest or maybe the family's head): 'Do you disentangle him?'

To which he must reply: 'Yes.'

Then he is asked: 'Who disentangles you?' Because the tangle-
ment is mutual.

The correct answer is 'God.'

'This', says Bateson, 'may be a post missionary addition to the
ritual.'

Obviously we can't start next Tuesday to get twenty or thirty
people and have them mean this when asked, and they must answer
and mean it. You must, therefore, devote from six months to three
years to working on every member of this network to the point
where they can come to this meeting and mean it. The final gathering of the whole group is in a sense a ritual affirmation of that
which has been gone through over the six months or three or four

year period. In this particular case they decided they would work towards a Ho'o Pono Pono and the members of the family started working on each other to plough up the ground.

From the moment they started to work on it the boy started to go straight. He is now doing very nicely at high school getting good marks and has been out of institutions for a couple of years. After some months they had what they regard as an abortive 'Ho'o Pono Pono.' They could not get everyone to talk straight but they are working on it and are expecting in two or three years time to have the real 'Ho'o Pono Pono'. It's as sophisticated as anything we do, possibly more sophisticated than anything we can do.

Speck's work in Philadelphia with networks is among the most sophisticated I know.

DIFFERENCES BETWEEN SOCIAL AND MEDICAL DIAGNOSIS

A few final remarks about social situations in relation to the medical model. Medical diagnosis finds its place in the context of a set of procedures in which all doctors are trained and which influences for life, all who have been trained in them. Essentially it is this. When one comes to see anyone as a patient, one listens to the complaint, takes a history, does an examination, institutes whatever supplementary investigations one feels to be necessary, arrives at a diagnosis, makes a prognosis if one can, and having done all that, one prescribes treatment. Complaint, history, examination plus investigations, diagnosis, prognosis, treatment. Diagnosis includes aetiology, where aetiology is thought to be known. Often it implies prognosis. In all cases it determines treatment: no rational therapy without prior diagnosis: it is reckless and irresponsible to attempt to treat anyone without having arrived at, at least, a tentative diagnosis on the basis of which one's treatment is instituted.

Now consider this model in relationship to the diagnosis of a social situation. One encounters a situation, defined in the first place by the people in it, and/or by agents in other situations. As soon as one is presented with any situation, one is interacting with elements of it, and hence, willy nilly intervening one way or another. As soon as one intervenes, the situation changes somewhat, however little. A doctor usually does not feel he intervenes, in this sense, in the processes of, say, cardio vascular failure or tuberculosis simply by hearing the complaint, taking a history, doing an examination. He has not started to intervene with a view to change until he begins his treatment, after he has done all that is necessary to arrive at his diagnosis. In our case, we are intervening in and changing the situation as soon as we are involved. As soon as we interplay with the situation, we have already begun to intervene willy nilly. Moreover our intervention is already beginning to change us, as well as the situation. A reciprocal relationship has begun. The doctor and the still predominantly medically oriented psychiatrist use a non reciprocal static model: history comes after the complaint; examination comes after the history; after this one makes a tentative or if possible definitive diagnosis: thereafter comes 'therapy'.

Diagnosis is dia: through; gnosis: knowledge of. Diagnosis is appropriate for social situations, if one understands it as seeing through the social scene. Diagnosis begins as soon as one encounters a particular situation, and never ends. The way one sees through the situation, changes the situation. As soon as we convey in any way (by a gesture, a handshake, a cough, a smile, an inflection of our voice), what we see or think we see, some change is occurring even in the most rigid situation.

We may feel that one way to change most quickly, and radically, and relevantly, a situation is to take one or two of the people 'in' the situation, 'out' of the situation, and 'give' them individual psycho-'therapy'. We engage in 'therapy' with a married couple, to get them to tell us how they see the situation, and to tell them what we think we can see, in the hope this interchange will help to change the situation. It is very naive indeed to expect that by telling people what we think we see they are doing they will stop doing it. Perhaps it is just as well that it is not so easy. We have discovered by now that it is usually 'water off a duck's back'. Whether in micro or macro situations, people seldom stop to think what they are doing, much less stop doing it, just because we 'make an interpretation', that is, tell them what we think they are doing and why. There are exceptions, but the strategy of intervening in situations through the medium of words by telling people what we think they are doing, in the hope that thereby they will stop doing it, because we think that they should not be doing what we think they are doing, is frequently vastly irrelevant to all concerned.

Social diagnosis is a continuous process: not a single moment. It is not an element in an ordered set of before - after events in time. In the medical model, such a sequence is the ideal, to which one tries to approximate in practice: complaint; history; examination; diagnosis; treatment. Intervention in social situations may have different phases: they overlap, contrapuntally. The phases cannot be chopped up into time slices.

What one sees as one looks into the situation changes as one hears the story. In a year's time, after one has got to know the people and their situation a little, the story will have gone through a number of transformations: often it will be very different from what one heard a year back; neither are necessarily untrue, neither are necessarily true. It is a different story, or one hears a different story. As the story is transformed as time goes by, so what one sees undergoes transformations. At a particular time one is inclined to define the situation in a particular way; this definition in turn changes the situation in ways we may never be able to define. One's definition of the situation may generate different stories. People remember different things, put things together in different ways. This redefines the situation as changed by our definition in the light of how it originally presented itself to us. Our definition is an act of intervention which changes the situation which thus requires redefining; it introduces a new factor. At any moment of time, in the continuous process of looking through, of diagnosis, we

see it in a particular way, that leads us to a non-definitive definition, subject to revision in the light of the transformations that this
very definition induces, prospectively and retrospectively. Medically,
our diagnosis of tuberculosis does not affect the fact that the person has tuberculosis. We don't change the illness by our diagnosis.
You don't convert a case of tuberculosis into a cardiac failure by
calling it cardiac failure. But suppose our diagnosis of a situation
is: This is a social crisis, due to the fact that this boy has 'got'
schizophrenia. We must treat the 'schizophrenia' in the boy, and the
social worker must help the relatives to cope with the terrible
tragedy of having a mental illness in the family and so forth. This
is not merely a medical diagnosis. It is a social prescription. As you
know, in my view, it is a gross misreading of the situation. In any
event, whether you agree with me on that point or not, there can
be no doubt that any such medical diagnosis also defines and changes
the situation. Such a definition may even be an 'aetiological factor'
in creating the situation one has defined: even creating at least a
very good imitation of the 'illness' one is purporting to cure. Social
situations are the field for the self-fulfilling prophecy. A self-
fulfilling diagnosis of the situation may lead to a situation approxi-
mating to the situation as defined.

One must not be naive. Who are the experts in such matters?
Certainly not many psychiatrists at present. We have no training
whatever in this respect, and have often been trained to be incompetent in this regard.

We all must continually learn to unlearn much we have learned,
and learn to learn much that we have not been taught. Only thus
do we and our subject grow.

ADDITIONAL READING

Ackerman N., Adolescent Problems: A Symptom of Family Disorder,
'Family Process', 1, 1962, pp. 202-13.
Cooper, D., 'Psychiatry and Anti-Psychiatry', Tavistock, London,
1967.
Foucault, M., 'Madness and Civilisation. A History of Insanity in
the Age of Reason', Pantheon Books, New York, and Tavistock,
London, 1967.
Goffman, E., 'Asylums. Essays on the Social Situation of Mental
Patients and Other Inmates', Doubleday-Anchor Books. New York,
and Penguin, Harmondsworth, 1968.
Haley, J., The Art of Being Schizophrenic, 'Voices', 1, 1965.
Handel, Gerald (ed.), 'The Psychosocial Interior of the Family: A
source book for the study of whole families', Allen & Unwin,
London, 1968:
Laing, R.D., Mystification, Confusion and Conflict, in 'Intensive
Family Therapy' ed. I. Boszormenyi-Nagy and J.L. Framo, Harper
& Row, New York, 1965.
Laing, R.D., Family and Individual Structure, 'The Predicament of
the Family', ed. P. Lomas, Hogarth Press, London, 1967.

Laing, R.D. and Esterson, A., 'Sanity, Madness and the Family, vol. I. Families of Schizophrenics', Tavistock, London, and Basic Books, New York, 1965.

Scheff, T., 'Being Mentally Ill', Aldine Books, Chicago, and Weidenfeld & Nicolson, London, 1967.

Speck, R.V., Psychotherapy of the Social Network of a Schizophrenic Family, 'Family Process', 6, 2, 1967.

Szasz, T., 'The Myth of Mental Illness', Harper, New York, 1961.

Zarlock, S.P., Social Expectations, Language and Schizophrenia, 'J. Human Psychol.', 6, 68, 1966.

3 THE TREATMENT BARRIER[1]

R. D. Scott

PART 1

My use of the term 'treatment barrier' refers to those obstacles to treatment which are created by the cultural view of mental illness prevailing in Western society. If dealing with issues in the relationships between the patient and others is an essential part of treatment, then the treatment barrier is the barrier that we must penetrate before treatment can begin. It should not be confused with the defence systems described by psycho-analysts.

The treatment barrier will exist whenever a person has been labelled as being ill by an authority, usually a doctor, whether the label be neurosis or psychosis. A mental hospital provides an excellent base from which to describe the treatment barrier. I will give two brief but very typical examples:

1. It is an everyday occurrence that a patient in hospital goes out for the day and creates a bit of trouble in the community by playing up. The patient is quite aware of acting so as to make trouble. When confronted by whoever he has upset he says, 'I'm from Napsbury' (mental hospital). No further questions are asked. The hospital doctor is rung up and held totally responsible for a person who, because he is a mental patient, is assumed to be not responsible for his behaviour. If the doctor does not take this view and act accordingly, then the community member may threaten to report the doctor to a higher authority.

2. The parents come to see the doctor about their son who is in hospital. The son asks, 'Can I go home?' Parents: 'We will have you home as soon as the doctor says you are well enough.' Doctor: 'He has no illness for which we need to keep him in hospital. It is between you and him whether he goes home.' The parents attack the doctor: 'But doctor he is ill; he stays up all night playing his guitar and stays in bed during the day. We cannot have him until he is well.' Doctor: 'It seems that it is the way he behaves which you cannot stand, and that is why you do not want him home.' 'But doctor, he is our son and we love him, we want him to get well.' Eventually, if the family show feeling, get angry, cry, begin to admit some real difficulties in their relationships, then the treatment barrier has been penetrated. If they succeed in forcing everything back onto the doctor in terms of 'illness', then the

barrier has not been penetrated.

We may notice from these two examples of the treatment barrier that different areas are involved:

The lay area. This has: (a) a public sector in which those concerned have no special relationships with the patient, and (b) a private sector, i.e. the cultural image of mental illness as it is used in family relationships.

The professional area. Here there are two main divisions: (a) the hospital and those working with in-patients, and (b) the community area, those working with patients in hospital and with their relatives. The professional workers may be psychiatrists, social workers, psychoanalysts, etc.

For most people the term 'mental patient' probably implies a person who has been in a mental hospital. The mental hospital patient and his illness may be regarded as the archetype through which the cultural images achieve a stark clarity which aids definition. The same cultural images are at work in any community setting in which there is a diagnosed patient; there, however, they appear in a more subtle form, but one which can, I believe, nevertheless provide a very effective barrier to treatment.

The presentation is in two parts: Part 1 gives a general survey of the areas in which the treatment barrier is likely to be operative and the manner of its operation in the different areas. An impression is also given of how awareness of the barrier has led to a refashioning of treatment policies in the hospital team with which I am concerned. Part 1 brings to view a massive cultural denial of the extent to which patients are agents who are capable of effectively exploiting the powerful forces which form the context of the situation of the mental patient. Part 2 (Scott, 1973) takes up the theme of the patient as an unrecognized agent. Research findings are used to show: (i) that patients are not merely helpless victims unable to determine their own fates, but that they may have a marked degree of agency which they use to attain certain ends; (ii) that patients are more aware of issues associated with these capacities than are their relatives, whose perceptions of the patient are obscured by the cultural image of mental illness.

ORIENTATION AND AIMS

There are three points:

1. The term 'mental illness' has replaced terms which now horrify us such as 'lunacy', 'insanity', 'insane heredity', 'pauper lunatic', which were used during the first forty years of this century. These latter terms imply alienation, banishment from society into asylums located away in the country, whereas the term 'mental illness' has been intended by the innovators in our culture to imply acceptance of the patient as a person in need of treatment as in the case of any other form of illness. It may therefore seem a paradox that through our experience I am forced to describe the cultural view of mental illness as a severe obstacle to treatment. I

wish to make clear that although I am describing only the negative aspects of the image of mental illness, I am aware of positive aspects too - I do not think I could have stood working in the asylums in the pre-war years.

The mental health services are being extensively refashioned. The process started in the late 1950s in this country, and it started at the top. On the basis of Tooth and Brooke's well-known 'turning of the tide' paper (1961), a blueprint was laid down.

It is the image of mental illness which has led us to the restructuring of the provisions for the treatment of the mentally ill which are now in the midstream of change. It is therefore important to look very carefully at the way in which the image of mental illness operates in the everyday world of our work.

2.   The above is a summary of the contemporary background. The aims of the present work are however purely practical. They are to define those aspects of the cultural view of mental illness which are antitherapeutic and, having defined them, to develop methods of treatment which can be effective in the existing social milieu. We cannot change society.

3.   I am not denying the existence of illness. I am concerned to differentiate areas in which tremendous confusion prevails. For instance, the majority of patients are admitted to mental hospitals for social reasons, yet our culture requires that all be labelled as 'ill'. Some patients are, by any standards, ill; but for the many whose problems are mainly social and interpersonal the label of 'illness' may place a barrier between them and their real problems.

Since we are concerned with the public image of mental illness in Western culture, it is necessary to review some of the literature in order to establish profiles for the generality of the image.

CULTURAL IMAGE OF MENTAL ILLNESS PROFILES DERIVED FROM THE LITERATURE

Profiles of: sick person, sick role, mental illness, mental patient, mental person, deviancy, legitimized deviant.

Parsons (1951, 1952) presents 'Health and illness as socially institutionalized role types'. The sick role is 'A partially and conditionally legitimized state', defined as follows:

(i) The sick person is exempted from certain of his social obligations (commitments, or obligations, taken over by others).

(ii) It is a condition that he is unable to recover by a conscious act of will, i.e. he cannot help it. Thus his disability is regarded as something for which he cannot be held responsible (*not responsible*), [2] but

(iii) He is obligated to want to get well. That is, he is responsible for seeking and accepting treatment. He must regard the sick role as an undesirable one.

(iv) He is regarded as being in need of competent technical help, and since he is obligated to want to get well, his status as a 'sick person' is conditional on his becoming a *patient*.

In consequence of these conditions the sick role may not be
granted if there appears to be inadequate evidence for the presence
of a *disease process* which would justify this role.

These definitions apply to illness in general. They are equally
applied to mental illness with the attendant difficulties and confusions which are later discussed. Here we need only note that any
admission to a psychiatric hospital requires that the person must
be labelled as 'ill', and that his illness must be seen as arising
from a disease process.

Erikson (1957) defines the public definition of mental illness
as follows:

(i) A breakdown of intellect, amounting to almost complete
loss of cognitive function, i.e. *loss of reason*, 'out of his mind'
(lacking *'insight'*).

(ii) This loss of rationality leads to the expectation that the
behaviour termed 'mental illness' must represent a serious loss
of self control, usually to the point of not being responsible for
his acts (*unpredictable, impulsive*).

(iii) The behaviour should be inappropriate and not reasonable
in the circumstances in which a person finds himself. (*Deviance*.)

Other authors, sociologists in particular, define mental illness
as a form of deviancy since it affects a person's behaviour. I do
not think that the term 'deviant' is applied to other forms of illness. The term appears to be confined to behaviour and not to
deviation from physical norms. Another attribute is, *helpless*,
unable to determine his own fate (*loss of agency*, or *volition*).
'Mental patient' is also sometimes seen as an *identity* rather than
as a role:

The danger of achieving a stabilized identity as a 'mental patient'
is greatest at a point in life where a person is struggling to
form an integrated identity (Talbot et al., 1964).

Pilowsky (1969) differentiates two sociological concepts: 1 the
sick role, as defined by Parsons, and 2 illness behaviour, as
defined by Mechanic:

The person is only entitled to the sick role provided he co-
operates in treatment with society's officially appointed delegates,
to get rid of this undesirable state. The patient may or may not
regard the role as undesirable, but by obligation those treating
him must do so.

Thus in the case of the mental patient who is not responsible,
absolute responsibility falls *by obligation* on the shoulders of
'society's officially appointed delegates' – the doctors.

The concept of illness behaviour is applicable to the actions of
the person as these are seen by others: 'the ways in which given
symptoms may be differentially perceived, evaluated, and acted
(or not acted) upon by different kinds of persons' (Mechanic,
1962).

The question of whether they are acted upon depends on the
'visibility' of symptoms as indicators of degree of deviancy:

The intervention in the case of 'assumed mental illness' by the
family or others in the community is highly dependent on the

visibility of symptoms. A person unable or unwilling to make
proper responses in his network of interpersonal relations is
regarded as : criminal or corrupt, if empathy is possible and
motivation attributable, or - sick or odd if the evaluator is at
a loss in empathizing.

Thus Mechanic makes it clear that whether a person is seen as
being 'ill' or not depends on somebody's view of what is 'ill' or
'well'. The expert is in a similar position, since in the majority of
cases there are no tests for mental illness other than what is provided by what a person says and does.

Mechanic makes the following important point which is completely
borne out by our daily experience: 'The person defined as mentally
ill is brought into hospital primarily as the result of lay decisions.
But the laymen involved usually presume that the patient is in
hospital as a result of medical decisions and expert knowledge.'

Kellert (1971) makes the same point: 'To a considerable extent
the psychiatric diagnosis functions largely to validate decisions
reached somewhere out in the community.'

We may note that this constitutes one of the nodal points in the
operation of the treatment barrier. This mode of placing responsibility onto the doctor enables the patient and his relatives to
evade the reality of the painful things they may have suffered,
and it places the doctor in a position of pseudo-authority which
is likely to impair his effectiveness in treatment.

Sarbin and Manusco (1970) provide evidence that the general
public will go a long way towards accepting and trying to understand disturbed behaviour, but once a person has had the official
seal of being mentally ill placed upon him, he is likely to be dis-
tanced and ostracized. His behaviour is then seen as being beyond
understanding, and in my experience beyond even the need for
understanding.

Families regularly use this cultural defence when, through the
pains and threats of their interpersonal conflicts, they reach a
threshold and suddenly see the behaviour of one member as being
beyond understanding. But this defence may increase anxiety,
for the behaviour of the member thus identified is now seen as
being even more unpredictable than before. At this point the family
is likely to turn to the doctor for confirmation of their view that
the member is mentally ill. A person whose behaviour is seen as
being unpredictable not only becomes an object of fear, he becomes
endowed, as we shall later be considering, with a potentiality for
a perverse sort of power. [3] This potentiality arises because of the
'closure' (Scott et al., 1967) involved in this defence which leaves
others unaware of whatever rationality the patient retains. As is
detailed in Part 2, the patient may then place his remaining awareness and agency in the service of the image of fear in which he
has been cast.

Star (1955), from the results of a national opinion poll, reports
that 'For most people mental illness is associated with violent and
unpredictable behaviour.'

During a psychotic crisis in a family there is an absolute dread

of the unpredictable - 'anything might happen'. But beyond this
there are definite and ultimate fears which I will indicate, since
the stereotypes of the cultural image quite specifically deny real
understanding of the mental hospital and its inhabitants, and
their relation with the community.

We have rated a number of parents of schizophrenics for what
they feared most: first came 'his becoming lost'; they feared that
the patient would become permanently out of touch - lost as a
person. Thus they feared ultimate separation; this was often
expressed as a fear of 'silence, of his not saying anything'. Second
came fear of violence, to the extent of fearing murder. From this
and much other evidence we know that the parents are not so
much threatened by those outward and visible signs of disturbed
behaviour, described by Mechanic for the general populace, as
they are by an *inner dread*, compared to which the stigma, as a
threat, is quite peripheral. This parental dread is about the fear
of 'his becoming lost'. It can best be pictured as a life-line felt
to exist between parents and patient. The parent(s) have to know
where the patient is, they cannot let him out of their minds, and
they behave as if their own lives literally depended on it (life-
line). In our experience the parental dread is not really concerned
with the fate of the patient, it is much more deeply concerned with
the survival of the involved relative(s) who are not in hospital.

The potentiality for anxiety in the situation described above is
obviously very great, and it may quickly rise above the threshold
of what can be endured at home. The hospital then *has* to have
the patient. The relatives, and, as we shall see, patients too,
usually assume that this is an *obligation* which is not open to
question. The hospital staff now become responsible not merely
for the patient, but for the *relationship* situation which exists
between patient and parents. Commonly the parent(s) want a son
or daughter tied in to their lives and they may use the diagnosis
of illness to secure this, and the patient may collude with an act
of identity murder. The hospital staff are required to be responsible for managing this situation, but they must see it entirely in
terms of disturbance in the patient.

I have outlined this aspect of the pathological inability to separate,
which typifies schizophrenics and their parents equally, because
it leads to an expectation that the hospital staff will assume total
responsibility for patients, and this expectation lies very close to
what is expected in our culture for the hospitalization of mental
patients in general.

In the next section I consider various areas in which the treatment barrier may operate. I start with the hospital where the issue
we are considering receives ultimate expression. From what has
been said it should be clear that the greatest forces acting on
hospital staff do not come from within the hospital, but are exerted
from the community. Community pressure is based on fear. The
form and intensity which this fear can take has been described above.
Any attempt to include relatives (from the community sector) as
an essential part of the hospital treatment situation is seen by them

as a violation of the rules prescribed by the cultural image of mental illness. The hospital is the physical expression of a cultural line dividing the ill from the well.

OPERATION OF THE TREATMENT BARRIER IN VARIOUS AREAS AND SOME IMPLICATIONS FOR TREATMENT

The hospital and the community
The description given earlier (example 2) of a meeting between family and patient is typical and stereotyped. It represents a revival of the original situation which led to admission. This original situation we term the 'first experience' of mental illness (Scott et al., 1967). Though it will have preceded the present admission, the first experience may have occurred on a number of previous occasions in connection with the present patient, or it may be a repeat of a parent's experience with the hospitalization of a close relative much earlier in that parent's life.

The essentials of the situation are, as Mechanic says, that it is a lay member in the community who makes the decision for admission and then immediately holds the doctor responsible for it as the 'expert' in mental illness. As in the example the parents tell the doctor what to say, and if he does not say it, the situation is likely to become very tense and threatening. If the doctor does comply with parents' expectations, as he is likely to have done on admission, he will be forced to draw a line which rigidly divides the ill from the well; human relationships are then maintained in a severed and disconnected state. The parents deny that forms of relationship threatening to themselves are relationships; they are seen as forms of disturbance in the patient. Thus symptomatology is maintained by the conventional approach whilst relationship issues are depersonalized and evaded.

A disconnexion from the circumstances surrounding admission, just described, is present in nearly all patients newly admitted, whether or not they are psychotic, and its form is extremely stereotyped. It is simply not done for a patient to know why he is in hospital or to want to be in hospital for any explicitly positive reason.

In the acute female admission ward we make the practice, at weekly meetings with all staff and patients present, of asking a few very simple questions: Why are you here? What has happened? Are you ill? Is there anything for which you would like some help? Do you want to be here? Almost all patients at these meetings attribute their being in hospital to the agency of others. Whilst this may be partly true, the patients themselves deny that they have taken any part in it; they have been brought in for some unknown reason: 'The doctor sent me in', 'A welfare officer came and took me away.' 'Why did he do it?' 'I don't know, there was no reason.' Or the patient may invoke psychotic forms of explanation, such as rays or telepathy, etc.

It is notable that it is extremely rare to be asked by a patient why they were brought into hospital.

Very few patients indicate that they have any responsibility for being in hospital. They know that the role of a mental patient is that he is *not responsible*, and has no agency or *volition* of his own by which he can determine his own fate. One patient summed up the rule governing the role by asking, 'Should a patient know why he is in hospital?'

Very few patients admit they want help, excepting perhaps 'a rest' or 'pills for nerves'. The role of a mental patient is that he *avoids committing* himself to anything; hence he is seen as being *without insight*.

Although patients do not admit that they want to be in hospital and often say they want to leave, when told they can leave at any time they wish - 'Now if you like' - it is exceptional for a patient placed in this position actually to commit himself to leaving.

Thus the majority of patients from the time of their admission fulfil all the attributions of the 'mental patient' which we have defined, to the letter.

By far the most striking of the above features of patient behaviour is the denial that they want anything from the hospital yet make no move to leave. Closely associated with this denial is the fact that over 90 per cent of admissions occur by crisis. This means that it is intolerable behaviour and not the seeking of treatment which led to admission. We have found that admission by crisis represents an escape from an intolerable situation and that this is equally true for both patients and relatives. Time and again it has been very evident that patients do not want to leave hospital, they want refuge, but this cannot be admitted. If patients were prepared to admit this need for refuge we would, in many cases, be prepared to grant it - conditionally. Rather than ask for what they want, or accept what they have been offered, patients go to almost any extremity of psychosis, or impulsive acting out, in order to secure admission unconditionally; and, having secured admission, they deny that they want anything from us. Patients, equally with relatives, act on the implicit assumption that we have got to take the patient. Thus patients avoid the human act of asking for what they want and of making a transaction with us about it.

In the case of schizophrenics this could be attributed to their well-known fear of commitment. But the avoidance of commitment extends to all types of patient. An intelligent, middle-aged, depressed woman, who knows quite well how to conduct herself, behaves in the same way. This makes it unlikely that we are dealing with a feature of illness 'per se', but rather with a cultural and learned response to the image of illness. We may term this the 'standard patient'. That this is a role which the patient actively takes, and which can obscure to others the degree of awareness and insight which he may possess, is investigated systematically in Part 2.

An approach to the treatment barrier
That most admissions deny that they want anything from us, yet
make no move to leave, creates an obvious barrier to treatment.
During the last two years members of my hospital team have been
developing an approach to this problem.

We discovered what lay behind the standard position taken by
nearly all individuals admitted by doing something we have never
dared to do before: challenge the role of the mental patient. At
the group meeting in the admission ward we, as a team, would
not take the medical counterpart of the mental patient role, but
instead adopt an approach in which we might say to a patient,
'You must want something from us since you do not leave. If you
could tell us about this we might be able to help.' We do not accept
denials of agency, and we remain unresponsive to psychotic types
of explanation. In this way psychotic ideas can sometimes be under-
cut in one session revealing more real issues, the hurts, despair,
conflict with others. The implication that we may ask a patient to
leave unless he can give some idea of what he wants from being in
hospital, [4] conveys to a patient that we are aware of the secret
source of power inherent in the patient role. This power lies in
the unstated assumption that we are obliged to have the patient
because he is a 'mental patient', i.e. an object of fear who might
do anything, and that it is we who will be responsible for what
he does. Hence he need give no reason for being in hospital nor
make any commitment about it. The unreality of the assumption
that we can be totally responsible for a patient's acts is especially
dangerous in the case of a patient threatening suicide. We have
had many examples in which this approach has checked suicidal
acting out.

The next step was to get the situation with the relatives into
the picture. For this purpose we have made it a condition of admission that the most involved relatives attend at least one ward
meeting soon after the patient comes in. Relatives, almost as much
as patients, avoid issues concerning the situation which led to
admission. Regularly they say that the doctor decided to admit the
patient, and regularly we have to ask them, along with the patient,
to describe what happened. Usually it turns out that things had got
intolerable at home, and that because of this the doctor had no
choice but to secure admission. At other times it may become clear
that a parent has manoeuvred the child into hospital in order to
keep possession and control of this child. By bringing to life the
situation between patient and relatives which led to admission, we
try to avoid being made totally responsible for it. Should we assume
this responsibility, by treating the patient and ignoring the
relationships, we would, in the last example, be making ourselves
into accomplices of the parents to ensure that the child remained
tied to them.

Results
The results of this approach have had a very marked effect on
the admission ward. Up to the time the policy was started in

January 1970, the ward had for years been subject to recurrent bed-pressure crises, over-crowding, violence, squabbling, and tension. Since January 1970 there have been no bed-pressure crises, which means that we can organize transfers on a rational basis. Breakages and the use of sedatives have gone right down. The ward has 44 beds. In the four months before starting the policy the average ward population (beds occupied on Wednesdays) was 38 patients, whose average length of stay was 28 days. Since starting the policy the ward population has progressively gone down: in the first six months of 1971 the average population was 13 patients whose average length of stay was 11.5 days. The admission rates were nearly the same in both periods, averaging 32.5 per month in the first, and 31.8 per month in the second period. The change has resulted from the average length of stay being reduced by more than a half. The readmission rate has remained about the same.

By using this approach we are able to get more control over the attitudes of the patient and relatives to admission. To this we attribute the great reduction in psychotic behaviour and also the associated disappearance of overcrowding. We do not yet know how it finally affects outcome for patients, but the reduction of in-patient load has freed staff to go into the community to deal with problems where they usually belong, i.e. between the patient and his involved others.

Hospital staff and the approach
The use of the approach has required staff to withstand a high degree of anxiety. It cannot be used by individual staff members, but requires a team organized from top to bottom. Staff who act in identification with the cultural image feel totally responsible; they feel that any failure on their part to take this total responsibility for a patient may lead to their being threatened by some authority. But, as we have seen, to be totally responsible for another person means the denial of the existence of human relationships with that person. The approach described introduces relationships; it could be called the human approach. It means that we do not act in complete uniformity to the very limited set of stereotyped expectations belonging to the cultural image and, as a result, relatives, and patients too, have tried threatening us with the highest authorities. Often this has been over so simple a matter as refusing to see a relative except in the presence of the patient, or only with the patient's permission (in order to keep relationships connected).

Under the present system, not only do relatives try to bind the staff to be totally responsible, but they also accord them only minimum status. That it is a community member who decides who needs admission, and who sees staff as 'expert' only when they do what they are told, and threatens them when they do not, may sound a caricature. It is not. Moreover, so long as staff collude with the traditional system they suffer a sense of shame and degradation that is, I believe, the most potent source of the inferior status associated with working in mental hospitals.

The traditional pattern is determined by fear. Relatives and community members are not so much holding staff responsible for the patient as requiring them to take care of their fears of mental illness, the fear which I have pictured as a life-line which can be cut.

It is crucial that staff differentiate the fear which community members convey to them, from their perception of the patient in his own right. If they are able to do this they will probably discover that they have been much too anxious about patients, and much too little concerned with the fears of community members.

In the coming section, I will leave this realm of ultimate fears and deal with everyday situations found in the community.

THE COMMUNITY SECTOR AND THE TREATMENT BARRIER

The issue is here more subtle. I will start in the out-patient department. I see a woman who complains of various symptoms including depression. Eventually it emerges that there is a bad marital conflict and that she is trying to get me to force her into hospital in order to escape the pain and stress, and perhaps also to punish her husband. I can approach the situation in two ways:

1. If my response is to offer help for the marital problem in terms such as 'You have told me that you have a bad problem with your marriage. I think that this is responsible for your depression. I would like to see you and your husband together', the wife may agree, but it is unlikely that I will get anywhere. Indeed she may well try to find another route into hospital – not that she has said she wants to come in, she has tried to make me say it.

2. Alternatively, I could say 'You have made it clear that you have a bad marriage problem and that you are suffering much depression because of it. Do you want help for this?' If the wife says that she really would like help about her relationship with her husband, the issue is put on an entirely new basis. She has committed herself to asking for help about her marriage, and it is up to me to say whether, and in what way, I think I might be able to help. If she says that she does not want help for her marriage problem, then I might say that I am not willing to give her the form of help for which I believe her to be asking, i.e. for admission, since I have found that if I admit a person in her position things work out very badly. At this point we might agree to part since I am not prepared to give her what she wants.

The first approach is unlikely to succeed because I have not dealt with the treatment barrier. Acting under the image of doctor and patient, I have prescribed marital therapy. But in taking this approach, I have treated her as a mental patient who does not know what she needs and have implied that she is incapable of knowing or deciding. I have secured no commitment on her part to seek help for her marriage, but only to do what I say.

THE COMMUNITY SOCIAL WORKER AND THE TREATMENT BARRIER

The picture I have given applies just as strongly to the community social worker. He is assigned 'referrals', that is to say, the head of his department receives patients referred for 'support', or help with family problems, sent by psychiatrists, GPs, etc. These cases are allotted to the staff. The social worker who then goes to the case often describes how he has had to use tact to 'get in', that is to say, he has had to persuade the family or the patient to allow him to come round and help them.

In one case a social worker told me that he had been referred a client who was a mother whose son was always getting into money trouble from which the mother rescued him. He described, quite correctly I thought, how this attitude of the mother was enabling the son to go on getting into trouble, and that this was a means of binding the son to her. I asked what was his position with the mother? He replied that he thought that he was a 'father-figure or husband'. I then inquired whether he had asked the mother if she wanted help with anything, such as managing her son. He replied that he had not. He just went round to help and give support to the mother who seemed pleased to see him. Now if this social worker had gone round to see the mother, and said that he had been sent round because they had heard there was trouble with the son, and after chatting with her had finally asked, 'Was there any help you want?', and she had said that she would like help about managing her son, then he would have been in a strong therapeutic position. As it was she had not asked help for anything, so that nothing he said to her was likely to have much effect. He then got very anxious: 'Supposing she did not ask for help?' He became terrified that he might be threatened by some authority for doing nothing about the case. His intense anxiety clearly confirmed that the image of mental illness and the treatment barrier were operative.

I find that social workers are, if anything, even more confused over their task than are hospital staff. They feel responsible to some authority for 'giving support', and that just as in the case of hospital staff, this leads to a failure to differentiate their own position with a family. It seems that even for patients not in hospital, they are still treated as being 'not responsible', and professionals have still to be totally responsible. The use of the medical model renders the social worker open to the challenge by their clients that 'She is ill, she should see the doctor'. The social worker in the community requires medical backing by a doctor who understands the importance of human relationships and who recognizes that many social problems become labelled medical through confusions in our present system.

THE TREATMENT BARRIER AND PSYCHOANALYSIS: PERMISSIVENESS

I have the impression that the treatment barrier can be operative also in psychoanalysis – the mere repetition of sessions without the question ever being asked, 'What do you want, what are you coming for?' Meanwhile the patient awaits cure.

It is also possible that because the patient cannot be expected to be responsible for unconscious impulses or fantasies, this may be used or confused with that permissiveness which is part of the cultural image of mental illness.

Because mental patients are seen as being not responsible for their actions, special allowances are made for them. A hall porter said to me, 'I don't know how you stand it.' 'Stand what?' I asked. 'Don't you get angry sometimes?', he replied. I said, 'Of course I do. I do not believe in encouraging a patient's unreality by acting in an unreal way.'

Relatives often have elaborate rituals for depersonalizing relationships with the patient by 'making special allowances so as not to upset him'. A patient may thus be treated as if he is invisible and yet be at the centre of family awareness. This unreal attitude is antitherapeutic, it can make patients extremely insecure. In the community I have stabilized a number of marriages simply by 'de-illnessing' them, by getting the other partner to be more real, to risk producing their own feelings and reactions instead of concealing them so as not to upset the patient.

CONCLUSION

Throughout the paper I have made clear how great anxiety is aroused when any of the basic assumptions belonging to the cultural image of mental illness are touched or questioned. For this reason the clinical procedures described cannot be put into operation without fully understanding the reasons for so working, and solid team backing.

I have been representing the hospital team, of which I am the leader, consisting of doctors, nurses and two psychologists. Although the paper is primarily a general sociological statement, the concepts have emerged out of a considerable change in the approach to treatment over the last two years. This change, both in conception and in action, has been initiated by various members of the team, and also from findings derived from the family research department attached to the team.[5] We are indebted to the community social workers in the Barnet Mental Health Centres who have helped us understand the community sector.

NOTES

1 Based on a paper given at a research seminar chaired by
Dr John Bowlby, Tavistock Institute of Human Relations, 21 April
1971. The material used in the technical part of this work is derived
from a project supported by the Department of Health and Social
Security.
2 The attributions in italics have become central to the image of
'mental patient'.
3 What is here described is the social context of a situation which
might be entirely social in nature, or which may contain a core of
illness in the sense defined by Parsons.
4 Nearly all admissions can do this. For the reasons given, most
patients behave as if they have not got a clue.
5 The Family Research Department is engaged in a project which
is supported by the Department of Health and Social Security.

REFERENCES

Erikson, K.T. (1957) Patient Role and Social Uncertainty: a
  Dilemma of the Mentally Ill, 'Psychiatry', 20, 263–74.
Kellert, S.R. (1971) The Lost Community in Community Psychiatry,
  'Psychiatry', 34, 168–79.
Mechanic, D. (1962) Some Factors in Identifying and Defining
  Mental Illness, 'Ment. Hyg.', 46, 66–74.
Parsons, T. (1951) Illness and the Role of the Physician: a Socio-
  logical Perspective, 'Am. J. Orthopsychiat.', 21, 452–60.
Parsons, T. (1952) Illness, Therapy and the Modern Urban
  American Family, 'J. Soc. Issues', 8, 31–44.
Pilowsky, I. (1969) Abnormal Illness Behaviour, 'Br. J. Med.
  Psychol.', 42, 347–51.
Sarbin, T. R. and Manusco, J.C. (1970) Failure of a Moral Enter-
  prise: Attitudes of the Public towards Mental Illness, 'J. Consult.
  Clin. Psychol.', 35, 159–73.
Scott, R.D. (1973) The Treatment Barrier. Part 2. The Patient
  as an Unrecognized Agent, 'Br. J. Med. Psychol.', 46, 57–67
  (see pp. 44–59, below).
Scott, R.D. and Ashworth, P.L. (1967) 'Closure' at the First
  Schizophrenic Breakdown: a Family Study, 'Br. J. Med. Psychol.',
  40, 109–45.
Star, S.A. (1955) The Public's Idea about Mental Illness (paper
  read to the National Association of Mental Health, Indianapolis).
Talbot, E., Miller, S.C. and White, R.B. (1964) Some Antitherapeutic Side Effects of Hospitalization and Psychotherapy,
  'Psychiatry', 27, 170–6.
Tooth, G.C. and Brooke, E.M. (1961) Trends in the Mental Hos-
  pital Population and their Effect on Future Planning, 'Lancet',
  i, 710–13.

PART 2[1]

I will restate my use of the term 'treatment barrier': that the
cultural view of mental illness which prevails in our society forms
a severe barrier to treatment whenever an essential part of treatment entails dealing with relationships between the patient and
others.[2]

In Part 1 (Scott, 1973) I surveyed the area, dividing it into
public and private sectors, in which professional staff, or lay
persons, might be involved in relationships with the patient.

Part 1 brought to view what appeared to be a massive cultural
denial of the extent to which patients may have awareness and
agency, and it gave an impression of the use which patients commonly make of this public denial of their capacity to retain such
faculties. This was seen as being a central feature of the barrier
to treatment.

In Part 2 we take up the theme of the patient as an unrecognized
agent, and use research findings to explore the issue in detail.
By means of our Family Relationship Test[3] we give evidence which
shows that a patient is more likely to be aware of issues in their
mutual relationships than are his parents. The results show that
the cultural image of mental illness places the patient in a position
to exploit an awareness which he is not seen as possessing, and
which he knows he is not seen as possessing. It is suggested
that a similar relationship is likely to hold between hospital staff
and the patient. Evidence is then given from the literature which
suggests that the patient, to an extent which is not usually
realized, is a knowing agent in determining outcome.

Empirical findings regarding patient's agency are contrasted
with conventional views that the patient is a helpless victim of
an illness, or of society, or of his family. The findings place a
perspective on conventional models of mental illness.

The patient's position: issues to be investigated
In Part 1 it was described how the majority of admissions were by
crisis. That is to say, a patient does not come into hospital for
treatment but comes as a result of an intolerable situation between
himself and others in the community. This mode of admission applies
equally to the really ill as it does to those suffering social problems
and interpersonal conflict. I described how, if we adopted an
approach which avoided acting in identification with the medical
counterpart of the role of mental patient, staff came to realize
that they were confronted by patients who, irrespective of whether
they were psychotic or not, 'informally' admitted or not, had a basic
attitude in common. This attitude was termed the 'standard patient'.
The standard patient presents in terms of the cultural image of
mental illness: he denies that he wants anything from us, he usually
makes no move to leave if offered the opportunity, and thus is
usually seen as being out of touch with reality, and lacking in
the insight that he is ill and in need of help and hospitalization.

However, I indicated that we had reason to suspect that patients knew they were mental patients, and that they accepted this identity, an identity which carried with it an assumption which was thought to be unquestionable, that we were obliged to have him. Thus the patient need show no commitment to wanting to help. Most admissions consist of people who appear to have difficulty in asking for help. Instead, they seek admission by crisis and go to almost any length to secure this. Thus they obtain unconditional refuge. This implies that patients may be active agents in setting a scene high in potentiality for a regressive evasion of reality and the problems of living. Our study, which shows that they have the necessary awareness for doing this, is now presented. It is followed by a summary of other studies showing that there is a group of patients who do exploit their hospital situation in a manner seldom perceived by staff.

THE STUDY

The profile of the standard patient applies to all types of admission, but schizophrenics are the most likely candidates to lack insight into their position. I will therefore use Family Relationship Test scorings for schizophrenics and their parents to explore the following issues:
1. Do patients lack insight that they are patients? Do they deny that they are ill?
2(a). How far are patients aware that their parents see them as patients, and of the extent to which they are seen as being ill?
(b) How far are parents aware of how the patient sees them?
3. Are parents more aware, or are patients more aware, of how they are seen by the other? Arising out of this, are patients or parents more in touch, or out of touch, with reality as far as awareness of issues in their mutual relationships are concerned?
4. How far are parents blind to what the patient thinks of them because of seeing the patient as ill?
5. How true is our proposition that the cultural image of mental illness places the patient in a position of power to exploit an awareness which he is not seen as possessing, and which he knows he is not seen as possessing? This question, and the formulation of it, is central to assessment of the patient's position and agency by means of the test.

The patient's position in relation to his parents as defined by the Family Relationship Test
The Test. The Family Relationship Test is an interpersonal perception technique. The essential details are given in Appendix I and II.
Appendix I shows the score form listing a series of terms which may be used to describe a person. It contains specific terms which enable family members to express how they use the cultural image of mental illness to describe themselves, and each other, and to predict what each of the others thinks of them (using the standard list of terms). The 'viewpoints' thus derived are listed in Appendix II. The two diagrams in Appendix II compare the scoring profiles

of seventeen community-centred and seventeen hospital-centred patients and their parents, the latter being patients with a chronic hospital outcome, and the former being patients living at home and in no danger of this outcome. The profiles express the degree of 'illness' or 'wellness' expressed in each viewpoint. Thus parents expect to be seen, and see themselves, as being 'well' (high black columns), whilst views referring to the patient (white columns) are all views attributing 'illness'. For details, see Scott and Ashworth (1965) and Scott et al. (1970).

Relationships within the nuclear family are radically reshaped when one member is first diagnosed mentally ill. An officially authorized line is then drawn between who is ill and who is well. When the difficulty is essentially interpersonal, as is commonly the case in marital conflict, the line falsifies the situation in the manner described in Part 1 of this paper. The couple nearly always present with one member labelled as 'ill'. Anyone with experience in conjoint therapy will know how difficult it then is to get the couple to face each other on an equal footing.

In cases in which the diagnosis of illness has a legitimate place, relationships can be even more crucial than in ordinary interpersonal conflict. This is so for schizophrenia, especially when the patient is a son or daughter who has been living with parents. One parent quite commonly sees the illness in terms of 'him or me'. This may be well based. Several of our parents have had psychotic episodes at the time that the patient achieved some independence in life. In these families the line dividing the 'well' from the 'ill' is critical. I have often been asked by those engaged in family therapy if I have ever known anyone who has dared tell a parent that they were as much in need of treatment as the patient. I never have. Parents have to be approached obliquely, using the patient. The fear of the direct approach to a parent, or even of involving a parent in a genuine relationship issue with the patient can be quite profound. It feels like 'lèse-majesté', a violation of the cultural mores; something like risking the destruction of everything a parent stands for in front of one of their children. What I have described as breaking through the treatment barrier if one is to reach real relationship problems, or real personality damage, always feels to some extent like violation of the cultural mores. Nowhere is this experience of violation so intense as it is in the families of schizophrenics. These families seem like sensitive crucibles of our culture.

Violation of the cultural and parental values in the families of schizophrenics is not the prerogative of professional staff. It is the patient himself who has the central position in this respect (Scott et al., 1970).

The two diagrams in Appendix II express the central issue around which revolves all that I have said about the treatment barrier. They give the Relationship Test scoring profiles typifying community-centred and hospital-centred patients. Community-centred patients spend the majority of their time out of hospital and are in no danger of becoming chronically hospitalized; hospital-

centred patients spend the majority of their time in hospital and
are very likely to end up being chronically hospitalized. The exact
criteria defining the two groups are given in Appendix II.

Both diagrams show that parents see themselves and expect
patients to see them as being 'well', and then there is an abrupt
drop down to the level of the white columns expressing views of
the patient - how patients see themselves, expect to be seen, and
are seen by parents. Across the drop we may run a line and with
some confidence term it the 'well-ill' line, an expression of that
officially authorized line which divides the ill from the well, as this
is seen by the family.

We may note that the profiles differ in one way only: community-
centred patients support their parents' identities, hospital-centred
patients see their parents below the well-ill line, i.e. as being
disturbed or 'ill', and the parents do not expect this. That a
serious violation of parental expectations is involved is shown by
the fact that a family crisis soon ensues if a hospital-centred
patient goes home to his parents; the patient is in danger of
spending the rest of his life in hospital, whereas the community-
centred patient can be ill at home provided he supports parental
identity. Other work (Scott and Montanez, 1972) has shown that
the parents are extremely dependent on the patient for support
of their sense of identity.

The specific issues concerning the patient's position - his insight,
awareness, agency - listed for exploration at the end of the introduction can now be examined with the aid of test scoring. The two
scoring profiles in the technical appendix are based on the crude
amounts of 'wellness' and 'illness' attributed in a viewpoint and
are composed of the aggregated scorings of seventeen families in
each profile. This reveals the general pattern but wipes out
individual differences. To examine the specific issues we must use
individual attributes and also consider family members as individuals.
Table 3.1 lists the main attributes by which the mother's view
of the patient differs from her view of herself, using ten community-
centred and ten hospital-centred scoring patterns. The table gives
the frequencies with which this set of attributions were used in the
six viewpoints involving the mother-patient relation. Father's
scorings are omitted in order not to overburden the table.

Evidence that mothers see patients in the cultural image of illness
Relative to how they see themselves, the mothers' highest scored
attribution for their view of the patient is *confused*, and the lowest
scored is *responsible*; *inadequate in the outer world* closely follows
confused. Of the 47 attributes in the test, *confused* and *responsible* (responsible not scored) are the most central to the cultural
image of illness. Thus we have confirmation that these mothers
have the cultural image of illness at the centre of their view of
the patient: they see the patient as being *not responsible*,
confused by illness, and thus unable to direct his own life, and
as being *isolated* and *detached*.

Table 3.1*　　Frequency of attributions scored in six viewpoints concerning the M-Pt
relationship: 10 families, max. score = 10

(M/Self = mother's view of herself; M/PT = mother's view of patient; M/PT/M = how mother
expects patient to see her; PT/Self = patient's view of self; PT/M = patient's view of mother;
PT/M/PT = how patient expects mother to see him. Attributions above the line are mainly
categorized as attributions of 'illness', the two below the line are central attributes of being
'well' parents as opposed to 'ill' patients.)

	M/Self	M/PT	M/PT/M	PT/Self	PT/M	PT/M/PT
Hospital-centred scoring (N 10 pts, 10 Ms)						
Confused	0	7	2	3	5	6
Sense of isolation	1	6	0	5	2	4
Inadequate in outer world	0	5	0	3	1	3
Emotionally inadequate	1	5	0	3	4	4
Dependent	1	5	1	5	6	5
Fearful	0	4	0	4	4	6
Detached	1	4	0	5	5	7
Secretive	0	3	0	7	3	7
Confusing	1	3	1	6	4	4
Suspicious	1	3	4	7	3	6
Responsible	8	3	8	4	6	2
Mixes well out	9	3	7	3	7	3
Community-centred scoring (N 10 pts, 10 Ms)						
Confused	0	4	1	7	2	5
Inadequate in outer world	0	4	0	2	0	4
Fearful	1	4	2	1	0	1
Detached	1	3	1	3	2	4
Confusing	0	3	1	5	2	6
Emotionally inadequate	1	2	0	3	0	2
Suspicious	0	2	4	5	1	4
Sense of isolation	0	1	0	4	1	2
Secretive	0	1	1	1	1	4
Responsible	9	3	6	3	8	4
Mixes well out	6	3	4	4	9	6

*These patients were admissions to hospitals other than Napsbury. The family was seen by
our research team once only, at the time of testing. Thus our influence on the family would
have been minimal.

Specific issues for examination

1.　Do patients lack insight that they are patients? Do they deny
that they are ill? In general terms (see diagrams in Appendix II),
patients see themselves as being ill and patients, to about the same
extent as parents see them. In specific terms (Table 3.1), they
also see themselves in similar terms to how their mothers see them,
but patients lay more stress on terms implying activity on their
own parts in their isolation from others – *secretive*, *confusing*,
suspicious.

　　2. (a) How far are patients aware of being seen as patients by
their parents? In general terms they are very well aware of how
their parents see them (Appendix II, diagram, col. 4, Pt /Par /Pt).

Regarding *confused*, we may note (Table 3.1) that patients see
themselves rather differently from how their mothers see them,
but they are very correct in their expectations of how their
mothers do see them in this respect.

(*b*) How far are parents aware of how the patient sees them?
The profiles in Appendix II show that the parents of hospital-
centred patients are quite adrift about how the patient sees them,
whereas the parents of community-centred patients are more or
less correct. This is probably due in part to community-centred
patients tuning in to how they know that their parents want to be
seen.

3. Are the parents or patients more in touch, or more out of
touch, with reality as far as awareness of issues in their mutual
relationships are concerned? Analyses 2a and b provide a general
indication that patients are more aware of how they are seen by
their parents than vice versa. But awareness belongs to an individual; hence to compare parents and patients we must use
individuals and individual terms, i.e. how far does a particular
patient perceive that his parent scores specific attributes about
him?

Correlations suggested that how parents expected to be seen was
determined almost entirely by how they saw themselves and not
by how patients saw them; whereas how patients expect to be seen
was determined by how parents saw them as well as by how patients
saw themselves. A role-image analysis [4] confirmed this: terms which
parents (correctly or incorrectly) expected were almost entirely
contained within the role image of how parents saw themselves,
i.e. they did not show awareness of terms which the patient saw
in them which were not contained in their own self-image; whereas
for patients, about a quarter of the terms correctly expected were
not contained in their self-image. That is to say the patients in
both groups were more able to stand aside from themselves and
to perceive correctly bits of their parents' views of them than their
parents were able to stand aside from themselves to perceive what
patients thought of them (the parents).

Conclusion. The above findings should not be overestimated.
Patients had a lot of incorrect expectations, but amongst these
were some very well perceived expectations. Parents on the whole
were not capable of this. Thus we may conclude that patients
showed an indication of being more aware of issues in their mutual
relationships than were their parents - that patients were more in
touch with reality in this respect. These findings have been confirmed in a number of other cases.

4. There is good evidence that parents fail to perceive what the
patient thinks of them because the cultural image of mental illness
blinds them. This is very clear in the cases of the parents of
hospital-centred patients. A glance at Table 3.1 will show how the
mothers are blind to the point of imperviousness about the negative
terms the patients saw in them. Anything threatening is seen by
the mothers as 'illness' in the patient and so is not applicable to
how their child sees them.

Table 3.2   Controlling: frequency of scoring in viewpoints

	Par/Self	Par/Pt	Par/Pt/Par	Pt/Self	Pt/Par	Pt/Par/Pt
Hospital-centred						
Mothers	3	0	4	6	6	1
Fathers	6	1	7	6	5	3
Community-centred						
Mothers	2	2	4	1	6	2
Fathers	5	1	4	1	7	2

Data are for the same series of 10 hospital-centred and 10 community-centred patients and parents as in Table 3.1. Maximum score = 10.

5.   The central theme of both parts of this paper is that the cultural image of mental illness places the patient in a position to exploit an awareness which, by reason of the image, he is not seen as possessing. That patients are aware of the possibilities of this position is indicated by the test term which implies agency, or power over others, more than the others - controlling.

The pattern shown in Table 3.2 is remarkably consistent for mothers and fathers right across the table. Parents, especially fathers, see themselves as controlling, and they correctly expect to be seen thus by patients. Very few parents see patients as controlling, and the patients know this, but six out of the 10 hospital-centred patients see themselves as controlling. The scoring implies that hospital-centred patients have an awareness of their potentiality for controlling others which they are not seen as possessing, and which they know they are not seen as possessing. We may add our own impression that patients usually control the family whether in hospital or at home, but the parents do not realize this because they see the patient as 'ill'. Likewise hospital staff usually fail completely to realize the extent to which a patient exerts active control. Community-centred patients do not admit this in their scoring; it is surprising that hospital-centred patients are prepared to score what it is difficult ever to get from them explicitly in words. But, in general, patients as well as many parents find it easier to reveal themselves in scoring rather than in words.

The test finding concerning parent's unawareness of the patient's attitude to, and view of his parent, is one of the most striking features of the scoring patterns we have examined. This unawareness need not be an expression of parental imperviousness; it could be an expression of the general cultural denial of the capacity of mental patients to have adopted agency and intention, which, as I showed in Part 1, has profoundly influenced the views of professional staff. [5] The use which patients may make of the public denial has been the subject of a growing, though fragmentary, body of work developing during the 1960s. This work shows that mental patients usually possess a well developed and adapted degree of agency and intention, but that these capacities are usually directed towards ends which are regarded as undesirable,

i.e. patients wanting to maintain their positions as patients in
hospital (or at home). I will summarize some of this work.

SUMMARY OF THE LITERATURE ON PATIENTS' AGENCY AND MOTIVATION

Although the work concerns patients in mental hospitals, most
of the findings are relevant also in less extreme cases. In Part 1
I showed how the treatment barrier could be operative in various
areas both for in-patients and for out-patients because in both types
of case the central issue for therapy is to harness the patient's
motivation and commitment.

Gordon and Groth (1967). They divided sixty patients into two
equal groups: 'stayers', those who by their attitudes were rated
as wanting to stay in hospital, and 'goers', those who by their
statements seemed eager to leave hospital. The two groups were
compared using Osgood's Semantic Differential for concepts relating
to the evaluation of home and relatives, neighbours at home,
hospital staff, discipline, control, etc.

The groups differed little regarding patients' attitudes to the
hospital. The most significant differentiation was obtained for how
patients evaluated their relatives and neighbours at home compared
to the hospital. The 'stayers' evaluated home as: unpleasant, bad ,
cruel, fathers as bad and cowardly, and neighbours as both bad
and sick. The authors concluded that the main obstacle to 'stayers'
leaving hospital was not symptomatology but poor relationships
with others in the community.

Unfortunately, the authors do not say whether the patients in
the two groups actually went or stayed. However, the findings
confirm what we have found scoring schizophrenic patients and
their parents on our Family Relationship test. Those who stay
see their parents as disturbed or ill (Scott et al., 1970).

Braginski et al. (1966). Two groups similar to those of the last
study were employed, 'old timers' and 'short timers'. The hypothesis was that the patients in the two groups would tend to
maximize the outcomes which it was inferred they desired by intentionally creating an impression likely to secure this outcome.
They used 30 MMPI items on the Social Desirability scale, and gave
the same set of terms to experimental and control groups on two
occasions which differed according to the oral instructions given:
one occasion the terms were introduced as being 'to find out how
ill you are', and on the other 'to find out how much insight you
have'. Scores of the two groups differed according to whether the
oral instructions pointed to illness or wellness; the 'old timers'
stressed ill and undesirable traits whilst the other group reacted
conversely to the instructions presenting a much more socially
desirable picture of themselves.

The authors concluded that mental patients are not helpless people
unable to determine their own fate, but
that patients' strategies are motivated and are powerful deter-

minants of the outcome of hospitalization by manipulating the
hospital milieu. The strategy is called 'impression management'.
Fontana et al. (1968). This is a similar study to the last and it
confirmed the findings.

The two groups were especially distinguished on the following two
variables: 'sick presenters' thought that they were much more under
the direction of others, and they scored much higher on the Family
Discord scale than did 'healthy presenters'; thus supporting Gordon
and Groth, and also our own finding that a patient's relation with
others outside hospital was more important than with patients or
staff in hospital.

The authors concluded that 'The creation of a sick incompetent
impression on others as an intermediate goal . . . is highly motivated', and 'patients are adept at managing their impressions on
others'.

In our experience the power of the role (which has become an
identity) of mental patient is tremendous. It is a power which
patients freely use: many times our patients have presented themselves at a police station, 'I'm from Napsbury'. They want a free
ride back. Or sometimes it is a demonstration of power on the eve
of being discharged. I might tell the police officer, 'It is very kind
of you to offer transport, but I think it would be better to let him
increase his self-reliance by finding his own way back.' The chances
are that the patient still arrives by police car, or else the patient
may then phone a relative who gets on to me and accuses me of
negligence and cruelty. It is practically impossible to let a patient
be responsible, and they know it.

The power of the role image is thought-stopping. One of the most
effective illness presenting moves is for a patient to express a
delusion or a hallucination to a psychiatrist. Normally this stops
any thoughts the psychiatrist might have regarding the patient's
motivation; instead the delusion or hallucination is seen as resulting
from some autonomous process. One may still hear a psychiatrist
diffidently asking a patient about 'voices', and getting him to
'admit' to hallucinations, and then fail to draw any conclusions
from the readiness with which a patient may speak of his voices
or delusions. Two papers describe how patients may simulate
symptoms of a previously psychotic state: Sadow and Suslick (1961)
and Ritson and Forrest (1970). Forrest told of how an audience at
one of our foremost psychiatric hospitals responded to his description of how patients could simulate psychotic symptoms; 'I was
received with utter incredulity', he said.

This expeditious use of psychotic symptoms is conscious and
intentional. But motivation with varying degrees of awareness
belongs to genuine psychotic symptoms too. We may find a patient
working himself up towards being hallucinated by acting in
accordance with a parent's fear of insanity in order to punish that
parent (Scott and Ashworth, 1969, p. 30). In the following case
the patient was probably not aware of her motivation.

On admission she accused the staff of intending to murder her
mother. Her doctor said to her: 'Perhaps you have done something

bad.' The girl responded: 'I have been bad, I have left my mother'; she then shouted: 'You are the devil.' The doctor said that he did not care for that approach and walked off. Two days later she came out of the psychosis. It became clear that the father was trying to bind his daughter to stay at home and to be involved with an invalid wife, and that he was doing everything in his power to make the doctor the 'expert' who pronounced his daughter mad. It was out of loyalty to her family that she had called her doctor 'the devil', that is when he refused to respond in the proper manner as the 'expert' in delusions.

I will conclude by setting the findings I have detailed of the patient as an unrecognized agent, against conventional models of mental illness.

MODELS OF MENTAL ILLNESS AND THE CULTURAL IMAGE

Our survey of the sick role in Part 1 of this paper showed that it was important to distinguish the sick role from the sickness, as well as from the person suffering from the sickness. In our culture the condition for the sick role is that the person has been disabled by an internal disease process for which he is not responsible. In physical illness the internal disease process is likely to be seen by others, and also experienced by the patient, as being somewhat peripheral to the person suffering it, though it is true that serious or dreaded physical diseases can greatly affect a person's sense of his own identity, as well as how he is seen by others. In the case of mental illness a person's sense of identity is also seriously affected, but in a very different way. In most cases of mental illness there is no evidence of a disease process other than what may be inferred from what a person says and does. The illness is not distinguished from the person. Thus a person who is not responsible for the illness he suffers becomes seen as a person who is not responsible. The sick-role mental patient becomes an identity, an identity which is not that of a person.

This aspect of our cultural image of mental illness has profoundly influenced most theories and views of mental illness and mental patients. The patient is seen as being the victim of forces over which he has no control and which affect his identity, i.e. he is seen as being a helpless person who cannot determine his own fate. This conventional view of a mental patient is common to views, or theories of mental illness which superficially may appear as being opposites:

1. The medical model. The patient is seen as the victim of an internal and autonomous disease process which to a greater or lesser extent has impaired his rationality and ability to function.

2. The sociological model. The patient is seen as being the victim of society. Often the hospital is seen as agent. Goffman is most representative (1958, 1959, 1961). He sees the mental patient not so much as a person who is uniquely ineffective in his own right, or through his own condition, but as being rendered so by

the massive power of the total institution to which society, intolerant of deviance, has compelled his admission. There is also
a mitigated version of the Goffman stereotype in which the hospital
is seen as a benign place to which a patient, rendered passive and
inadequate by his illness, clings.

3. The family model. In family studies the patient is commonly
seen as the victim of his family, and his agency in becoming a
victim may be muted to the point of invisibility. Laing and Esterson
(1964) are representative of this aspect of the conventional view of
a patient. The disease is no longer seen as being inside the patient
but has been placed outside him. The family is the disease and the
patient the helpless and innocent victim.

In model 2, and to some extent 3, the person has been identified
with the sick role and causality is then attributed to the sick role.
Szasz (1961, 1967) has seen this and, as a result, has described
mental illness as a 'myth'. But Szasz himself fails both to make
and to consider the distinction between the sick role and illness,
so that his work seems unreal and unconvincing.

My presentation has been from a stand-point placed midway
between the interpersonal and the sociological. For years I have
been working on the intimate details of the family relationships of
our patients, and have been impressed with the way in which their
conceptions of mental illness formed the main barrier to the treatment of the severe disturbance and psychopathology which was
frequently present. More recently I have emerged out of the family
hinterland into the light of day, and seen how many abnormalities
in family relationships are based on the cultural image of mental
illness. It then becomes clear that the image of mental illness prevailing in our culture itself formed a barrier to treatment; more
in some cases than in others. The issue was then taken up by my
hospital team. In Part 1 I described how our understanding of the
way in which patients, community members and professional staff
used the image had considerably altered the treatment policy of
the team. In Part 2 I have given details of the patient's position,
showing how the image of illness obscured awareness of a patient's
agency and motivation, in a way which seemed designed to enable
patients to continue as patients and for the community to promote
this and bear the expense for doing so.

NOTES

1 Based on a paper given at a research seminar chaired by
Dr John Bowlby, Tavistock Institute of Human Relations, 5 May 1971.
The material used for the technical part of this work was derived
from a project supported by the Department of Health and Social
Security.

2 For admissions to hospital this needs putting in perspective:
in the case of about 80 per cent of all individuals under 65 years of
age admitted to Napsbury, dealing with relationships does not form
an essential part of treatment - physical treatments and the refuge

function of the hospital suffice. But, as shown in Part 1 (Scott, 1973), an appreciation of the issues concerning the treatment barrier can greatly improve the functioning of a ward and staff efficiency. In the remaining 20 per cent the treatment of relation-ships is often essential since untenable relationships between the patient and his significant others in the community commonly form a severe obstacle to leaving hospital.

3 An interpersonal perception technique described later in this paper.

4 Role image: for a group of patients and parents the average frequency of scoring of attributions in any one viewpoint is calcu-lated, and the role image is made up by terms scored with a fre - quency of the nearest whole number above the average, or more.

5 Whether, or not, imperviousness is involved may be assessed by exploring the sensitivity of a parent to the feelings and attitudes of persons other than the patient.

REFERENCES

Braginski, B.M., Grosse, M. and Ring, K. (1966) Controlling
  Outcomes through Impression Management: an Experimental
  Study of the Manipulative Tactics of Mental Patients, 'J. Consult.
  Psychol.', 30, 295-300.
Fontana, A.F., Klein, E.B., Lewis, E. and Levine, L. (1968)
  Presentation of the Self in Mental Illness, 'J. Consult. Clin.
  Psychol.', 32, 110-19.
Goffman, E. (1958) The Characteristics of Total Institutions, in
  'Symposium of Preventive and Social Psychiatry', Washington DC:
  Walter Reed Army Institute of Research.
Goffman, E. (1959) The Moral Career of the Mental Patient,
  'Psychiatry', 22, 123-42.
Goffman, E. (1961) 'Asylums', Garden City, New York: Doubleday-
  Anchor.
Gordon, H.L. and Groth, L. (1967) Mental Patients wanting to stay
  in Hospital, in T.J. Scheff (ed.), 'Mental Illness and Social
  Process', New York: Harper & Row.
Laing, R.D. and Esterson, A. (1964) 'Sanity, Madness and the
  Family', London: Tavistock.
Ritson, B. and Forrest, A. (1970) The Simulation of Psychosis:
  a Contemporary Presentation, 'Br. J. Med. Psychol.', 43, 31-7.
Sadow, L. and Suslick, A. (1961) Simulation of a Previous Psychotic
  State, 'Archs Gen. Psychiat.', 4, 452-8.
Scott, R.D. (1973) The Treatment Barrier. Part 1, 'Br. J. Med.
  Psychol.', 46, 45-55 (see pp. 30-43 above).
Scott, R.D. and Ashworth, P.L. (1965) The 'Axis Value' and the
  Transfer of Psychosis: a Scored Analysis of the Interaction
  in the Families of Schizophrenic Patients, 'Br. J. Med. Psychol.',
  38, 97-116.
Scott, R.D. and Ashworth, P.L. (1969) The Shadow of the Ancestor:
  a Historical Factor in the Transmission of Schizophrenia, 'Br. J.
  Med. Psychol.', 42, 13-32.
Scott, R.D., Ashworth, P.L. and Casson, P.D. (1970) Violation
  of Parental Role Structure and Outcome in Schizophrenia: a Scored
  Analysis of Features in the Patient-parent Relationship, 'Soc.
  Sci. & Med.', 4, 41-64.
Scott, R.D. and Montanez, A. (1972) The Nature of Tenable and
  Untenable Patient-parent Relationships and their Connexion with
  Hospital Outcome, in Y. Alanen (ed.), 'Proceedings of the Fourth
  International Symposium on Psychotherapy of Schizophrenia',
  Amsterdam: Excerpta Medica.
Szasz, T.S. (1961) 'The Myth of Mental Illness: Foundation of a
  Theory of Personal Conduct', New York: Hoeber.
Szasz, T.S. (1967) The Myth of Mental Illness, in T.J. Scheff
  (ed.), 'Mental Illness and Social Process', New York: Harper &
  Row.

APPENDIX 1

The Family Relationship Test
The mother, father, and patient, are asked to use the set of terms listed below to describe:

How they see themselves
How they see each other
How they expect each of
the others to see them

These are
termed
viewpoints.

Your view of _____

Below is a list of descriptive terms. Tick off those you think apply.

N	Demanding	S	Secure
	Popular	I	Left out
N	Anxious	N	Confusing
	Respectful	I	Confused
N	Sensitive	S	Generous
	Devoted to family	N	Dependent
S	Understanding	S	Self-confident
S	Sociable at home	N	Obstinate
S	Responsible	I	Sense of isolation
N	Emotional	S	Mixes well out
N	Quick-tempered	S	Careful with money
S	Reasonable	I	Self-doubting
I	Emotionally	I	Misjudging
	inadequate	N	Helpless sometimes
S	Considerate	S	Open to correction
N	Timid	N	Easily led
I	Inadequate in outside	S	Tolerant
	world	S	Easy to talk to
S	Strong-willed	N	Jealous
	Controlling	N	Fear of control by
S	Affectionate		others
I	Detached	N	Nervous
N	Uneasy with	I	Secretive
	strangers		
N	Submissive	I	Suspicious

Classification: by and large families of schizophrenics use: I terms to attribute 'illness', S terms to attribute 'wellness' (S for strong), N terms to attribute nervousness not amounting to illness. The classification is not given on the actual score form.

APPENDIX II

The following viewpoints are used in the present context:

Viewpoints	Abbreviations
How parents see themselves	Par /Self
How patient sees himself	Pt /Self
How parents see the patient	Par /Pt
How patient sees his parents	Pt /Par
How parents expect patient to see them	Par /Pt /Par
How patient expects his parents to see him	Pt /Par /Pt

The crude amount of 'wellness' or 'illness' attributed in a viewpoint is measured by

$$\frac{\text{No. of S attributes}}{\text{No. of I attributes}}$$

scored in that viewpoint. This is termed S /I ratio - the higher the 'weller'. Using the S /I ratios of the six viewpoints listed above, the diagram shows typical community-centred and hospital-centred scoring profiles. The figures in the diagram represent the aggregated scoring of seventeen community-centred patients and their parents, and seventeen hospital-centred patients and their parents.

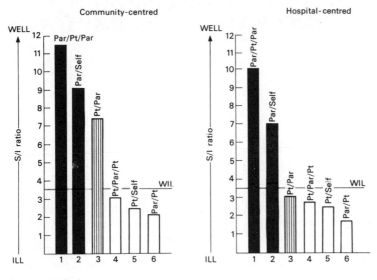

FIGURE 3.1

WIL = WELL-ILL LINE (Above the line are 'well' views; below
the line are 'ill' views).

Community-centred patients are defined as spending < 70 per
cent of the two years after first admission in hospital. They are
very unlikely to become chronically hospitalized. Hospital-centred
patients spend > 70 per cent of the two years after first admission
in hospital. They are very likely to become chronically hospitalized.

4 A GROUP-ANALYTIC APPROACH TO CONJOINT FAMILY THERAPY

A. C. R. Skynner

INTRODUCTION

The dynamic interlocking nature of family relationships, where the
demands of instinct and society, impulse and control, may be served
by different family members, has received increasing study in
recent years. Bowlby (1949) reported the bringing together of
parents and referred child, during their individual treatments, for
occasional joint sessions. Other landmarks include Sperling's (1951)
description of the manner in which the child acts out its mother's
repressed needs and Henry and Warson's (1951) concept of a family
core neurosis which affects all members. Fisher and Mendell (1956)
in a particularly interesting attempt to objectify this idea, applied
various projective tests to two or three generations of several families. They concluded that 'each family tends to be characterised
by a special "flavour" or "atmosphere". The projective responses
of the members of a family manifest certain themes in common, as if
there were a key motif that concerned the members of this particular
group. Illustratively, in 1 family all 7 of the members, at 3 different
generation levels, show an unusual preoccupation with themes of
exhibitionism and self-display.' Their impression that 'this transmission process occurs primarily in terms of what is denied, forbidden and concealed' is highly relevant, since the focus of family
therapy is on facilitating intercommunication in these forbidden areas.
   Amerongen (1954) and Hallowitz et al. (1957) illustrated a growing
recognition of the value of including fathers in the therapeutic effort.
Ackerman (1958, 1959, 1966a, b, c, 1967), demonstrated the potential
of working with the whole family, including siblings, though his
theories are limited by their basis in individual rather than group
dynamics and his techniques by a corresponding excessive activity
on the part of the therapist. Prince (1961) has described joint treatment of mothers and young children, pointing up particularly the
direct information to be gained from physical movements and the
highly supportive and reassuring effect, on both mother and child,
of witnessing the latent love which lies beneath overt hostility and
other defences. Martin and Knight (1962) outlined an intake procedure at the Tavistock Clinic during which both parents met together with the whole clinic 'family'. Howells (1962) treats the designated patient as the family member who may be most obviously

handicapped but may also be a scapegoat or an ambassador.

Bell (1961, 1962) views child psychiatric problems as examples of blockage of communication in the family network, as a result of which there is regression from symbolic communication to preverbal signs. A rigid, inflexible pattern of response and role-playing develops from which the family can be freed only by an outsider who can translate the stalemate of symptoms and condemnation back into a symbolic form that permits discussion and resolution of the conflict.

A number of authors and teams have developed increasingly group-centred theories of family functioning in association with research into schizophrenia. These enquiries have tended, until recently, to develop rather separately from the research into conjoint family therapy of the broader range of diagnostic categories occurring mainly within the field of child psychiatry, but each is now increasingly shedding light on the other. The concepts of the 'double-bind' and of 'family homeostasis' produced by the Palo Alto group (Bateson et al; 1956) are early examples. Bowen (1960) comments on similar observations of symbiotic pairing of 1 marital partner with a schizophrenic child, thereby excluding the spouse. Lidz and his colleagues (Lidz, 1963; Lidz et al; 1966) have noted disturbances they describe as marital 'schism' and 'skew', with associated weakness of the normal generation boundaries in families producing schizophrenic members. Satir (1964) has developed a detailed and generally applicable technique from this specialised background.

The Philadelphia team (Friedman et al; 1965), though restricting their study to families of schizophrenic patients, have explored and formulated general problems of family therapeutic technique with remarkable frankness and clarity. They are particularly interesting on issues raised by co-therapy and by the power struggle which they believe must ensue when therapists interact with a pathological family system. The University of Texas Medical Branch team (MacGregor et al; 1964) studying a broader range of problems among adolescents, and using an intensive investigatory and therapeutic technique whereby a team and family interact in various combinations for two full days, has produced some of the most interesting concepts regarding family dynamics, particularly in their detailed exposition of the relation between different forms of marital pathology and corresponding levels of developmental arrest in the children. Ferreira (1963) speaks of 'family myths' - fantasies shared by a family which preserve self-esteem at the cost of self-deception and breakdown of some of its members; and Laing and his colleagues (Laing and Esterson, 1964) have made careful studies supporting the notion that schizophrenic disorder can be brought about by pressures to distort the perception of reality.

It appears to be no accident that the best published work is increasingly produced by teams rather than individuals. Sager (1968a) has commented on the way that treatment of the family together has been paralleled by a tendency for teachers to allow their students to learn by being present throughout the treatment process, or to act as co-therapists, rather than by supervision of the students' cases alone or through hearing carefully edited accounts of the

teacher's work. This has led to refreshingly frank studies of co-
therapy and team-work, and to a more open examination of the
therapist's role, the effect of his personality, and so on. At the
same time, growing interest in this field has led to conferences
where attempts have been made to integrate existing knowledge.
(Ackerman et al; 1961, 1967; Cohen, 1964).

A number of authors require special mention because of their
contribution to specific problems. The University of Texas team
(MacGregor et al; 1964) has paid particular attention to therapeutic
procedures which are based more on example and identification than
on insight and intellectual processes. Minuchin and Montalvo (1966,
1967) have carried this type of research even further and have
developed special techniques, based on role-playing and identification, for treating culturally deprived families. Parsloe (1967) has
written on the use of similar methods through home visits and
Roberts (1968) has reported on principles we have developed for
working with deprived families.

Sager (1968b) has contributed an excellent paper on selection for,
and induction to, family group therapy, while among others Ackerman (1958, 1966 a, b, c) Scherz (1962) and Skynner (1967b) have
attempted to formulate indications and contra-indications for the
technique.

More recently a number of authors (Leichter and Schulman, 1968;
Blinder, 1965; Curry, 1965; Durrell, 1969; Powell and Monahan,
1969) have given interesting accounts of multi-family therapy – the
simultaneous treatment of several families together. This approach
combines many of the advantages of family and of 'stranger' group
therapy and is a particularly promising field.

With the exception of Bell (1961, 1962, 1964), however, little
consideration has been given until recently to the theory and technique of therapeutic group interaction in this context. General
theories of group functioning have tended to develop in association
with the therapist-constituted 'small group of strangers', or with
'T' groups or analytically-orientated training groups. In family
therapy, much interesting work has been done in studying the
typical structure and interaction of families with particular types
of pathology, but the therapeutic interventions have tended to be
based either on one-to-one techniques or on 'common-sense', spontaneous responses by the therapist.

Recently, some extremely fruitful ideas, with the aim of applying
group and system theory to family interactions, have been put
forward by a number of authors, particularly Brodey (1967) and
Scheflen (1967); I propose now to outline some possible developments of group analytic theory in this direction.

THE GROUP-ANALYTIC APPROACH

The Group-Analytic method is described by Foulkes (1948, 1964)
and Foulkes and Anthony (1957). In the latter they state of the
Group-Analytic approach:

'No programme or directions are given, so that all contributions arise spontaneously from the patients' (p. 28).

'All communications are treated as the equivalent on the part of the Group of the free association of the individual under psycho-analytic conditions. There is also a corresponding relaxation of censorship' (p. 28).

'All communications and relationships . . . are seen as part of a total field of interaction, the Group Matrix' (p. 28).

'All Group members take an active part in the total therapeutic process' (p. 28).

'The Group tends to speak and react to a common theme as if it were a living entity, expressing itself in different ways through different mouths. All contributions are variations on a single theme, even though the Group are not consciously aware of that theme and do not know what they are really talking about' (p. 219).

This concept of an unconscious common group pre-occupation, is, of course, a feature of other theories and techniques such as those of Whitaker and Lieberman (1964), Bion (1961), Ezriel (1950) and others. All these have important lessons for us but the Group-Analytic approach differs from them, I believe, in the following important respects: first, its simultaneous recognition of the individual and its willingness to focus on his more personal psycho-pathology when this is indicated (always, however, within the context of the Group as a whole); secondly, its recognition of the vital therapeutic functions performed by the group towards the individuals and the emphasis that it is the therapist's primary task to facilitate these; and thirdly, its affirmation that the Group as a whole, if its communications are sufficiently understood, stands in a position of authority to the therapist, correcting his own distortions and limit-ations and including him in the treatment process in so far as this is necessary and he can tolerate it. In the small group of strangers (usually about seven or eight) which meets with the therapist in the process of group-analysis, the therapist or conductor thus functions mainly as a catalyst who facilitates the inherent therapeutic potentialities of a well-selected group, a translator who recognises and interprets the group themes as they emerge in the same way as a psychoanalyst links and makes meaningful the apparently dis-jointed and meaningless associations of the analysand.

SOME DIFFERENCES IN THE NATURE OF THE FAMILY GROUP

Now all this does apply to the family group as well, but some modi-fications and elaborations appear necessary due to certain vital differences. In the first place, the issue of authority and control can largely be avoided in conventional 'small group' technique with adults by selecting patients who have different and conflicting views so that they are likely, despite temporary defensive coalitions, to cancel out each other's extreme attitudes and to represent a reasonable degree of 'normality' as a whole even if they do not do so individually. The members are also chosen in such a way that, in the long run, no individual will be so powerful and dominant in relation to others that he can impose his will to prevent change and growth in the whole situation. Finally, the patients more commonly chosen tend to have reasonably well developed ego and super-ego functions; they are, in other words, adult enough to ensure that there is sufficient capacity for self-control in the group as a whole to require that the therapist be an authority only in so far as he is an expert with special knowledge.

None of these conditions is ensured in family groups. There are usually great differences in the strengths of the family members from the point of view both of their maturity and of the power that society vests in them by virtue of their roles. In the children at least, self-control may be limited, and if one works with the more inadequate types of families, often referred to child guidance clinics and other community services, the parents may be defective in this regard, too. Further, from the group-analytic point of view the family could hardly be a worse-selected group, since they share a common psychopathology and can be expected to collude to conceal vital information and to oppose changes which will threaten a long-established family equilibrium.

I believe these facts explain the more active, controlling role that all family therapists appear to have found necessary in their work, though it has taken some time for theory to catch up with practice and in the literature the conceptual focus was at first on enabling information to be shared through the more passive, neutral therapeutic interventions usual and appropriate in the group of strangers in which group-analysis was first developed. Active, challenging, stimulating interventions are, nevertheless, striking in the protocols of most workers in this field as well as in more recent theoretical contributions (Ackerman, 1958, 1966a, b, c, 1967; MacGregor et al; 1964; Friedman et al., 1965; etc.) and I believe that group-analytic theory needs to be clarified and extended to include this particular dimension. What follows is an attempt to contribute to this, and to describe the principles by which I have come to operate.

THE FAMILY AS AN EVOLVING STRUCTURE REQUIRING INTER-COMMUNICATION OF MEMBERS FOR COHERENCE AND DEVELOPMENT

First, following a group-analytic approach, I believe that there is a certain correspondence of structure and function between the group and the individual, so that concepts pertaining to the one are, to some extent, applicable to the other. Each is an assembly of parts which, to function effectively, need to be related to one another in a way which will produce a balanced and harmonious whole. Failure to maintain this balance comprises disorder or disease, whether 'physical' or 'psychological', and leads to destruction and conflict rather than creation and growth, or at least to arrest of development or regression to more primitive forms of functioning, in group and individual alike.

Since the system is dynamic and constantly changing, adequate communication must exist between the parts and the whole, whereby harmony and balance are preserved. In the individual, dissociation of an emotion may lead to impoverishment of normal functioning as well as the appearance of seemingly meaningless symptoms which interfere with the effectiveness of the whole organism; for example, fear of negative feelings leading to dissociation of aggressive impulses, which may result in a weakening of the personality in situations requiring assertiveness, as well as headaches, muscular tensions or other symptoms which operate as handicaps to effective living. In the group we see similar phenomena when one member becomes the chosen (and to some extent self-chosen) container of some aspect of personality which is unacceptable to the others. This individual is then used as a scapegoat to be attacked and rejected and will be seen as, or will become, disruptive; eventually he will be excluded, when another member may become the container in turn. In families, many authors have made us familiar with the role often served by the sick or mad child, the delinquent, the child who is said to be always jealous, and so on. In the case of the group, as with the individual patient, the task of the therapist is to bridge these dissociations in order to establish communication between the disconnected fragments of the total system. Most people who have written on family therapy have explicitly emphasised this function of facilitating inter-personal communication, as the therapists' central task. To do this, of course, corresponding aspects of the therapist's personality must be adequately integrated already. Persistent scapegoating or harmful subgrouping, like persistence of an undesirable dissociation in the course of individual psychotherapy, must always to some extent reflect a split within the group leader or therapist himself.

The first requirement, then, is that communication must be possible to link the various parts of the system together to permit them to form an integrated whole, whether we are dealing with an individual, a family, or a culture.

HIERARCHICAL STRUCTURE - AUTHORITY

However, the parts of the group, like the parts of the individual, are not all on one level but require to be arranged in a certain hierarchical order if they are to function effectively. No one disputes this in the organisation of the central nervous system, where lower centres are under the dominance of higher, or in the individual where more basic drives and instincts require to be subordinated to ego controls and these in turn to super-ego sanctions. But groups and families also have an optimum type of organisation which must involve a form of dominance hierarchy and while there is again a range of possibilities of varying effectiveness, it appears that breakdown of the authority structure - whether through the loss of control of a nation by its government, abdication of responsibility by a father, or destruction of the cortex through birth injury – leads to unco-ordinated release of tendencies which can be damaging to the whole system, however valuable these may be within proper bounds and in their proper place. On the other hand, excessive restriction of the lower by the higher leads to other forms of disturbance, like the emotional impoverishment of the severe obsessional or the lack of creativity which can occur in a social system where individual initiative is suppressed. This principle underlies the second main function of the family therapist, as I see it, which is to intervene and take control of the family situation where necessary, handing back responsibility when a more healthy form of interaction and control has been established by the thera- pist's example. Among various possibilities, a rigid authoritarian father may be suppressing initiative and denying individuality; a penis-envying mother may be preventing a passive father from taking his proper place in family decisions; or a child may be tyrannising the parents by playing upon their excessive need to avoid frustration or separation anxiety.

What constitutes the most effective authority structure is too little explored, and the subject arouses such strong emotion, especially in a time of change like today, that dispassionate thought about it is not easy. No doubt the requirements are different at different stages of the development of an individual, family or culture. In time of war or great danger a more definite hierarchy may be necessary for the survival of a society, while young children can be made anxious, as we know, by a degree of freedom for which their limited self-control makes them unfitted. At other stages a more flexible pattern, permitting a greater sharing of responsibility, may be required to give freedom to explore new patterns of development. Certainly the actual patterns and cycles seen in therapeutic and training groups or in therapeutic communities suggest that the most effective authority structure is a compromise between that degree of control which gives security but limits change, and that openness and freedom which permits development and growth but contains a danger of chaos and destructive conflict if carried too far. We appear to be living in a period when this issue is very much under examination and the so-called 'student revolts' can be very instructive when seen as a search for systems of communication and control more appropriate to present conditions. Anthropologists and ethologists can no doubt help us to apply these principles to the family, so that we may see if there are any natural invariant requirements in the relationship of male and female parents despite cultural variations. It seems likely that persistent authority conflicts between the parents, whereby each undermines and denigrates the other, would create disturbances in the children, and in our own culture my impression is that families operate best where each parent respects the other and shares responsibility, but where the father is accorded ultimate authority. It may be that a matriarchal pattern works equally well where this is culture-syntonic. Cross-cultural investigation is needed to clarify this.

CHILD DEVELOPMENT VIEWED AS A SERIES OF CHALLENGES TO MASTER GROUP SITUATIONS OF INCREASING COMPLEXITY

I have presented the need for communication between parts of the system, and the need for hierarchy within it whereby some parts are dominant to others, as if these two principles were separate. But I think this is only a limitation of my own capacity to understand and formulate the problem for I can see dimly that these two considerations are merely two aspects of the same thing, two ways of viewing the concept of order. However, these two simple principles, which comprise the theoretical justification for the therapist's role in facilitating communication and exercising control, describe correspondences between the individual and groups in general. But the family is a very special kind of group, since it acts as a bridge between the individuals of one generation and those of the next, giving a series of provisions, demands and challenges whereby the dependent infant evolves to an autonomous adult. These successive challenges may be seen, from one point of view, as requirements that the individual shall learn how to relate to increasingly complex group situations. The first dyadic relationship with the mother requires the recognition of another individual, of boundaries, separateness, and responsibility for loving and preserving another. The second challenge, requiring a further relinquishing of omnipotence, involves an encounter with paternal authority, demanding compromises between instinctual drives and the welfare of the family as a whole or of larger social units. (This challenge may be mediated by the mother but it is surmounted or not, in my experience, to the extent that the mother herself accepts the authority of the father, who in turn is more related to the outside world and so the representative of its values in the home.) Awareness of the parents as a pair, and as a sexual couple with a special relationship from which the child is excluded, is a further challenge which requires the child to cope with this exclusion and the jealousy it inevitably arouses, as well as the loss involved in accepting one sexual identity at the price of the other. The need to struggle and share with siblings at home and peers at school entails a further step towards the interdependence characteristic of adulthood. Adolescence finally brings pressures, both internal and external, thrusting the individual out of the family to find his main support among his peers, to mate and begin the process again, as leader this time of a new family group. The family therapist needs to be aware of this developmental sequence in order to see where a given family situation may be depriving its members of the opportunity to meet and master some crucial developmental stage.

PRACTICAL ARRANGEMENTS

All these remarks apply, if they are true at all, to any form of work with the family together; but what I particularly wish to describe is an application of these principles to a technique of therapeutic con-

sultation characterised chiefly by the use of rather widely spaced
interviews and the expectation that the main work will be done by
the family itself between the sessions. I will begin by describing
some practical considerations.

As in other approaches, the whole family is expected to attend;
both parents are vital and at my clinics the first letter to the family
expresses the importance of the father's presence as well as our
willingness to try to accommodate to his difficulties over obtaining
time off. In the approach I am describing all the siblings are invited,
too; their presence is often the crucial factor in opening up the
interview by breaking some family collusion and initiating a vital
communication. Though Bell (1961, 1962) has suggested that children under 9 are better excluded because of their limited ability to
communicate by verbal means, we find their participation is generally
helpful and rewarding provided the therapist acts as a communicative
link by connecting their non-verbal behaviour and play with the
more verbal contributions of the other members. For instance, at a
point where male potency was being implicitly questioned during a
family consultation carried out at a home visit, a young boy ran out
and rushed back waving a stick, and the stick then kept changing
hands, its possessor at any moment appearing to be the temporarily
dominant member of the family grouping. In another interview, at a
stage where the parents were speaking of the effect of their child's
sleep disturbance on their sexual relationship, the 2-year-old concerned began making coital movements against the mother. We find
that even the baby can be usefully included, and the way others
relate to him and his responses from moment to moment are often
illuminating.

Sometimes the family problem is felt to be so intolerable that it is
left behind in a member who stays at home. This must often be
accepted and the interview can be effective nevertheless if the
absent member is 'brought alive' in the interview by asking the
family to talk about his behaviour in detail to help the therapist to
understand him, since the more the projection is clarified, even
without comment, the more its illusory and defensive nature will be
recognised and pointed out by another member of the family. The
therapist will tend to be cast in the role of the absent member and
care must be taken not to respond unconsciously to this projection,
especially where the therapist is the same sex as an absent parent.
Provided one does not make this error one can of course start with
those who attend and then work towards including the others. At
first a parent may be unable to share the children with the partner
until they have got something for themselves.

As to time, an hour and a half is desirable, and most family therapists recommend it. I have come to use an hour in most cases because
of shortage of time, and have learned to work within it, but even
an hour and a quarter is a great advantage. Apart from this, I find
arrangements can be flexible and I personally prefer a certain infor-
mality. All participants should be able to sit in a rough circle with
play equipment, if needed, within the circle so that play activity can
be seen by all and included in the discussion. I encourage children

to sit and participate verbally, and how they respond to such requests from me or the parents gives important information which can
be taken up, but whatever they do can be included and used. Seating and change of seating at different sessions can be very informa-
tive. One father sat opposite me, then beside me, then away again
as he passed through phases of hidden conflict, identification and
growing independence. Who takes the lead at any time, who withdraws, the capacity to share the conversation or the need to inter-
rupt or to establish pairing relationships if there is more than one
therapist, all give as much information as the things which are said.

FOCUS ON GROUP INTERACTION IN THE HERE-AND-NOW

Beginners to family therapy often find it difficult to get the consultation started. The essence of the technique I use lies, I believe, in
the personal involvement of the therapist in the family's difficulties
in communication. By having no more preliminary contact or information than is essential to see whether the interview is necessary at
all, and to ensure that all the family come, the therapist is automatically exposed to all their difficulties of communication and control
from the very beginning as he tries to understand why they are
seeking help and what the problem may be. This is inevitably uncomfortable and frustrating but if it is possible to break through
this to an awareness of what is happening, in the here-and-now of
the interview situation, the understanding is in some way shared
with the family in a truly organic way and has an impact on everyone present that is often dramatic. A detailed history enables the
therapist to understand only intellectually and in advance, out of
time with the true rhythm of the family and out of touch with its
living experience. It is certainly more comfortable but I find it takes
away my main usefulness. Operating with limited information, the
therapist becomes in a sense one of the family, and has to find a
solution from that point, not from outside it; it does not seem unreasonable that such a solution found from inside should be of more
value to the family itself.
   It may be worth saying at this point that what the therapist has
to find, is almost always something that is missing; this one would
expect, of course, if one starts from the premise, supported by
much experimental work, that family difficulties are derived mainly
from what is concealed and denied, and so not communicated. This
valuable insight that there are advantages to operating without prior
intellectual understanding I owe partly to Winnicott (1965). When I
first attended his seminars on his technique of individual therapeutic
consultation I found it very hard to understand why he insisted on
seeing the child without a preliminary interview with the parents. It
seemed to me that whatever he could do without a history could be
done even better if he had one, but later I came to see that there
were similar principles involved in my work with families and found
his evident sharing of the child's struggle to reach an understanding of its problem, and his formulation in terms of 'meeting the

challenge of the case' very meaningful in terms of this different type of experience.

This avoidance of prior information is one factor which, from the beginning, helps to keep the responsibility for solving the problem squarely on the family, with the therapist as a helper who may be more expert in facilitating communication but who can never know as much about them, while seeing them in this fashion, as they do themselves. This is very much in contrast to conventional procedures, where the therapist is often the recipient of confidential knowledge about each member which cannot be shared with them all and where the therapist can consequently be looked to with some justification as the only person with the information required to resolve the difficulty. Even so, most families will try to escape responsibility by going no further than presenting the problem in terms of apparently meaningless symptoms in one child and then waiting for the 'expert' to provide a solution as they might expect a general practitioner to make a diagnosis on some spots and prescribe some medicine. This projection of the 'expert' role is at first difficult to avoid, but often the family will expand upon the problem if one resists too quick a response. Though I am sure that there are other ways of meeting this difficulty, I have found three approaches particularly helpful in moving from the initial presentation of symptoms in one member of a family to the real problem in the family as a whole. First, one can insist that the symptom is usually a hidden communication and ask 'What is it saying to us?' By suggesting that the system represents some blocked communication one gives sanction for that communication to be made, and sooner or later a member of the family is likely to make it in a clearer form. Second, it is often fruitful to ask what the 'effect' of the symptom is on the rest of the family, since this includes everyone in the discussion, and often leads to the 'cause'. Third, one can ask for a detailed, play-by-play account of family interactions centring around a symptom as a substitute for actually seeing them interacting at home. This nearly always leads to the reproduction of the actual conflict in the interview itself, though in different form. An authority conflict in the home will appear, for instance, in the actual way the family describes it, and this can then be commented on. In these and other ways the family is led from the presenting complaint to its meaning as part of a family problem, which can then be explored.

TRANSFERENCE AND THE THERAPIST'S ROLE

I shall say little about the therapist's role, yet the way the therapist is used is the most interesting aspect of all and I am sure an understanding of this would throw light on many other puzzling questions about the nature of the therapeutic factors in different forms of treatment. All therapists I have met who have practised family therapy have noticed that they behave in a much more spontaneous, open and natural fashion than they do when practising individual or other forms of group therapy. While this seems to be demanded by the needs of the situation it is not clear to me why this is so. One reason, perhaps, is that one intuitively sees the advantages of keeping primitive transference feelings within the family, and spontaneous, active behaviour by the therapist counteracts the projection of fantasy on to him just as passive 'blank-screen' behaviour facilitates it. Infantile projections and distortions are clarified as they exist between the family members and the fact that no time is required for such types of transference to develop or be resolved in relation to the therapist is no doubt one reason why such rapid changes are possible, and why each brief intervention is somehow complete in itself.

Transference must exist, of course, but it would seem that the role projected on to the therapist is less an idiosyncratic and personal one than a culturally accepted projection of certain universal parental qualities. The easy, relaxed feeling experienced by the therapist in a well-functioning family session suggests that the more uncomfortable projections characteristic of individual or group psychotherapy are not taking place, at least in a large proportion of cases. I have found that the ambivalent transferences, to which psychotherapists are more accustomed, do indeed occur where more ambivalence is released within the family system than the members can cope with. For example, in a middle-class family with two teenage sons, adolescent rebellion and the ambivalence natural between children and parents had been dealt with through an excessively permissive attitude, which obliged the children to inhibit their natural assertiveness. As it became apparent that the jealousy between the children served the purpose of displacing and containing parent-child and marital conflicts, and the latter came into the open, communication began to block and negative transference to the therapist emerged, displaced to a colleague at another clinic who referred the family. Without interpretation of this negative transference the family would probably have found reasons for failing the next session and discontinuing treatment, perhaps making it impossible to return for help by dealing with the hostility between family members by forming a paranoid attitude to the clinic.**Following interpretation, the family did indeed decide to terminate, but did so through a conscious decision that further therapy at that time might involve more pain than the problem warranted, since they were satisfied with the considerable, though limited, improvement already attained.

Donnelly (1966) has suggested that successful treatment of a family, whatever the method, requires that the therapist be seen as more powerful than the dominant parent, yet able to use this power for the benefit of the family rather than to fulfil personal needs or to protect himself. I have already attempted to provide a theoretical justification for this requirement earlier in this paper, but something more needs to be said about the problem from the point of view of technique and the demands it makes on the therapist. In my experience, the therapist needs to intervene and challenge family members only on rare occasions, and on reviewing my records and recollections, these have all been instances where communication was being restricted to avoid discomfort to some members, at the cost of the long-term benefit of the family as a whole. The therapist's use of authority is thus based on his responsibility for representing the demands of reality; it has, in other words, the same basis as the normal authority of the parents. This is conditional, of course, on the therapist's own authority over himself, and this, in turn, is based on his ability to face his own 'inner reality', his ability to take responsibility for himself.

However, the less the therapist takes control in this way the better, for what the family achieves for itself is far more valuable than what is given to them by others. Usually, the therapist can sit back a bit after a crucial intervention, for some previously inhibited family members are thereby emboldened to continue to open up the discussion in a more fruitful way.

It is surprising how little the therapist in fact needs to control the emotional interaction, apart from this. Bowlby (1949) and Bell (1962), among others, have both commented on the safety of the method despite the alarming (to the therapist) intensity of emotional exchange. Beginners commonly fear that the situation may get out of hand and produce harmful effects through continued negative interaction after the family have returned home, if not in the interview itself. I have tried to follow up all cases where I have had fears of this kind, and have not yet encountered one where my anxieties were justified. Indeed, one is often astonished to find how a seemingly disastrous interview in fact had a beneficial effect.

My work with training groups, as well as my personal experience, clearly shows that anxieties of this kind, as well as difficulties in taking control, have their origin in fantasies related to the therapist's own childhood experiences. A personal psycho-analysis or group analysis, or participation in a training group run on group-analytic lines, is therefore of great value.

GROUP VERSUS INDIVIDUAL RELATIONSHIPS

All forms of group psychotherapy require of the therapist a special form of attention, akin to the wide, unfocused visual attention we all automatically adopt when we are alert for some expected stimulus but uncertain of the direction from which it will come. Those used to individual psychotherapy often complain that they forget the group, focusing instead on individuals in turn in the way one may focus visually on an object which grips one's attention, neglecting the field in which it occurs.

This needed 'wide' attention comes partly with practice, partly perhaps with a reduction in the therapist's own need to be intimately related in a one-to-one fashion, but it can only be struggled for. Once attained, it automatically relates the therapist to the group as a whole, so that he is never unaware of it even though he may communicate with one person at a time.

I used to believe that I also took a neutral position between members of a family, until tape recordings showed that I frequently took sides. I now believe that an overall fairness is essential, but that siding with children or parents from time to time is not only inevitable but often meaningful and useful, as well as acceptable to the family, provided one acknowledges what one is doing, tries to formulate the reason one has been led to take sides, and remains open to criticism and further discussion. The therapist then includes himself in the treatment process and may find his reaction has some real justification, subsequently acknowledged by the family, or he may see that it is due to some personal identification. In any case it will be corrected automatically as the interview proceeds. The therapist's ability to be unfair, and to be criticised and corrected for it, can provide an important example for some families where the need to be rigidly fair and reasonable is a problem.

Zuk (1968a, b, c) has in fact based a whole technique of family therapy on deliberate siding, with the object of breaking down an excessive avoidance of conflict. The tendency to side with the referred patient evidenced by Laing and his colleagues (Laing and Esterson, 1964) seems, on the other hand, based more on an identification with the patient role and a simple reversal of values within the schizoid solution, whereby the patient is regarded as normal, the family mad, instead of vice versa.

FREQUENCY OF MEETINGS AND DURATION OF TREATMENT

As it is such a fundamental factor in my own technique, I must say something about the frequency of sessions I find most effective. An interval of three weeks seems ideal and several families have said spontaneously that less frequent sessions prevent continuity while more frequent ones prevent their digesting and utilising fully the consequences of each session. I have also found that meeting more often encourages the development of strong transference feelings towards the therapist, including a more dependent and passively receptive expectation that the therapist will do the work and provide the answers. This is a perfectly valid way of working, of course, but it operates through different mechanisms and according to a quite different time scale, similar to individual or 'small-group' psychotherapy. Three-weekly sessions keep responsibility squarely on the family, and exploit to the full the fact that the family continues to work at the problem between the sessions. While the changes may be limited in degree, they are great in total effect, and the intensity of the process even at this frequency has to be seen to be believed.

It has been my experience that this technique either produces striking and satisfactory change within a few interviews - often only one or two, rarely as many as ten - or, on the other hand, it provides early, clear indications that the balance of motivation is against change, without at least a heavy investment of therapeutic time and skill.

The cases dealt with have been those referred to a children's hospital and child guidance clinics in different types of areas. Clearly the same principles would not apply in general to severely disturbed families producing schizophrenic members, though my

experience has been that even very severely disturbed families who
seem hopeless at first sight can often make limited but worthwhile
gains. General principles regarding the suitability of this approach
for different types of problem and personality remain to be worked
out, though I have tried to summarise our current findings elsewhere
(Skynner, 1967b).

OTHER CONSIDERATIONS

I have not dealt with the issues of having two or more therapists
conducting family groups, though this is widely practised at my own
clinics as elsewhere. It introduces additional complications as well
as advantages though it does not alter the fundamental principles
set out above. Our experience in combining individual or marital
sessions with family therapy is also not dealt with here, though
the case illustration which follows contains an example of such a
combination. Generally speaking, we have found it possible to be
extremely flexible in combining different techniques, provided the
therapists have confidence in themselves and each other, and are
able to discuss their own reactions to the family and each other
frankly.

Little has also been said about the extent to which communication
requires to be restricted in family sessions. In fact, it has become
clear that probably anything can be discussed, including the
parents' and children's sexuality, though the timing is as important
as in other therapeutic work. Anxieties about discussing the parental sexual relationship in the family interviews prove to be related
more to the therapist's guilt over primal scene fantasies than to
real disadvantages.

A more detailed consideration of the ways in which communication
takes place in family sessions would require a paper of its own. In
psychoanalysis and individual psychotherapy verbal interpretation
of underlying feelings may play the main part, but in groups of all
kinds, where people are face to face, expressive posture, action
and example become increasingly important.

Our own work in poor districts of east and north east London confirms the findings of others that with more intelligent and educated
families greater reliance can be placed on verbal communication, insight and conscious understanding; while with more limited families
good results can still be obtained provided the focus is more on
education by example. In the latter conscious verbalisation of the
process is unnecessary and indeed often undesirable, when limited
goals need to be set.

For instance, the therapist may meet the needs of the children
for attention and communication, or for patient firmness and containment of overactivity, demonstrating to the parents that these
approaches are more effective than passive indulgence or punitive
suppression; or the parents, having their needs met in these ways
themselves, are able to internalise the therapist and the skills he
demonstrates; or the therapist may tacitly give permission for a more

free release of feeling in an inhibited family by behaving in a more spontaneous way himself, showing that he can be childish at times without losing his effectiveness in general. Examples of all these will be evident in the transcript of a session at the end of this paper.

CASE ILLUSTRATION

I shall now outline the course of a series of five family consultations which illustrate several of the points I have made. The interviews were all tape-recorded so that the accounts are reasonably accurate, though the difficulties of condensing five hours of family interaction into such a brief compass will be appreciated. The case is atypical since the identified patient and the mother had received between them several hundred hours of individual treatment over the previous twelve years, with temporary improvement but without basic change in the family dynamics. The case was therefore better documented than the usual family consultations become and the individual histories were available in a way that is not usually possible or even necessary in this type of family work. This is helpful from the point of view of examining the technique, but I had in fact had no contact myself with this family before the consultations to be described began and I came to them more or less blind, having forgotten by the time I saw them the conference at which they were presented because individual treatment had become blocked. I deliberately avoided reading the case notes until the family sessions were completed, though I have of course done so for the purposes of this presentation.

Case history
I will introduce the family very briefly. Pam, the referred patient, was a girl of almost 14 at the time of the first family session, and had a history of repeated separations from the mother, beginning at the age of 10 months, which had clearly damaged the relationship between them. The original symptoms twelve years earlier included destructiveness and hostility to the mother, together with depression and separation anxiety which took the central place as she grew older, as well as difficulty in spelling. As she entered adolescence, behaviour problems including stealing, truanting and sexual acting-out gained prominence.
     The mother was a vulnerable, unstable person, with several admissions to hospital for severe depression; during one of these, lasting almost a year, the children had been taken into care and had not seen her throughout this time; she felt herself to be intellectually and socially superior to the father, an aggressive, forthright 'rough diamond'. Just as Pam, the referred patient, had been used all her life as the container of all the family's unacceptable aspects, Sara, three years older and 17 at the time I first saw her, was the receptacle into whom all the family's good qualities were projected for safe-keeping. Their appearance was in line with this:

Pam, sullen, bad-tempered, evasive, poorly controlled, sitting
clumsily slumped in her chair; Sarah sitting calm, straight, with a
clear level gaze, gentle yet naturally commanding respect.

At the first interview, I invited the family to put me in the picture
about the current problems. The mother at once expressed intense
anxiety about Pam's stealing and truanting, while the father was
more concerned about Pam's failure to return home at the proper
time at night, clearly fearing sexual misbehaviour. Pam hung her
head, looked miserable and as if about to cry, and angrily refused
to contribute. The elder sister, Sarah, opened up the conversation
several times: first by saying that father was too strict; then that
Pam lost all her friends by being too possessive; and later that she
felt Pam was jealous of her and that this was partly caused by the
unfair treatment of the parents, who praised her (Sarah) and
blamed Pam.

Most of the early part of the session was nevertheless devoted to
Pam and her difficult behaviour, and attempts to clarify this led us
to focus on the way Pam always felt herself to be deprived and left
out. Here it was possible to confront Pam with the fact that she was
in fact depriving herself by the way she was refusing to participate
in the interview, despite our attempts to include her.

The conversation then moved on to criticism by the children, and
later mother, of father for being rigid and restrictive, particularly
in his refusal to allow his daughters to have boyfriends. This was
then partly explained by the way he expressed unhappiness at
losing his former close relationship with Pam as she entered adolescence and made more contacts outside the home. Next, as the
girls described their enjoyment at fooling about with father, tickling
and teasing him, the first criticism of mother, until then carefully
avoided, began to appear as they complained that she would 'moan'
and sulk when father and daughters behaved in this way. The
mother now became increasingly tense and uncomfortable, as if
angry yet ashamed and attempting to conceal her annoyance. The
rest of the family, suddenly realising this, became silent and behaved as if paralysed. I pointed this out, and the mother encouraged
them to speak freely, but they clearly felt she could not tolerate
criticism. I tried to bring the situation more into the open, pointing
out how mother had seemed to opt out of a rivalry situation with the
two daughters. Father's next statement that he treated wife and
daughters 'just the same', did nothing to improve matters and I
questioned whether this was appropriate!

At this point the interview suddenly turned into a discussion of a
marital problem, the mother complaining that father was unsympathetic and did not try to understand her disability, the father
countering by saying the mother spent all her time talking to doctors
and social workers instead of asking for help from him.

One of the functions Pam served in the family was clearly demonstrated when on several occasions they escaped from the marital conflict by uniting to attack Pam again, but this ceased, and the marital
conflict resumed, each time I pointed out this defence.

When it was time to stop, the father and daughters appeared in-

volved and interested, and keenly accepted the offer of a further
joint interview, but the mother appeared angry and upset that I
was proposing no special treatment 'for Pam'.

This account illustrates clearly, I hope, the general pattern of
development I expect from a first interview. This begins with the
presentation of the problem as the family at first views it – usually
as an inexplicable problem located in one individual – and leads
naturally, by encouraging exploration of the problem and interaction
by the whole family under the stimulus of the therapist's attempt to
grasp the difficulty, to the emergence of a coherent and explicable
family pattern and to pathology in other members or the marriage
itself.

We have become very flexible over combining different methods of
treatment and in this case, because of the mother's history and her
agitation at the end of the first session, she was offered appointments as she needed them with the p.s.w. who had been treating
her for some years (later on the mother gradually gave these up).
Seen individually in this way a week later, the mother was still
angry that I was 'not going to do anything for Pam'. I had been
'casual', had not seemed worried about the extent of her anxiety.
She had felt 'utterly defeated'. Yet she admitted she was pleased,
nevertheless, that the focus had not been on Pam, and she was preoccupied with my remark that she (mother) had appeared not to be
emotionally involved in the discussion, despite her attempts to
appear so. Pam, it seemed, had left the interview 'on top of the
world' and had stayed in for two evenings after it.

The interval between the first and second interviews, due to
pressure on evening appointments, was two months and this was
too long. Nevertheless the pattern had changed and even though
the parents began by accusing and blaming Pam as if nothing had
altered Pam was in fact strikingly more open, co-operative and
appreciative. She participated more helpfully in the interview and
this greater responsiveness contrasted sharply with the rejecting
behaviour of the parents who seemed to refuse to see the improvement demonstrated before them; I felt angered by the way they
seemed determined to destroy any progress we made.

Sarah hesitantly supported Pam, and the argument gradually
developed from a focus on Pam's behaviour to the familiar quarrel
of adolescence with adulthood, especially over symbols of sexual
freedom, an important change in the family structuring.

The third interview was arranged after only a month's interval, a
spacing which was subsequently adhered to, and progress was more
satisfactory. The session began with the usual attack by the parents
on Pam, but the realignment reached at the previous session had
persisted and the girls were now united in criticism of both parents,
while the parental coalition, though partly defensive against the
marital conflict, was also more secure and healthy as compared with
the previous pairing of each parent with one of the children. Indeed,
it was Sarah, the 'good' one, who this time received the main attack
from father. Nevertheless, movement was blocked by the parents'
refusal to acknowledge any share in the difficulty and every approach

to understanding would be negated by subtly destructive manoeuvres.

At some point in the interview I realised that I was failing to deal with this straightforwardly in response to my fear that to pursue the truth might risk the mother's sanity, and decided that the danger must be risked and, if necessary, coped with. I then confronted the parents with what I saw as their failure to involve themselves honestly in the transactions, and, as if released by my more active control of the situation, the parents at once began to speak of their feelings of failure and inadequacy. This led, in turn, to a sharing of feelings of concern and responsibility by the children, and painful recollections of the early separations and the mother's illnesses appeared.

At the fourth interview, a dramatic change was evident in the entire family, dating from the previous session, both parents now showing warmth and almost weeping with relief as if they had passed through a depression too deep to risk acknowledging at the time of its greatest intensity. The children both expressed very positive feelings in return and, since the previous interview, all the initial complaints had been in abeyance. Pam was co-operative and helpful, and they were getting on well.

In the rest of this fourth session we focused on the family problem of envy which, by making them deny their contribution to the solution of the problem as well as of my own, led them to feel they had no persisting control of the situation and so to fear a relapse. The fifth session, to which father was obliged to come late, revealed the parents' diffuse ego boundaries and the mutual projection which constantly occurred between them; this was an object lesson in the dangers of treating one parent alone. Also at this session the mother's need to keep Pam ill, or to keep her own illness in Pam, was pointed out by Sarah in relation to the intense separation fears of mother and indeed of both parents.

The sixth session was the last of the treatment series (though follow-ups have continued for two years) and all improvements had persisted in general though Pam became a problem for a time again in school when mother was admitted to hospital for hysterectomy early in the year. Pam had a good report from school, later, had been helpful and friendly about the house, and had become a comfort and support to mother, who almost wept at the warmth of Pam's response and now seemed able to reveal and let the children satisfy her own needs in a way she had not been able to do before. The improvements have since been maintained.

EXAMPLE OF FAMILY INTERACTION

It is extremely difficult to convey the experience of a family interview in words, but one can get closer to communicating its intensity, liveliness and impact with an actual transcript. What follows is the second half of the third family interview in the case just described, taken from the tape recording. I have chosen it rather than another excerpt since, although it shows me in a less favourable light than other excerpts might do, it was clearly the crucial episode. Soon after it begins I confront the parents with my view that they are avoiding the real issue of their own involvement. This is done too violently, due to my having avoided expressing this too long for fear the mother might become mentally ill again (in fact, she went from strength to strength from this point on!), but perhaps my own 'bad' behaviour freed the others to communicate more freely. It will be seen how the children follow by much more direct and open complaints and criticisms of the parents, and how the parents, in turn, react in a more open and fruitful way. Although the situation seems quite unresolved at the end, what followed at home was ultimately constructive and led to the dramatic improvement of the next (fourth) session. My own role in this crucial session, it will be apparent, was much more that of an active authority than a neutral, passive interpreter of the communications being made. It is important to emphasise that other sessions did not involve this degree of active intervention, and that I have chosen this extract rather than another not because it is typical but because this aspect of conjoint family therapy is likely to be the most difficult for those accustomed to an analytic technique to accept and utilise.

Transcript begins almost half-way through the third family session

Pam: Yes, but every time you was ill you always seemed to blame it on me, didn't you? (Imitates mother's voice): Well, you made me ill, you did that, yes, you did.

Mother: Rubbish, that's something of your own making, Pam.

Pam: No, because even when I said it to you, you said 'That's right'.
          Few seconds' silence

Doctor: (To Mother): You did say this last time, if I may remind you, and it was something I didn't pick up but you did in fact say Pam made you ill.

Mother: About Pam's making me ill?

Doctor: Yes. Maybe it's not true, but we must face this and see what it is about.

Mother: I have been taking Pam to child guidance ever since she was 2 years old and it's just a coincidence I had three nervous breakdowns during that period, since Pam was 2.

Doctor: You think there may be no connection?

Mother: I think there may be some connection. It is, as you say, a vicious circle.
          The tape fades out here. Tape not changed over.
          A few minutes lost.

Father: (Speaking of his previous close relationship with Pam): . . . at one time I couldn't pick me cap up without 'Where are you going? Let's come with you.' Then she just changed and she is just the opposite now, and she doesn't want to know anything. Whether or not it's since she has been to this new school.

Mother: (Interrupting): You can't blame schools, you can't blame people.

Father: Well, it's somewhere, isn't it?

Mother: It's no good blaming other people, and it's no good blaming schools.
Doctor: Then who are you going to blame?
Father: Well, where is it, then? It's got to be somewhere.
Mother: (To Doctor): Well, you know, in a round-about way, you have hinted that it could be him and me.
Father: Not necessarily.
Mother: It must be.
Doctor: (Angrily): I didn't hint . . . I said I was just always puzzled that it's all Pam. That's the story every time you come, it's all Pam. Pam is bad, B-A-D, and there is nothing wrong with you, that's what you tell me every time.
Mother: But I know there is something wrong with me.
Doctor: You don't. You tell me over and over again how you never put a foot wrong anywhere. I wish I could do as well as that.
Mother: (Interrupting): There is a lot wrong with me. I'm irritable . . . nasty-tempered . . . .
Father: Ah, now, when we say we haven't put a foot wrong, well, as regards the children you might say we done the best for them as we know how.
Doctor: That I accept.
Father: I am not going to say that we done everything for them that we could have done because there's times when we couldn't - when you hadn't got it to do with. I don't quite know how to put it. I mean I know myself I can be quite nasty at times, but regarding having everything they wanted and what they wanted to do more often than not they done it.
Pam: Sarah has, put it that way.
Father: (To Pam): Well, you have, yes, you have.
Sarah: (To Pam): But, Pam, you don't realise when I was your age I had exactly the same restrictions. I had to be in at 9 o'clock and if I wasn't in at 9 o'clock. . . .
Pam: (Interrupting): I have to be in at half-past eight.
Sarah: That's when I was 14, 9 o'clock.
Father: (Angrily): What about Saturday night? What was going on on Saturday night when I went down and sorted out about twenty yobbos down there?
Pam: Oh, there wasn't!
Father: Well, what was they, then?
Pam: About five.
Father: Chasing you up and down the stairs, trying to pull your trousers off. Well, that's not right!
Pam: No, they wasn't.
Father: Yes, they was. If I hadn't caught you they would have done.
Pam: They were trying to chuck me in the bushes.
Father: I've got a good pair of eyes, you know.
Pam: Trying to chuck me in the bushes.
Father: I've got a good pair of eyes.
Pam: . . . and go and ask if you want to.

Father: I asked you which way it was but you wouldn't tell me,
          would you?
Pam: I don't split, like some people.
Sarah: (To Pam): Are you referring to me, Pam? How do I split?
          What have I split on?
Father: (Interrupting): Well, I . . . .
Sarah: (To Pam): There is a lot I know about you that I could say,
          mate.
Father: (To Doctor): The trouble is there is nothing out in the
          open. They won't bring it out in the open.
Doctor: No? Well, I feel it just doesn't come in the open anywhere.
          I would say the same to you; in some way you don't come
          out in the open either, as I experience you. You (to
          parents) certainly don't come in the open.
Father: Well, I can't say anything more open than what I have said
          already. Because there is nothing more that I know that I
          can tell you, other than what I have already told you. As
          regards coming out in the open, I mean I air my views with
          the best of people, I don't care who they are or anything
          else. I mean I have argued with Sarah many a time. But
          the point is, I mean, I have always been plain straight
          talking. I don't care who they are or what they are. If I
          have got something to say I'll say it. I don't care who I
          offend or who I please. I speak me mind.
Doctor: Yes, that's quite true in a sense. . . .
Father: (Interrupting): The point is, I have been in trouble over
          it two or three times with the missus as well over it, she'll
          tell you that, but the point is, we can't get to know any-
          thing from Pam, because she just won't tell you. Sarah
          knows a lot more than what she'll say, but she won't say
          anything. All this business of not splitting and that, I
          mean it's a load of hogwash to me. I mean if there is some-
          thing going on like that that shouldn't be, then it should
          be let out and sorted out, that's my way of thinking. But
          if you just bang your head against a brick wall, then that's
          it, you can't do nothing about it. You just don't get any-
          where. You can't do anything.
Mother: (To Doctor): Do you think Pam would be better seeing you
          on her own?
Doctor: Who thinks that?
Mother: Would Pam be more open on her own with you?
Doctor: I don't think it would help because I don't think she is the
          whole trouble.
Pam: I don't want to keep coming here . . .
Doctor: (Interrupting): I am seeing you as a family because I think
          the problem is in the family, and I am seeing you together
          and I don't think seeing Pam on her own is going to make
          any difference.
Mother: But Pam doesn't contribute to this at all, does she?
          She doesn't say anything.
Doctor: (To Mother): Neither of you contributes, neither you nor

Pam contributes. Sarah and her father both (To Father and Sarah), you are quite correct, you are pretty direct and you both got at each other, you said what you really think, both got a bit upset and a bit further forward – (To Mother again) but both you and Pam somehow sit back, you withdraw and I can't feel your feelings; it is as if you are sitting behind yourself and are not involved in it. Neither of you seem to *feel*, that's all I can say. (To Father and Sarah): *You* both feel, certainly.

Mother: I don't know what else to do. I have given you and told you everything I feel and I just don't know what to tell you.

Doctor: (To Mother): Well, I rather think the trouble is that you don't feel. Pam doesn't feel, you don't feel. This is what the trouble is about – this lack of feeling. You know, while I have been here with you I can feel you (to Father) feeling and I can feel you (to Sarah) feeling. I can't feel either (to Mother and Pam) of you feeling. You are not feeling, you are not there, you are not in yourselves at the moment, and I feel the lack of it, I feel I don't make any contact with either of you, and there is something important in this; something has gone wrong between you because of it.

Mother: You mean Pam and me?

Doctor: Yes. That's the best I can say at the moment, though there's more to it than that, between all of you.

Mother: What can I do?

Father: If Pam would air her views a bit. . . .

Doctor: (To Mother): What are you – what are you. . . .

Mother: What am I?

Doctor: What are you? I don't know who you are, I don't know who you are.

Mother: I'll tell you what I am. I'm irritable, I am nasty-tempered, I feel rotten most of the time, little things upset me. . . .

Doctor: Then why did it go wrong between you and Pam when it didn't with you and Sarah? It's gone all right with her, but something has gone wrong between you . . . and why?

Sarah: It's lack of trust, that's what I think it is, because Mum trusts me implicitly in whatever I do, but with Pam it's 'Oh, dear what's she doing? Oh, where's me purse? Where's me pay?' She doesn't trust her.

Doctor: Why? Why is it different?

Father: Well, you can't trust her. . . .

Mother: I can't. . . .

Doctor: Well, now you can't, but this must have started somewhere.

Mother: It started when we first found out that Pam was helping herself, out of my purse and out of her father's wallet!

Doctor: Well, I don't believe it, I think it started long before that. These things don't suddenly start, the roots were there long ago. It might be nonsense, but I think it's true (the tape blurs here), there was something wrong from very early on.

Father: Well, the only thing that I can see is that it must go back

	to when the wife was away at the mental hospital, when I had Pam on my own.
Doctor:	Yes?
Father:	When they finished up, they went away to a children's home.
Sarah:	And it's the worst place I have ever been to, honestly.
Mother:	So Pam blames me for that; that's something I can't help.
Sarah:	But before we were sent away to that place I will say that for Daddy, he did ask us if we wanted to go or not – well, he asked me, anyway.
Father:	(To children): The point was, in the finish I couldn't have looked after you if I wanted to because I couldn't even walk, talk, stand or anything else in the finish. That's how I was.
Mother:	(To Doctor): I'd like to know a bit more about this feeling you have about Pam and me. I am interested in this because truthfully I come out with everything that I feel, everything that I can think of.
Doctor:	Well, if you don't feel any more than you said then there is something missing. It doesn't add up. It's too good to be true, it just isn't right, there is something wrong somewhere.
Mother:	What isn't true?
Doctor:	(To parents): What you describe. There is something wrong, something I don't hear about. I don't hear it from either of you.
Mother:	Well, Pam doesn't say anything, so you can't hear anything from Pam, can you?
Doctor:	No.
Mother:	At least I do make an effort.
Doctor:	Yes.
Sarah:	(To Mother): You don't say your *true* feelings, do you?
Mother:	What do you mean about my true feelings?
Sarah:	Well, the impression I get, you only seem to sort of half say what you think.
Mother:	What I think?
Sarah:	What you really think.
Mother:	Well, if I say that to the Doctor, what I really think then where do I stand? I told Doctor exactly what I feel that I am worried sick about Pam.
Doctor:	(To Mother): And I have said quite honestly to you that this is how I experience you, that you don't seem to feel. I feel you are behind your feelings, you are not there, being good and bad, black and white, both at the same time. You are somehow standing behind yourself, not really feeling. I can't get hold of you anywhere. I wonder what this feels like to the children?
Sarah:	(To Mother): All the time you say all the good things you give Pam and you never say anything about the bad things that you give her.
Father:	Well, what's this about bad things?

Mother: What sort of bad things?
Sarah: (To parents): No, not just you, both of you. You are
            explaining about giving everything we want and every-
            thing like that - you do, that's true - but you don't say
            well, you are always moaning, or something like that, or
            telling her off or having a go at her. I can't really put
            into words what I feel.
Father: Well, I have said that, haven't I? I do go on and I give a
            few wallopings. I give you a few in your time. I mean,
            that doesn't make any difference.
Pam: (Bitterly about Mother): If I have done anything wrong
            she moans, she moans, she moans, she moans, there's
            no stopping her.
Sarah: (To Mother): It's true, you start on one thing and you
            never let it drop, all the time.
Mother: Because I'm worried about it, Sarah, that's why . . .
            Both girls together: (It's not possible to hear what is
            being shouted).
Sarah: (To Mother): Then you start on about pyjamas: 'Oh, dear,
            pyjamas all over the place', another minute and then, 'Oh,
            dear, these pyjamas all over the place'. You just have to
            keep on and on . . . and then 'Just look at all the pyjamas
            over the place this morning' - you keep harping on it.
Doctor: What would you prefer to that?
Sarah: Well, you only have to be told once, 'Put your pyjamas
            away' or 'Oh, these pyjamas', but then you don't have to
            say anything more than that. It's already in your mind
            that the pyjamas are on the floor.
Father: The point is that they are not shifted, are they?
Doctor: (To Sarah): If they are not moved, what then?
Sarah: They are:
Mother: Pam takes her pyjamas off in the morning, irrespective of
            where they are, they are left there.
Pam: The other day you said 'Put your pyjamas away' and I
            hadn't even taken mine off!
Father: Yes, but that was only this morning; they were put away
            this morning.
Pam: . . . I hadn't even taken mine off!
Father: The whole point is if Pam would turn round and say about
            these things what's going on and get them here now, then
            we can clear it all up. We know what we are doing of, we
            know what's worrying us and there we are.
Pam: (It isn't possible to hear all she is saying but she is
            imitating her father saying: 'Were you talking to him -
            Yobbo').
Father: Well, they are yobbos, aren't they?
Sarah: Every boy is a yobbo unless he is sitting there and, you
            know, being very quiet.
Mother: But I went over this with Pam. I have no objections to her
            talking to boys at the gate.
Pam: Yes, but Daddy has.

Father: No, I haven't.
Mother: Whilst talking at the gate with a crowd of girls and boys
          there's nothing going on. There's nothing wrong.
Father: As I said to you, I don't mind you talking to them, but
          I'm not having you sliding off with them, that's what I
          said to you.
Sarah: Pam thinks she is being unjustly treated because she
          thinks that she is old enough to do as she likes. She
          keeps saying. 'When I'm 14 I'm not coming in at half-past
          eight, I'm not.'
Pam: I'm not.
Sarah: She seems to think she is (Pam interrupts here but it is
          not possible to hear what she is saying). Well, you do,
          you think you should be allowed in about 12 o'clock every
          night.
Pam: No, I don't
Father: (To Pam): It's very seldom that you are in at half-past
          eight! You come in at half-past eight, I'll grant you that,
          invariably for about two minutes. Then it's 'Oh, can't I
          go down to the bus stop?' and it's about half-past nine
          time you get back.
          (Several minutes omitted here, while the argument contin-
          ues. Doctor suggests several times that Father is rigid
          about the issue.)
Father: No, I say it's the same with Pam, now she says she has
          been down there looking at television, now if I turn round
          and say, 'Right, you are not to go there no more', it
          wouldn't make much difference.
Doctor: (To Father): Well, you know that you are rather rigid
          about this. You say, 'Well, that's what I say and you must
          do as I tell you'. I know that a father must. . . .
Mother: (Interrupting): Well, you must exercise some control.
Doctor: Yes, I was just going to say the father must have authority,
          and must be respected, but on the other hand it can come
          to a point where a vicious circle starts and you then say
          'No', all the time, and because you say 'No' such a lot,
          they think 'Oh, to hell with it, I'm not going to do anything
          they tell me', and it all gets worse and worse. This seems
          to be something that has happened. It's a very difficult
          situation for everybody to get out of. That's why I am
          hoping you can get out of it by talking in this way. I
          think you will both have to come half-way to meet each
          other.
Pam: I know Daddy loves us and everything, but he just doesn't
          realise that we are growing up. I mean even I'll be 14 in
          three weeks' time.
Father: So you are, so you are a big girl.
Sarah: But you look on us as 11 years old. He doesn't seem to
          understand that I am actually 17 and she is nearly 14.
Doctor: Well, she thinks she is older than she really is and he
          thinks she is younger.

Sarah: I know, everybody does. I always thought, 17, you know, really getting on, you know.

Doctor: Well, you will have to come half-way to meet each other, you know.

Pam: Well, I don't mind coming in at nine, but if I want to go out somewhere and it's - 'Be here at half-past nine' - you just about get fed up with it then.

Doctor: (To Pam): Well, I think you don't want to accept any authority from parents and, if you can feel they are bad and unfair and rotten to you and beastly and, you know, never do anything right, you then feel you don't have to obey them in any way at all and this is the position you have got yourself in, where you can feel free to do anything because you feel they are just rotten parents.

Pam:) They are talking about coming in late but it is not possible
Sarah:) to hear what exactly is being said.

Pam: As soon as I leave school I'll just get away!

Father: Get away where, mate?

Pam: Anywhere.

Doctor: Well, we have to stop for today . . . and we'll fix another appointment. . . .

Father: We did get moving in the finish.

---

*This article first appeared in the 'Journal of Child Psychology and Psychiatry and Allied Disciplines', 1969: 10; 81-106.
**The family has now returned for further treatment, and confirmed that our conclusions were generally correct.

REFERENCES AND SELECTED BIBLIOGRAPHY

Items of particular value to those seeking to use the conjoint family approach within the field of child psychiatry are marked with an asterisk.

Ackerman, N.W. (1958) Toward an Integrative Therapy of the Family, 'Am. J. Psychiatry', 114; 727-33.

*Ackerman, N.W. (1959) 'Psychodynamics of Family Life', Basic Books, New York.

Ackerman, N.W. (1966a) Family Psychotherapy - Theory and Practice, 'Am. J. Psychotherapy', 20; 405-14.

*Ackerman, N.W. (1966b) Family Therapy, in 'American Hand-Book of Psychiatry', ed. S. Arieti, Basic Books, New York.

*Ackerman, N.W. (1966c) 'Treating the Troubled Family', Basic Books, New York.

*Ackerman, N.W., Beatman, E.L. and Sandford, S.N. (eds) (1961) 'Exploring the Base for Family Therapy', Family Service Ass. New York.

*Ackerman, N.W., Beatman, F.J. and Sanford, S.N. (eds) (1967) 'Expanding Theory and Practice in Family Therapy', Family Service Ass., New York.

Amerongen, S. (1954) Initial Psychiatric Family Studies, 'Am. J. Orthopsychiatry', 24; 73-83.

Bateson, G., Jackson, D, Haley, J. and Weakland J. (1956) Towards a Theory of Schizophrenia, 'Behav. Sci.', 1; 251-64.

*Bell J.E. (1961) Family Group Therapy, 'Publ. Hlth Monogr.' no. 64, US Publ. Hlth Serv., Washington, DC.

*Bell, J.E. (1962) Recent Advances in Family Group Therapy, 'J. Child Psychol. Psychiat.', 3; 1-15.

Bell, J.E. (1964) The Family Group Therapist: an Agent of Change, 'Int. J. Group Psychother.', 14; 72-83.

Bion, W.R. (1961) 'Experiences in Groups', Tavistock, London.

Blinder, M.G. (1965) 'MCFT': Simultaneous Treatment of Several Families, 'Am. J. Psychotherapy'., 19: 559-69.

Boszormenyi-Nagy, I. and Framo, J.L. (eds) (1965) 'Intensive Family Therapy', Harper, New York.

Bowen, M., Dysinger, R.H. and Basamania, B. (1959) The Role of the Father in Families with a Schizophrenic Patient, 'Am. J. Psychiat.', 115; 1017-20.

Bowen, M. (1960) A Family Concept of Schizophrenia, in 'Aetiology of Schizophrenia', ed. D. Jackson, Basic Books, New York.

Bowlby, J. (1949) The Study and Reduction of Group Tensions in the Family, 'Human Relations', 2; 123-8, chapter 1 above.

Brodey, W. M. (1959) Some Family Operations and Schizophrenia, 'Archs. Gen. Psychiat.', 1; 379-402.

Brodey, W. M. (1967) Processes of Family Change, in 'Expanding Theory and Practice in Family Therapy', ed. N.W. Ackerman, F.L. Beatman and S.N. Sherman, Family Service Ass, New York.

Brown, G.W. and Rutter, M. (1966) The Measurement of Family Activities and Relationships, 'Human Relations', 19; 241-63.

Bruch, H. (1966) Changing Approaches to the Study of the Family, in 'Family Structure, Dynamics and Therapy', ed. I. Cohen, Psychiat. Res. Rep., no. 20, Am. Psychiat. Ass.

Bursten, B. (1965) Family Dynamics, the Sick Role, and Medical Hospital Admissions, 'Family Process', 4; 206-16.

Cheek, F.E. (1965) The Father of the Schizophrenic, 'Archs Gen. Psychiat.', 13; 336-45.

Clarke, A.H. (1967) The Dominant Matriarch Syndrome, 'Br. J. Psychiat.', 113; 1069-71.

Cohen, I.M. (ed.) (1964) 'Family Structure, Dynamics and Therapy', Psychiat. Res. Rep. no. 20. Am. Psychiat. Ass., Washington,DC.

Curry, A.E. (1965) Therapeutic Management of Multiple Family Group, 'Int. J. Group Psychother', 15; 90-5.

Cutter, A.V. and Hallowitz, D. (1962) Different Approaches to, Treatment of the Child and his Parents, 'Am. J. Orthopsychiat., 32; 152-8.

Davis, D.R. (1968) Interventions into Family Affairs, 'Br. J. Psychiat.', 41; 73-9.

Day, J. and Kwiatkowska, H.Y. (1962) The Psychiatric Patient and his 'Well' Sibling, 'Bull. Art. Ther.' 2; 51-66.

Donnelly, J. (1966) Aspects of the Treatment of Character Disorders, 'Archs Gen. Psychiat', 15; 22-8.

Durrell, V.G. (1969) Adolescents in Multiple Family Group Therapy in a School Setting, 'Int. J. Group Psychother.', 19; 44-52.

Ehrenwald, J. (1963) Family Diagnosis and Mechanisms of Psycho-social Defence, 'Family Process', 2; 121-31.

Esterson, A. Cooper, D.G. and Laing, R.D. (1965) Results of Family-oriented Therapy with Hospitalized Schizophrenics, 'Br. Med. J.', 2; 1462-5.

Ezriel, H. (1950) A Psychoanalytic Approach to Group Treatment, 'Br. J. Med. Psychol.', 23; 59-74.

Faucett, E.C. (1962) Multiple-client Interviewing: a Means of Assessing Family Processes, 'Soc. Casework', 43; 114-20.

Ferreira, A.J. (1963) Family Myth and Homeostasis, 'Archs Gen. Psychiat.', 9, 457-63.

Ferreira, A.J. (1967) Psychosis and Family Myth, 'Am. J. Psychother.', 21; 186-97.

*Fisher, S. and Mendell, D. (1956) The Communication of Neurotic Patterns over Two and Three Generations, 'Psychiatry', 19; 41-6.

Fleck, S. Cornelison, A.R. Norton, N. and Lidz, T. (1957) The Intrafamilial Environment of the Schizophrenic Patient, 'Psychiatry', 20; 343-50.

Fleck, S. (1960) Family Dynamics and the Origin of Schizophrenia, 'Psychosom. Med.', 12; 333-44.

Fleck, S. (1963) Psychiatric Hospitalization as a Family Experience, 'Acta Psychiat Scand.', supp 169. 39.

Fordham, M. (1953) A Child Guidance Approach to Marriage, 'Br. J. Med. Psychol.', 26; 197-203.

Foulkes, S.H. (1948) 'Introduction to Group-Analytic Psychotherapy', Heinemann, London.

*Foulkes, S.H. (1964) 'Therapeutic Group Analysis', Allen & Unwin, London.

*Foulkes, S.H. and Anthony, E.J. (1957 - second edition 1965), 'Group Psychotherapy: The Psychoanalytic Approach', Penguin, Harmondsworth.

*Friedman, A.S. et al. (1965) 'Psychotherapy for the Whole Family', Springer, New York.

Gehrke, S. (1967) Survival Patterns in Family Conjoint Therapy, 'Family Process', 6; 67-80.

Glasser, P.H. (1963) Changes in Family Equilibrium during Psychotherapy, 'Family Process', 2; 245-64.

Gralnick, A. (1962) Family Psychotherapy: General and Specific Considerations, 'Am. J. Orthopsychiat.', 32; 515-26.

Grotjahn, M. (1960) 'Psychoanalysis and the Family Neurosis', Norton, New York.

Grunebaum, H. and Christ, J. (1968) Interpretation and the Task of the Therapist with Couples and Families, 'Int. J. Group Psychother.', 18; 495-503.

Gullerud, E.N. and Harlan, V.L. (1963) Four-way Joint Interviewing in Marital Counselling, 'Soc. Casework', 43; 532-6.

Hallowitz, D., Clement, R. and Cutter, A. (1957) The Treatment Process with both Parents Together, 'Am. J. Orthopsychiat.', 27; 587-607.

Hare, E.H. and Shaw G.K. (1965) Mental and Physical Family Health, 'Brit. J. Psychiat.', 111; 461-71.
Henry, J. and Warson, S. (1951) Family Structure and Psychic Development, 'Am. J. Orthopsychiat.', 21; 59-73.
Howells, K.G. (1962) The Nuclear Family as the Functional Unit in Psychiatry, 'J. Men. Sci.', 108; 675-84.
Jackson, D.D. and Weakland, J.H. (1961) Conjoint Family Therapy, 'Psychiatry', 24 (suppl.); S30-45.
Jackson D.D. and Yalom, I. (1966) Family Research on the Problem of Ulcerative Colitis, 'Archs Gen. Psychiat.', 15; 410-18.
Jackson, D.D. (1967) Differences between 'Normal' and 'Abnormal' Families, in 'Expanding Theory and Practice in Family Therapy', ed. N.W. Ackerman et al. Family Service Ass, New York.
Kellner, R. (1963) 'Family Ill Health', Tavistock, London.
Laing, R.D. and Esterson, A. (1964) 'Sanity, Madness and the Family; Vol I, Families of Schizophrenics', Tavistock, London.
Langsley, D.G. et al. (1968) Family Crisis Therapy - Results and Implications, 'Family Process', 7; 145-58.
Leichter, E. and Schulman, G.L. (1963) The Family Interview as an Integrative Device in Group Therapy with Families, 'Int. J. Group Psychother.', 13; 335-46.
Leichter, E. and Schulman, G.L. (1968) Emerging Phenomena in Multi-family Group Treatment, 'Int. J. Group Psychother.', 18; 59-69.
Lidz, T. (1963) 'The Family and Human Adaptation: Three Lectures', Int. Univ. Press, New York.
*Lidz, T., Fleck, S. and Cornelison, A.R. (1966) 'Schizophrenia and the Family', Int. Univ. Press, New York.
*MacGregor, R., Ritchie, A.M., Serrano, A.C. and Schuster, F.P. (1964) 'Multiple Impact Therapy with Families', McGraw-Hill, New York.
Martin, F. and Knight, J. (1962) Joint interviews as Part of Intake Procedure in a Child Psychiatric Clinic, 'J. Child Psychol. Psychiat.', 3; 17-27.
Mendell, D. and Fisher S. (1958) A Multi-generation Approach to Treatment of Psychopathology, 'J. Nerv. Ment. Dis.', 126; 523-9.
Minuchin, S. et al. (1964) The Study and Treatment of Families that Produce Multiple Acting-out Boys, 'Am. J. Orthopsychiat.', 34; 125-33.
Minuchin, S. (1965) Conflict-resolution Family Therapy, 'Psychiat.', 28; 278-86.
Minuchin, S. and Montalvo, B. (1966) An Approach for Diagnosis of the Low Socio-economic Family, in 'Family Structure, Dynamics and Therapy' ed. I. Cohen, Psychiat. Res. Rep. no. 20, Am. Psychiat. Ass.
*Minuchin, S. and Montalvo, B. (1967) Techniques for Working with Disorganised Low Socio-economic Families, 'Am. J. Orthopsychiat.', 37; 880-7.
Mittlemann, B. (1952) Simultaneous Treatment of Both Parents, and their Child, in 'Specialised Techniques in Psychotherapy', ed. G. Chowski and J.L. Despert, Basic Books, New York.

Patton, J.D. (1957) Joint Treatment of Adolescent and Mother, 'Dis. Nerv. System.', 18; 220-2.

*Parsloe, P. (1967) Families which do not come to Clinics, in 'Child Guidance From Within: Reactions to New Pressures', Proc. of 23rd Interclinic. Conf. Nat. Ass. of Mental Health, London.

Powell, M.B. and Monahan, J. (1969) Reaching the Rejects through Multifamily Group Therapy, 'Int. J. Group Psychother.', 19; 35-43.

Prince, G.S. (1961) A Clinical Approach to Parent-child Interaction, 'J. Child Psychol. Psychiat.', 2; 169-84.

Rafferty, F.T., Ingraham, B. and McClure, S.M. (1966) The Disturbed Child at Home, 'J. Nerv. Ment. Dis.', 142; 127-39.

Roberts, W.L. (1968) Working with the Family Group in a Child Guidance Clinic, 'Br. J. Psychiat. Soc. Work', 9; 175-9.

Robinson, B. (1968) Family Based Therapy, 'Br. J. Psychiat. Soc. Work', 9; 188-92.

Rosenbaum, P. (1961) Patient-family Similarities in Schizophrenia, 'Archs Gen. Psychiat.', 5; 120-6.

Rutter, M. and Brown, G.W. (1966) The Reliability and Validity of Measures of Family Life and Relationships in Families containing a Psychiatric Patient, 'Soc. Psychiat.', 1; 38-53.

Ryle, A. (1967) 'Neurosis in the Ordinary Family', Tavistock, London.

Sager, C.J. (1968a) An Overview of Family Therapy, 'Int. J. Group Psychother.', 18; 302-12.

*Sager, C.J. (1968b) Selection and Engagement of Patients in Family Therapy, 'Am. J. Orthopsychiat.', 38; 715-23.

*Satir, V. (1964) 'Conjoint Family Therapy', Science and Behaviour Books, Palo Alto.

Schaffer, L. et al. (1962) On the Nature and Sources of the Psychiatrist's Experience with the Family of the Schizophrenic, 'Psychiatry', 25; 32-45.

Scheflen, A.E. (1967) Explaining Communicative Behaviour: Three Points of View, in 'Expanding Theory and Practice in Family Therapy,' ed. N.W. Ackerman, F.L. Beatman and S.N. Sherman, Family Service Ass. New York.

*Scherz, F.H. (1962) Multiple-client Interviewing: Treatment Implications, 'Soc. Casework', 43, 114-20.

*Skynner, A.C.R. (1967a) Diagnosis Consultation and Co-ordination of Treatment, in 'Child Guidance From Within: Reactions to New Pressures', Proc. of 23rd Interclinic. Conf. Nat. Ass. of Mental Health, London.

*Skynner, A.C.R. (1967b) Indications and Contra-indications for Conjoint Family Therapy, 'Int. J. Social Psychiat.', 15 245-9.

Sonne, J.C., Speck, R.V. and Jungreis, J.E. (1962). The Absent-member Manoeuvre as a Resistance in Family Therapy of Schizophrenia, 'Family Process', 1; 44-62.

Sperling, M. (1951) The Neurotic Child and his Mother - a Psychoanalytic Study, 'Am. J. Orthopsychiat.', 21; 351-64.

Szasz, T.S. (1959) The communication of distress between child and parent, 'Br. J. Med. Psychol.', 32; 161-70.

Westman, J.C. et al. (1963) Parallel Group Psychotherapy with the Parents of Emotionally Disturbed Children, 'Int. J. Group Psychother.', 13; 52-9.

Whitaker, D.S. and Lieberman, M.A. (1964) 'Psychotherapy through the Group Process', Atherton Press, New York.

Winnicott, D.W. (1961) The Effect of Psychotic Parents on the Emotional Development of the Child, 'Br. J. Psychiat. Social Work', 6; 13-20.

Winnicott, D.W. (1965) Clinical Study of the Effect of a Failure of the Average Expectable Environment on a Child's Mental Functioning, 'Int. J. Psychoanal', 46; 81-7.

Zuk, G.H. and Rubinstein, D. (1965) A Review of Concepts in the Study and Treatment of Families of Schizophrenics, in 'Intensive Family Therapy', ed. I. Boszormenyi-Nagy and J.L. Framo, Hoeber, New York.

Zuk, G.H. (1968a) The Side-taking Function in Family Therapy, 'Am. J. Orthopsychiat.', 38; 553-9.

Zuk, G.H. (1968b) When the Family Therapist takes Sides: a Case Report, 'Psychother.', 5; 24-8.

*Zuk, G.H. (1968c) Family Therapy: Formulation of a Technique and its Theory, 'Int. J. Group Psychother.', 18; 42-58.

5   WORKING WITH THE FAMILY GROUP*:

some problems of practice

Gill Gorell Barnes

Working with the family group is a complex subject, and lends itself
to a variety of theoretical formulations. It engenders a literature
that tends to be both verbose and obscure, inflating the mystique
of the concept 'family group', and making it at times difficult to
believe that knowledge and skills are involved which are commonly
practised by all social workers in their everyday contact with
families, and with groups of other kinds. The aim of this paper is
not to present family group work as the solution to all the problems
with which we are confronted in our differing agencies, but to consider some of the advantages it offers, some of the difficulties it
presents, and to indicate how the skills involved may highlight
problematic aspects of technique in other areas of our work.

THE FAMILY AS A SUBSYSTEM

In 1961 Lidz wrote a central text about family subsystems, in which
he outlined the model of a family as a social institution, a subsystem
of the larger society in which we live and into which the child must
emerge.[1] He postulated three concepts on which effective family
functioning should rest, which may be held to form the crude basis
for family group work assumptions. The first is that there should
be an effective parental coalition with appropriate sharing of roles,
providing the child with role models to follow into adulthood; the
second is that the generation boundaries should be maintained, so
that the unmet needs of the parents should not spill over inappropriately on to the children; and the third is that appropriate sex
linked roles should be maintained between the parents. On reading
these, as simplified here, we are immediately confronted with the
discrepancy between this ideal model of family functioning, and the
reality that we are presented with in our work, and, very probably,
in our own families of origin and current existence, where our ideas
may be said to have been formed and confirmed. However, we may
still hold to this model as our ideal. As an alternative way of thinking about family systems I would like to point to the thinking that
has been done about linguistically inaccessible, 'deprived' families –
developed by Bernstein in this country[2] and Deutsch,[3] John,[4]
Pavenstedt,[5] and others in America – which outlines the role of

families as the conveyors of ideas related primarily to a societal
subsystem. I would like to refer particularly to the work of
Minuchin et al,[6] who, in their very detailed book 'Families of the
Slums' outline the problems and methods of working with families
from highly restricted areas of society, conditioned chiefly by
poverty and the non-availability of achieving integration into the
larger system of social status, achievement and values. Their
expectations and hence their models, have thus been limited through
generations.

Although we may regard our society as more homogeneous and less
divided than the urban areas of America on which this work was
based, many of the findings are none the less highly relevant, and
are particularly important in assisting us to focus on our limited
ability to help people change, while their potential for change is
constricted by the conditions in which they live and which inevitably
shape their outlook, their hopes, their myths, and their structures.
Where members of such a family are referred as 'disturbed' to any
agency we have to consider whether within the context of their own
family they are indeed behaving unusually, or whether the family
norms and the area subsystem are conflicting with the world outside.
This larger and continuing social work topic is relevant to consider
here as it may affect the way the family and the social worker/thera-
pist will interact. Their conjoint meeting may be contained within a
larger circle of expectation from the school, the doctor or hospital,
the social services committee or the courts, who will have their own
expectations of what this interview will achieve, and the kind of
changes, often anticipated as controls, which will result.

The gap between other peoples' expectations of what we can or
should do, and our own practice, is one current in many aspects of
social work but the therapist in a family group situation seems to
me to crystallise some of the dilemmas affecting intervention generally.
The different kinds of approach outlined below will make this clearer.

INTERVENTION IN THE FAMILY GROUP

The family is a unit which functions twenty-four hours a day, which
makes it an extremely complex group to work with. The therapist,
(and I propose to use that word as interchangeable with social
worker) is allowed into that group for an extremely limited portion
of time. Despite this he hopes effectively to change their interaction.
It seems to me that in this relative weakness of the therapist in the
face of group cohesion lies the potential strength and the potential
danger of family work, since it appears to encourage a swiftness
and freedom of movement that is much greater than work with individuals will allow. In seeing the whole family the therapist may fear
that he will be overwhelmed by group denial or rebuffed by long-
standing collective defences and he may not anticipate that he will
find strengths that can be mobilised that he would not have been
aware of had he seen the individual client on his own. (I am excluding from this discussion the much described but rarely found

'schizophrenogenic family' who form the core of a large body of
written work, but only a small percentage of the actual family work
done in social work agencies and in local authority clinics such as
my own.) Being a group, the average referred family may be seen
as containing among them more potential for changing the patient/
client's situation, than he could bring on his own. This is particularly so where the referred person is a child. These indications
for health give the therapist some reassurance that his interventions
are unlikely to harm the unit he is treating, the group as a whole,
although individuals within it may be made angry, deflated or
depressed. It is rarely that the whole group at any one time is reduced to a state of non-functioning while some maladaptive piece of
interaction is being shed and a new one considered.

Whatever goals of treatment are collectively formed with the family,
members will move towards the achievement of these at different
paces. This elasticity is an asset in coping with any change that may
have been promoted during a family interview, and ensures that there
will be ways of coping with new ideas that have been introduced, and
new perspectives that may be confronting the family. The reverse
of the group potential for health is that the family may also be
strong in blocking any individual move towards change; and may in
refusing to contemplate this, reinforce one another. If what has
been said is too painful they can resort to familiar collective defences
and denials. It is this group strength however, that may encourage
the freedom of movement that seems to characterise family therapy.
In practice it is difficult to say whether this occurs because people
who choose to work with families happen to enjoy working in this
way, or whether there is in fact something within the family group
which releases this kind of spontaneity.

In the theory of family therapy, this freedom is generally accepted
to be to do with the containment of the potential projections in the
situation within the members of the family group itself. Where the
therapist is more active and real, the infantile projections and
distortions that occur remain among the family members, and can
there be pointed out, examined and clarified as they appear in the
room during the session. This containment may also speed up the
movement towards co-operative problem solving since the therapist,
of necessity removed from the ongoing group by not being a family
member, does not have to concern himself so closely with the effects
of his interjection as they will affect the therapeutic relationship
with him, but only as they will affect the interaction of the family
members with one another. In practice this will mean risking a
greater exposure of himself to attack from different members, for
whom he has moved too fast or too far, and he has to be prepared
for this. He has also to be sensitive to the capacity of the group
as a whole for change, and avoid becoming seen as the outside
aggressor, who provokes a collective and defensive withdrawal.

If the characteristic medium of the work does not lie in the individual therapeutic relationship, we must consider the alternative
approaches on which the family worker can draw. The division I am
proposing below is crude, and must only be regarded as a first

attempt at differentiation of approach. At one end of a continuum is
the group analytic approach, which has been fully documented by
Dr Skynner in one of his three full articles in 'Social Work Today',[7]
and at the other end is the emphasis on behavioural modelling which
has been more fully documented in America.[8] I do not see either
approach as clearly isolated from the other, but the implications of
each source are different for the conduct of the therapist. Before
we consider the values and differences of these two approaches
there are some general points about the role of the therapist that
need examination.

THE ROLE OF THE THERAPIST

In contrast to clinical work with individuals, the transference elements of the therapist's relationship with the family are on the whole
ignored in the family group discussion. If an interpretation is made
about this it is usually in terms of a generalised parental model,
and the particular significance for that family or individual is often
not explored. None the less it is utilised and both the value and the
dangers of this need to be considered. If it is accepted that swiftness, directness and freedom of movement, together with risk-
taking in interpretation are all elements that characterise family
therapy, how do we then define the boundaries of the therapist's
role? If it is accepted that direct intervention in order to change
behaviour is one of his chief tools, how do we limit his power? In
individual work the professional guidelines are generally clear regarding pace and self determination – in theory if not in practice;
but in work with the family it is taken as a central premise that
the therapist has the right to intervene in order to change interaction; to comment, criticise, and bring the weight of his feeling
and experience to bear on the observed discrepancies he sees before
him. The danger in this, as in other areas of our work, lies in
oversimplification; in the assumption that the therapist knows better
than the family the way through the thickets before him because he
has clear pre-planned paths mapped out. He holds certain tenets
about the desirable qualities in family life which will in practice be
shaping his intervention, and it may be that going as they do, unstated, they remain unquestioned; where we might feel that to
question assumptions is a necessary part of our social work role. We
all hold basic assumptions, but where the family is being worked
with as a group the unstudied transference potential of the therapist,
particularly as the behaviour shaping end of the spectrum of work
is approached, may lead to the family being directed towards standards of behaviour that they are not equipped to meet, and towards
values which are less appropriate to them than they are to the
therapist. This problem is lessened where therapist and family are
from the same social backgrounds, as they are in the professional
training courses run in Philadelphia[9] and heightened where the backgrounds and experiences are entirely different, as they are more
likely to be in England.

A further danger of work with the family group is that it is
usually described in terms of family pathology, rather than family
health. Since only a small percentage of the families we see would
be capable of achieving the realisation of the family model I outlined
above, which serves as a prototype of sociological models of the
family; and since there is an absence of alternative internalised
models available to the therapist I feel there is a danger that an
assessment may more often be made of family failure, often based on
the assessor's own unrecognised idealisations, rather than on a recognition of the success the family that is being seen have achieved
in the face of multiple difficulties. If we became more skilled at recognising what made for health in a family situation, in spite of non-
traditional family features, we might build up a range of models more
suited to the subtlety and variety of human need and adaptability.
We need to look at the models offered by single-parent families,
many of whom would be highly successful in meeting their childrens'
needs if they did not have so much prejudice to face, much of which
has become institutionalised. We need to look at patterns of com-
munal child-rearing, to gain new insights into what makes for family
health. The problem of stereotype in role goes deep in our society,
and many of the families I have seen over the last year are, I believe,
facing the strain of not aligning with themselves as they think they
ought to be. This strain is particularly apparent in the area of sex-
linked role models. Expectations of what a spouse should be are, as
we know, brought in from our own early experience and unresolved
infantile conflicts, but there is also the larger societal expectation
which reinforces certain aspects of 'role' and 'model'. Parents are
asking themselves how on the one hand as a mother or father they
feel that they can manage best to be a good one; and on the other
whether their view and inclination will match up to the standard of
professional behaviour they feel society holds of them. The dichotomy between the expectation they hold of themselves, based in
part on the internalised fantasy of what society expects of them;
and the reality of what they have been able to achieve, has formed
one of the key core conflicts in many of the families presenting at
the clinic. It is here that the therapist has to do some fundamental
work on his own assumptions about the proper behaviour of parents,
since his own intervention can easily reinforce the precariously
held, socially acceptable superego ideal, without his ever pausing
to consider sufficiently whether he indeed knows what the most
effective model of family functioning should be.

These dangers of doctrine or dogma affect many areas of our work,
but they are possibly more pronounced in a family group situation.
In individual work we are more inclined by long held professional
tradition to allow the client to work upon his own problems, and
produce his own solution. In work with peer-based groups members
will not accept unquestioned the assumptions of the therapist if
more than one of them experiences these as discrepant. In a family
group, where the balance of power is unequal, the danger of mis-
using professional authority may be increased. This is particularly
so as we approach that area of work which may be seen as the be-

haviour shaping end of the spectrum, since this approach is more likely to be used with lower income, less verbally able clients, whose needs may be seen by the therapist as requiring an authoritarian approach.

A FAMILY INTERVIEW: THE TWO APPROACHES

I see family work as a spectrum, with the group analytic approach, and the behavioural approach at opposite ends. The unit for intervention is the family, with whom the therapist will join for a prescribed space. If he favours a group analytic technique, he will, for the ninety minutes they meet together, participate as a group member, struggling to understand the problem as it presents itself in the room. He may have prior information about the family which he chooses to share with them, so that what is known is known to all. He may simply wait to see which aspects of the problem they will choose to bring. He will not structure the interview by asking set questions, or taking a formal history. If there are other significant figures involved in the problem who are not family members they may be invited to join in the initial assessment of the family problem. The process of understanding what is going on is shared within the group as it occurs to the therapist, thus keeping the struggle towards a solution always within the group as a whole. A comment made to any one member is made within the nexus of the group interaction, any internal state or piece of communication being constantly linked to the family framework surrounding them.

The therapist in theory then allows his power to be controlled by what the group will permit. The disadvantages of this approach clearly lie within the potentially pathological limitations of the group, which may prevent the movement of any one member towards a healthier position. The family may bind together to conceal forbidden areas, to protect a long preserved equilibrium, and thus work against the freeing of the individuals within the group.

It may be at this point in the interview situation that the two kinds of approach overlap. Whichever framework the therapist initially saw as guiding his intervention, his job will have been to point out the dissociations, to make clear the different needs and expectations, conscious as well as unconscious, that are not being met within the family; and at the same time to point out to them the reality which they present to him. He has to let them know what he perceives as missing in their interaction, not only what he feels they see as missing in one another. His techniques for doing this will vary, and the more disorganised or unsophisticated the family the more likely it is that he will rely on role playing, modelling, cognitive interpretation and intervention related towards the observable changing of behaviour. Not only does he suggest what needs to be done, he has to demonstrate how it is to be done. The group interpretative approach, with no alternative method of behaviour offered, will be the less effective the more physically, cognitively and verbally impoverished the family, since the client will be correspondingly unable to change his behaviour as the result of a piece of verbal interaction. The connection between words and action will need to be made explicit. In the move from group analytic to behaviour shaping this will mean abandoning distance, joining the family's affective axis, and using the medium of exchange to which they are accustomed. If all serious points are made as jokes, the therapist may have to become a joker. Where a premium is placed on winning arguments, he will have to make sure that he scores telling points. (In many West Indian families for example, a high value is placed on good 'disputation' and to offer criticism in this way may thus be acceptable.) By exaggerating the prevailing mood, the therapist may try to make key family members perceive their effect on others, as he, the therapist, has affected them. He may have to introduce emotional content, where it is inappropriately lacking, and help family members to discriminate between the relative importance and intensity of family issues, where all are inappropriately treated as the same. Minuchin has defined this ability to gear intervention to the appropriate family mood – without being dragged into their modes of organisation that inhibit change – as accommodation versus suction. The therapist has to be aware of the family's ability to receive a message at any given moment, and gear the intensity of his comments accordingly.

How is he using his relationship with the family here? If he is hoping to offer a useful model which they can imitate, he has to abandon the role of passive commentator, leave his 'professionalism' behind, and enter vigorously into the family crossfire. By experiencing the intensity of feeling as though he were a family member himself, he will be using the transference in order to teach from within and produce behaviour with which individual members can identify. It will be subtly different from their own, sufficiently so for old maladaptive systems to be unbalanced. He will demonstrate new ways for them to talk to each other, and new ways in which each can be approached.

ROLE PLAYING AND AUTHORITY

It may be useful here to summarise the rationale for this kind of directive intervention. The psychotherapeutic approach has been broadly criticised as not being relevant to large sections of the population because of its traditional stress on a permissive environment, a non directive attitude on the part of the therapist and a free associative atmosphere. It relies on the patient remembering past events and exploring the way these affect him now. The argument for an alternative approach has become structured around the low income patient, although there are many kinds of client, not only those in low income brackets who welcome the authoritarian approach. The low income patient is seen as seeking advice, suggestion, attention to physical problems, support, authority, warmth and structure. Goals may have to be short-term and concrete, information that leads to action will be welcomed and direct intervention, particularly in crisis situations will be more valuable than the

giving of insights. The worker will reach out to the client, rather
than waiting for the client to adopt his norms; he will encourage
movement and doing on the part of the client and he will concentrate
on what can be achieved in the future, rather than seeking for the
blocks of the past. This intensive mobilising of ego resources is
combined with the worker's consistent support, encouragement, and
reward.

While the above approach and the use of authority that it implies
is an essential feature of much social work and psychiatric activity,
the potential for the abandonment of the ideal of 'co-operative problem solving' causes me concern. This approach relies on the dependence of the client on the therapist; and there is always a danger
that in accepting this authority we may be offering the client an unhelpful model of how problems can be solved. I find there is a continual dilemma between attempting a democratic problem-solving
approach, particularly in a family situation where the models are
being offered to children as well as parents; and recognising that
there are clients who because of the way they have been raised and
the hierarchies they have already incorporated, may never be able
to use the democratic model. The therapist has to consider in each
case whether he will play into already incorporated models, and
become the authority figure who provides structure and reinforces
traditional authority carrying patterns within the family; or whether
by doing this he might not be recreating and reinforcing patterns
which we might in the long term wish to see families managing without. The therapist is always in danger of accepting a culture pattern which offers authority as a solution to other people's problems
without considering whether he believes that to play into a class-
based pattern of this kind will ultimately be the most useful thing
for a family in our society. The borders of education and therapy
are in this sense often hazy, and we cannot afford not to consider
what it is we are trying to achieve for the families who seek our
help in the broadest sense. This may pose us with the fundamental
question of whether we are going to be agents of change helping
families towards new and better models of functioning, or whether
we are in fact conservers of what we have been taught to believe is
right; ideas that are not necessarily opposed, but that are not always sufficiently recognised as different. We are constantly caught
between helping families and the individuals within them to find and
be selves to which they can be more true, and helping them to be
more in tune with what society, and we inevitably, as its repre-
sentatives and reared as we are within aspects of the same system,
believe to be right, normal and healthy. Deviation from traditional
patterns will be as hard for us to accept as it is for others, although
it is often clear that health is better achieved where people have
broken with tradition.

UNRESOLVED DILEMMAS

It may be that the lack of fixed models in work with the family
group is healthy, since there will always be a need for variety and
flexibility in approaching this complex unit. However we need to try
and isolate the components of technique so that they can be studied,
criticised and further developed. In the work I have done I would
distinguish the processes involved from dynamic psychotherapy in
the lack of regression among group members in the course of treatment, and in the lack of projection of unconscious contents and
images onto the therapist. However, from dynamic psychotherapy
the ideology has incorporated the belief in the contractual approach,
the use of identification with the therapist, and the belief in co-
operative problem solving whether or not this has always been carried into practice. In the reliance upon the manipulation of conscious
processes, and upon suggestions rather than the uncovering of unconscious processes through the medium of the relationship, it may
be said to come rather within the group of non-dynamic therapies.[10]
From the group analytic approach it has incorporated the concept of
the free association of any one member as helping us understand
something about the group as a whole: the concept of the common
theme which links with the work on family neurosis,[11] and the
myth.[12]

Dr Skynner has written that the therapist's use of authority in
the family group situation is based on his responsibility for representing the demands of reality. He may be provoked to take a more
active controlling role than he would consider in a peer-based
group because of the unbalanced power structure of the family
group. He uses his power, as a good parent would do if consulted
by the family. If we can indeed say that his power has the normal
authority of parents it is clear that this is placing a direct reliance
on the transference, just as the behavioural approach aims to teach
from within, using the authority of the therapist to provide role
models that can be followed. If the family group situation leads to
the therapist having certain universal parental qualities projected
on to him it gives him a heightened power; and the fact that he may
not make the family aware of this transference, while he himself
utilises it to achieve change within the group, means that he needs
to be fully aware of what he is doing, and not deluding himself
about the nature of the skills he is practising.

INDICATIONS OF CHANGE

Given these dilemmas of practice we need to understand something
about the effect of the intervention on the family. How can we tell
if they are being helped, since despite all the problems of practice
this is always our aim. I offer below a few pointers that show a
family as functioning more successfully, however we have gone
about our work.

1 Individuation. We can see that things are better where family

members are treating one another as real people; and not as aspects
of some previously held internal conflict, in which each held a role
(probably unrecognised and unstated).

2   Loosening of bonds. Where the family struggle has become less
intense, members are allowed to form and gain from relationships
outside the family. This is particularly important for children who
may have been isolated from their peers by carrying age-inappropriate
roles.

3   Relief. Once the family have discovered that nothing dreadful
has happened following a change in the constellation, they are encouraged themselves to go further in exploring how things can be
improved. Often it is the first step in changing anything that is
the most difficult because of their fear of what may happen if an
old pattern is abandoned.

4   Enjoyment. This comes through in sessions, but is often openly
discussed in terms of the shared things families have enjoyed doing
together. This means they now have positive things to say about
one another instead of purely negative things and the good effects
of this are self reinforcing.

5   The ability to solve things at home. Instead of bringing un-
solved problems, family quarrels, etc., to the sessions for the
therapist to adjudicate upon, family members do the work themselves
in between sessions. This is obviously a necessary preliminary to
giving up regular family treatment sessions.

PRESSURE FOR CHANGE

To achieve change at its own pace a family requires time, which
agencies hard pressed for time and for resources may find difficult
to allow. The appeal of the more direct behaviour changing approach
is clear. Work with the family group can move far from dynamic
understanding in its emphasis on the importance of interaction and
reinforcement patterns; but effective intervention must involve the
therapist in the understanding of processes underlying behaviour.
If he can see the client in the nexus of his social background as
well as his family circle he is more likely to utilise this dynamic
understanding appropriately, and if the method of his approach is
one in which both client and worker find satisfaction he is less likely
to retreat into attitudes that are ultimately unhelpful. Trying to
help families find solutions that work is a difficult and frequently
long-term job, but simply to reinforce socially acceptable frame-
works of role patterning and behaviour will not help the underlying
and uncomprehended needs. The struggle to find ways of having
these met is what is causing disturbance in the family group, and
only when the worker can see what these are will he be in a position
to help them see that some needs cannot be met; that the way they
are attempting to do so is causing harm to those they are most
deeply involved with; to help them through the pain this recognition
will cause and then to begin the work of finding new solutions. That
these may only be partially satisfactory may be as difficult for the

therapist to come to terms with as it is for the family, as it may involve him in giving up the fantasy component in his own solutions.
Only when this is done on both sides, however, can we begin to
find solutions that will permit and promote growth.

CO-THERAPY

I have not touched on the value of working with a co-therapist,
which is a topic that deserves longer consideration than I will give
here. Working in pairs helps in many ways in a family group situation. At the most basic level it provides support when embarking
on these potentially stormy waters, and also a second, objective
stance from which to confirm one's own assessment of family functioning. In practice the co-therapist helps to prevent sidetracking
by particular areas of family pathology which touch a chord in the
therapist, and prevents from being ignored aspects of family functioning which the single therapist may feel unable to touch because
of his own defences. Overreaction or underreaction are less likely
when there are two people involved. There is always the danger of
attempting to refashion one's own family of origin in work with the
family group, and of projecting one's own unresolved struggles with
parents into the situation.[13] It is less likely that this will happen
where there is another worker.
   Co-therapists can also break up systems of communication that
are preventing the real expression of feeling taking place. They
can change repetitive patterns by turning to one another; can
clarify confusion by discussing their own confusion with one
another in the family session and can help the family to look at what
is going on by openly speculating and discussing it. One therapist
may be more able than the other to express taboo feelings which
the family cannot manage; for example sexual or hostile feelings towards his own parents, siblings or children. Therapists may often
disagree about what should and shouldn't be tackled in the material
the family is presenting; and a successfully resolved disagreement,
taking place within the context of the session, can be a very useful
experience for the family. However, this requires a great deal of
work outside the sessions, so that the family do not get involved in
unresolved quarrels between the therapists.
   My view is that co-therapy can only be successful where the workers involved are able to share on an equal basis with one another,
and where they can hope to work together over a reasonable period
of time. The conflicts that are aroused in the course of work will
not otherwise be either expressed honestly or looked at openly;
and while they may never be fully resolved, it requires at the least
an awareness of their existence before the family gain from the experience of having two workers involved.

ACKNOWLEDGEMENTS

With thanks to the staff of Woodberry Down Child Guidance Unit;
Dr Robin Skynner; Dr Minuchin and the clinic staff who made a
visit to Philadelphia very enjoyable, and to Dr John Barteaux who
shared many family sessions with me.

---

*Based on a paper given at the invitation of the Child Guidance
Special Interest Group at the Study Conference of the British
Association of Social Workers at Scarborough in October 1972.

REFERENCES

1 Theodore Lidz, 'The Family and Human Adaptation', Internat.
   Psychoanal. Library, 1964.
2 Basil Bernstein, Language and Social Class, 'Brit. F. Sociol.',
   1960, 11 271-7. Social Class and Linguistic Development: a
   Theory of Social Learning, in A.H. Hasley, Jean Floud and
   C.A. Anderson (eds), 'Education, Economy and Society', New
   York, 1961, 288-314. Social Class Speech Systems and Psychotherapy', 'Brit. F. Sociol.', 1964, 15, 54-64.
3 M. Deutsch, The Role of Social Class in Language Development
   and Cognition, 'Amer. F. Orthopsychiat.', 1965, 35, 78-88.
4 Vera P. John, The Intellectual Development of Slum, Children:
   some Preliminary Findings, 'Amer. F. Orthopsychiat.', 1963, 33,
   813-22.
5 Eleanor Pavenstedt, A Comparison of the Child Rearing Environment of Upper Lower and Very Low-Lower Class Families, 'Amer.
   F. Orthopsychiat.', 1965, 35, 89-98.
6 S. Minuchin, B. Montalvo, B.G. Guerney, B.L. Rosman and
   F. Schumer, 'Families of the Slums', Basic Books, 1967.
7 R. Skynner, A Group Analytic Approach to Conjoint Family Therapy
   'Social Work Today', 2, no. 8, 15 July 1971, chapter 4 this volume.
8 'Families of the Slums'.
9 Personal communication. At Philadelphia child guidance clinic
   family therapists without prior social work experience are now
   being selected from the same community networks as the major
   body of client referral, and given a two year intensive training
   course in working with family groups. The clinic is under the
   direction of Dr Minuchin.
10 The Association of Psychotherapists, 'Psychotherapy, Definition
    and Training', Report of the Working Party (with thanks to Miss
    Sally Hornby MA).
11 Seymour Fisher and David Mendell, The Communication of
    Neurotic Patterns over Two and Three Generations, 'Psychiatry',
    19, February 1956, 41-46.
12 Antonio Ferreira, Family Myth and Homeostasis, 'Arch. Gen.
    Psychiat', 9, 1963, 457-63. (These last two references may be
    found synopsised in Norman Bell and Ezra Vogel (eds), 'A

Modern Introduction to the Family', Collier-Macmillan, London, 1968.
13   Ivan Boszormenyi-Nagy and James Framo (eds), 'Intensive Family Therapy', Harper Medical Press, 1965.

6 FAMILY MYTHS USED AS DEFENCE IN CONJOINT FAMILY THERAPY

John Byng-Hall

This paper examines the role of the family myth as a defence in psychotherapy with the family. The technique of giving psychotherapy to the whole family in a group is called conjoint family therapy and has been used increasingly within the last few years (Ackerman, 1971). This expansion of interest and practice has created a need for concepts and interventions which take the whole family into account, but which are close enough to a therapist's previous conceptual formulations for him to be able to integrate them within the new frame of reference.

The idea of family myth was first put forward within the context of systems theory by Ferreira (1963, 1965), who considered it to be a family defence mechanism. He defined it as the pattern of mutually agreed, but distorted, roles which family members adopt as a defensive posture and which are not challenged from within the family. Ferreira considered that these roles could provide a useful blueprint for social action but at the same time reduce the family's flexibility and capacity to respond to new and unrehearsed situations. Hence if a family is overloaded with family myths it produces a pathological system. The myth represents a compromise between family members so that each individual's defences are maintained through the myth. Thus threats to the myth also threaten the individual's defences, and changes in individuals threaten the family myth. Thus the concept of family myth provides a framework which can link individual to family psychopathology.

The term 'myth' has been used in a number of ways, some of which emphasize the creative enriching role of myths (Jung, 1951). As Ferreira points out all families probably have and need their myths. This paper will, however, concentrate on clinical situations where the quality or quantity of the mythology represents pathology.

Ferreira considered that the myth's function was to maintain homeostasis, but in his papers he did not describe in any detail either the factors that might disturb the family equilibrium or the origins of the myth.

The present paper attempts to throw some light on how family myths are formed, and why. It also tries to indicate how the concept of family myth can be broadly related to psychodynamic theory and discusses some ways in which the idea provides a conceptual framework for therapeutic interventions during a family therapy session.

The clinical background to the paper is the writer's experience in conjoint family therapy with, at the time of writing, some fifty families seen in a number of settings. He has also had secondhand experience of a slightly larger number of similar families through case conferences, family therapy workshops and by supervising other therapists. The designated patients were mostly adolescents, some of whom had been referred to an out-patient clinic, others to an in-patient adolescent unit. The clinical setting, but not the details of the family therapy techniques, within the adolescent unit have been described in a paper by Bruggen et al. (1973). Co-therapy has normally been used, and the length of treatment has varied from one meeting to two years, and the frequency of meetings varied from once a week to once a month – usually fortnightly. Individual meetings have lasted from one to one and a half hours (the present writer prefers the longer time). The diagnoses of the designated patients have included neurosis, personality disorder and psychosis.

FAMILY ROLE IMAGES

During a meeting the family conveys to the therapists a great deal about how they relate, how they see each other, and their feelings about what they see in each other. The various images and perceptions within the family are both numerous and highly complex, as Laing et al. (1966) indicated. The therapists may, however, be able to build up a picture of three patterns of images which are relevant to family myth: (i) ideal-self images – the behaviour towards which each strives or pressures others to adopt; (ii) the consensus role images – those roles that together they agree each actually occupies; individuals away from the family group may admit to secret reservations about the validity of these images, thus the consensus role images represent a group phenomenon; (iii) repudiated images – family members may be specific about these but they can often only be inferred from the rising anxiety, or the diversionary techniques which occur when certain topics are raised or sequences of interaction are initiated. The degree of vehmence or disgust with which the roles are denied or attributed to someone else can convey the quality of the repudiation. In other families, observable, often non-verbal, patterns of interaction occur of which they are unaware.

Roles are not static attributes but are defined by the quality of interaction between people. The language of theatre can help to give the added dimension to describe the scene of a family group. The theatre as a model for family therapy has been discussed by Kantor and Hoffman (1966). They point out that the paradoxical and incompatible qualities of human relationships may be explored through the theatre. The therapists may observe these conflicting themes during a family meeting. Thus the family (consensus) script and main observable drama may centre, say, on a fight, full of disgust between father and daughter. Another opposite (repudiated because taboo) theme may be revealed by a sexually tinged glance and the fight may then be seen to be providing father-daughter interaction to the exclusion of a lifeless, depressed mother. The entire family may vigorously deny the presence of any incestuous sexuality. The battle is, parents say, to try to make sure that daughter remains a 'good' (ideal) girl.

Family myth is related to the general area of how one drama, re-cognized by all, hides and controls another, perhaps diametrically opposed, repudiated family scene. Dream material presents a useful analogy to illustrate how the myth might be seen. The patient pro-duces the manifest dream material, but remains unaware of the latent content. The myth is equivalent to the manifest content, but, as with dreams, the therapist may be able to discern both aspects, manifest and latent, and the defensive disguises which are operative in the session.

FORMATION OF FAMILY MYTHS

Family myths may originate in an unresolved crisis such as a failed mourning, a desertion or an abortion; the image of the lost person can become resurrected in a remaining member of the family. Scott and Ashworth (1969) discuss how the 'shadow of the ancestor' may be recreated in a 'psychotic' child, where there has been a psy-chotic episode in a family member in the past. Frequently, however, when the precise historical origins of myths are lost, they may be sought in the collusions set up by the marriage, which are later extended into the family. Skynner (1969) suggests that families which use projection, splitting and denial extensively are particu-larly, perhaps only, suitable for conjoint family therapy. These families tend to use family myths as defence. Dicks (1963, 1967) discusses in detail marital collusions based on splitting mechanisms using object relations theory (Fairbairn, 1952). In brief, two basic types of collusion relevant to family myth formation occur.

The first form of collusion may become established through a marriage based on the sharing of a similar split. The same split-off, denied aspects of themselves are seen as lying outside the home. Each idealizes the other and their relationship. This leads to a formation of a joint 'false self'. This form of rather brittle defence is likely to create an impoverished restricted relationship; for in-stance, 'we are lucky we are not bothered with too much sex like so many people are'.

In the second type of collusion Dicks hypothesized (1967, p. 63) that mating was based on attraction to a partner who was uncon-sciously perceived as a symbol of the 'lost' (because repressed) aspects of the subject's own personality. If both partners are attracted on the same basis, then a marriage of opposites occurs. Each spouse finds his or her split-off aspects in the other, thus both sides of the split, e.g. aggressive/submissive, are represen-ted in outward and visible form (say an aggressive husband with a submissive wife), and in a more hidden form in the reverse order (wife's repressed aggression and husband's denied submissiveness)

but which may emerge as the overt pattern occasionally. This unacknowledged aspect of the marriage may have been hidden from
view by idealization and sexual urgency of courting and early
marriage. When each is confronted solidly by the denied part of
himself present in the other, there is a potential for either using
the complementary nature of the marriage constructively, and mending internal splits, or for establishing a collusive defence. Each can
attack and disown the feared or unacceptable aspects of himself or
herself when it shows in the other, thus maintaining defences. This
can lead to the cat and dog type of marriages which can neither
mend nor break up.

These collusive marital systems will have to incorporate the children
into what will become family myths if the parents' defences are to
be maintained. It may be that those marriages which are defending
against unresolved child-parent difficulties are likely to recruit
children into major roles in the defensive system. Marital defences
erected around difficulties in handling genital sexuality, violence
or leaving home are likely to be strained by adolescents whose own
maturational problems in these areas are brought into the family.

A number of mechanisms are involved in recruiting offspring into
roles in the parents' inner worlds. Stierlin et al. (1971) showed how
the parental assumptions about their adolescent's capacity for autonomy influences their offspring's actual ability to leave home. Shapiro
(1967) used the term 'delineation' to describe the view or image that
one person had of another. Defensive delineation by the parent
resulted in a distortion of the parent's image of the adolescent.
Shapiro showed that this can be related to the defensive organization of the parent's character structure and his or her object relations. The defensive delineation of the adolescent by the parent
defined and limited the adolescent and, Shapiro felt, contributed to
the adolescent's disturbance. Although Shapiro discusses each
parent's separate delineation of an adolescent, he did not discuss
whether the parental defensive systems interlocked and, if so, how
it affected the adolescent. If the hypothesis is correct, that the
collusive marital defence system may have to incorporate the adolescent within it, then it may be expected that the parents' defensive delineations could at times overlap, each reinforcing the other's
impact on the adolescent.

Where the parents' marriage is based on mutual idealization, producing a 'joint false self', children may be linked to the marital collusion by processes of secondary identification and projective identification (these concepts used in the way suggested by Rycroft,
1968, p. 67). The adolescents can be required to confirm parental
self-images by not damaging the basic integrity of the parental
'good' internal objects which are being reinforced by identification
with 'good' children. The reciprocal process of children identifying
with parents is, of course, part of normal development, but it can
also play a part in the mechanism of mutual idealization. Repudiated
images are either projected out of the family or denied altogether.
The family consensus image approaches its ideal image. This may
lead to impoverished family life with family myths that give similar

roles to all members, reflecting life styles such as: 'we are a united/happy/peaceful/intellectual family'. To these families in which such a view of themselves is based on a capacity to enjoy this way of life but at the same time contain within it the angry conflictual aspects of family life – in other words those families that can tolerate ambivalence – the term 'myth' would not be applicable. It would be appropriate, however, if the consensus script denied and hid the opposite feared or taboo drama, i.e. a disintegrated/ unhappy/turbulent/impulse-ridden family.

This type of collusion tends to be brittle and its integrity depends on members both fitting the role assigned by adopting the family life-style sufficiently to reaffirm it, and by paying enough lip-service to sustain other members' idealization of their self-images.

The B family

The Bs married on the basis of a shared view that their parents gave each of them a near perfect adolescence, despite intolerably difficult war conditions. They shared a feared inner drama that their fury about having been given no autonomy might break loose and shatter their precariously balanced families of origin. The couple set about providing a perfect upbringing for their children in a world which they felt was full of rebellious, unpleasant, badly brought up youths. Their boys, not surprisingly, found the role of 'perfect' adolescent, proof of 'perfect' upbringing impossible. They proceeded, with some relish, first one, then the other, to become the most unacceptable 'yobs', Hell's Angels, in the neighbourhood. It seems that they identified with the denigrated image of youth with which the family was so preoccupied and fascinated. When the family was seen as a group, the glints in the parents' eyes as some dastardly exploit was recounted revealed the vicarious excitement involved.

As the boys' intense problems with aggression and autonomy burst through the brittle idealization of the family, the parental defence shifted from collusive projection out of the family to projection on to the adolescents.

The family myth which initially maintained homeostasis was: 'the children are being brought up perfectly despite a decadent world.' After this myth was exploded, an uneasy equilibrium was re-established around another myth that 'the boys are doing awful things that the parents would not even dream about'.

The family's preoccupation with the adolescents' attempts to angrily break out of the home may have helped to control and hide from awareness the parents' potential to do the same with the consequent disintegration of the whole family. Bell and Vogel (1960) considered that the scapegoat child's role was to divert attention from parental break-up which would be a more fundamental disaster to the family.

Where the marriage is one of opposites, of the 'cat and dog' variety, the extension of the collusive defence into the family is more complex. The children may attract and confirm the role images which fit the parents' split internal objects, e.g. 'aggressive' and 'submissive', 'sexual and asexual'. Identification and projection tend to draw the children into one or other of the parents' camps, with each camp viewing its own role as striving towards an ideal and the other as playing a denigrated role. Parents may, on the other hand, mend some of their differences by both viewing a child as bad. The same value may be attached by all to a role, say 'bad', by the 'bad' person accepting a damaged self-image, while preserving his own idealized internal objects through images assigned to other members.

In these families the family myth is equivalent to a consensus part/counterpart script which can provide a dramatic framework on to which each can project his own repressed, split-off aspects, while at the same time confirming a self-image that he can tolerate. At the least, such a family myth can preserve for him an ideal object safe somewhere in the fabric of the family. This allows the family to live together.

The C family

Angela C, 16 years old, had started threatening suicide and was considered to have gone mad by her family. Mr C's mother had committed suicide, his sister had had a psychotic breakdown in adolescence and his father had been hospitalized for phobic states in middle age. The GP's greatest anxiety was whether Mrs C would damage Angela in the violent fights she had with her. There was a history of Angela's having always been a bit more awkward than her good, bright brother Derek, but that long before she showed serious signs of disturbance, in family rows Mrs C would shout and scream that Angela would go mad and commit suicide. Angela was not told of her paternal grandmother's suicide and so related the idea of suicide exclusively to herself. One of the family's views of itself presented in the first family meeting on referral for hospitalization was that Angela was absolutely mad and bad, and that Derek was completely sane and very good. The latter fact was repeatedly stated by father, which seemed strangely out of context in the middle of a highly emotional meeting. The preoccupation with the children's roles tended to overshadow a similar parallel but definite view that mother was scatty and irresponsible, father sensible and responsible, the pillar of the family. Subsequent meetings revealed the distortion involved in these views. Angela was indeed disturbed, this showed vividly in meetings, but even there at times she emerged as the most sensible person, and when away from the family her symptoms rapdily diminished. Father emerged as a highly disturbed and disturbing person. Anxiety within the family rose very high when he showed signs of serious depression. Mother turned out to be the one who managed the family affairs very effectively, as well as earning a higher wage than her husband. Derek turned out to be a rather limited boy, capable of being angry and difficult at times.

The marital collusive defence seemed to be for mother to accept the assumed role of 'scatty', thus defining father as the sane one, which defined mother as the easygoing, nice one. In this way father gained some respite from an inner family script in which he was the only one of his family of origin who had not (yet) gone mad or committed suicide (his father broke down at Mr C's present age). Mrs C had, she felt, a vindictive, ruthlessly efficient, nagging mother whom she consciously rejected as a model, but her secret efficiency within the C family revealed the depth of her identity with her mother. She was, however, consciously able to feel, 'I am so muddly, I have to be organized by my husband, so unlike my mother who organized my father.' Her anger, however, erupted whenever she was attacked. The story given indicated that when Mr and Mrs C had rows, Mr C had denigrated Mrs C as 'nutty'. The attack was deflected by Mrs C, with venom added, towards Angela by screaming that Angela would go mad or commit suicide. As this also fitted Mrs C's expectations for Angela, she was delineated, to use Shapiro's term, as mad by both parents. For mother to return the accusation of 'mad and suicidal' to father would have broken the collusive family myth supporting father in the assumed role of reliable and sane. Father found further support in this role image in confirming that sons can after all remain completely sane, like Derek.

The family myth at referral was that the females, mother and daughter, but especially daughter, were mad, scatty and incompetent in contrast to the males, father and son, who were sane, sensible and competent. The feared drama controlled and hidden by this was of father becoming deeply depressed and killing himself, after being nagged by an efficient, dominating wife.

There is some evidence to suggest that the adolescent's view of his parents is of fundamental importance. When Scott et al. (1970) examined the factors relating to whether hospitalized schizophrenics remained mainly in hospital or within their families over a two-year period, they found that the variable which separated these two groups was the designated patient's view of his parents. If he violated the parental role image, seeing them as 'sick' while they saw themselves as 'well', the patient spent most of his time in hospital. If the parental role images concurred, both patient and parents viewing the parental role as 'well', the family remained intact. In family myth terms, it may be that all family members need to agree broadly with the role images of the myth. Those who do not may upset the homeostasis so much that they have to leave home. Angela indicated that she would no longer share the otherwise consensus view of herself as the only mad one. She shouted in a wild manner that her parents and Derek were mad. This merely confirmed in the eyes of the rest of the family the view of her as mad, but it may have also played an important part in the family's wish to separate from her.

STABILITY OF MYTHS

Family mythology represents a body of beliefs that the family has about itself and its members which has some stability conferred by having been repeatedly confirmed by family consensus over the years. It represents the final compromise, necessary for staying together, between each individual's need to have himself seen by others in a particular light, plus the rest of the family seeming to provide the supporting drama which gives substance to the image. Family homeostasis is maintained while each finds at least the minimal support that he needs within this fabric.

In some families there are probably many layers of family myths, each related to particular areas of family functioning, and providing each member with a part within the family scenes related to those tasks. Clearly some layers are more precarious than others, and the various changes occurring within the family will threaten the relevant myth in different ways.

It will be clear that the family myth represents role images. The capacity to maintain the images without testing them against reality varies from family to family and from individual to individual. These variations will indicate the degree to which individuals have to fit or be recruited to concrete roles within the myth. A key mechanism is the way in which cues are given out and received when an individual's self-image cannot be challenged further without catastrophic results, or when he has to be supported by counterpart images accepted, or counterpart roles actually played, by others. When challenge is felt, rightly or wrongly, to be too dangerous, an ever-increasing disjunction between private and consensus views occur; individuals become stranded with the mistaken impression that others agree with their own self-images, or they may be faced with the impossible task of trying to live up to someone else's unreasonable and irrefutable expectations.

The myth eventually loses its capacity to provide even minimal support to individuals, one of whom might break down, or the myth may be exploded, the family regrouping around another one. Frequently it is the adolescents who irrevocably challenge a myth, and they then risk becoming the repositories of the denied parental shared fantasy, as did the boys in the B family.

RESTATEMENT OF CONCEPTS OF FAMILY MYTH, INCLUDING ITS HYPOTHETICAL FUNCTION

Definition of family myth
Those family role images which are accepted by the whole family together as representing each member. This gives each an allotted role in a particular pattern of interaction. The images of interaction are, however, either distortions of, or only a segment of, observable behaviour. The integrity of the role images is not irrevocably challenged from within the family and hence may come to have some degree of permanence.

Function
The function is twofold: to hide from awareness each member's own repudiated, because feared or taboo, inner potential roles; and to

help restrain members from enacting those roles overtly.

Mechanism
The family myth establishes the role images at some distance, from
where they create most anxiety. This is done either by enabling
those most anxious about entering particular roles to play counterpart roles to their own disallowed roles, or by refocusing on the
repudiated drama as it manifests itself outside the family or in a different generation. At a whole family level, the overt drama and
dramatic image hide and prevent, often by reversal, a family drama
felt to be potentially calamitous.

FAMILY MYTHS IN TREATMENT

As families approach the clinic they are frequently in a state of flux,
with defences breached. Inasmuch as the family uses family mythology,
they will have the potential to establish a new collusive defensive
system, recruiting the therapist into a role in the mythology and
blinding him with the myth images. Or they may establish a therapeutic alliance with the therapist and give up maladaptive defences.
The family is likely to be trying to re-establish the currently
breached or threatened myth, and will attempt to recruit the therapists into it. This gives the therapists important diagnostic clues
as to the nature of the myth and the area which requires urgent
attention, but which also has the greatest potential for change. The
deeper, more recalcitrant, family myths emerge later in therapy.
    The clinical material presented by Ferreira (1963) suggests that
a direct, straightforward challenge to the myth may lead to a clos-
ing of the family's ranks in support of the myth, or, if the myth is
suddenly exploded, to termination with that therapist. The technique of reducing the sway of family mythology requires a balance
between a respect for the family's defensive needs and a capacity
for not colluding in it.
    Space does not allow for a detailed account of the therapist's
verbal interventions or of how the transference may be interpreted.
Another paper is required. A general indication of the place of the
myth in treatment will be given.

*Difficulties perceived as either inside the individual or within
the family system*
A feature of family myths is that certain characteristics are often
perceived as residing in particular individuals. One variant of this
is that the problem, which may become further defined as the 'illness', is seen as residing *only* in one person. This can be seen as
a type of family myth. This statement in turn reveals one of the
drawbacks of the term 'myth', which may seem to imply 'untrue'.
Yet those adolescents or children arriving at the clinic who are
defined as the patient by their families and referring medical
agencies are usually highly disturbed and can be assigned to a
diagnostic category. The idea of family myths, then, implies the

use of roles and role images to hide other, even more disturbing, conflicts. Thus the word 'only' becomes pivotal within the phrase 'only in one person'. Families arriving at the clinic vary in their views of the designated patient from that of the 'only' problem to that of the person providing the ticket of entry for the family. Families using myths as defence are probably more likely to see the patient as the problem.

In those families chosen for family therapy the therapist openly confronts the family myth with his own view, embodied in the form of therapy offered, that in this family it is the family system which needs to change. Much of the early work of therapy deals with the feelings about this and establishes a therapeutic alliance with the whole family. The anger and disappointment of all family members must be dealt with.

Frequently particular members of the family become spokesmen for different feelings towards the therapists. This reveals a lot about the role structure of the family. The adolescent may express the anger openly by stating that he never wanted to come anyway, and is certainly not going to come again. The parents protest that they want to come. It may take most of the session to clarify that, at another level, the adolescent is furious that he was not seen on his own and hence given the major share, and that his parents never wanted to be involved therapeutically. If this work is not done, the adolescent, secretly supported by his parents, may opt out of treatment. The family can sometimes impose their myth model on the therapist, despite whatever the therapist does. He is seen by them as playing the role of psychiatrist to the adolescent, confirming the patient role. After months of treatment, during which the parents seem to accept the family focus, father's admiring glances at the therapist revealed 'isn't he so clever doing it this way to give James the impression that he is not mad'. The 'myth' cannot be dropped until the parents' anxieties about their own sanity have been dealt with.

A number of effects are produced if the therapist, right from the first session stops the meeting at times to clarify what has just been happening between family members, and its consequences. First, it gives the therapist some breathing space. Second, it indicates to the family that it is their relationships which are the focus of the therapeutic effort. Third, it gives the family a research model of pausing to think about the consequences of its actions. Patterns of interaction which clarify the role of the adolescent as 'the problem' can be particularly fruitful. The adolescent may, for instance, become tiresome at the moment that parents seem to be about to disagree, thereby drawing attention to himself and making sure that they unite in tackling his problem.

Polarization within the family
Family members may polarize around tasks at home or in the group. This may represent a manifestation of family myth roles. A useful technique is to explore the service that each performs for the others in taking on roles in the myth, following this with an examination of

the price paid in doing so. The management of the adolescent's autonomy is frequently a source of polarization.

The D family

    The family myth was that father was impossibly strict with his daughter; the women somehow had to deal with this difficulty. What emerged in meetings was that mother subtly provoked the girl into rebellious activity, throwing the onus on to father to set all the limits. The therapist explored how father saved mother from being in any way bad or restricting, like her own dominating mother, by his setting of ridiculously early bedtimes, which mother clearly had to resist. Mother, by being excessively indulgent, pushed father into a disciplinarian role and thus saved him from facing his own soft tenderness, something on which his family of origin had placed a taboo. The daughter expressed all the anger for both parents. The price in lost capacities was then counted; father gave up his tender, warm loving potential, mother, gave up her assertive capacities and the respect of her daughter, the girl isolated herself from the warm exchanges with her parents that she needed and longed for. Later, polarization diminished, with mother becoming more assertive and father less rigid, and the daughter testing limits less often.

    This approach, which emphasizes mutual protection, has advantages over demonstrating how each family member forces the other into representing his own unacceptable parts, a technique which can lead to mounting fury within the family, each angrily demanding that the others change their ways. Another advantage is that, in demonstrating the lost function, a healthier model of interaction is provided by implication. Restrictive family defences are more likely to be retained if the alternatives are sensed to be catastrophic and no new models are available.

    The concept of family myth is particularly useful when multiple projections are occurring within the family. A quite simple central theme can be kept in the therapist's mind throughout a session or period of work. This can provide a prompt to the therapist that work has to be done to see how each member articulates with the myth, and hence with the others' defences. This work with each individual can then include much of the subtlety and expertise derived from working with individuals, in this way linking intrapsychic work to group processes. The overall aim is to help replace understanding based on myth roles and projection with empathy. Disagreements can then be tolerated on the basis of allowing the other his point of view, and are more likely to lead to resolution of the problem than to polarization and mutual denigration.

The family myth's impact on the therapist

The countertransference phenomena, used in the way that Sandler et al. (1970) suggest, may include not only the emotional responses aroused by the family, but often seems to include a high level of pressure to add action to the affect i.e. to play the role assigned in the family mythology. This phenomenon may occur because a number

of family members, taking up each other's cues, all start viewing
and responding to the therapist as if he had certain characteristics.
   One session started with the father complaining that his son said
nothing. After a constant bombardment of complaints by the parents,
the therapist found that he himself was stumbling over his words;
he suddenly realized that he was speechless. Exploring this phenomenon helped the family to see that the boy was not only being
stubborn; the rest of the family was also assigning this role to him.
   Families who have one member designated as psychotic often leave
the therapists feeling mad or confused. This can offer a similar
opportunity to demonstrate to the family what they do to people.
   One advantage of having a co-therapist is that it allows one therapist to become absorbed into the family system because he knows
that this co-therapist will rescue him. For instance, when the therapist mentioned above was rendered speechless the mother exchanged
a secret glance with the co-therapist which indicated, 'What can you
do with a dumb clot like this?' The co-therapist was able to show the
family how the 'speechless' therapist was being isolated as 'the
problem' by non-verbal agreement between the rest, which he was
not allowed to see, and hence to combat.
   Co-therapists often find that they re-enact a family myth. So many
taboo topics seem to relate to what men and women do to each other
and how children intrude, that having a male and a female therapist
seems most appropriate. They can also represent grandparents in
the transference.

The E family
   A male therapist found that he was being treated as if he was very
delicate. The family became concerned about a sore elbow which
he assumed to have because he was holding it. But he also
sensed at another level that anything he said or did was treated
as if it was potentially hurtful to his woman co-therapist. He
found himself almost making an interpretation which would have
undermined his co-therapist. He felt protected by the family but
paradoxically treated as highly competent by them. This led,
after examining the contradictions, to an understanding of the
family myth that women are highly competent and tough, and men
and boys weak and sickly. The teenage son had been referred
with 'an illness', thought to be a brain tumour by mother. The
taboo topic was mother's cancer, which had been operated on before the marriage, and the real fear was of women becoming weak
and dying, especially if ill-treated by rough men.
   On another occasion the woman therapist complained to her co-
therapist before a session that she seemed to be developing flu.
When the family came into the room the male therapist sat down
almost immediately, instead of remaining standing until the family
started to sit, which is what the female therapist did and which he
usually did. This led the family to concentrate its concern and
attention on the male therapist's health. The mother's probing
questions were felt to be attacking, rather than caring, by him.
This helped to clarify how the teenage son first invited concern

about his health and then felt attacked, which indeed he was, by
having all the sickness 'dumped' on to him. Later it transpired
that the woman therapist had been developing only a mild cold and
that the male therapist had not been aware of the significance of
his sitting down early. It seemed then that the therapists had
somehow picked up the family's acute anxiety about any illness in
women, and how the men were used to divert anxiety away from
this.

Although it may be important to be able to experience, and hence
know, the role assigned by the family, often by becoming identified
with one of the family members either past or present, it is even
more important that the therapist then disentangles himself from such
a role, otherwise he will just become swallowed up by the family
system. Disturbed families have an amazing capacity to induce collusive denial systems between the therapists themselves. It often
emerges that the family seems to latch on to the therapist's particular
blind-spots, which in itself provides an interesting comment on the
natural history of collusive systems. Therapists, whether they like
it or not, are often used as role models. For the therapists to become
involved in the family mythology closely enough to be felt to be almost part of it, but to maintain the capacity to break out of the collusions, can, it may be argued, provide a major avenue for change.
Inertia occurs when therapists become involved in collusions of
which they remain unaware. Therapists who imagine that they can
remain detached are likely to fall into this trap.

One danger is for the therapist to ally himself with the adolescent,
against the parents, seeing the adolescent as merely victim. This
deprives the adolescent of his most valuable asset, which is his
ability, and need, to take responsibility for what he puts into the
family system. If he sees his parents as responsible, and can use
the therapist as a model to support this view, then his grievance is
justified. He can then concentrate his psychic energy on attacking
the rest of the family, who are then much more likely to need to
refute the attacks by seeing his anger, plus their own, as a 'bad'
part of the adolescent. In this way the family polarizes with each
member's inner script, casting someone else as the devil, and hence
no one taking responsibility for his own difficulties, with consequent loss of capacity to put things right. The dangers of violating
the parental role image have already been discussed.

The best way of enabling the therapist or therapists to disentangle from the family script is to ensure adequate discussion and
working through between the sessions. This should ideally be done
in supervision, or in the setting of a discussion group of practising
therapists. Co-therapy teamwork relationships in family therapy are
discussed in a paper by Rubinstein and Weiner (1967).

DISCUSSION

The significance of the idea of family myth rests partly on the importance of the phenomenon in its own right, and partly on its position

as a bridging concept between psychoanalytic psychology and systems theory.

Ferreira (personal communication 1972,) still finds the family myth concept useful in therapy. He has not, however, found it amenable to research techniques. It is hoped that the present restatement will provide scope for operational definitions.

Beels and Ferber (1969), observing and comparing many well-known American family therapists, noticed that those who concentrated on systems theory considered that psychoanalytically orientated therapists were unscientific; the psychodynamic therapists considered that the systems purists were naive. Perhaps both viewpoints have some validity.

Family myths bring form and content together; when intrapsychic content meets in interpersonal interaction it produces form, the system of role images. Family images can be examined through interpersonal perception tests done separately, followed by a consensus record completed within a family group. Content may be explored clinically and through projective testing.

Some family myths can be related directly to life events and painful experiences within the family more readily than can unconscious fantasy. On the other hand, unconscious fantasy itself clearly articulates in some way with the repudiated taboo or feared drama hidden, and hence perhaps perpetuated, by family myths. Family myths may provide one bridge between life events and unconscious fantasy, a potentially fruitful source of inquiry.

If the hypothesis is correct that consensus role images are needed for families to live together, then it has important implications for working with families who are extruding one member. To establish a new, more reality-based, consensus may be more urgent a task than to elucidate the nature of the break up of the old consensus.

In those families with an adolescent referred for hospitalization (Bruggen et al., 1973) the reason for admission has to be understood by all within a family group. What emerges is that the only reasons which everyone, including the professionals can understand and agree about are in terms of the parents not being able to cope or manage the adolescent at home. This painful piece of reality provides a new, less fantasy-prone, focus of attention than that of 'mental illness'. Parents may be more able to accept the role image of 'cannot cope' or 'needing a rest' than that of 'crazy', which they are forced to direct exclusively towards the child. The details of the family psychopathology emerge later, but this approach can lead to some adolescents avoiding hospitalization, and it provides a basis for reunion for those who are admitted; the family can agree when parents can cope again and when the adolescent is manageable once more.

The main objection to the use of the concept of family myth is that the term 'myth' means many things to many people. The writer has considered numerous other words or phrases which could be used instead, such as family beliefs, credo, role expectations or collusive defence.

The rich and varied usage given to myth, however, enables it to encompass more aspects of the clinical phenomenon: its legendary or historical component, the support given through the explanations it offers; but also its drawbacks because it is a commonly held belief that is untrue. Using a new term would mean burdening the literature with more jargon.

Ultimately, the justification for using the idea of family myth will depend on any understanding that it offers and on future research findings.

ACKNOWLEDGMENTS

I am indebted to Dr Bruggen, Dr Hunter and Dr Hyatt Williams, whose patients provided me with the clinical experience. I would like to thank them and many other staff members of the Tavistock Clinic and Hill End Hospital for their support and helpful suggestions. I learnt much from my various co-therapists.

REFERENCES

Ackerman, N.W. (1971) The Growing Edge of Family Therapy, 'Fam. Proc.', 10, 143-56.
Beels, C.C. and Ferber, A. (1969) Family Therapy: a View, 'Fam. Proc.', 8, 280-332.
Bell, N.W. and Vogel, E.F. (1960) The Emotionally Disturbed Child as the Family Scapegoat, in N.W. Bell and E.F. Vogel (eds), 'Modern Introduction to the Family', London: Routledge & Kegan Paul.
Bruggen, P., Byng-Hall, J.J. and Pitt-Aitkens, T. (1973) Reason for Admission as a Focus of Work for an Adolescent Unit, 'Br. J. Psychiat.', 122, 319-29.
Dicks, H.V. (1963) Object Relations Theory and Marital Studies, 'Br. J. Med. Psychol.,' 36, 25-9.
Dicks, H.V. (1967) 'Marital Tensions: Clinical Studies Towards a Psychological Theory of Interaction', London: Routledge & Kegan Paul.
Fairbairn, W.R.D. (1952), 'Psychoanalytic Studies of the Personality', London: Tavistock.
Ferreira, A.J. (1963) Family Myth and Homeostasis, 'Archs. Gen. Psychiat.', 9, 457-63.
Ferreira, A.J. (1965) Family Myths: the Covert Rules of the Relationship, 'Confin. Psychiat.', 8, 15-20.
Jung, C.G. (1951) 'Introduction to a Science of Mythology', London: Routledge & Kegan Paul.
Kantor, R.E. and Hoffman, L. (1966) Brechtian Theatre as a Model for Conjoint Family Therapy, 'Fam. Proc.', 218-29.
Laing, R.D., Phillipson, H. and Lee, A.R. (1966) 'Interpersonal Perception', London: Tavistock.
Rubinstein, D.R. and Weiner, O.R. (1966) Co-therapy Teamwork Relationships in Family Therapy, in G.H. Zuk and I. Boszormenyi-

Nagy (eds), 'Family Therapy and Disturbed Families', Palo Alto, California: Science and Behaviour Books.

Rycroft, C. (1968) 'A Critical Dictionary of Psychoanalysis', London: Nelson.

Sandler, J., Holder, A. and Dare, C. (1970) Basic Psychoanalytic Concepts. IV. Counter-transference, 'Br. J. Psychiat.', 117, 83-8.

Scott, R.D. and Ashworth, P.L. (1969) The Shadow of the Ancestor: a Historical Factor in the Transmission of Schizophrenia, 'Br. J. Med. Psychol.', 42, 13-32.

Scott, R.D., Ashworth, P.L. and Casson, P.D. (1970) Violation of Parental Role Structure and Outcome in Schizophrenia, 'Soc. Sci. Med.', 4, 41-64.

Shapiro, R.L. (1967) The Origin of Adolescent Disturbance in the Family: some Considerations in Theory and Implications for Therapy, in G.H. Zuk and I. Boszormenyi-Nagy (eds), 'Family Therapy and Disturbed Families', Palo Alto, California: Science and Behaviour Books.

Skynner, A.C. (1969) Indications and Contra-indications for Conjoint Family Therapy, 'Int. J. soc. Psychiat.', 15, 245-9.

Stierlin, H., Levi, L.D. and Savard, R.J. (1971) Parental Perceptions of Separating Children, 'Fam. Proc.', 10, 411-27.

7 INDICATIONS AND CONTRA-INDICATIONS FOR THE USE OF FAMILY THERAPY

Sue Walrond-Skinner

Family therapy can be defined as the psychotherapeutic treatment of the family system using as its basic medium conjoint interpersonal interviews. It includes many sub-specialities, the most important of which is conjoint marital therapy – which addresses itself to the marital system, in the same way that family therapy focuses on the family system. For the purposes of this annotation, the literature referring to indications for both family and marital therapy will be discussed.

A variety of problems confront the theorists who would attempt to define the conditions which indicate or contra-indicate the use of family psychotherapy as the treatment of choice for emotional psychiatric and behavioural disorders. Not least of these is the immaturity of the subject itself – family therapy having been recognized as a valid psychotherapeutic modality for barely twenty years. Stein (1969) for example, writes of the 'experimental, evolutionary and partial quality of most investigations in the family field'. Hence it would be true to say that family therapy is still at a 'pre-theory' stage of development, with practitioners and researchers simply lacking sufficient experience of their subject to be able to offer anything approaching a definite set of conditions for its use. Empirically based and properly controlled outcome studies into the effectiveness of family therapy are almost entirely lacking (Wells et al., 1972) and whilst work specifically focusing on the outcome of conjoint marital therapy has been rather more widespread (Gurman, 1973; Gurman and Rice, 1975) this too is inconclusive. Lacking too is any established taxonomy of family types which would enable the practitioner to move outside traditional psychiatric nosology into a genuine systems framework of interpersonal disorders (Walrond-Skinner, 1976).

The practitioner, working at this pre-theory stage and requiring some guidelines for case selection, develops working metaphors to describe the conditions which appear to him to respond favourably to treatment. Skynner (1976), for example, talks of a 'kind of sandwich distribution regarding the suitability for group treatment whereby the most primitive levels of development and the more sophisticated levels could use group situations fruitfully . . . while the level intermediate between these 'top' and 'bottom' levels requires a dyadic relationship.' Obviously, such metaphors, arising out of the day-to-day experience of the practitioner, provide fruitful ground for developing hypotheses. The danger arises when apparent confirmation of the metaphor's accuracy occurs subtly over time. It then becomes enshrined not as the product of controlled research, yet inappropriately takes on the status of scientific fact.

A further difficulty needs to be borne in mind. The term family therapy describes a modality, which in turn embraces a complex range of methods, each employing treatment techniques specifically suited to the particular approach being used. Modality, method and technique - each is addressed to a different level of therapeutic functioning and the sometimes muddled and contradictory statements made about treatment indications may result from a confusion between these three levels. For example, family therapy might be dismissed out of hand because the family seems poorly motivated to come to the clinic; shows little interest in gaining insight into its difficulties and is beset by grave environmental problems of a material nature. What may at first seem a contra-indication for the modality, may turn out instead to be a contra-indication for one of its methods (in this case, the psychoanalytic approach) and an indication for another (in this case, the structural approach). The major part of this annotation is concerned with the current state of discussion regarding indications and contra-indications for the modality not its widely differing methods or technical approaches.

A final problem worth mentioning is the fact that few writers have attempted to assess the relative merits of family therapy versus other psychotherapeutic modalities with the same kind of problem, an exception being the work of Wellish et al. (1976). As the report of the Group for the Advancement of Psychiatry (1970) points out 'the problem is whether there are indeed particular conditions that respond more easily to family therapy than to other forms of treatment.' This report found that in considering the indications for family therapy compared with other types of therapy, 83 per cent of questionnaire respondents expressed interest in comparing the outcome of family therapy with various forms of individual psychotherapy, whereas only 47 per cent made a conscious choice between family therapy and any form of group psychotherapy. As regards a comparison with other types of treatment interventions such as behaviour modification, chemotherapy or in-patient treatment, the situation is even bleaker, a notable exception being the work of Langsley et al. (1968), where the effects of family therapy are compared with the effects of hospitalization.

A search of the literature from approximately 1960 to 1976 is disappointing in that it reveals little in the way of any growing sophistication in its attempts to refine the clinical conditions in which family psychotherapy may appropriately be used. However, with these caveats in mind, some of the approaches that are made to the problem will be considered.

THE 'EXCLUSIVE APPROACH' POSITION

For some, the question of indications or contra-indications simply does not arise. All symptomatology becomes, for these practitioners, amenable to change through the intervention in and manipulation of the individual's most salient psycho-social system - usually his family. Family therapy (or systems therapy as it is more usually described in this generic context) is thus regarded as a new orientation to problems of mental illness, and since systems must be adapted to individuals, not individuals to systems, family therapy or systems therapy is considered to be almost universally appropriate in its application.

THE 'TREATMENT OF LAST RESORT' POSITION

At the other extreme are those who employ family therapy when all other treatment modalities have failed, and the failure of other treatment interventions is hence the criterion for employing family therapy. This approach has meant that family therapy has been tried out in an impressive array of 'untreatable situations'. Chronic schizophrenia, recidivism, child abuse, drug dependency, have all been exposed to family therapy, the treatment choice being made on the basis of absence of any alternatives.

THE 'DIAGNOSTIC AID' POSITION

A different view from either of the above, is often adopted by practitioners who are mainly committed to their own discipline and its traditional tools and practices, rather than to the full-time practice of family therapy - be they psychiatrists, social workers or clinical psychologists. Conjoint family interviewing is seen as an aid to promote the more effective use of individual, group or in-patient treatment and is used either initially as a diagnostic aid to treatment selection or as an intermittent event during a crisis phase of therapy - for example, when a child is to be returned to his parents after a period in a children's home. A series of family interviews may be conducted after a schizophrenic patient has returned home in order to maintain his improvement in the community; or a once-off conjoint interview may be arranged to try to discover why a successfully treated individual has found that his symptoms have recurred. The selection of family therapy for brief periods is based on the need to unlock intra-psychic or interpersonal resistance which may occur during the course of another treatment modality.

THE DIFFERENTIAL TREATMENT POSITION

Despite the difficulties discussed in the opening section, this fourth group embraces all those practitioners who endeavour to select family therapy as the treatment of choice from a range of possible treatment interventions. As has already been stated, the criteria used for selection derives more from ongoing clinical experience of 'what works' than from hard research findings. One of the reasons why comparisons are difficult is that practitioners are working from very different theoretical stances and hence from different basic assumptions, so that categories are often contradictory between one writer and another. Moreover, as with any other type of psycho-therapy where the therapist's own self is such a vital ingredient in the therapeutic process, the practitioner will necessarily use very personal yardsticks for drawing up his own list of indications and contra-indications, depending on the type of families and situations with which he knows he can or cannot work.

INDICATIONS

1   Symptomatology, of whatever kind which is felt by the prac-titioner to be embedded in a dysfunctional system of family relation-ships. Wynne (1965), for example, states that some form of family therapy is indicated 'for the clarification and resolution of any structural intrafamilial relationship difficulty'. Here the approach is essentially directed towards the family system, with less regard being paid to the presenting symptom as an indicator of whether or not to employ family therapy. In summary, wherever the identified patient's presenting problems are seen to be expressing the pain or dysfunction of the family system, family therapy automatically be-comes the treatment of choice, unless there are specific indications to the contrary. (This would be the traditional position by all the major writers on family therapy.)
2   Clinical situations which are presented transactionally by the patient in terms of a relationship rather than in terms of an indi-vidual family member's symptomatology. For example, dysfunctional situations which are presented by one or both parties as marital conflict; difficulties involving sexual dysfunction; relationship dif-ficulties occurring in other intimate interpersonal systems such as unmarried heterosexual or homosexual couples; parent/child or parent/adolescent problems presented as involving the system or sub-system as a whole. Where family members are themselves per-ceiving their difficulties in relationship terms, it is usually felt to be retrogressive for the practitioner to offer a form of treatment which focuses on one party only. The method or sub-speciality of family therapy chosen may not of course be the treatment of the whole family group on its own. In preference, the practitioner may select conjoint marital therapy (where marital or sexual problems are presented); kin network therapy (where a wide circle of rela-tives, friends and work associates appear to be intricately involved in the problem); or multiple couples/family therapy (where strong positive or negative transference feelings prevent the therapist from working effectively with the marital pair or family on its own, or where the therapist is felt by the family to be too overpowering, for

example, where the family has a poor sense of group identity
(Lacquer, 1972). For some practitioners, multiple couples work is
always the treatment of choice for marital problems (Framo, 1973).)

3   Family therapy is routinely employed by a large number of
practitioners in different types of separation difficulty (although
this is also given as a contra-indication by some, who feel that individual or stranger group treatment is more appropriate when an
adolescent is trying to separate from his family or when a marriage
is breaking up). In these situations, individual, group or in-
patient treatment may often be employed by the therapist alongside
family therapy (Byng-Hall and Bruggen, 1974).

4   Writers working largely from within a psychoanalytic conceptual framework highlight the usefulness of family therapy when members of a family are 'functioning at a basically paranoid-schizoid
level, with part object relationships, lack of ego boundaries and extensive use of denial, splitting and projection' (Skynner, 1969). The
rationale used is that in these families, basic psychological features,
normally located within the individual, are 'scattered' between
family members. Hence it is only by assembling the whole group,
that the therapist can hope to attend to the various split off and
projected intra-psychic attributes of each individual. Family therapy
enables individuals to reality test some of their paranoid phantasies,
hopefully with positive effect, enabling each to begin to reintegrate
the projected negative parts into themselves again.

5   Finally, family therapy has been successfully employed with
'hard to reach' disorganized families who would not normally be able
to mobilize sufficient resources to enable them to participate in a
sustained therapeutic programme. Again, the use of family therapy
with low socio-economic, severely deprived families with poor verbal
skills is sometimes cited as a contra-indication; but Minuchin et al.
(1967) as well as many others have convincingly shown that family
therapy, employing an active, directive approach to problem-solving,
is often the only intervention that is likely to be effective.

CONTRA-INDICATIONS

1   Practical limitations. The physical or psychological unavailability
of crucial family members is the first practical consideration for the
family therapist to bear in mind. Family members may either be
dead, geographically distant or completely unmotivated to engage in
any type of therapeutic work. On the other hand, it may be the
absence of appropriately experienced and personally suitable therapists that prevents the employment of family therapy in a particular
agency or area, even when families seem well motivated and where,
from other points of view, family therapy would be indicated.

2   Often family therapy is contra-indicated because the situation
has been presented too late to offer the family therapist much hope
of bringing about constructive change. In other words, the prognosis may simply be too poor to warrant the necessary expenditure
of effort. Ackerman (1966) for example, cites as a contra-indication

'the presence of a malignant irreversible trend towards break-up of family which may mean that it is too late to reverse the process of fragmentation'. Here, of course, those family therapists who engage in divorce therapy would not necessarily agree, though even those would generally admit that the desire to separate relatively undestructively would be a necessary pre-requisite for commencing treatment.

3   The dangers of engaging in family therapy with some families are frequently alluded to, where the emotional equilibrium is so precariously maintained that attempts at changing the relationship system may precipitate a severe decompensation on the part of one or more family members. Many apparently highly stressful interpersonal situations are ego-syntonic for the individuals involved, and attempting to upset this balance may mean that the last condition becomes worse than the first (Pittman and Flomenhaft, 1970). It may also be felt to be psychologically dangerous to engage in family therapy where one or more members are organically ill, since the sessions might either increase the level of stress intolerably for that member or might raise unjustifiable 'magical' hopes in other family members that the family member's organic symptoms will be removed.

4   Families where one or more members are depressed are often considered to respond poorly to family therapy, since the depressed member may find it difficult to participate meaningfully in conjoint sessions, or to share a therapist. The same rationale may contra-indicate family therapy for severely emotionally deprived individuals. However, in both of these situations the use of individual psychotherapy for the symptomatic members, in conjunction with the conjoint sessions may well enable family therapy to be productive.

5   Finally, it may sometimes happen that the family therapist is asked to take on the treatment of a family by an agency such as a court or school and where, unbeknown to the therapist, there is a hidden agenda to be fulfilled (Zuk, 1976). The family therapist may suddenly find himself forced to collude with an external decision-making process where, for example, his prior commitments of confidentiality to the family is called into question by a third party. Families where child abuse is suspected may, for example, involve the family therapist, if he is not extremely careful in making written statements or court appearances in favour of one part of the family against the other - a position which is always inimical to his role as therapist to the whole system. It may ultimately be quite harmful to the family to begin treating these situations via family therapy, where there are severe entanglements between the other agencies involved in the treatment.

REFERENCES

Ackerman, N.W. (1966) 'Treating the Troubled Family', Basic Books, New York.
Byng-Hall, J. and Bruggen, P. (1974) Family Admission Decisions

as a Therapeutic Tool, 'Family Process', 13, 443-59, chapter 9 below.

Framo, F. (1973) Marriage Therapy in a Couples Group, in 'Techniques of Family Therapy - A Primer', D.A. Bloch, Grune & Stratton, New York.

Group for the Advancement of Psychiatry (1970) 'The Field of Family Therapy', vol. VII, Mental Health Materials Centre, New York, p. 558.

Gurman, A.S. (1973) The Effects and Effectiveness of Marital Therapy - a Review of Outcome Research, 'Family Process', 12, 145-70.

Gurman, A.S. and Rice, D.G. (1975) 'Couples in Conflict - New Directions in Marital Therapy', Aronson, New York.

Lacquer, H.P. (1972) Mechanisms of Change in Multiple Family Therapy, in 'Progress in Group and Family Therapy', ed. C.J. Sager and H.S. Kaplan, Brunner/Mazel, New York.

Langsley, D.G., Pitman, F.S., Machotka, P. and Flomenhaft, K. (1968) Family Crisis Therapy - Results and Implications, 'Family Process', 7, 145-58.

Minuchin, S., Montalvo, B., Guerney, B.G., Rosman, B.L. and Schumer, F. (1967) 'Families of the Slums', Basic Books, New York.

Pittman, F. and Flomenhaft, K. (1970) Treating the Doll's House Marriage, 'Family Process', 9, 143-55.

Skynner, A.C.R. (1969) Indications and Contra-indications for Conjoint Family Therapy, 'Int. F. Soc. Psychiat.', 15, 245-49.

Skynner, A.C.R. (1976) 'One Flesh, Separate Persons - Principles of Family and Marital Psychotherapy', Constable, London.

Stein, J.W. (1969) 'The Family as a Unit of Study and Treatment', Regional Rehabilitation Research Institute, University of Washington School of Social Work. Washington, DC.

Walrond-Skinner, S. (1976) 'Family Therapy - the Treatment of Natural Systems', Routledge & Kegan Paul, London. (Chapter 9 outlines a development in the construction of family taxonomies and gives references to the main attempts which have been made.)

Wellish, D.K., Vincent, J. and Kelton Ro-Trock, G. (1976) Family Therapy versus Individual Therapy: a Study of Adolescents and their Parents, in 'Treating Relationships', ed. D.H. Olson, Graphic, Iowa.

Wells, R.A., Dilkes, T.C. and Trivelli, N. (1972) The Results of Family Therapy: a Critical Review of the Literature, 'Family Process', 11, 189-207.

Wynne, L. (1965) Some Indications and Contra-indications for Exploratory Family Therapy, in 'Intensive Family Therapy', ed. I. Boszormenyi-Nagy and J. Framo, Harper & Row, New York.

Zuk, G. (1976) Family Therapy: Clinical Hodgepodge or Clinical Science? 'F. Marriage Family Counseling', 2, 299-303.

Part 2

APPLICATION

8 FAMILY THERAPY IN ADOLESCENT PSYCHIATRY

Peter Bruggen and
Graham Davies

INTRODUCTION

Disturbance in adolescence
There are differences of opinion about the incidence and significance
of disturbance in adolescence. Some, for example Anna Freud (1958),
expect trouble and difficult relations with parents and almost regard
adolescence as a psychiatric disorder in its own right; while others
criticize such views for tending to become self-fulfilling prophecies
(Anthony, 1969). It is not surprising that, from the clinical perspective, adolescence looks stormy; but studies which have attempted
to look at an unselected sample of adolescents find that most young-
sters negotiate this transitional period without severe problems or
marked conflict with their parents. Studies by Henderson et al.
(1971) in Australia, Leslie (1974) in an industrial town in northern
England and Rutter et al. (1976) in the Isle of Wight show a pre-
valence of psychiatric disorder of between 14 and 21 per cent.
Rutter et al., in their study, which was of 14-year-olds, found
that alienation from parents was not common, though petty disagreements about clothes, hair and going out were more so.
   The impression that disturbed adolescents have more communication
difficulties with their parents has support from the Isle of Wight
study, and the consequent generalization of their difficulty in communicating distress and finding help may partially account for a
referral rate that is lower than would be expected on the basis of
epidemiological studies (Baldwin, 1968).

Why family therapy?
Although the causal relevance of the family to adolescent disturbance
is not easy to determine conclusively, Rutter et al. show that
'psychiatric disturbance is associated with various indications of
family pathology'. Interestingly, when compared with the views of
clinical writers on the family, cited below, this study found that
the one 'association reaching statistical significance in new disorders arising in adolescence was that of marital disharmony'.
   A study which compares the organization and interaction in families with an adolescent designated as schizophrenic, as delinquent
or as well-adjusted (in each case with controls who were neither
delinquent nor schizophrenic) is that of Stabenau et al. (1965).

The structure of the three family types were shown to be different. Lewis et al.'s (1976) seven-year study of forty-four research volunteer families as well as of 'dysfunctional families' with designated patients identifies several discriminating variables. A study which strongly indicates the effectiveness of family therapy in comparison with normal in-patient treatment is that of Langsley et al. (1968 and 1969).

There are, therefore, good empirical grounds for the increasing turning of attention to the family of the adolescent in trouble.

In the last analysis, however, 'family therapy is not a treatment method but a clinical orientation that includes many different therapeutic approaches' (Haley, 1975a). This is fundamental. Family therapy is the result of taking seriously the fact that we are all part of one another and that individual experience or behaviour is always in a social context, the most significant and enduring of which is clearly the family. The family therapist's view of pathology is broader than that of one who studies pathology in the individual. The possibilities of intervention are therefore broader and ramify into the extended family and social network (Bowlby, 1949; Hansell et al., 1970; Attneave and Speck, 1973; Garrison, 1974).

Further reasons for interest in the family approach in the psychiatry of adolescence
When one member of a family reaches adolescence, that family necessarily enters a phase of transition. The adolescent member is shaping up to change various roles, of which three are particularly relevant to the family: he is becoming independent and may leave the family; he is forming sexual relationships; he may become a parent himself. The family system must alter in response. Each family member, especially each of the parents, has to undergo complementary role change; at the same time echoes reverberate in each person among his memories and archaic conflicts connected with infantile and childhood situations. It is for these reasons that problems thrown up by adolescents are family problems par excellence. It is when these undercurrents, stirred within and between each member, are felt as excessive that there is a family with pathology - or, as it more often presents, a family with a pathological adolescent.

In the experience of all psychiatrists there must have been occasions when the treatment they are carrying out was interfered with by the relatives of the person they were trying to treat. From the family therapy point of view this is to be expected since if the adolescent is the 'symptom bearer' for the family then for him to 'get better' is to threaten other family members with the need to face their own problems. Such 'interference' can become the object of therapeutic work when the family is seen together.

Williams (1975) argues that, however skilled many therapists may be in developing one-to-one relationships with individuals, in most situations the family resistances will prevail. He argues that the sense of control which a therapist feels is illusory. While this comfortable, reassuring experience of good systematic psychotherapy is going on, covert and subtle sabotage is taking place behind the scenes, in the wider field of the whole family. On the other hand, bringing the family together allows for such resistances to be broken through together.

A typical example of this experience is quoted by Williams. A teenager and his mother had been seen in separate diagnostic sessions several years after the father's death. Both talked about this but neither showed appropriate affect. Seen together, another phenomenon was observed. Whenever the boy's talk turned to his feelings about his father, his mother would say 'Your father was a good man and it isn't proper to talk about him' or she would go on to talk about how hurtful it would be if they 'dredged up the past'. Family interviews helped to free the mother to be able to give her son permission to delve into his feelings of rage and depression about his father's death. Certainly, an attempt to get the boy to reach the same point in individual therapy could have been made, but, Williams writes, the consequent conflict of loyalty would have been immense. On the one hand, there would be his own wish for relief and on the other his awareness of his mother's wish for the continual burial of feelings.

Offer and Vander Stoep (1975) point out how, in family therapy, it can be demonstrated for all to see that the overtly unacceptable behaviour of an adolescent may be stimulated or supported by other family members and how it may 'reflect a tension in the whole family system'. Furthermore, the apparently disturbing behaviour of the adolescent may in fact be comforting to the parents in that it gives a problem outside themselves to worry about. 'When the acting-out behaviour stops, other parts of the family must show overt conflict for example, the marital disharmony between father and mother does not come up to the surface until the acting-out of their adolescent child has stopped.'

Family therapy exposes, and so enables the family to see, the full plight of their relationships. Whitaker (1975) describes an adolescent girl, Sue, suffering from a 'psychotic breakdown', coming from a family described as close, friendly and warm. After half-an-hour of a family session, one of the adult siblings said she did not know why her father went on like that, and reminded him that her mother had been in a mental hospital and that two of the other children had had treatment. Here was a family with well-kept secrets to whom 'the honesty of an intimate, loving family and open communication was unknown'. Whitaker writes, 'The family consultation thus enabled Sue to get some sense that she was not the black sheep of the family and allowed mother and father to at least have the honour of facing life the way it was and of expressing their anxiety and concern in some better way than by hiding it.' A different kind of reason is given by Glick and Hesler (1974) when they write of the threat that particularly hostile adolescents may pose to the therapist. 'In treating a family with an adolescent "authority problem", inclusion of the entire family group can dilute the adolescent's feelings about the therapist.' The relevance of the adolescent's ability to deflate our image of ourselves should not be underestimated.

A very practical reason suggested for family therapy is to help keep the adolescent out of hospital (Bruggen, Byng-Hall and Pitt-Aikens, 1973). By helping a family in a crisis to continue to contain a young person, the start of a career as a mental patient may be avoided.

The impact of McGregor's work with adolescents is quoted by Offer and Vander Stoep (1975). Intervening with multidisciplinary teams for a very limited time, he exposed parental interactions which were arresting the development of the children. The interaction of the team itself in working with the family served as a useful model for the family in its struggle to develop more adaptive problem-solving techniques. This conclusion is supported by the work of Langsley et al. (1968 and 1969).

But the introduction of family therapy into a clinic can be disquieting. Haley (1975b) has pointed out how the usual hierarchical position of staff is upset by the ability of people in different disciplines to carry out family therapy and that the value of much medical training is lowered.

INDICATIONS AND CONTRA-INDICATIONS

'When all therapy is considered from a family orientation, one cannot say that family therapy is indicated in one case and individual therapy in another. From the family point of view individual therapy is, in fact, one way of intervening in a family' (Haley, 1975a). True, but the 'conjoint' interview with two generations, parents and children together, is generally seen as essential to what is meant by 'family therapy' and Haley does go on to admit the question of whether to see the designated patient alone or with the group - the family. On this opinions differ. Whitaker (1975) wishes to suggest family therapy as a modality for every adolescent patient and certainly sees no contra-indications if the family is available and the therapists are willing to struggle. Others, more cautious feel that family therapy 'need not be presented as a panacea, a substitute for all other approaches or even appropriate in all cases as a total self-contained service' (Group for the Advancement of Psychiatry, 1970, p. 543).

Views on indications and contra-indications tend to be linked with the two principal theoretical approaches in the family therapy field. These are the systems approach, which has its origins in general systems theory (Bertalanffy, 1956; Grinker, 1976), and the psychoanalytic approach, which stems from the individual and group-analytical traditions. Therapists who are more oriented towards the systems approach are inclined to find fewer reasons to exclude families than are their more psychoanalytic colleagues.

1. *On the basis of diagnosis or family pathology*
Therapists from a psychoanalytic background assess individuals and families according to views of psychodynamic intrapersonal and interpersonal forces. Thus Wynne (1965) saw family therapy as

being indicated in particular situations, notably
(a) where there is a failure in an adolescent to emerge from a
symbiotic dependency relationship with a parent ('separation
problems').
(b) where each member of a family projects qualities or feelings
on to another ('trading of dissociations'), and
(c) in the families with a schizophrenic member, where there is
'collective cognitive chaos and erratic distancing'.
It was in this context that he had used the terms pseudo-mutuality
and pseudo-hostility (Wynne et al., 1958).

In discussing conjoint sessions (in which two or more generations
are seen together), Skynner (1976) distinguishes between the task
of diagnosis - 'securing information about the family system and its
relevance to the problem as presented by the referrers' - and
treatment - 'the attempt to change the state of affairs thus clarified'.
He goes on to write:

For diagnosis there are no objections at all to conjoint sessions,
and ideally an attempt should be made to see a family together at
least once at the beginning or at least in the course of any form of
treatment whatsoever. Only in this way can one be sure that one
has not missed a family involvement crucial to the treatment of the
presenting problem. To fail to see the family is equivalent to a
physician deciding not to carry out a full physical examination in
the case of organic disorder - permissible for the experienced,
but a calculated risk nevertheless.

Skynner uses the theory of emotional development put forward by
the psychoanalyst Melanie Klein (1946; Segal, 1973) to describe
three levels of group and family functioning. In a 'sandwich' distribution of suitability for family therapy, 'the most primitive level
of development and the more sophisticated levels could use group
situations fruitfully, though in different ways', whereas individuals
in families between these 'top' and 'bottom' levels need a two-person,
or dyadic, relationship for therapy.

Individuals in families representing the 'bottom' layer of the sandwich make extensive use of 'paranoid/schizoid' functioning, with
vague and fluctuating ego boundaries. In such a family, one member
will project a part of his 'self' on to another member, who then
accepts these projections and performs certain functions 'on behalf
of' the projector. As mutual projections switch around, problems
appear in different family members and there is much 'splitting',
in which one member may experience himself as having no anger
while feeling that someone else shows too much. (These ideas compare interestingly with those of Shapiro and Zinner (1976), described later.)

In the 'top' layer, Klein's 'depressive position', with the capacity
to contain negative feelings without projecting them, is securely
established. Ambivalence and separateness can now be faced; negative
affect, difference and conflict in family sessions can be used constructively.

Conjoint sessions, working with the first group as an 'organism'
of which the family is part and with the second group as an assembly

of individuals, often produce rapid change.

In the 'middle' layer, families function as if Klein's 'depressive position' were not yet securely established. There are capacities to contain negative feelings without projecting them and to tolerate some ambivalence, but frustration and rage are easily aroused by absence or by a perceived rejection. Such families are very dependent on positive relationships, both with each other and with the therapist. 'Uncovering of strong negative feelings in the course of family sessions can lead such families to flee, and even the awareness of differences of attitude and of separate identities can be experienced as a threat of abandonment. At this level, therapeutic emphasis needs to be on secure, reliable, dyadic relationships.'

Some feel that certain kinds of psychopathology in one family member may prevent the family from doing the work of therapy (e.g. Guttman, 1973), but much must depend on the setting of the therapy and on the techniques which the therapists feel able and willing to use.

2. *On the basis of social class and deprivation*
Therapists of a systems orientation, particularly Minuchin et al. (1964, 1967), have led the way in working with families who are severely disadvantaged and disorganized. This would seem to be because of the style of this approach, in which the therapist is inclined to be more a 'conductor' than a 'reactor' (Beels and Ferber, 1969) and the techniques to be more oriented towards the 'behaviour' end of the intervention spectrum than a verbal and 'experience' end (see Figure 8.1).

The more reflective, passive approach derived from conventional psychoanalytic treatment is ineffective with severely deprived people. Bychowski (1970) gives an account of the difficulties for such children and adolescents in their ego development, and Cobb (1972) is critical of the published attempts to handle such problems. Limited goals, emphasizing growth potential and flexibility, have been found to be more effective with 'multideficit' families (McKinney, 1970).

Skynner (1976) suggests 'that the label "unmotivated", often applied to these families by child guidance clinics, might better be applied to those therapists who are unwilling to put themselves out to meet their special needs'.

THEORY AND TECHNIQUE

The different concepts of family therapy in adolescent psychiatry can be seen as particularly relevant to various points on a dimension that has 'experience' at one end and 'behaviour' at the other (see Figure 8.1).

In any individual or group activity, both experience and behaviour exist and interact. A change in one affects the others. (Fear leads to trembling; trembling reinforces fear. If father is seen to tremble, the whole family feels more afraid.)

The two main perspectives, the psychoanalytic and the systems, have their standpoints at opposite ends of this dimension. Each necessarily affects the whole, but its characteristic point of intervention, or leverage, is different.

From the psychoanalytic perspective, at the 'experience' end of the continuum, talk is in terms of 'assumptions', 'perceptions', 'images', 'myths' - as belonging to individuals in the family or to the family as a whole. The fundamental technique is the interpretation; the communication, to the family, of the therapist's way of understanding them.

From the systems perspective, on the other hand, talk is in terms of family interactions and family functioning. The systems therapist thinks in terms of 'subsystem', 'boundary', 'implicit rules', etc, but it is fundamental to this approach that he does not talk with the family in these terms. Rather, within the framework of such concepts, he acts directly on the family structure in order to change its form.

In selecting from the writings of therapists of particular persuasions to describe these two perspectives further, we do not wish to exaggerate the differences nor to suggest that using one approach means excluding the other. The writers quoted below make specific reference to adolescent problems.

The psychoanalytic perspective
Zinner and Shapiro (1972, 1974; Shapiro and Zinner, 1976) draw upon Bion's (1961) theory that small group behaviour is determined by shared, unconscious fantasies of the members of the group as well as by reality-oriented thinking directed towards the fulfilment of specific and overt tasks. They apply this to a family with adolescent children dealing with its 'central task' of helping the development of the offspring as individuals. To be successful at this task means to restructure the family group and this is threatened, they argue, by 'demands placed upon the child to collude with the unconscious assumptions of family life which are implicitly striving to maintain the *status quo ante* in family relations'. Unfulfilled and unrecognized unconscious needs in the parents lead to children being subjected to a 'variety of parental coercions' which 'interact with the child's own instinctual requirements, to fix him as a collusive participant in the family's hidden agenda'.

The process defined is carried out by aspects of actions or statements by the parents, which communicate the parents' image of the adolescent to him. Zinner and Shapiro call these communications 'delineations' and describe them as 'part and parcel of parental behaviour', and write that they 'constitute the raw material for adolescent internalization and consequent identification'. Thus, the adolescent identifies with distorted images of himself and 'in this fashion, his own subjective self-experience is likely to be affected by his parents' efforts to diminish their own anxiety'.

The psychoanalytically oriented family therapist is able to make observations and to offer interpretations based upon study of accumulated delineating statements. The interpretations concentrate on the mechanisms of projection and projective identification. (In projective identification, A projects something on to B, and B, unconsciously or otherwise, as the recipient of the projections, colludes in providing vicarious gratification for the other.) Indeed, Zinner and Shapiro see these mechanisms and their interpretation as basic to the understanding and changing of the phenomenon described in so many different ways; that people interact with others 'as if they were not themselves but someone else'.

British papers in this tradition have included those of Byng-Hall (1973, 1975), Byng-Hall and Miller (1975); Cooklin (1974); Dare (1975); Lewis (1970) and Skynner (1962, 1969, 1976). Another group of writers whose ideas have had considerable influence are associated with the name of R. D. Laing (Laing and Esterson, 1964; Laing, 1970; Laing, 1971).

The systems perspective
For the systems family worker the family itself is the system, 'in that a change in one part of the system is followed by compensatory change in other parts of the system' (Bowen, 1966). The therapist studies over-functioning in one part (for example, domination by one parent), under-functioning in another part, and dysfunctioning or collapse of the total system. He sees dysfunctioning encouraged by the family's tendency to see him as 'healer' and to wait for him to accomplish his work. Rather, he aims to establish himself as 'consultant' or 'supervisor' - 'to help family members become "system experts" who could know the family system so well that the family could readjust itself without the help of an outside expert, if and when the family system was again stressed'. A 'sick' or delinquent member is a powerful force in such a system, maintaining it as it is.

The system analyst works on the interaction between the two systems, the family and the therapist. The main concern is to change the experience of the family members; 'insight' may or may not result.

Minuchin (1974) is an active therapist believing that change takes precedence over insight. He may behave like a distant relative. He intervenes in space, in seating, in behaviour; he manipulates mood and even meals. He uses authority, and believes that 'supporting the parents' responsibility to determine family rules secures the child's right and obligation to grow and to develop autonomy'.

Boundaries are the rules defining who participates in a system and how. Minuchin intervenes in the family system in order to modify the subsystem boundaries, and it is where there is a family member diagnosed as having anorexia nervosa that his work most clearly and dramatically stands out. He aims to release the anorexic child from a deviant relationship. He manipulates the system to precipitate a crisis. By the second session at latest, the family have a meal with him to facilitate 'the creation, within the field of eating, of a strong, interpersonal conflict', which then takes precendence over the 'symptom'. In this way, the symptom of anorexia, with its accompanying tremendous anxiety about death, disappears, and subsequent therapy can concentrate on the real underlying problems of the conflicts within the family or the marriage. (Support for the idea of enabling family conflicts to be explored by removing the anxiety about death comes from work on admitting the child to hospital simply because it is a place where people are less anxious about dying (Bruggen, 1976).)

Minuchin's repertoire is wide. He sides with, or against, individual members during sessions. He sees members individually. He gives tasks; he challenges family members to exaggerate or continue a symptom. He will compete with, or outdo, individual members of a family with certain behaviours (for example, by shouting at the children more loudly than the mother does, so that she becomes protective of them) or he will support the adolescent sub-group. His structural family therapy is a therapy of action, aiming 'to modify the present, not to explore and interpret the past'.

Technique
The variety of technical manoeuvres and their coherence in family therapy are represented in the Diagram.

At the analytic end of the spectrum, interpretation and confrontation are important. The interpretation is directed to the individual or the family group and speaks to feelings and perceptions, presenting a reappraisal of what is going on. Family members, if they hear and at some level accept this alternative understanding, will change their behaviour. (The movement is from left to right in the diagram.) In confrontation, the therapist describes what he sees people to be doing. This can be said with varying degrees of insistence or feeling and can be a powerful boundary-strengthening intervention (Skynner, 1974)

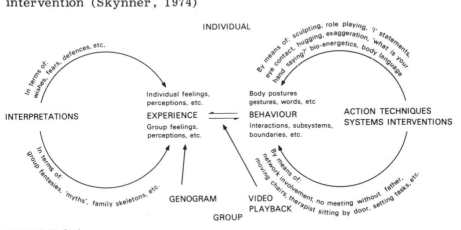

FIGURE 8.1

Whatever the theoretical approach, it seems hard to question the fact that to be successful in family therapy, the therapist exercises a great deal of control over the process. There is always the effect of modelling, but the degree to which a therapist is willing to make explicit his position as a rule-setter varies greatly.

The analytical ideology and the use of words as the main therapeutic tool make it more difficult to acknowledge the power of
selective response and non-verbal reinforcement. On the other
hand, the therapist working in ways represented at the systems
end of the Diagram uses interventions which are more likely to
involve the settings of tasks, the distribution of the family in
space, or the explicit prohibition of certain interactions. This
highlights his position as determiner of rules within the session
and makes his acceptance of it more natural. It is important to
appreciate that the pathological patterns of interaction that are
seen as needing a change may be described by therapists of either
persuasion in similar terms, but that the techniques of intervention
chosen impinge more directly on either the experience or the behaviour of the family in order to effect that change.

A comprehensive and clear breakdown of techniques from the
systems perspective is given by Minuchin (1974).

Several writers of both perspectives say that, as well as the
conjoint family sessions, individual sessions are advisable with the
adolescent to support the growing autonomy of the age group. The
value of both individual and family sessions in the treatment of
'borderline' adolescents is carefully argued in a recent paper by
Shapiro et al. (1977).

Other perspectives and techniques

A. *Action techniques*
At the behaviour end of the Diagram can be placed methods which
are loosely grouped together as 'action techniques'. They come from
various theoretical backgrounds. In contrast with the group interventions of a systems nature, these techniques are directed more
towards the individual, and this is represented by placing them in
the upper half of the Diagram.

(i) Family sculpting (Simon, 1972; Papp, Silverstein and Carter,
1973). The subject is invited to create a tableau, using the professional and family people in the room, to represent a particular
family situation. Individuals are then asked to state what they
have been feeling and changes may be made in their positioning.
This technique is often recommended when therapists are feeling
'stuck' with a family. It is one of the best known of the action
therapies and is carefully explained with diagrams, by Walrond-
Skinner (1976).

(ii) Role-playing. In some ways derived from psychodrama
(Moreno, 1946), role-playing has similarities to sculpting but is
more active. A recent incident, described with little affect by a
family, may be 'brought to life' by its being role-played by the
members present.

(iii) Exaggeration (Levitsky and Perls, 1972) is a part of the
modern gestalt (Kempler, 1973) approach, which in a number of
ways helps people to retain responsibility for themselves and
their 'symptoms'. Someone saying 'I hate you' would be encouraged
to 'say it again' and to 'say it louder', until it changes. Similar

encouragement may be given to the exaggeration of gesture.

'I' statements (not accepting someone saying 'When I was a child you were lucky ever to see your father', but rather, 'When I was a child *I* was lucky ever to see my father'), 'no gossipping' (not talking about someone in the group, but talking to them) and eye contact are further examples.

(iv) Touch between family members or with therapists may obviously occur during sculpting and role-playing. The powerful effects of touch are noted by Rueveni (1975) in describing the group hugging a distressed member near the end of a network meeting.

Bioenergetic assertive techniques (Palmer, 1973), in which the postural and expressive cues associated with a feeling (such as shouting or clenching a fist with anger) are worked with, introduce the whole field of body language, a development of the concept of 'muscular armour' (Reich, 1948) as the way in which feelings are contained in posture and muscular tension. A family member may be encouraged to uncross arms and legs (which may be seen as a bodily way of holding in feelings) or an adolescent asked 'What is your foot saying?' as it taps the air.

B. *Genograms* (Guerin and Fogarty, 1972)
This is a family tree, constructed as a shared task, on a blackboard, for all to see. It is a powerful integrative tool, often enabling family members to feel involved with each other's backgrounds in a new way and sometimes freeing them, as the diagram on the blackboard grows, to share hitherto closely kept secrets.

The genogram's relation to analytic techniques is reflected by its representation towards the left of the Diagram.

C. *Video playback* (Berger, 1970)
This tool offers uniquely forceful opportunities for confrontation (often of the most supportive nature).

D. *Vector therapy* (Howells, 1971)
Vector therapy works on the forces within a family and their directions. Thus, an emotional force can be changed in magnitude (father's aggression is diminished), in direction (father abuses mother instead of child), in duration (father works away from home and spends less time there) and in quality, as when one force replaces another (father treats his child with kindness instead). From the Institute of Family Psychiatry in Ipswich, Howells' work on the vector model has appeared strangely isolated from the rest of the family therapy literature and movement. One of the many important aspects of work which he mentions is the need to pay attention to the physical setting and seating arrangements for therapy sessions.

E. *Multi-family groups* (Kimbro, et al., 1967 and Harrow, 1970)
Individual family members can see other families in process of dealing with their own difficulties in multi-family groups which combine

some of the advantages of both traditional group and conjoint
family therapy. Multi-family groups are probably more commonly
used when one family member is an in-patient.

Therapeutic pitfalls
Stierlin (1975) writes of the problems resulting from 'any deviation
from a therapeutic position of involved impartiality' (a deviation
which, incidentally, he defines as 'counter-transference'). Over-
active therapists stir up the family but still fail to build trust,
whereas the over-passive miss their chance to move into the family.
He writes of the temptation to side with the powerful, 'sick' victim
member of the family against the apparent victimizers, the parents.
Such a therapist fails to realize the immense power which such a
victim, often designated as schizophrenic, may have over the
parents. Stierlin described a 'spiral of negative mutuality' stirred
up by a therapist consciously or unconsciously siding with the
victim against his parents, supporting, with his medical authority,
the adolescent's 'masochistic power ploy' and stirring up the parents'
guilt. He continues, 'A parent can usually discharge this increased
guilt only by assuming an even harsher punitive and blaming –
that is victimizing – stance *vis-à-vis* the adolescent, who, his own
unconscious guilt rising, will be driven to further live up to his
parents' victimization of him, thereby deadlocking him and them
even more tightly.' The other serious deviation from Stierlin's
'involved impartiality' is siding with the 'victimized' parent. In this
case, there may be a tendency for therapists to encourage punish-
ment in the guise of firmness, authority, or setting limits, and
these warnings can be set alongside the views of those who advocate,
in working with adolescents, firmness and confrontation (Winnicott,
1969; Bruggen and Pitt-Aikens, 1975) and the need for the law to
be observed (Davies, Riddle and Wolfenden, 1975).
    Also, therapists may unwittingly compete with the parents and
try to be, or be seen as 'better' parents than they. If this happens,
it is essential for it to be dealt with. Minuchin (1974) emphasizes
the need to balance one's interventions, not ignoring any subsystems entirely.
    One way of responding to the difficulty of working with families
has been the use of therapeutic teams.

Therapeutic teams
Most family therapists work, not singly, but with a co-therapist,
and believe that without a colleague a lone therapist may be
'swallowed up' by the intense experience, or at least so preoccupied with some aspects of the session that other, important,
matters are missed. So co-therapists can check each other: one
can be deeply involved in the intense, even exciting, experience,
while the other remains less so. A vivid metaphor for this kind of
division of labour between co-therapists is where one plays at the
net and the other towards the back of the court, as in tennis – a
metaphor used by Hyatt Williams of the Tavistock Clinic. Henderson
and Williams (1973) have also argued that some of the best work is

done when therapists, discovering that they are split, struggle towards a resolution in front of the family. The intensity of feelings engendered in therapists must be recognized; it is not uncommon for family therapists to feel full of anger, love, laughter, or for their eyes to be full of tears.

To have therapists support and consult each other in front of families can offer a more constructive model for handling differences (Bruggen, Byng-Hall and Pitt-Aikens, 1973). Many people see special advantages in having the co-therapists of opposite sexes. There is an obvious training advantage in having one more experienced and the other a novice. The role of nurses as family therapists is described in Smoyak (1975).

Solow and Cooper (1975) emphasize how co-therapists may need to be 'advocates' for one member of the family. They may have to counter such forces as are shown when parents imply that it is normal for every adolescent to take an overdose at one time or another, or, on the other hand, imply that some normal teenage behaviour is a symptom of serious illness.

How co-therapists get on with each other can make or mar the therapy and adolescents are highly skilled at detecting and exploiting any split between staff. Johnson and Szurek (1952) have advised that collaborating therapists should be 'unambivalent, uncompetitive and entirely cooperative' with each other. A less idealistic approach has been to advocate that an institution should be structured (Bruggen, 1973) to open communications and facilitate confrontation, to maximize involvement in decision-making and to minimize the chance of staff breaking down under stress.

Howells (1971), emphasizing that one therapist is of one mind, is against co-therapists.

RESEARCH

Traditionally, psychiatrists have seen themselves as doctors treating specific illnesses in individual patients. In more recent years, however, as Maxwell Jones (1974) has told us, some have been 'questioning the whole approach to "illness", which may be relevant to medical and surgical conditions but which may be actually harmful in psychiatry'. Such workers are more likely to regard psychiatric illness as a way of handling problems of living. Similarly, the type of research familiar in the writings of those who take the more medical view is seldom applied to family therapy. The intercommunication of ideas between family therapists at conferences is usually based on participation rather than on evaluation of data presented in lectures. Sharing with other professional workers the experiences of families is often found to be inestimably helpful by those already practising in this field, but is unlikely to impress or influence the sceptic.

A 'bridging' study is that of Langsley et al. (1968 and 1969). The psychiatrists' decision to admit was reversed in 150 controlled cases, and family crisis therapy was offered instead. No one from

this group was admitted to psychiatric hospital during the period
of treatment, which averaged 5 to 8 sessions. Compared with the
control group's in-patient treatment, the family therapy led to
one-fifth as long loss of social functioning, one half as many subsequent admissions of one-third the length, and cost one-sixth
as much. In 'The Treatment of Families in Crisis', Langsley and
Kaplan give an account (Chapter 5) of the handling of an 18-year-
old girl showing a schizophrenic breakdown. Bringing the family
together, bringing into the open, but then not dwelling upon,
the sexuality between the girl and her father, using phenothiazines
for the girl, being available on the telephone for the family, involving the grandmother and energetically interacting with other
rehabilitation agencies are all described in some detail.

Langsley's general thesis that family work can prevent admission
to psychiatric hospitals has had some confirmation in work with
adolescents in this country (Bruggen, Byng-Hall and Pitt-Aikens,
1973). A particular development of it has been, not to reverse
an admission decision nor to decide on no admission, but rather
to leave the decision-making to those in parental authority. Psychiatrists are therefore working, not as experts who make the best
decision, but as workers who study and assist the decision-making
abilities of the parents within the family (Byng-Hall and Bruggen,
1974).

The most comprehensive review of quantifiable interaction research into family therapy is by Riskin and Faunce (1972).

CONCLUSION

The impression given in the literature that each person working
with the families of adolescents does so exclusively from one particular standpoint is strengthened by listening to their talk. It seems
to be a characteristic of adolescent units that the staff put forward
a particular point of view with confidence, enthusiasm and idealization.

An in-patient unit's work, involving as it does taking care of the
child on behalf of the parents, fits readily into systems terms. On
the other hand, the essentially *understanding* work of those units
involved in family therapy with the exploration and the re-examining
of feelings, perceptions and interactions, can be seen as a psychoanalytic approach. Both are effective and compatible.

Perhaps both are necessary. Freud's (1910) paper, ' "Wild"
Psychoanalysis' can be seen as a warning against neglecting the
systems aspects of the technique by failing to carry out certain
'technical rules'. At the other extreme, in bioenergetic assertive
techniques, the therapeutic intention described (Palmer, 1973,
p. 245) in a textbook of behaviour therapy, is 'to heighten the
vividness or reality of an individual's experience or recollection of
a feeling'. Such a change in experience is one that an analyst would
wish. Furthermore, the most non-directive analyst may yet, by
implication, give an injunction (e.g. 'Do not take illegal drugs'),

and the least interpretative action-oriented therapist does, by implication, interpret (e.g. 'You do have angry feelings inside').

It is in the integration of the approaches, as well as their development and the production of more quantifiable research, that the challenge of family therapy in adolescent psychiatry now rests.

ACKNOWLEDGMENTS

We would like to thank the Young People and their Families Workshop of the Adolescent Department, Tavistock Clinic, for their suggestions; Mrs Faith Raven for her helpful improvements to the script, and Mrs Wenna Gilbraith for producing it.

REFERENCES

Anthony, E.J. (1969) The reactions of adults to adolescents and their behavior, in 'Adolescence' (ed, G. Caplan and S. Lebovici), New York and London: Basic Books, pp. 54–78.
Attneave, C.L. and Speck, R.V. (1973) 'Family Networks', New York: Vintage Books.
Baldwin, J.A. (1968) Psychiatric Illness from Birth to Maturity: an Epidemiological Study, 'Acta Psychiatrica Scandinavia', 44, 313–33.
Beels, C.C. and Ferber, A. (1969) Family Therapy: a View, 'Family Process', 8(2), 280–318.
Berger, M.M. (ed.) (1970) 'Videotape Techniques in Psychiatric Training and Treatment', New York: Brunner/Mazel.
Bertalanffy, L. von (1956) General System Theory, 'General Systems', 1, 1–10.
Bion, W.R. (1961) 'Experiences in Groups', London: Tavistock. (Republished as a Social Science paperback in 1968 by Tavistock Publications.)
Bowen, M. (1966) The Use of Family Theory in Clinical Practice, 'Comprehensive Psychiatry', 7, 345–74 (pp. 351, 353).
Bowlby, J. (1949) The Study and Reduction of Group Tensions in the Family, 'Human Relations', 2, 123–8, chapter 1 above.
Bruggen, P. (1973) Multi-disciplinary or Inter-disciplinary? Paper read at the residential conference of the Child Psychiatry Section of the Royal College of Psychiatrists, University of Sussex, September 1973.
Bruggen, P. (1976) The Role of the Hospital-based Adolescent Unit, in 'Mental Health in Children', vol. III, New York: PJD Publications, pp. 731–42.
Bruggen, P., Byng-Hall, J. and Pitt-Aikens, T. (1973) The Reason for Admission as a Focus of Work for an Adolescent Unit, 'British Journal of Psychiatry', 122, 319–29.
Bruggen, P. and Pitt-Aikens, T. (1975) Authority as a Key Factor In Adolescent Disturbance, 'British Journal of Medical Psychology', 48, 253–9.

Bychowski, G. (1970) Psychoanalytic Reflections on the Psychiatry of the Poor, 'International Journal of Psychoanalysis', 51, 503-9.

Byng-Hall, J. (1973) Family Myths used as Defence in Conjoint Family Therapy, 'British Journal of Medical Psychology', 46(3), 239-50, chapter 6 above.

Byng-Hall, J. (1975) Conjoint Family Therapy, in 'Adolescence and Breakdown' (ed. S. Meyerson), London: Allen & Unwin, pp. 119-34.

Byng-Hall, J. and Bruggen, P. (1974) Family Admission Decisions as a Therapeutic Tool, 'Family Process', 13, 443-59, chapter 9 below.

Byng-Hall, J. and Miller, M. (1975) Adolescence and Family, in 'Adolescence: the Crisis of Adjustment' (ed. S. Meyerson), London: Allen & Unwin.

Cobb, C.W. (1972) Community Mental Health Services and the Lower Socio-economic Classes: a Summary of Research Literature on Out-patient Treatment (1963-1969), 'American Journal of Ortho-psychiatry', 42, 404-14.

Cooklin, A. (1974) Family Preoccupation and Role in Conjoint Therapy. Paper read to the Royal College of Psychiatrists, June 1974.

Dare, C. (1975) The Classification of Interventions in Child and Conjoint Family Therapy, 'Psychotherapy and Psychosomatics', 25, 116-25.

Davies, G., Riddle, P. and Wolfenden, A. (1975) Render unto Caesar, 'Therapeutic Education', 3(1), 13-19.

Freud, A. (1958) Adolescence, 'The Psycho-Analytic Study of the Child', vol. XIII, pp. 255-78.

Freud, S. (1910) 'Wild' psycho-analysis, in 'The Complete Psychological Works of Sigmund Freud', vol. XI, London: Hogarth Press, 1957, pp. 219-27.

Garrison, J. (1974) Network Techniques: Case Studies in the Screening-Linking-Planning Conference Method, 'Family Process', 13(3), 337-53.

Glick, I. D. and Hesler, D. R. (1974) 'Marital and Family Therapy', New York: Grune & Stratton, p. 106.

Grinker, R. R. (1976) In Memory of Ludwig von Bertalanffy's Contribution to Psychiatry, 'Behavioural Science', 21(4), 207-18.

Group for the Advancement of Psychiatry (1970) 'The Field of Family Therapy', New York: GAP Publication, no. 78, p. 543.

Guerin, P. and Fogarty, T. F. (1972) The Family Therapist's Own Family, 'International Journal of Psychiatry', 10(p), 6-22.

Guttman, H. (1973) A Contra-indication for Family Therapy: the Pre-psychotic or Post-psychotic Young Adult and his Parents, 'Archives of General Psychiatry', 29, 352-5.

Haley, J. (1975a) Family Therapy, in 'Comprehensive Textbook of Psychiatry' (ed. Alfred M. Freedman, Harold I. Kaplan and Benjamin J. Sadock), 2nd edition, Baltimore: Williams & Wilkins, vol. II, p. 1881.

Haley, J. (1975b) Why a Mental Health Clinic should avoid Family Therapy, 'Journal of Marriage and Family Counselling', 1, 3-13.

Hansell, N., Wodarczyk, M. and Handlon-Lathrop, B. (1970)

Decision Counselling Method: Expanding Coping at Crisis-in-transit, 'Archives of General Psychiatry', 22, 462-7.

Harrow„ A. (1970) A Nursing Approach to Multiple Family Group Therapy, 'Proceedings of the Fifth Conference of the Association for the Psychiatric Study of Adolescents', Edinburgh.

Henderson, A. S., Krupinski, J. and Stoller, A. (1971) Epidemiological Aspects of Adolescent Psychiatry, in 'Modern Perspectives in Adolescent Psychiatry' (ed. J. G. Howells). Edinburgh: Oliver & Boyd.

Henderson, E. and Hyatt Williams, A. (1973) Transference in Family Therapy. Paper read at Tavistock Clinic Family Therapy Conference in July 1973.

Howells, J. G. (1971) Family Group Therapy, in 'Modern Perspectives in Adolescent Psychiatry' (ed. J. G. Howells), Edinburgh: Oliver & Boyd, p. 421.

Johnson, A. M. and Szurek, S. A. (1952) The Genesis of Anti-social Acting out in Children and Adults, 'Psycho-analytic Quarterly', 21, 323-43.

Jones, M. (1974) Psychiatry, Systems Theory, Education and Change, 'British Journal of Psychiatry', 124, 75-80.

Kempler, W. (1973) 'Principles of Gestalt Therapy', Costa Mesa, California: Kempler Institute.

Kimbro, E. L., Taschman, H. A., Wylie, H. W. and MacLennan, B. W. (1967) A Multiple Family Group Approach to some Problems of Adolescence, 'International Journal of Group Psychotherapy', xvii, 18-24.

Klein, M. (1946) Notes on Some Schizoid Mechanisms, 'International Journal of Psychoanalysis', XXVII(3), 99-110. (Republished 1952 in 'Developments in Psycho-Analysis' (ed. J. Riviere), London: Hogarth Press.)

Laing, R. D. (1970) 'Knots', London: Tavistock.

Laing, R. D. (1971) 'The Politics of the Family', London: Tavistock.

Laing, R. D. and Esterson, A. (1964) 'Sanity, Madness and the Family', London: Tavistock.

Langsley, D. G. and Kaplan, D. M. (1968) 'The Treatment of Families in Crisis', New York: Grune & Stratton.

Langsley, D. G., Flumenhaft, K. and Machotka, P. (1969) Follow-up Evaluation of Family Crisis Therapy, 'American Journal of Orthopsychiatry', 39(5), 753-9.

Leslie, S. (1974) Psychiatric Disorder in the Young Adolescents of an Industrial Town, 'British Journal of Psychiatry', 125, 113-24.

Levitsky, A. and Perls, F. S. (1972) The Rules and Games of Gestalt Therapy, in 'Gestalt Therapy Now' London: Penguin Books, p. 172.

Lewis, E. (1970) Family Treatment. Paper read to the Psychotherapy Section of the Royal Medico-Psychological Association.

Lewis, J. M., Beavers, W. R., Gossett, J. T. and Phillips, V. A. (1976) 'No Single Thread: Psychological Health in Family Systems', New York: Brunner/Mazel.

McKinney, G. E. (1970) Adapting Family Therapy to Multideficit

Families, 'Social Casework', 51, 327-33.
Minuchin, S. (1974) 'Families and Family Therapy', London: Tavistock. pp. 14, 59, 154, ch. 8.
Minuchin, S., Auerswald, E., King, C. H. and Rabinowitz, C. (1964) The Study and Treatment of Families that produce Multiple Acting out Boys, 'American Journal of Orthopsychiatry', 34, 125-33.
Minuchin, S. and Montalvo, B. (1967) Techniques for Working with Disorganized, Low Socioeconomic Families, 'American Journal of Orthopsychiatry', 37, 880-7.
Minuchin, S., Guerney, B. G. Jr, Rosman, B. L. and Schumer, F. (1967) 'Families of the Slums; an Exploration of their Structure and Treatment', New York, London: Basic Books.
Moreno, J. L. (1946) 'Psychodrama', New York: Beacon House.
Offer, D. & Vander Stoep, E. (1975) Indications and Contraindications for Family Therapy, in 'The Adolescent in Group and Family Therapy' (ed. M. Sugar), New York: Brunner/Mazel, pp. 145-60.
Palmer, R. D. (1973) Desensitization of the Fear of Expressing One's Own Inhibited Aggression: Bioenergetic Assertive Techniques for Behaviour Therapists, in 'Advances in Behaviour Therapy', vol. 4 (ed. D. Rubin), London: Academic Press, p. 245.
Papp, P., Silverstein, O. and Carter, E. (1973) Family Sculpting in Preventive Work with 'well families', 'Family Process', 12(2), 197-211.
Riskin, J. and Faunce, E. (1972) An Evaluative Review of Family Interaction Research, 'Family Process', 11, 365-455.
Rueveni, U. (1975) Network Intervention with a Family in Crisis, 'Family Process', 14(2), 193-203.
Rutter, M., Graham, P., Chadwick, O. F. D. and Yule, W. (1976) Adolescent Turmoil: Fact or Fiction? 'Journal of Child Psychology and Psychiatry', 17, 35-56.
Reich, W. (1948) 'The Function of the Orgasm', New York: Orgone Institute Press. (Reprinted in 1968. London: Panther.)
Segal, H. (1973) 'Introduction to the Work of Melanie Klein' (especially chapters 3, 5 and 6). London: Hogarth Press.
Shapiro, E., Shapiro, R., Zinner, J. and Berkowitz, D. (1977) The Borderline Ego and the Working Alliance: Indications for Family and Individual Treatment in Adolescence, 'International Journal of Psychoanalysis', 58, 77-87.
Shapiro, R. and Zinner, J. (1976) Family Organization and Adolescent Development, in 'Task and Organization' (ed. Eric Miller). London, New York, Sydney, Toronto: John Wiley.
Simon, R. (1972) Sculpting the Family, 'Family Process', 11, 49-57.
Skynner, A. C. R. (1962) Comment on Implications of Recent Work in Conjoint Family Therapy for Group Analytic Theory, 'Group Analysis', 5.
Skynner, A. C. R. (1969) A Group-analytic Approach to Conjoint Family Therapy, 'Journal of Child Psychology and Psychiatry', 10, 81-106, chapter 4 above.

Skynner, A. C. R. (1974) Boundaries, 'Social Work Today', 5(10), 290-4.
Skynner, A. C. R. (1976) 'One Flesh: Separate Persons. Principles of Family and Marital Psychotherapy', London: Constable, pp. 225, 228 and 238.
Smoyak, S. (ed.) (1975) 'Psychiatric Nurse as a Family Therapist', New York: Wiley.
Solow, R. and Cooper, B. (1975) Co-therapists as Advocates in Family Therapy with Crisis-provoking Adolescents, in 'The Adolescent in Group and Family Therapy' (ed. M. Sugar), New York: Brunner/Mazel, pp. 248-61.
Stabenau, J. R., Tupin, J., Werner, M. and Pollin, W. (1965) A Comparative Study of Families of Schizophrenics, Delinquents and Normals, 'Psychiatry', 28, 45-59.
Stierlin, H. (1975) Countertransference in Family Therapy with Adolescents, in 'The Adolescent in Group and Family Therapy' (ed. M. Sugar), New York: Brunner/Mazel, pp. 161-77.
Walrond-Skinner, S. (1976) 'Family Therapy. The Treatment of Natural Systems ', London: Routledge & Kegan Paul (especially chapter 7: Action Techniques).
Watzlawick, P., Beavin, J. H. and Jackson, D. D. (1967) 'Pragmatics of Human Communications', London: Faber & Faber.
Whitaker, C. (1975) The Symptomatic Adolescent - an A.W.O.L. family member, in 'The Adolescent in Group and Family Therapy' (ed. M. Sugar), New York: Brunner/Mazel, pp. 205-15.
Williams, F. (1975) Family Therapy: its Role in Adolescent Psychiatry, in 'The Adolescent in Group and Family Therapy', (ed. M. Sugar), New York: Brunner/Mazel, pp. 178-93.
Winnicott, D. W. (1969) Adolescent Process and the Need for Personal Confrontation, 'Paediatrics', 44(5.1), 752-6. Reprinted in Winnicott, D. W. (1971) 'Playing and Reality', London: Tavistock Publications, ch. 11, pp. 143-50.
Wynne, L. C. (1965) Some Indications and Contra-indications for Exploratory Family Therapy, in 'Intensive Family Therapy: Theoretical and Practical Aspects' (eds I. Boszormenyi-Nagy and J. L. Framo), New York: Harper and Row.
Wynne, L. C., Ryckoff, L. M., Day, J. and Hirsch, S. I. (1958) Pseudo-mutuality in the Family Relations of Schizophrenics, 'Pschiatry', 21, 205-23.
Zinner, J. and Shapiro, R. (1972) Projective Identification as a Mode of Perception and Behaviour in Families of Adolescents, 'International Journal of Psycho-Analysis', 53, 523-30.
Zinner, J. and Shapiro, R. (1974) The Family Group as a Single Psychic Entity: Implications for Acting Out in Adolescence, 'International Review of Psycho-Analysis', 1, 179-85.

APPENDIX   Examples of sessions in which an attempt is made to integrate various approaches

The setting
Every detail of the way staff conduct themselves defines the form of the boundary between the Adolescent Unit at Hill End Hospital and the family. The family's boundary control is further influenced by the Unit working on their 'executive subsystem' by insisting that those in authority (the parents) should make the admission decision (Byng-Hall and Bruggen, 1974) and review this decision in face-to-face meetings. (It may also induce a 'large change' (Haley, 1975a) in the marital subsystem, by insisting that the decision to admit should be explicitly agreed by both parents, if they share authority, in front of the adolescent.) The adolescent's need for explicitness and the right to have a say, as well as the parents' responsibilities, backed by legal rights and duties, are both recognized.

While a statement about offering a break to the family in crisis suggests a systems approach, the simultaneous presentation of an opportunity to explore and re-examine their feelings, perceptions and interactions, acknowledged or not, is an explicit engagement in psychoanalytic work. Whether change precedes insight or insight precedes change is not an issue; both are welcomed.

Insight is seen as having two aspects:
(a)   into what is called 'the unconscious' - the unacknowledged and relatively inaccessible ways in which we perceive the world as if it were the one we inhabited as infants or children, and
(b)   into the ways in which behaviour so resulting is reinforced, engendered or sustained by those with whom we interact.

Increase of insight in either sense makes the individual more able to exercise choice. The essential assumption is that to exercise this choice is always possible, however great the pathology.

The psychoanalytic work finds its place in interpreting with the family the memories and infantile or old conflicts which make it so difficult for the family to adjust to or accept change. Just as there are rearoused, in the 'inner world' of the adolescent, anxieties associated with separation and parental relationships, so too are stimulated in the adult members earlier anxieties to do with giving birth, sexuality and autonomy.

The physical setting is also important. It is intended that meetings start on time, at a fixed time and for a set time; in privacy, with no telephone, no interruptions and with windows that will not be stared into from outside. Chairs are comfortable, similar, in a circle and with no table in between. (One therapist may position himself in the circle so that if anybody wishes to leave precipitately the therapist has to be moved first.) There is a carpet on the floor to generate a feeling of warmth and to make action techniques more acceptable. The therapists do not smoke or take notes, nor do they make asides that cannot be heard by all members of the meeting.

Case 1

To admit this 14-year-old boy, his parents had to say why in his
presence. They had not seen him for eighteen months because of
their anxiety about his violence when they did. Those looking
after him had stopped even talking about his mother and father
after he had attacked them whenever they were mentioned.

During the admission meeting, while he was being restrained from
attacking his parents with any movable object in the room, he
smashed a nurse's spectacles and tugged out some of a doctor's
hair. He was given an injection of chlorpromazine, because the staff
were anxious about further things like that happening, and the
meeting continued.

In the next family meeting, after discussion with his parents,
the therapists from the Unit, the community social worker and
his parents all held him with close body contact, while he tried
to bite, and hurled abuse continually. His mother did get bitten
deeply in the shoulder. He was held for over one and a quarter
hours in this way. When he shouted 'I hate you!' at his mother, he
was encouraged, repeatedly, to 'Say it again'. What he said changed
from abuse to the expression of some of the more primitive anxieties
underlying it. He shouted, 'You want to eat me.' But, more fundamentally, the quality of body contact changed from that of fear and
hate on both sides to that of more warmth and acceptance.

An interpretation was put to the whole family. Perhaps their
anxiety about meeting together was not just because of fear of
violence. Perhaps it also represented the fear, in each one of them,
of re-experiencing some of the strong feelings of their very early
childhood.

At the end of the one and a quarter hours the boy asked to sit
on a chair and said he would behave 'like a 14-year-old'. This
he did for the last fifteen minutes of the meeting, during which he
turned to his father, saying, '*You*'re not so bad after all.'
Immediately after this meeting he went into a group with the other
adolescents and talked in a new way about his parents.

Case 2

Anna was in tears, and her mother was telling her to be more
reasonable. It was suggested that Anna was crying for both of
them and that Mrs Smith's own 'reasonableness' covered many tears
for her bereavement. No discernible change followed this interpretation: the tears and bickering continued.

To move from this impasse, Anna was invited to sculpt the home
situation as she saw it, using the people in the room. She placed
her mother on a chair, in a corner, with her hands in position for
mending clothes. She chose one of the therapists to take the role
of herself, at the other end of the room, sitting at the table, with
her hands still in position for writing homework. Another therapist
was chosen for the role of her father, now dead, sitting beside
her and looking at her homework. Anna was then asked to take 'her
own place' and the people involved asked what they were feeling.
Mrs Smith felt lonely; Anna felt nothing (but had stopped crying

and had been working on the sculpt in a business-like way), and the staff member playing the role of her father felt cold.

Anna was invited to rearrange the sculpt 'as you would like it to be'. She placed all three of them standing in a circle: she and her mother were looking at 'father' and he was looking at Anna. Again they were asked what they were feeling. Mrs Smith felt better. Anna felt good, and the staff member (who had tears in his eyes) said he was feeling sad that he had to leave them. Mrs Smith then cried, saying that she had loved her husband and missed him too. Then she moved towards her daughter. Anna shouted to her mother to keep her hands off and became as cold as her mother had been at the beginning of the session. Mrs Smith stopped crying, sat on the floor and said, 'I do feel, you know.' A therapist commented that she spoke with no conviction and, as in bioenergetic assertive techniques, she was encouraged to shout more and more loudly and to open her hands. A therapist, with hand on her back, shouted with her.

While Mrs Smith worked at this, Anna giggled and ridiculed her. The therapist who had been in the role of her father felt very angry with Anna (and afterwards shared with his colleagues that he felt like ordering her out of the room), went over to her and asked her if she would please support her mother as her mother had supported her in the sculpt. Anna leaned forward and looked up at him, her eyes full of tears. The therapist held her in his arms as she sobbed quietly for most of the remaining half hour of the session.

Mrs Smith went on to say that after her own father died she had been sent to an Approved School, a fact that she had kept secret from Anna. She added that Anna and her mother, whom she had hated, had the same look in their eyes.

Two connected interpretations were made by one of the therapists. 'When you, Mrs Smith, are hating Anna, I think you are partly still feeling hatred towards your mother, whom you see in Anna.' 'And you, Anna, when your mother is behaving as if she were hating you, now know that she is probably putting on to you feelings that are "meant" for her own mother. So you might not need to retaliate.'

Comment
These two examples are given, not as evidence of the value of family therapy (in fact, the adolescent in one case made a markedly improved adjustment to boarding school, and in the other case was expelled within two weeks), but simply to demonstrate how techniques may be combined.

The first case illustrates how bringing the parents and the boy together brought the feared violent behaviour into the family. Sharing, with the parents, the task of holding and restraining the boy and, at the same time, encouraging him to repeat what he was shouting, were followed by two changes. Warm feelings were experienced by those holding him and he expressed fears which had not been noticed beneath the violence. The interpretation about fear of experiencing other strong feelings, not to do with violence, could then appear more meaningful.

In the second case, sculpting brought mother and daughter working together, at least for a time. When the mother went on to show her feelings and the daughter was supported so that they could continue to work together, then the mother was able to share a secret. This in its turn suggested two interpretations which were made in a climate changed, by the preceding work, from the unresponsive one of the start of the session.

9 FAMILY ADMISSION DECISIONS AS A THERAPEUTIC TOOL

John Byng-Hall and
Peter Bruggen

INTRODUCTION

Some potential dangers behind incorrect admission decisions
Despite the well-known dangers of separating children from their
parents, of institutionalism, and of pathological identity formation,
the need for more psychiatric beds for adolescents continues to be
pressed in England. Little is known about the results of the failure
to admit these adolescents who, it is said, should be in hospital.
Do they end up in penal institutions, leave home for some undesirable sub-culture, or are they more likely to kill themselves? How
are these, and related questions to be answered?

*Measuring the effect of 'treatment' on 'illness' is unlikely to
provide data for admission decisions*
A major part of medical practice is the monitoring of the effect of
a specific treatment on a particular diagnosed illness. The major
variable is the treatment process itself, and the efficacy of different treatments can be compared. When a patient is referred for
admission, the decision involves a choice between treatment as an
in-patient and treatment as an out-patient. In pediatric practice,
where treatment procedures may be specific, home care services
have been offered as an alternative to hospitalization (1). The
physician's admission decision can then rest on his management
role as the person who can provide and supervise various settings
for his specific treatments. This leaves the choice between home
or hospital to him. Research and clinical experience can be expected
to sharpen the pediatrician's capacity to match the admission
decision to the best outcome.

In psychiatric practice, however, the situation is much more
complex. Illness concepts are imprecise and their validity is often
unproven; therapeutic processes are varied and diverse. The
multiple effects of separating a person from his family are added
to the altered treatment setting. No single variable remains.

*Offering family crisis therapy instead of trying to decide which
cases to admit*
A search of the literature shows that little has, in fact, been
written of the reasons behind changing patients' status from out-

154

patient to in-patient (4). Brandon (3) suggests that there should
be a critical evaluation of the use of hospital admission in psychiatry,
and Langsley (8) has demonstrated the arbitrary quality of psychiatrists' admission decisions. In a group of 150 randomly selected
patients whom the duty psychiatrist had decided to admit, Langsley
reversed that decision and offered out-patient, family crisis therapy
instead. Langsley's decision was based only on his capacity to
offer family therapy. The patients had to continue to live in their
own families; diagnosis and severity were not taken into account.
Langsley compared this group with a control group of 150 patients
who were routinely admitted to the high-quality hospital involved.
At a six-month follow-up, he found that there was no discernible
difference between the groups in social functioning, although the
family therapy treatment had cost only one-sixth as much as the
hospital treatment. The experimental group spent less time away
from their normal roles, and they were statistically significantly
less likely to be admitted to a mental hospital at all than were the
control goup likely to be readmitted. Their findings suggest that
if a psychiatrist's skills are devoted to deciding whom to admit to
hospital, the pay-off is likely to be low, but if his skills are
directed into management and especially into providing family
crisis therapy, then the pay-off may be high.

Langsley did not suggest, however, that, for those living in
families, hospital should be ruled out completely. Some of his
family therapy group did require admission later.

Could a referral for admission be made into a more constructive
event than that provided by a blanket decision not to admit, but
to offer family therapy instead? Before proceeding to this question,
the processes of decision-making require further scrutiny.

DECISIONS

Framework required for effective decision-making
1.   The choice issues. Clear alternatives must be available if there
is to be a real choice. Some of the consequences of making each
potential choice need to be known in order to weigh the alternatives.
2.   A stable decision-making structure. It must be clear who carries
the authority for a decision and that the person or persons will
have sufficient support in carrying out that decision and in any
future revision of the decision. If someone else can at any moment
change the decision, then power lies with the potential reviser
and not with the original decision-maker. The endowment of
authority and the mechanism for changing or maintaining the site of
authority all have implications for any decision, especially if it is an
unpopular one.

Consequences of decision-taking: form as important as direction
In the process of taking a decision, the direction of the choice
taken will have certain consequences, but the decision-making
structure itself may be molded or altered. By redefining who makes
the decision and how it is taken, a change in form may be produced

that will have a continuing influence on the effectiveness and direction of future decisions. In the situation of crisis, which is usually present at the point of admission, there is a potential for new solutions, adaptive or maladaptive, to be developed (Caplan, (6)).

By taking over authority from parents, the psychiatrist may consolidate family pathology
Ferreira (7) showed that families with disturbed members have an impaired capacity to make decisions. When a younger adolescent is referred for admission, the parents often no longer know what is happening, nor what to do. A high degree of ambivalence may be manifest in the request for admission; to some degree both family and child may wish to be rid of each other.

Traditionally, admission decisions are made by psychiatrists, while the parents' role is limited to accepting or rejecting the psychiatrist's 'advice.' Acceptance of decision to admit can ease the referrer's anxiety, as well as rapidly reduce a number of family tensions by:
(a)   Meeting the need for separation;
(b)   Reducing the anxiety about hostility ('You only have to leave home because we want the best treatment for you,' implying that it is an act only of love and is without rejection);
(c)   Removing the pain of decision-taking within the family;
(d)   Shifting responsibility from the parents and sharing it between the psychiatrist, who makes the decision, and the adolescent, who is clearly labeled as the problem.

Although other, new, tensions may arise as a result of admission, it is easy to see that in the future, if the family faces another intolerable crisis situation, they will be likely to seek the same solution. The higher re-admission rate of Langsley's (8) control group may support this hypothesis. Because admission is primarily a psychiatrist's decision, the impact on the family's social system is to shift the assumed site of potential solutions from the area of the family living arrangements to some mysterious knowledge and skill held by the psychiatrist to be practiced on the identified patient. Thus the group that needs to tackle the problem, that is the family, hands over authority to the psychiatrist, giving him most of the status and power (although as all psychiatrists know to their chagrin, the adolescent may rapidly deflate this image).

A central problem, as we have seen, often lies in the breakdown of parental (especially paternal) authority. The psychiatrist, in taking over the role of decision-maker, even if it is a decision not to admit, may further undermine the family's authority structure and thus consolidate the pathology.

Therapy aimed at returning authority to a more appropriate site
The need for psychiatric patients to take back responsibility for their actions and decisions is well recognised. A major tenet of theory in out-patient psychotherapy is the importance of the

patient becoming free to make his own decisions. In some in-patient therapeutic communities, the major responsibility for admission and discharge decisions is given to the patient group (10).

Obviously however, when disturbed younger adolescents do not control themselves but push their families hither and thither, firmer parental control is appropriate in providing the framework within which a measure of internal control can be learned or re-gained. To give an adolescent overt or covert deciding rights over admission in these circumstances would be a collusion with family pathology. Therapy should aim at returning viable authority to the family unit – that is to the parents within the family group.

Admission criterion of 'family failure to cope' allows parents to decide about admission
In the face of the lack of adequate specific diagnostic criteria for the admission of younger adolescents, the multi-disciplinary psychiatric team at Hill End Adolescent Unit* considers that the relevant 'diagnosis' indicating in-patient rather than out-patient treatment is that of the family being unable to manage with the adolescent at home. That is, separation at that time is felt to be inevitable. As the only people who can decide whether they can cope or not are the family members, they are the only ones who can appropriately make the decision. The unit aims to provide the setting of a family group in which parents can make a real and effective decision – either to continue to cope with the adolescent at home or to ask the unit to cope on their behalf until they can manage again. This offers the opportunity for authority to be re-established where it really counts – within the family. In a number of cases, re-establishing a functioning family system before admission in fact avoids hospitalization. In one year in only 50 per cent of families seen was an adolescent admitted, despite admission being presented as a possibility to all referrers (5).

Other implications of the psychiatrist relinquishing authority over admission decisions
Traditionally, it is the psychiatrist's role to define the boundary between in-patient and out-patient. If he does not admit enough patients, then the beds are empty and the hospital team is out of work. And empty beds make it difficult to resist tiresome patients. On the other hand, if he admits too many or too disturbed patients, then his staff will not be able to cope. His professional group is likely to put pressure on him if he goes to either of these extremes.

If the psychiatrist hands over the admission decisions to parents, the unit will still be able to take only as many as it can cope with. The psychiatrist can adopt a policy of offering parents the admis-sion only if there are always vacancies. Putting clients on a waiting list when parents are saying that they cannot cope at that moment is not offering parents the opportunity to decide. Instead, it is the unit's limits and not the family's that are determining the admis-sion decision.

Given that there are always vacancies, a psychiatrist who allows parents authority over admissions decisions may run the risk of having empty beds and idle staff - and having to justify this to the authority that finances the unit. This can be extremely difficult.

A psychiatrist's authority comes partly from his role within the organization but is maintained by his clinical knowledge and skill. He must be prepared to justify his view that giving admission decisions to parents is, in his opinion, more profitable than spending time devising assessment procedures himself. Families and professionals must be told about the policy. A great deal of personal authority has to be maintained to withstand the pressures from all concerned, who may expect, and be more comfortable with, a psychiatrist who takes decisions and keeps beds full.

Family authority structure
There is considerable confusion about the terms used, and the many factors involved in, the concept of family power structure, as Stafilios-Rothschild (12) pointed out in her review of research in this area. Yet it is essential for therapists to be aware of all the facets of family power struggles if they are to help families resolve pathological patterns of authority. There is no suitable alternative to the therapist gaining clinical experience of families trying to decide and of the pressures exerted upon him and upon each other in the process.

UNIT ADMISSION PROCEDURE

Understanding the reason for admission
The unit staff decided early in its history that admission should be only for an understandable and understood reason. This reduces the potential for the adolescent to create fantasies about his own madness as the reason for admission. It also puts the onus on staff to make sure that the first criterion of any effective decision-making is met, i.e. that those involved should know something of the issues inherent in admission choice.

The unit also makes a major point of clarifying who has legal responsibility for admission. (Just tracing this out with the family and observing discrepancies, e.g. that the adolescent actually controls the situation although his parents have the legal power, can provide the therapeutic framework in which the broken-down family authority can be restructured.) The staff's family therapy skills can then be focused on removing blocks to the proper functioning of family authority.

After a decision to admit or not, the unit supports the parents in their decision either by (a) keeping the admitted patient until the parents decide to discharge, or (b) in the case of a decision not to admit, by offering a bed for the future, should the parents change their decision. This often has the effect of supporting the family's coping mechanisms and helps to secure the second element of effective decision-making, namely a stable decision-making structure.

Families do not, however, exist in isolation, and if the family

decision is to be supported, then all those people already involved
with the family must be brought into the picture. Work starts with
the referring agent, and the importance of the long-term professional worker is repeatedly emphasized during the family's contact.

Work with referral agencies
Nearly all referrals come from professionals, mostly social workers
or psychiatrists. The referral indicates that the professionals feel
that what they can offer is in some way inadequate compared with
the specialized treatment that may be available in hospital. The
identified patient may, or may not, be on the verge of having to
leave home - which is the point at which the unit considers admission. It is important that only those cases where admission seems
likely are seen. This is not only to save professional time, but also
to avoid introducing a 'mental patient set' into the problem-solving
structure of families, thus rendering a suitable family solution less
likely.

The situation is discussed over the telephone with the referrer.
The unit's admission policy is described, and it usually becomes
clear whether admission is a current issue. If not, the referrer
is told that a bed will be available if coping breaks down some time
in the future. (Some referrers have reported that this sort of
support helps them to feel they can go on managing their patient
at home.)

An offer to meet the referrer is made if he or she wants to discuss
the management of the case, or if admission seems a likelihood. This
meeting is held as soon as possible and with all the important professional people involved in caring for the family. A satisfactory plan
for managing the adolescent within the community may emerge from
these meetings. But in those cases in which admission remains
likely, the referring professional will be invited to take part in the
family meetings before, and during, admission, as well as to continue the care after discharge. The unit aims at supporting referring professionals through the management of a crisis and specifically
avoids taking over from them.

Work with families

First meeting In order to avoid implying that admission is a fore-
gone conclusion, the first meeting with the family takes place outside the unit, usually in the referrer's office. It is offered within
a few days of referral. The unit team, consisting of psychiatrist,
psychiatric nurse, and social worker, tells the family that a bed
is available and describes the facilities of the unit. The team also
ensures that the family have details of community support so that
they know what to expect if they choose not to ask for admission.

It is emphasized that younger adolescents are admitted only if
they cannot be treated while remaining at home and that admission
is a serious step. The site of responsibility for decision-making
is made clear: it is in the parents, and both parents have to be
present and in agreement, that is if they still share legal custody.

Staff openly discuss anxieties about admission and the uncertainty behind the treatment situation. The unit provides a bed and a roof, but, as far as treatment is concerned, can be sure only of providing the setting for it. Whether family members can make use of the therapeutic possibilities in the family meetings, group meetings, and other interactions, is not certain. This must depend partly on the family's wish to make it work and partly on the level of professional skills that have been acquired by the staff.

The family are asked why they are considering hospitalizing the adolescent. Symptomatology, if presented, is dealt with in terms of how it affects the family, rather than for its diagnostic significance. During the discussion, which should include both the situation of the family and the resources of the community, family members may start using phrases like 'cannot go on like this any longer,' 'my wife must have a rest,' 'we need a break.' Such phrases are accepted as understandable and acceptable reasons for considering admission, but the family is offered a second meeting, during which they will see the unit, before making the final decision.

On the other hand, if the family decides they can cope, they are told that the unit's offer of admission still stands, if in the future the situation changes.

Second family meeting   This occurs at the unit within a few days of the first meeting. During this intervening time, the difficulties may have remained or increased, or the family will have had an opportunity to move toward a coping situation.

At the unit the family are shown round. They are then left alone for further discussion before being joined by the unit team for the second family meeting. Some time may be spent on further clarifying issues of admission choice, but early in the meeting the parents will be asked if they are managing better. If they have not moved toward a coping situation, they are asked if they are going to decide on admission on the basis of the particular reason that emerged at the first meeting. The authority structure within the family, which will probably have revealed itself in the first meeting, frequently becomes even more sharply delineated as a focus for the psychotherapeutic interventions of the staff.

One particular family situation is worth mentioning here. This is when the overt decision-making rests with one member of the family, e.g., father, who does all the talking and says that he has made a decision, whereas the influential person is someone else, perhaps mother, or the adolescent. The 'puppet' leader may well reveal his secondary role by desperately attempting to pick up cues from the staff about which way they want him to decide. Mother or adolescent may be quite content to leave father in this position, hiding their own views and feelings. Skill is required in getting the whole family to discuss each other's attitudes. If the unit staff feels that the decision is unsupported, they say so. They say they feel uncertain and may wonder if, in that case, the adolescent is also unsure and hence may think of running away from the unit to

test whether his parents really meant that he should be admitted?
The parents are asked what they would do if the adolescent did
arrive home in the next day or two. This question frequently
clarifies the issues of how strongly the parents feel, how much
they support each other, and who is in charge.

Asking the family to make up their minds about whether they
want their boys or girls to leave or stay often opens up the previously denied cross-generational coalitions and incestuous ties.
Once the conflict is made overt, it can be worked upon.

Admission agreements provide criteria for discharge
When the admission agreement is put into words at the end of the
meeting, it states who has decided upon admission, for what reason,
and how it could end or be revised. For example: 'Mr and Mrs Smith
decided to admit Harry because father can't stand it any more and
mother is too worried to allow it to go on any longer. Harry will
stay in hospital until things have changed so that this is no longer
so. The agreement will not be changed except at a similar meeting,
which might be called by any of the present members.'

The agreement provides a problem-solving focus for the therapy,
both in the family review meetings every two to three weeks and in
the work of the unit staff with the adolescent. Because study of
those factors that were creating the need for separation is central
to the work, it can be seen to have the aim of reuniting the family
as soon as possible. It also provides the criterion for discharge.

Review and discharge
At one of the regular family meetings that monitor progress of the
adolescent in the ward, and the family in the community, the
parents must eventually fix a discharge date. The staff may say
what has happened; they also make interpretations. The need for
the family support system to be reconstructed positively and the
danger of institutionalization are both stressed. The after-care
resources of the referrer, or other community agencies, and the
availability of re-admission to the unit are presented before the
family – but it is for the parents to say when they can cope again.

Therapeutic techniques: underlying concepts
As a theoretical and training frame of reference, staff have a
psychoanalytic ethos set within a framework of crisis (6) and
attachment (2) theories. The emphasis on 'coping' produced by
this decision-making focus has led to a systems type of family
therapy that has similarities with structural family therapy as
described by Minuchin (9). In his parlance, an attempt is made
to restructure the family authority pattern. The parental subsystem is firmly given the executive role, and the therapists then
counter any attempts to use the designated patient to detour
parental conflicts that appear. Interpretations are used also, however, to help disentangle dysfunctional systems. Space, especially
between the adolescent and his family, is used therapeutically,
but the responsibility for handling it is left largely to the family.

Unlike Minuchin's technique, seating arrangements are not usually changed by the staff during family meetings.

The longer the adolescent remains in hospital, the greater becomes the attempt to understand with the family the historical origins and the underlying incestuous or aggressive dynamics involved. The unit attempts to integrate psychodynamic concepts and practice within a systems approach, avoiding a polarization into either viewpoint.

Locating the appropriate site of authority
It is hoped that by defining who can make which decision where, each person's task of 'owning' his or her own part of the dysfunctional system will be easier. The unit uses the handling of its own authority as a model. The theme within the ward often becomes, 'We, the staff, are in charge of how the place is run but will consult you, the patients, about decisions we make. Your parents are in charge of whether you stay or not and have discussed what they found difficult to cope with. You are in charge of your part of the difficulty but can consult us in your attempts to change.'

Previous staff training
A great difficulty this creates within the professional workers is how to deal with the results of previous training. The psychiatrist, trained to advise and to admit patients, may become impatient while parents relearn the art of decision-making. All members of staff, feeling that they are establishing a helpful rapport with patients, may be anxious and distressed by an apparently premature discharge decision made by parents, although they can find reassurance in the unit's re-admission policy.

CASE ILLUSTRATIONS

The contact with one family has already been described in some detail by Raven (11). The following vignettes show how the admission decision may provide a turning point in those cases in which parents are still in charge. The more complex problems in which authority rests with someone other than the natural parents, perhaps a guardian or a social services department, require a separate paper.

Case 1
A 14-year-old boy was referred for admission with the strong suggestion from the referrer that his thought disorder and bizarre behavior was schizophrenic. The parents, in the first meeting, wanted a diagnosis and advice. Neither was forthcoming from the unit staff, but a second meeting was arranged at the unit.

The situation was unchanged at the second meeting. The boy, an only child, had been up all night concocting worrying chemistry experiments, and talked nonsense all day. His parents seemed to be at the end of their tether yet could themselves make no decision.

After forty minutes of a difficult meeting in which great pressure
was put on the unit staff to advise, the father said, apparently
in desperation, that he would go back to their general practitioner,
who had known them a long time, and ask him for advice. It was
put to the family that the parents seemed prepared to do anything
rather than make a decision themselves.

Thereupon father decided upon admission, mother supported him,
and, within six weeks, after a short trial period at home, the boy
was discharged by his parents and was back at school.

Case 2
A 15-year-old girl had her first psychotic breakdown over a period
of three days and was referred by her general practitioner and
consultant psychiatrist for admission.

When confronted with the need for them to make the decision in
the first family meeting, the parents reviewed the events of the
past few days with their daughter and son. The son pointed out
some inconsistencies in the parents' behavior, and the unit psychiatrist interpreted their sad feelings about the children growing
up. The unit social worker interpreted the girl's anxiety, attributing it to the fear that she might yet be tricked and admitted to
hospital on the authority of the doctors and against her parents'
will. The girl then spoke, which reassured everyone. The parents
could cope and decided to continue to work with the general
practitioner, who had been present throughout the meeting, and
arranged an appointment with him.

Case 3
A 13-year-old, promiscuous, drug-taking girl had been suspended
from a 'special' school where she had been receiving psychiatric
treatment. The psychiatrist at the school asked the unit to admit
the girl for treatment until she was well enough to return. The
unit team member suggested that the unit would not feel competent
to say when a particular child was well enough to return to a
particular school; that must be the executive decision of the headmaster. But after a meeting with the referring professionals, the
family was seen.

The unit staff head had learned that the father had deserted his
wife when the girl was a baby and so agreed to see only the girl
and her mother together with the social worker from the local
authority to whom the mother had gone for help. It was understood
that the mother had custody of the child. In the family meeting,
however, enquiry disclosed an unusual feature of the separation.
The mother had not obtained legal, sole parental rights – these
remained, theoretically, shared between both parents. The unit's
criteria for decision-making were not fulfilled and so, although
the mother insisted that she could not cope, admission was refused.
It was pointed out that if the girl were admitted on the mother's
authority, father, although he had not been on the scene for
twelve and a-half years, could turn up at the unit and legally discharge the girl. He could not be considered bound by the admission

agreement to abide by the arrangements pending another meeting.
That this must also be a disturbing uncertainty for the girl was
confirmed by the social worker, remembering that in an earlier
psychologist's report emphasis had been placed on the girl's
search for her father.

The mother took her daughter away and agreed to explore the
legal procedures for obtaining sole parental rights.

The mother and daughter did not meet the unit staff again,
but we were told by the social worker that a few days later the
mother had confided in her that, in fact, there had been no husband. She had not been married and so had all along had full
parental rights. The social worker helped her client to share her
secret with her daughter. A family taboo was broken, and they
were able to cope again.

Case 4

An acutely phobic, 15-year-old girl was admitted to the unit after
a second meeting in which her method of wresting authority and
decision-making from her parents had been demonstrated, interpreted, and controlled.

She sat between her parents but close to her father, whom she
eyed, smiled at, and gently touched. Later, when the father was
thinking aloud about her admission, she turned to her mother,
whispered, cried, and then tried to clamber on top of her. Her
father tried to pull her back, whereupon she fell to the floor and
vomited, immediately promising to return to school and to behave
at home if they would only take her away. Her father was certain,
but her mother hesitated, so the girl knelt on the floor in front
of her. Her father told her to sit down and her mother repeated
the order. She obeyed.

A demonstration had been made by the girl, an interpretation
given by a nurse, and control supplied by the father and mother.

She was admitted to the unit to give them a break, during which
the parents were able to resume their life together. When they felt
ready to have her home, she was seen to be a less fragile person
and hence less capable of controlling through 'illness.'

Case 5

In an admission meeting at the unit, John, who was 14, was to stay
because his parents would not tolerate his behavior. Throughout
the meeting his father did most of the talking while his mother
looked anxiously at her husband and the male members of the staff.
John sat close to his mother, and she smiled at him from time to
time.

At the close of the meeting, in the formal summary of the admission agreement, the words 'and none of us will change this agreement except at another meeting' were noticed to coincide with
John's eyes meeting his mother's. 'Hey,' interrupted the member of
staff who had observed this. 'What does you two looking at each
other like that mean? What will you do mother, if John rings you
up and says he is being bullied or runs home and cries and says

"don't send me back"?' John's mother immediately admitted that she would try to keep him at home. An entirely new area of parental interaction was exposed by the mother's apparent acquiescence but simultaneous, silent sabotage of her husband's authority. Delay of the admission and a further meeting at a later date were suggested, unless the mother was able to give a firm and convincing assurance that she would support her husband. She did.

DISCUSSION

We cannot escape from the problem of evaluation, yet the many factors involved make the tasks seem overwhelmingly complicated. Some of the advantages and disadvantages of this way of working were discussed in a paper by Bruggen et al. (5). Short term advantages included (a) a relatively short admission (average three-and-a-half months) and (b) only 25 per cent of referrals led to admission. These two factors led to vacancies being present most of the time, despite a catchment area population of four-and-a-half million with only fifteen available beds. In this setting family decisions themselves, it may be argued, contributed to the empty beds, completing a complementary cycle of factors.

The clinical impression is that families frequently used the opportunity fruitfully for setting out in new directions and that the institution avoided much of its potential for labeling and consolidating symptoms. At least the unit's impression can be checked against the user's impression. Referrers wanting a cure for their patients find not only that their own assessment does not clinch admission, but also that they are caught up in a lot of work throughout the patient's contact with the unit that can involve uncomfortable confrontations in an unfamiliar clinical mode. How many found this opportunity exciting and creative? How many withdrew and avoided using the unit in the future (another factor in low bed usage?)? How many adolescents denied lengthy 'treatment' merely found an even less 'desirable' solution, such as drugs or criminal subculture, or deteriorated eventually to become chronic inmates of mental hospitals? A follow-up study to explore some of these issues is under way.

Eventually, a properly controlled study should be conducted with three randomly selected groups. The first two would represent Langsley's groups, i.e. (a) routinely admitted on duty psychiatrist's decision, (b) admission refused and crisis family therapy offered, while in the third group (c) the family would make the decision.

One of the authors (J. Byng-Hall) now does some work for a local authority in a residential setting. As many of the children are taken into care because their parents cannot cope, he has found that the family decision model, with modifications, is readily usable. Could it have application in other situations, for example, when the admitted person is adult or elderly?

NOTE

* The unit, consisting of a 24-bed villa with small school and gymnasium attached, is situated in the grounds of a general psychiatric hospital, twenty miles north of London.

REFERENCES

1   A. B. Bergman, H. Shrand and T. E. Oppé, A Pediatric Home-Care Program in London - Ten Years' Experience, 'Pediatrics', 1965, 36: 314-21.
2   J. Bowlby, 'Attachment and Loss, Vol. I: Attachment', London: Hogarth Press, and New York: Basic Books, 1969. 'Attachment and Loss, Vol II: Anxiety and Anger', London: Hogarth Press, and New York: Basic Books, 1973.
3   S. Brandon, Crisis Theory and Possibilities of Therapeutic Intervention, 'Brit. J. Psychiat.', 1970, 117: 627-633.
4   P. Bruggen, The Role of a Hospital-Based Adolescent Unit, in D. V. Sira Sankar (ed.), 'Mental Health in Children, Vol. III', New York: PJD Publications, 1976.
5   P. Bruggen, J. Byng-Hall, and T. Pitt-Aikens, The Reason for Admission as a Focus of Work for an Adolescent Unit, 'Brit. J. Psychiat.,' 1973, 112: 319-29.
6   G. Caplan, 'Principles of Preventive Psychiatry,' London: Tavistock Publications, 1964.
7   A. J. Ferreira, Decision-Making in Normal and Abnormal Two-Child Families 'Fam. Proc.,' 1968, 7: 17.
8   D. G. Langsley and D. M. Kaplan, 'The Treatment of Families in Crisis', New York: Grune & Stratton, 1968.
9   S. Minuchin, 'Families and Family Therapy,' Cambridge, Mass.: Harvard University Press and London: Tavistock, 1974.
10 R. N. Rapoport, 'Community as Doctor,' London: Tavistock, 1960.
11 Faith Raven, Admission and Discharge in an Adolescent Unit: a case study, 'Soc. Work Today,' 1973, 4: 98-103.
12 C. Stafilios-Rothschild, A Study of Family Power Structure: a Review 1960-1969, in C. B. Broderick (ed.), 'A Decade of Family Research and Action', Minneapolis, USA: National Council on Family Relations, 1972.

10 ILLNESS IN THE FAMILY:

a conceptual model

Bryan Lask

INTRODUCTION

In the course of his work the family therapist often meets clients
with physical illness. The temptation to ignore it as belonging to
the individual and his doctor must be avoided. The illness can
play a vital part in family homeostasis, be the cause of much discord, or the end result of family disharmony or stress:
- The parents of a severely subnormal 10-year-old boy coped
magnificently with him in their own home. Family life proceeded
as well as possible, and all the family seemed happy and contented.
The only problem was that the mother had severe vaginal bleeding
for which no cause could be found. . . .
  In considering the psychological aspects of physical illness,
the conceptualisation may be at:
  (a)   an individual level using such models as
        (i)   intrapsychic - the application of psychodynamic
              theory to the relationship between the individual
              and his illness;
        (ii) personality typology - the idea that certain personality
              types suffer specific illnesses, e.g. the rigid, obses-
              sional migraine sufferer;
        (iii) individual life-stress - an accumulation of stressful
              life-events can precipitate physical illness (the linear
              causal chain).
  (b)   a dyadic level focusing on such considerations as
        (i)   mother-child interaction, e.g. the mother's anxiety
              or over-protectiveness may aggravate or maintain
              the illness;
        (ii) object-loss phenomena, i.e. the loss of a good object
              which may be a loved one or perhaps health;
        (iii) husband-wife interaction, e.g. in a poor marriage the
              wife may find she can only gain her husband's atten-
              tion by being ill.
  (c)   a family level
  Grolnick (1972) has related the above models to psychosomatic
disorders, but they are equally applicable to any form of illness.
The complex interplay between an individual's illness and his
family was stressed over thirty years ago (Richardson, 1949) at

167

a time when illness was first being recognised as playing an important part in family equilibrium. General practitioners (e.g. Lask, 1966; Hopkins, 1959), and paediatricians (Apley, 1963; Weller, 1975; Miller et al., 1960) have reminded us of this, but as Weakland (1977) has pointed out, there needs to be a far wider application of the family interaction viewpoint to illness and disease. I intend to expand this theme and elaborate upon the application of the family model to any physical illness.

DEFINITIONS

At this point, I wish to clarify what I mean by certain general terms.

The word 'psychosomatic' is commonly used but with many different meanings. A useful definition is that – 'a psychosomatic disease is one in which psychological factors are of considerable importance in causing, aggravating or maintaining the physical symptoms.' Minuchin et al. (1975) distinguished between primary and secondary psychosomatic symptomatology. In the primary type, a physiological disorder is already present, e.g. in asthma the patient is born with a labile bronchus which all too readily goes into spasm producing the characteristic wheeze; the psychological component is the aggravation or maintenance of the illness due to emotional arousal. In the secondary type of psychosomatic disorder there is no preceding physical problem, but there is transformation of emotional conflict into physical symptoms as, for example, in anorexia nervosa or tension headaches. Whilst this may be an important distinction, I agree with Lipowski (1975) that 'the concept of psychosomatic disorders represents a misleading and redundant diagnostic grouping.' It is, I would suggest, more fruitful to discard the concept of 'psychosomatic disorder', and instead take a 'psychosomatic approach' to all patients whatever their disease. In this way the intimate interplay between psychological, social and biological factors is given due consideration in every patient whatever the disorder.

Open-systems family model
This term refers simply to the broader concept that causation is viewed as a circular process. It may be applied to many concepts besides family psychopathology. A very clear description of general systems theory as applicable to families is provided by Walrond-Skinner (1976). Where there is illness in a family, the open-systems model recognises an interplay between the 'sick' family member, his illness, and the patterns of involvement and interaction within his family (see below). It also acknowledges the significance of the doctor, the employer or teacher, and peers (Balint, 1977; Lask, 1966).

WHY DO WE NEED A FAMILY MODEL TO UNDERSTAND ILLNESS?

In attempting to unravel the complex interaction patterns of a family with a sick member, it seems essential to have a theoretical framework upon which to structure the necessary formulation. What can be offered by the individually based models to help us in this respect?

The learning theorist's model of seeing all behaviour, including 'illness behaviour' (Cautella, 1977) as learned, seems naive and simplistic. The psychodynamic approach leans too heavily on intra-psychic phenomena, which may be acceptable when studying an individual, but seems inadequate when investigating the rich network of interaction around an illness and the involved persons. The personal construct approach similarly needs considerable expansion to account for family equilibrium, whilst the linear causal chain view pays no heed to complex and subtle feedback processes. Even mathematicians have entered the arena with catastrophe-theory which attempts to explain anorexia nervosa in a geometrical manner (Zeeman, 1977).

The family model broadens the focus from the sick individual to the role of that individual and his illness within the family system, the effect the family has on the illness, and the significance of extra-familial elements. Within such a framework, various theoretical viewpoints may be integrated (Walrond-Skinner, 1976) and different therapeutic modalities employed.

APPLICATION

Several components need to be considered when formulating the problem as part of an open-system:
1 Physiological status
2 The sick individual
3 Extra-familial factors
4 The family unit

1 *Physiological status*
In considering the sick individual's physiological state, we can recognise three different categories of illness: (a) organic; (b) 'psychosomatic'; and (c) psychiatric.

(a) The ill family member may be suffering from a clear-cut organic condition such as malignancy or a congenital disease (which even the most enthusiastic supporters of psychogenic causation would be pressed to explain in psychogenic terms). (b) The illness may be one in which psychological factors do seem to have an important role in causation or maintenance although the manifestation of illness is physical. Examples include asthma, diabetes, peptic ulcer, anorexia nervosa and hypertension (high blood pressure). (c) Finally, the illness may be a so-called 'psychiatric' illness such as depression, or schizophrenia, in both of

which the neurochemical and neurophysiological processes remain
unclear, but the most overt change is in the individual's mental
rather than physical state.

Many would argue that such a distinction is anachronistic. None
the less it is made, and has various ramifications. In the organic
category the idea that psychological factors are at all relevant
may be treated with scepticism, and treatment is often exclusively
physical. 'Psychosomatic' illnessses seem to arouse the most con-
troversy with proponents of either physical or psychological
causation taking up extreme positions. 'Psychiatric illness' also
causes disagreement with some arguing for an environmental and
others a biochemical cause. Treatment is often confined to either
chemical or psychological methods.

In fact, stress can trigger either physical or emotional symptoms
as is shown in Figure 10.1, which demonstrates that the whole
debate about category of illness can be seen to be irrelevant. Due
attention needs to be paid to all aspects of the individual, obviously
including the physiological state.

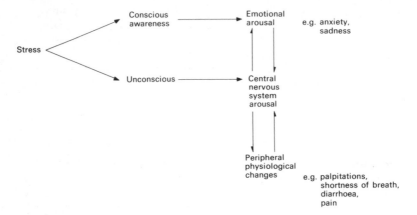

FIGURE 10.1 Physiological pathways of stress (modified from
M. Lader)

2 *The sick person as an individual*
Various aspects of the individual's psychological make-up need
consideration.

(a) Personality. Although there is very little evidence to show
that specific personality types suffer particular illnesses, given
that an illness or predisposition to illness exists, then the personality type may contribute to the problem. Thus, the business
executive with a peptic ulcer who continues to drive himself because of his competitiveness and forcefulness may aggravate his
symptoms. The timid and sensitive child with eczema unable to
tolerate teasing at school may resort to more scratching and thus
an exacerbation to avoid the school problem.

A 30-year-old professional woman divorced her psychiatrist

husband two years after he developed an unresolved 'identity-crisis'. She chose as her second husband a man who was completely the opposite in behaviour to her first, being ambitious and very keen to please. The reconstituted family consisted of mother, step-father, Carol, 8, and Simon, 5. Carol displaced her unresolved angry feelings about her father on to her step-father, who, unwilling to be like father, and thus supported by his wife, failed to express any of his own distress at the situation, and within three months had suffered a heart-attack.

(b) Suggestibility. 'Suggestion' is a term which summarises a complex set of psychological phenomena. Suffice to say that it can play an important part in producing and relieving a wide range of physical symptoms. Most research has been done with pain (e.g. Melzack, Wetsz and Sprague, 1963) and asthma (e.g. Godfrey and Silverman, 1973). The widely-recognised effectiveness of placebos (Rachman and Philips, 1978) must be attributed in the main to suggestion. The degree of suggestibility of any individual plays a part in determining the course of his illness and the response to treatment.

Jean, 9, had become psychologically dependent upon a strong steroid ointment to control her eczema. Without it the itching was extremely distressing. When a dummy (harmless) ointment was substituted without Jean being told, there was no deterioration. This was the first step in an ultimately successful rehabilitation.

(c) Attitudes to illness. The sick person can manifest a wide range of attitudes to his illness from the one extreme of over-involvement in which he 'gives in' and finds his life taken over, to the opposite extreme of 'denial' of handicap, with determined efforts to continue regardless. This attitude spectrum is portrayed in Figure 10.2. The ideal is one of optimal realistic accaptance, for neither extreme represents a healthy adjustment and either can lead to greater problems (Lask, 1979).

(Attitude spectrum applicable to the individual or important persons in his life)

FIGURE 10.2 Attitude spectrum

Denial
A white middle-class professional couple had adopted two West Indian children, after failing to have children of their own. When the children were 7 and 5, the wife developed multiple sclerosis. The illness ran a typically fluctuant course with times of normality and other times when she would be confined to a wheel-chair. Neither adult could admit to the severity of the illness, and they

characterised their lives by trying to do as much as possible, and
be as normal as possible. Any suggestion of weakness or vulnerability in any member of the family was suppressed and perfection
was demanded. As the elder child approached adolescence and
started seeking some autonomy, his age-appropriate behaviour was
forbidden and he was increasingly infantilized. Ultimately, he ran
away and committed a variety of offences, necessitating his being
taken into care.

Overacceptance
Frances, 11, started having 'migraine attacks' every week. At the
first indication of a headache she would take to her bed in a
darkened room, and insist on silence in the house. Her family would
creep around on tiptoe for fear of upsetting her, and 'normal'
family life came to a halt. Her parents became increasingly distressed and unable to express their irritation, leading to a build-up
of unresolved tension and exacerbation of Frances's headaches.

   (d) Conflicts. These may be internal and unconscious as defined
in psychoanalytic theory, or internal and conscious as, for
example, in the down-trodden office worker who can not cope with
his boss's demands and whose peptic ulcer then 'plays up' to
resolve the conflict of whether or not to go to work. Conflicts may
also be external to the individual. Children are often caught up
in marital conflict and used as go-betweens or buffers. Lask and
Kirk (1979) have demonstrated how childhood asthma can be aggravated and maintained by marital conflict, and Minuchin et al. (1975)
have stressed the role of the sick child in parental conflict avoidance in a variety of illnesses.

The odd couple
An oddly assorted couple, an American ex-hippie art dealer, aged
45, and his orthodox Jewish wife, 40, had two children Tony, 15,
and Linda, 11. The parents argued constantly about their respective
life-styles, drawing in the children whenever possible. Linda
developed a wide variety of physical symptoms for which no organic
cause could be found, and which only resolved after three marital
therapy sessions in which the parents learned to seclude the children from their conflict.

3 *Extra-familial factors*
Consideration here is given to stressful events arising outside the
family such as examinations, interviews or change of job, and the
attitudes of significant persons such as doctors, teachers or
employers. The attitude-spectrum described earlier is just as
applicable to extra-familial people.

   A 40-year-old librarian, who considered himself a professional
failure became depressed. His employer was unsympathetic and
intolerant, and eventually caused him to be sacked. His wife who
had a rather manic personality was unable to comfort her husband
nor express her own concern. She became increasingly accident-
prone and on two occasions caused fires in the home. The 8-year-

old son, Martin, equally unable to express directly his own anxieties about the apparent disintegration of his parents developed recurrent fevers for which no organic cause could be found. In therapy he told his parents: 'I feel safer not going to school so I can watch Mummy.'

4 *The family unit*
As when working with any other type of family, consideration must be given to how the family functions. Attention is paid to how the family copes with feelings and conflicts, the roles of each member, the boundaries between individuals and generations, the alliances and identifications, and the scapegoating, secrets and myths. Each person can react to an illness in the family in a multitude of ways, which themselves may vary within the same individual from one time to the next. Such reactions are comprehensively reviewed by Pless and Pinkerton (1975) and major features to be observed are the spectrum of attitudes from over-protection with reorganisation of family life-style, to rejection or denial (see Figure 10.2) and the emotional responses such as anger, guilt, despair, fear or resentment.

Over-protective parents
Freddy was a plump, friendly, bright 13-year-old with quite severe eczema and asthma. His father was a large, amiable, tough, illiterate man, who adored his children, and had managed to conceal his illiteracy and run an office-cleaning business. Mother was a warm and grossly overprotective woman with a wide range of neurotic symptoms. She was unable to allow the children any maturity, and still washed Freddy daily to ensure it was done properly, so that his eczema may improve. The family had organised itself around Freddy's asthma with the parents working shifts to ensure someone was always at home in case he became ill. He insisted on the house being very warm to 'help his chest' although this was unnecessary, and the family spent every spare penny to effect this. There seemed no way in which Freddy could escape the enmeshment despite his own insight: 'Does Mum's worrying make me have attacks?' The parents, too, were trapped, mother by her neurosis, and father by his illiteracy and dependency. The whole interacted to reinforce Freddy's asthma. The family's attitude to the medical profession and the medication prescribed may also be of significance.

Gaynor, 11, had such severe asthma that control was only obtained by taking strong steroid tablets. Her parents were unable to discuss their concern regarding the medication with the paediatrician, nor could they hide their concern from Gaynor. She consequently refused to take the tablets, and her asthma spiralled out of control.

The rejecting parent
The opposite end of the spectrum is illustrated in the following case.

Ivan was a 13-year-old with an unpleasant, chronic, inflammatory bowel disease leading to pain and diarrhoea. He was an unhappy and inhibited child suppressing much of his feeling, and using his illness as the only means he had to gain comfort from his tired and depressed mother. She was bitterly resigned to her fate of having married an insensitive and dominating man, who had long since rejected Ivan because of his weakness and lack of masculinity. The whole family (there were four other children) were unhappy and rejecting of Ivan as a way of 'keeping in with father'. Ivan's role of scapegoat and recipient of such hostile rejection aggravated the bowel disorder and perpetuated the vicious cycle.

The illness itself may have a special role in the family. It may serve to evade conflict, be used as a scapegoat for all the family's problems, or be a reason for avoiding sexual contact.

Throughout this paper the case examples illustrate the effect the illness has on the family, and the family on the illness. Where attitudes to illness are of optimal realistic acceptance, and family function is satisfactory, then the illness is not required for homeostasis.

Much has been written about specific family constellations being linked to particular symptoms or illness, and few diseases have escaped the often uncritical research of the more eager student of the family system. This area has been comprehensively reviewed by Meissner (1966) and Grolnick (1972), and it is clear that the research methodology is almost invariably inadequate, and that the reported studies focus not so much on family interaction patterns, as on individuals or dyads. Where the families as a whole are investigated there are rarely any control groups, so we need not be surprised when different writers find opposing family patterns for the same disease. It is insufficient to make claims for a specific family pattern in, for example, ulcerative colitis (Jackson and Yalom 1965) or childhood psychogenic pain (Liebman et al., 1976) without controlling for at least the presence of chronic or recurrent illness, as Jackson and Yalom themselves acknowledge.

The Philadelphia team (Minuchin et al., 1975) have done as much as any group to advance our understanding of the family interaction viewpoint of physical illness. They have described a general type of family constellation that encourages somatisation of emotional conflict. Three factors in conjunction are considered by them to be necessary for the development of psychosomatic illness in children:
1 the child is physiologically vulnerable;
2 the family has four transactional characteristics:
  (a) enmeshment   (b) overprotectiveness
  (b) rigidity   (d) lack of conflict resolution
3 the sick child plays an important role in the family's conflict-avoidance.

Elsewhere (Lask, 1980), I have questioned the scientific validity of these findings, although from a clinician's viewpoint there is no doubt that such a family constellation seems to occur commonly with childhood illness.

The detailed application of this model to childhood asthma has been described elsewhere (Lask and Kirk, 1979) and its more general application is illustrated in Figure 10.3 There is a circular interaction between the illness, the family, and the individual's psychological state, and extra-familial factors. There is no specificity in terms of attitudes, personality-types or family constellations or transactional characteristics. It recognises the wide range of each of these, and emphasises the interaction between the components. There is no insistence that the illness plays a vital part in family equilibrium but allows for that possibility. It is applicable to children or adults, and may be extended to include more than one sick family member. It is well documented that a delicate equilibrium may be maintained between two or more sick persons within a family, e.g. Richardson, 1949; Hopkins, 1959; Cobb et al., 1969. In addition, the model is equally applicable to whichever point on the 'psychosomatic' spectrum the illness lies.

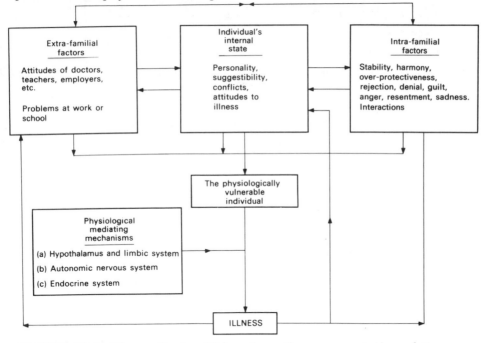

FIGURE 10.3 Illness Cycle. This schematic representation of the system's approach to understanding illness within the family is a modification of such models as proposed by Mattson (1975) and Pinkerton (1971) for the understanding of childhood asthma.

To complete the picture it is worth noting that an internal physiological open-systems circuit is in operation coinciding with the external system described above. Figure 10.4 demonstrates how that system operates and links with the external system. Thus it can be seen how the individual's physical symptom may be regulated by both internal and external influences.

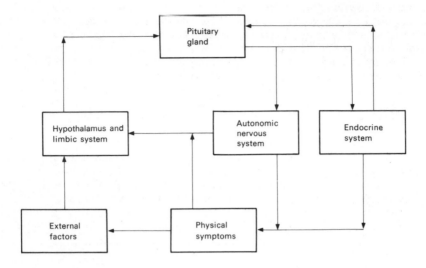

Key: Pituitary gland — secretes hormones which promote the activity of other endocrine
        glands, e.g. the thyroid, the ovaries, the adrenals.

   Endocrine system — concerned with energy metabolism, activity, sexual function.

   Autonomic nervous system — concerned principally with internal adjustments of the organism.

   Hypothalamus and limbic system — (i) that part of the brain concerned with the
                                    integration of 'messages' received from
                                    other parts of the body, e.g. sleep,
                                    appetite, temperature control, sexual
                                    behaviour, etc.

                                  (ii) centre of emotional behaviour.

   External factors — physical and emotional stresses, thus including family responses.

FIGURE 10.4 Internal physiological system

MANAGEMENT

The family therapist may encounter a family containing physical
illness in a variety of ways: (a) The family may be referred for
reasons other than the illness, which becomes a 'chance finding'.
(b) The referring agent may refer the family because of concern
that the illness is taking its toll on family life. (c) The illness
may be considered to be 'psychological'.

When using the theoretical framework discussed earlier, the
family therapist's approach to the illness and the family will not
depend upon whichever of the above conditions apply. The
physical manifestation of the problem is genuine and of intense
significance to the sufferer and his family. However, the importance

of the environment in the precipitation and maintenance of the
disorder varies. Thus, whilst the therapist conveys his belief in
and concern for the illness, he may consider it necessary to
focus on other aspects of family life. However, asking for details
of the illness not only conveys interest in the problem but may shed
light on precipitating and maintaining factors, as well as the way
in which the family react to and handle it. Using the illness as a
focus, it is possible to observe the mood of the family, its coping
methods, its communications patterns, its boundaries, alliances,
sub-systems, and conflicts.

[I do not believe that any illness arises as a symbolic expression
of conflict or suppressed instinct, (indeed there is no evidence
at all that this is ever the case) but its very existence is an
important aspect of family life. Here I take issue with authorities
such as Pincus and Dare (1978) who consider asthma, for example,
as being 'the literal suffocation of the anger which cannot be
expressed'. Certainly, some asthmatics have difficulty in expressing
anger (as do many non-asthmatics) but many asthmatics are well
able to give vent to their feelings.]

The place of the illness in the family will be included in the
formulation. Whether it be determined by organic or psychogenic
processes or a combination of the two, the illness is considered in
a similar way to other interruptions in normal family life, whether
that be a bereavement, adverse social circumstances, loss of
employment, move of house, etc. The significance of any illness
will vary from one family to another depending upon attitudes,
adjustment, marital stability, family harmony and homeostasis.
Thus the aims of treatment, and strategies and interventions used
will be determined not by the quality of the illness but the part
it plays in family life.

Focusing on the illness may be a necessary strategy but equally
the family may be using the illness as a pathological adaptation to
maintain, for example, homeostasis inappropriately, and thus the
therapist may need to move away from it. To illustrate the varieties
of intervention, I have included a series of case examples.

The correct 'medicine'
Janice, 11, was referred to the psychiatrist after investigations of
her severe headaches had excluded an organic cause. The family
consisted of father, 40, who had an important and responsible
job as a town planner. He seemed a nice, caring man who suffered
from migraine and high cholesterol levels in the blood.

Mother, 39, had devoted herself to the family, and presented as
a delightful and caring person. Janice was tense and depressed,
but at times shared her parental warmth, as did the second child,
Sarah, aged 9.

The first family session revealed no obvious dysfunction, and in
the second a sculpt showed a closely knit but not totally enmeshed
family, with only Janice in her sculpt portraying a hint of dissatisfaction, by asking Sarah to change places with her. Further
exploration of this led to Janice expressing previously concealed

resentment about a variety of issues. The parents expressed surprise at this revelation and agreed that as a family, dissatisfaction
was not discussed, for fear of upsetting father and aggravating
his heart condition. Father in turn had not discussed his own
worries to avoid bothering the family. The therapist commented
that it seemed that they needed to have a good row. At the next
session, father was more relaxed and mother was glowing. In the
interim they had 'had a very good row', with mother ending up
throwing a vase at father, whilst the children were out with
friends. On return when Janice discovered the reason for the
broken vase, she herself expressed anger at her parents 'for
having the row "the doctor ordered" ' whilst she was out. The
family all felt as if the air was cleared, and neither Janice nor her
father had further headaches, an improvement maintained at a
two-year follow-up.

Here, the fear of expressing negative feeling lest it should aggravate two illnesses that father suffered had led also to a vicious
cycle of perpetuating one of his disorders (migraine) whilst in-
ducing another in one of the children. 'Permission' to be angry
was the only medicine required, as this not only made safe bad
feelings but helped the parents to start resolving rather than
bottling-up conflict.

Not all families with psychogenically-determined physical symptoms
are so easy to help.

The B family consisted of father, 40, mother, 40, Celia, 12, and
David, 6. Father worked as an odd-job man for a small firm but had
been off sick for six months with pain and weakness in his left
arm and leg. He was an over-polite, talkative man who used words
and humour to cover feelings. His first marriage had ended in
divorce. Mother, Irish, worked as a receptionist in a night-club
from 8 p.m. to 4 a.m. She was rather passive in the sessions and
seemingly irritated by it all. Celia had been referred by a paediatrician because of severe headaches for which could be found no
organic cause. She was a lively, attractive, pseudomature girl,
who was at stage school. David, an equally attractive and lively
lad, whose behaviour was more age-appropriate, also attended
stage school.

Early interviews with the family revealed an over-close relationship between father and Celia, with the quality of both sibling
rivalry and marital conflict. Mother was peripheral to the family,
and David seemed self-contained. The obvious resentment of
mother's night-job, shared by father, Celia and David, was denied
when pointed out, as was any 'bad' feeling, e.g. when Celia was
irritated by a therapist's statement she turned away and sulked,
refusing to admit to her distress. She then complained of a severe
headache. It was not possible to gain a picture of the parental
relationship, as they spent so little time together. Any observations on this were deflected and Celia's or father's symptoms
discussed instead.

In formulating the problems of this family, there was unresolved
parental conflict, detoured through the children, with a peripheral

mother, and a cross-generational alliance between father and
Celia, which in itself was conflict-ridden. In addition, bad feelings
were denied and somatised. The aims of therapy were to restore
the appropriate generation boundaries, exclude the children from
the parental conflict, and encourage direct expression of painful
feeling. The prediction was that should the aims be achieved, the
symptoms of both Celia and father would disappear.

The denial was so strong, that this family proved very difficult
to work with. A family sculpt to help overcome this demonstrated
how extreme was mother's outside position, and how over-close the
relationship between father and Celia. The discussion of this included much expression of sadness by father and children, but
by the next session all this was again denied. In the following
session, the family were shown a video of the sculpt in an attempt
to reactivate the sadness. Mother's reaction was to say, 'I prefer
to work at night, there's more excitement there than at home.'
Succeeding sessions clarified the parental conflict but both parents
and Celia successfully diverted discussion of this to Celia's headaches. Two sessions were arranged in which the parents were
seen alone. Father managed to spend most of the first session
discussing his own symptoms, whilst mother remained silent. In
the next session the same process occurred, until as the therapist
expressed his despair of ever helping them, mother suddenly
complained of father's drinking (a problem never previously discussed). The therapist suggested a further session to pursue this,
and predictably the parents 'denied' any such problem. The therapist then said that clearly they preferred physical symptoms to
attempting to solve their problems, and that as they had chosen
that style he had no more to offer. Immediately, mother blurted out
that father's first wife had been a persistent nagger, and he had
divorced her, so she dare not complain in case the same happened
again. Father said his first wife had driven him mad. The therapist
ended by saying that under these circumstances, he did not think
anything could change. The next session, the final one of the
contract, was for the whole family. The therapist tried to recreate
what had happened in the previous session, the parents denied
it and Celia cried. The therapist said that unless the parents could
understand Celia's tears there was no point in continuing. Father
swore at the therapist, his first overt expression of anger towards
him. Both parents then asked for further help with their marriage.

A new contract of four marital sessions was agreed, followed
by a final family session. These followed the same pattern as before,
and the therapist felt increasingly angry with himself for agreeing
to the contract. In the fourth session the therapist admitted his
failure, and apologised for wasting their time. Mother immediately
attacked father for being unpredictable and contrary. The therapist
made no effort to pursue this. The final family meeting was extremely lively, characterised by vigorous arguments between Celia
and father with mother once more on the periphery. The therapist
pointed out how nothing had changed, at which Celia said things
had changed because she could get angry now, and did not have

headaches. The therapist said he did not think this would last unless the parents could start working things out together, instead of letting Celia and father fight for them.

At a follow-up six months later, the parents were behaving more appropriately, with some discussion between them of how to manage the children. There had been no further rows between Celia and father, mother was thinking of giving up her job, and both Celia and father were relatively free of physical symptoms and father was back in full-time employment. He talked more openly of his own depression.

Returning to the formulation, it was clear that both father and Celia were somatising their distress, and that the lack of parental conflict resolution and the close and ambivalent relationship between Celia and father were the major contributing factors. It took the therapist a long time to realise that the only way this family could be helped was by the use of the paradox. The family's insistence on using the physical symptoms to avoid discussion of other problems had defeated the therapist, despite his awareness of the process.

The strength of the denial, the somatisation and the detouring of conflict are all characteristic of families containing psychogenically induced physical illness. Not all are as resistant as this, and certainly conventional treatment methods should be tried first, particularly making safe the expression of bad feelings (as in the first illustration), and the re-locating and resolution of conflict.

At a much more serious level, illness can give rise to very genuine fears and consequent inappropriate management.

Fear of death
Mrs M's first husband died of asthma, aged 30, one year after the birth of twins. She remarried two years later, and her second husband adopted the twins. By the age of 6, both children had severe steroid-dependent asthma. Mother was intelligent, friendly and warm; she concealed her fear of further deaths and consequent desire to protect the children by adopting an opposite posture of denial of the severity of the illness. Her equally intelligent and caring second husband joined her in this reaction. They were adamant that the children should not know the cause of their real father's death. These attitudes were compounded by an additional fear that 'giving-in' to the asthma may make it worse. The marriage was stable and harmonious. The children's own fears and curiosity about their father had not been acknowledged.

The profound denial led to situations in which when one or other child developed an asthma attack, the doctor would not be called. Inevitably the condition worsened until the child would have to be rushed to hospital as an emergency.

The aims of treatment in this family were to help the parents towards a more realistic acceptance of the asthma, with consequent more appropriate handling. The means of achieving this required acknowledgment of the fears of death which the whole family (unknowingly) shared.

The children's play provided the key in that it was almost exclusively about illness, hospitals and dying. The fears of loss were
gradually expressed and shared openly. Mother particularly was
encouraged to acknowledge the terror one of the children experienced during the attack. Previously she had been unable to do
this, feeling it may lead to giving-in. The other twin responded
to this by directly saying she was frightened she would die.
    Half-way through therapy mother suffered a slipped disc, and
missed two sessions which focused on the problems of coping without her. The final (sixth) session was characterised by her en-
forced dependency which had facilitated her ability to tolerate the
children's own fears and dependency.
    At follow-up a year later, both children were considerably
improved and not requiring steroid treatment.
    In this family the fears had led to denial, with inevitable in-
appropriate management and subsequent deterioration of the
asthma. The inability to discuss the first husband's death had
compounded the problem, but fortunately the insistence on maintaining the secret did not impede therapeutic progress.

The secret that had to be revealed
Revealing a secret in a family meeting can often have a dramatic
effect on physical symptoms.
    Maureen, 8, had been admitted with severe abdominal pain for
which no organic cause could be found. The family consisted of
mother and father, both in their 30s, Sally, 11, Maureen, and an
aging maternal grandfather who lived with them. An interview with
Maureen alone, and a meeting with her parents added little to an
understanding of the problem. The only items of relevance were
that maternal grandfather was suffering from early senile dementia,
and that Sally had suffered a first attack of asthma about the same
time as Maureen's pains started.
    A family meeting was arranged. Little dysfunction was observed.
Eventually the therapist asked Sally why she thought Maureen had
tummy-aches. Sally replied that it was since grand-dad had got
into bed with them. The parents had not known of the grandfather's sexual approaches to the two sisters, who had since been
frightened both of their grandfather, and of telling their parents.
As a result of this revelation the grandfather was moved out of
the family home, and the symptoms disappeared. When symptoms
recurred a year later, the parents were able to talk to Maureen
about what might be upsetting her, and a further hospital consultation was not required.
    The skewed subsystems in the B family described earlier had been
the cause of tension headaches in one family member, and incapacitat-
ing limb symptoms in another. The next illustration shows how the
reverse may apply - an illness may lead to generational skewing,
with the production of a 'parental child', and a second illness.

The parental child
Dick, 8, was referred to the psychiatrist to help prepare him for
major surgery for ulcerative colitis with resulting ileostomy (arti-
ficial opening of the bowel on the abdominal wall). Neither the
paediatricians nor the parents had felt able to explain the operation.
A meeting with the family, consisting of Dick, his parents and a
younger brother, John, aged 6, showed that Dick was a 'parental
child', carrying considerable responsibility for decision-making,
and 'disciplining' John. The parents were warm, caring, pleasant
people who seemed unable to assert themselves in this respect.
Father particularly was quite passive. In addition he suffered from
ankylosing spondylitis, a potentially crippling spinal deformity,
which had caused him to have a very stiff spinal column, and
limited neck movements (the therapist did not discover this until
the end of therapy, having considered him to be simply 'tense'!).
Dick denied any concern regarding his disease, an operation, or
his position in the family.
   Although inhibited affect was a major feature in Dick's personality,
the chosen focus was the inappropriate generation-skewing. The
aim of therapy was to strengthen both the parental and the child
subsystems. This was achieved by instructing the family not to
make any effort to change but for the parents to record each
incident involving Dick inappropriately taking responsibility.
Within two weeks, Dick's 'interfering' (as it was re-labelled) had
virtually ceased despite the instruction not to change. The therapists
expressed concern that such a dramatic and unasked-for change
had occurred, predicted relapse, and instructed the family to
revert to normal behaviour and to continue to record interfering.
At the next session a blank sheet was presented. In addition,
Dick and John spent most of the session giggling and fooling about.
The parents felt they had been tricked by the therapists and
expressed concern that they did not have control themselves.
The therapists agreed with the latter concern and advised the
parents to do as they wished for the next fortnight and not to
keep a record for the therapists. The interfering recurred immediately, but after three days the parents spontaneously and unitedly
forbade Dick to interfere. It stopped again, and did not recur.
Coincident with this change in family functioning, the overt manifestations of the ulcerative colitis, frequent and bloody diarrhoea,
also improved. At the end of the therapy (six months later) Dick
was asymptomatic, and his dosage of (very powerful) medicine had
been dramatically reduced to safe levels.
   In this family it seemed clear that the generational skewing had
thrown an intolerable burden on Dick who, unable to express his
concern overtly, somatised it and presented it through his disease.
The parents, wary of being too firm with him, and passive themselves, tolerated this and perpetuated a vicious cycle. Because the
therapists had not realised that father had a serious physical
illness, they had not incorporated this in their formulation. Retrospectively, it was possible to see how Dick's position as 'parental
child' had arisen. Because father was forced to 'take it easy and

avoid stress', mother had stopped using him as a partner in the executive sub-system, and had brought in Dick instead. Thus the family's unhealthy adaptation to one illness had precipitated or aggravated another.

Successful outcome at follow-up will be determined not only by the maintenance of appropriate boundaries and remission of the ulcerative colitis, but also stability of the ankylosing spondylitis.

Interventions do not have to be particularly complex or sophisticated. Indeed, once some understanding of the family's contribution to the problem has been gained, frightening symptoms may be controlled by very simple methods. This may help the family to cope more appropriately in future - as in the next illustration - or serve as a 'rescue operation' for a sick child, with no family change - as in the succeeding example.

Therapist - magician or 'quack'?
Jane, 8, and Ann, 5, were the daughters of a member of the government of the day, and his much younger wife. Ann developed a rare skin complaint the cause of which is unknown, and required frequent hospital attendances. Within a week of Ann's first hospital attendance, Jane developed a loud, persistent, cough, sufficiently severe to cause her admission to a respiratory unit lest she should have serious lung disease. It soon became clear that the cough was in fact a vocal tic. At the family meeting, father's peripheral role in the family was obvious as was mother's inability to cope with two demanding children. The therapist felt a resistance to change on the family's part, and was himself going on leave the next day. Consequently, and unusually for him, he prescribed a tranquilliser for Jane, and asked a student colleague to 'keep an eye' on the situation. The student had two meetings with Jane and her parents. Jane complained of a feeling of isolation in the family. The student suggested that father should spend half an hour each evening talking with Jane. Her tic/cough vanished after the second session. At the next family meeting, when the therapist returned, mother attributed this to the medication and was effusively grateful to the therapist for the prescription. There was little doubt in anyone else's mind that the tic was a means of gaining attention in a family where what little of this was available had been diverted to her sick younger sister. When the latter was finally admitted to hospital for investigation, the tic returned but the mother was able to involve the previously peripheral father, and before she could request more medicine, the tic disappeared.

The student who had never treated a family before had quickly understood the basis of the problem and had devised a simple and effective remedy.

Therapist as knight in shining armour
Rosemary, 6, had nearly died on several occasions from asthma. The paediatrician was so worried he asked for psychiatric help. Individual psychotherapy had no impact. The psychiatrist then decided on a family interview which again shed no light on matters.

It was only when an interview with the extended family was held
that any impact was made. A long-standing silent hostility existed
between father and maternal grandmother (they had not spoken
to each other for seven years, despite sharing the same house).
None the less they disagreed strongly on the upbringing of the
children, and expressed their differences through mother and the
children. Rosemary particularly acted as a go-between, and given
her asthmatic sub-strata it was not surprising that the tensions
were such that her asthma became dangerously severe.

After the adults had been confronted with their joint mishandling
and instructed not to use the children in this way, Rosemary's
asthma dramatically improved despite the fact that the war of
silence continued unabated.

Therapist as 'marriage-breaker' or 'life-saver'?
Nick, 11, was the only child of warring parents. The battlefield
was the home, and family life was scarred by the constant sniping.
In addition to his other problems, Nick had unstable diabetes,
i.e. despite insulin injections and a rigid diet it was not possible
to control the blood sugar levels. Consequently, he would frequently
develop a diabetic coma and require hospitalisation and resuscitation.

The therapist insisted that the parents confine their fighting to
themselves, and not draw in Nick to take sides, or to use him as
a weapon. The parents complied, but having lost what was in
effect a safety-valve, they found each other intolerable, and
separated. Nick's diabetes immediately became, and remained,
stable. His successful role as a marriage-saver had been at the
cost of his health, and a danger to his life. The therapist could
be accused of breaking up a marriage, or complimented on possibly
saving a life.

This latter-day doctor's dilemma in less extreme forms is not
unfamiliar to the family therapist involved in physical illness.
The ideal is to help the child limp to the sidelines and then assist
the parents to find less damaging solutions to their conflicts. This
is often easier said than done, as illustrated in the next example.

Another boy with ulcerative colitis, Paul, 13, was referred on the
day of the operation to remove his diseased bowel. He had refused
to go to the operating theatre until he could discuss the implications
of the ileostomy - an understandable objection! His mother hovered
in the background in an equally understandable state of agitated
distress. The operation was a success and Paul recovered rapidly
and adjusted well. A family meeting had been arranged to help with
the early convalescent period, and also to evaluate whether family
dysfunction may have contributed to the disease, and was likely to
continue to do so. Paul had a small piece of bowel left, and if
this could be preserved for a few years then the ileostomy might
be reversed.

The family were very tense - father would always initiate discussion after a long silence, Paul would immediately mock him, and
he would be joined in this by the other child, Bill, 12. Mother
would sit silently, rarely sharing her thoughts. When she did speak

it was to make a scathing comment about her husband. The pattern
was clear. There was severe parental disharmony with considerable
unresolved conflict and a cross-generational alliance between mother
and the two sons against father. This was an intolerable position
for Paul, and with no easy escape, somatisation was inevitable.

A contract of twelve fortnightly meetings was agreed with the
family. The aims were as follows: 1 to help restore appropriate
boundaries between the parental and sibling sub-systems; 2 to
assist the parents to confront each other and find a resolution to
their conflict; 3 to help Paul feel safe in expressing some of his
more painful feelings.

In the second session, Paul criticised his mother for signing
the consent form for the operation, wanting to know why his
parents had not signed it together. Obvious explanations such as
father being at work, met with the reply, 'How would you feel
having a bag attached to your tummy?' This apparent non sequitur,
considered in the context of his life-experience and the family's
pattern of relationships, was the first sign of change. Not only
was he now different from the pre-operative Paul, physically, but
also emotionally. He was for the first time challenging his parents,
and asking them why they did not work together (sign the form
together) instead of against each other. Sensing his new-found
power he launched a blistering attack on both parents. Paul's
further attacks on mother were countered by Bill's criticisms of
father. The next two sessions were manifested by Bill and Paul
battling with each other, and the reader will realise far more quickly
than did the therapists that the boys were arguing on behalf of
their parents, who sat in silent bewilderment. In the final sessions
of the contract the therapists put an embargo on the boys speaking
for their parents. The whole family found this impossibly difficult,
and eventually the boys were told to watch their parents through
the one-way screen. It was only then that the parents started
talking to each other.

A new contract was agreed in which the parents were to meet with
the therapists three times a month, and in the fourth week the whole
family would meet. Progress was very slow and characterised by
various crises, the most significant of which was mother's decision
to spend Christmas with Bill, in her own parents' home abroad,
whilst Paul and father stayed in London. On return, the sessions
focused on the meaning of Christmas to each partner, and this
highlighted deep religious differences. It became clear that on this
issue, like many others, they were irreconcilable. Mother stormed
out of a session, saying that everyone was against her. Father
rang to say he thought that the sessions were too painful for her,
and that she would only return for a final meeting. This was
arranged for the whole family. The therapists recapitulated on
what they thought had happened, particularly emphasising how
once the parents had learned to keep the boys out of their relationship they had found each other immovable on important issues.
This had clearly felt as if the therapists had imposed something
painful into their relationship.

Despite the crises and painful experiences, Paul remained physically well, and at a one-year follow-up had no signs of recurrence of the colitis. Aims 1 and 3 had been met successfully, but the second aim of helping the parents was not achieved.

Sometimes it may be prudent to aim only for restoration of appropriate subsystems, without attempting to explore further the marital difficulties.

CONCLUSIONS AND SUMMARY

In all illness there is an intimate interplay between psychological, social and biological factors. This interaction needs due consideration whatever the illness, physical, psychological or a combination, in childhood or adult life.

The 4-tier model emphasises the respective relevance of 1 the biological component; 2 the individual's psychological state; 3 extra-familial factors; and 4 the family contribution. By understanding the nature of these various components of the individual's network, the focus may be broadened from the illness per se to incorporate all the relevant factors in the environment. Within this framework varying theoretical viewpoints may be integrated, and different therapeutic models employed. The 'family interaction model' recognises that family interaction patterns may trigger or maintain psychophysiological processes. The resulting physical symptoms can function as a homeostatic mechanism, regulating family transactions.

The family therapist may assume that symptoms in an individual member of a family are often an expression of disturbed family function, and so consider the whole family as the patient. Treatment commences with 1 meeting the whole family; 2 active exploration and discussion of family interaction; 3 formulation of family function including the role of the illness; 4 determination of a relevant focus upon which therapy may be concentrated.

The most common goals are: 1 the promotion of more realistic attitudes to the illness, e.g. encouraging relatives to do things they fear, such as comforting, controlling, or allowing freedom; 2 the expression of suppressed emotions, especially the fear of death and resentment towards the patient; 3 the resolution of marital problems, or avoidance of detouring them through a sick family member; 4 the increased involvement of a peripheral parent and the reduced involvement of an overinvolved parent.

The therapist 1 acts as a catalyst for family interaction; 2 helps the family to see how it functions in relation to the illness and everyday life; 3 encourages appropriate, coping reactions; 4 helps the family alter inappropriate behaviour.

ACKNOWLEDGMENT

I am indebted to many colleagues for their help in the formulation and treatment of these families.

REFERENCES

Alexander, F., French, T. and Pollock, G. (1968) 'Psychosomatic
  Specificity', University of Chicago Press.
Apley, J. (1963) Family Patterning and Childhood Disorders,
  'Lancet', 12 Jan., 67-70.
Balint, M. (1977) 'The Doctor, His Patient and the Illness', Pitman
  Press.
Block, J. (1969) Parents of Schizophrenic, Neurotic, Asthmatic and
  Congenitally Ill Children, 'Arch. Gen. Psychiat.', 20, 659-73.
Cautella, J. (1977) Illness Behaviour, 'J. Behav. Ther. & Exper.
  Psychiatry', 8, 45-52.
Cobb, S., Schull, W., Harburg, E. and Kasl, S. (1969) The Intra-familial
  Transmission of Rheumatoid Arthritis, 'J. Chronic Disease', 22,
  193-295.
Godfrey, S. and Silverman, M. (1973) Demonstration of Placebo
  Response in Asthma, 'Journal of Psychosomatic Research', 17,
  293-7.
Grolnick, L. (1972) A Family Perspective of Psychosomatic Factors
  in Illness, 'Family Process', 11, 457-86.
Hopkins, P. (1959) Health and Happiness and the Family, 'Brit.
  J. Clinical Practice', 13 (5), 311-13.
Jackson, D. and Yalom, I. (1965) Family Research on the Problem
  of Ulcerative Colitis, 'Arch. Gen. Psych.', 15, 410-18.
Lask, A. (1966) 'Asthma, Attitude and Milieu', Tavistock.
Lask, B. (1979) Emotional Considerations in Wheezy Children,
  'J. Royal Society of Medicine', 72, 56-9.
Lask, B. (1980) 'Institute of Family Therapy Monograph, vol. II',
  Academic Press.
Lask, B. and Kirk, M. (1979) Childhood Asthma - Family Therapy
  as an Adjunct to Routine Management, 'Journal of Family Therapy',
  1, 33-49.
Liebman, R., Honig, P. and Berger, H. (1976) An Integrated Treat-
  ment Programme for Psychogenic Pain, 'Family Process', 15 (4),
  397-406.
Lipowski, Z. (1975) Psychiatry of Somatic Diseases, 'Comprehensive
  Psychiatry', 16 (2), 105-23.
Mattson, A. (1975) Psychological Aspects of Childhood Asthma,
  'Paediatric Clinics of North America', 22, 77-87.
Meissner, W. (1966) Family Dynamics and Psychosomatic Processes,
  'Family Process', 5, 142-60.
Melzack, R., Wetsz, A. and Sprague, L. (1963) The Role of Sugges-
  tion in Pain Tolerance, 'Experimental Neurology', 8, 239-47.
Miller, F., Court, S., Walton, W. and Knox, E. (1960) 'Growing Up
  in Newcastle upon Tyne', Oxford University Press.
Minuchin, S. et al. (1975) A Conceptual Model of Psychosomatic
  Illness in Children, 'Arch. Gen. Psych.', 32, 1031-8.
Pincus, L. and Dare, C. (1978) 'Secrets in the Family', Faber &
  Faber.
Pinkerton, P. (1971) Childhood Asthma, 'British Journal of Hospital
  Medicine', 6, 331-8.

Pless, I. and Pinkerton, P. (1975) 'Chronic Childhood Disorder',
  Kimpton Publications.
Rachman, S. and Philips, C. (1978) 'Psychology and Medicine',
  Penguin Books.
Richardson, H.B. (1949) 'Patients have Families', New York:
  Commonwealth Fund.
Stewart, L. (1962) Social and Emotional Adjustment during
  Adolescence as Related to Development of Psychosomatic Illness
  in Adulthood, 'Psychol. Monographs', 65, 175–215.
Tomm, K.M., McArthur, R. and Leahey, M. (1977) Psychological
  Management of Children with Diabetes Mellitus, 'Clinical Paedi-
    atrics', 16 (12), 1151–5.
Walrond-Skinner, S. (1976) 'Family Therapy. The Treatment of
  Natural Systems', Routledge & Kegan Paul.
Weakland, J. (1977) 'Family Somatics' – A Neglected Edge, 'Family
  Process', 16, 263–72.
Weller, S. (1975) The Patient is a Family, 'World Medicine', 19
  November, 36–8.
Williams, J.S. (1975) Aspects of Dependence-Independence Conflict
  in Children with Asthma, 'J. Child Psychology & Psychiatry',
  16 (3), 199–218.
Zeeman, E.C. (1977) 'Catastrophy Theory – Selected Papers 1972',
  Reading, Mass., USA: Addison-Wesley.

11 MOURNING AND THE FAMILY

Dora Black

INTRODUCTION

> He first deceased, she for a little tried
> To live without him, liked it not and died.
> (Sir Henry Wootton, sixteenth century)

Our folklore, enshrined in these lines, has only recently been
studied systematically. That bereavement can kill we now know from
researchers (Young et al., 1963; Parkes et al., 1969; Rees and
Lutkins, 1967) who have shown that there is an increase in the
mortality rate of widowers within the first year of bereavement –
that one can die of a 'broken heart'. Less dramatically, bereaved
spouses also suffer an increase in physical and mental illness
(see Parkes, 1972, for a review of research studies). More recently,
we have looked at the effect on children of the death of a parent
(see Black, 1978, for a review) and on parents of the death of a
child (see Burton, 1974, for reviews) or a stillbirth (Lewis, 1976)
and have found similar increases in ill-health. For bereaved children
the effects of parental death outlast childhood (see Granville-
Grossman, 1968 and Birtchnell, 1972) and influence their suscepti-
bility to depression and alcoholism in adult life, as well as their
chances of successful marriage and parenting. What is the reason
for these associations? Can we isolate the aspects of death and
deprivation that cause morbidity and mortality? And if we can, is
there a way to intervene early to prevent them? In this chapter
we will examine the normal processes which occur in the individual
and in the family and which are set in train by the death of a
loved one. We will look at some of the ways that grief can go wrong
and what can be done to help. Finally, we will explore whether we
can prevent some of the unpleasant consequences of bereavement
and especially in this context consider the use of family therapy.

DEVELOPMENTAL APPROACH TO GRIEF AND MOURNING

> It is better to have loved and lost than never to have loved at
> all   (English folk saying)

The concept of loss plays a central role in theories of personality, especially as developed by psychoanalytic writers. The death of a parent is seen as predisposing children to the development of maladaptive coping strategies such as denial and producing constricted personalities. In the literature there is often no clear distinction between the loss of a parent by death and by desertion or divorce. Similarly, few writers distinguish between deprivation of a parent or spouse (loss) and the privation (lack) of one. Rutter (1972) clearly separates these concepts of loss, lack and distortion. He is referring to aspects of parenting, but the concepts hold good in a more general context. You cannot lose what you have never had. There is evidence that lack (or privation) of a parent or spouse has consequences different from deprivation or loss. Our folklore confirms the belief that to have and to lose is different from to lack. 'It is better to have loved and lost than never to have loved at all.' But it is more complicated than that. Our uniquely human possession, language, enables us to articulate dreams, hopes and longings. These we all have and these too can be lost. We are only affected adversely by the loss of someone or something to which we are attached. Bowlby's (1969 and 1973) approach to an understanding of attachment is important in making sense of the phenomena of loss. He draws together observations of ethologists and clinicians in a hypothesis which is plausible and able to be tested. Bowlby suggests that the observed strong tendency of infants to attach a caretaker to them is a behaviour which had survival value in the environment in which human beings evolved; that of the jungle. There, wild animals and other dangers lurked, and any infant not close to an adult would be unlikely to survive. Those infants with weak attachment behaviour died out by natural selection and thus was bred into us the very strong attachment behaviour present today.

If attachment is biologically necessary to survival, nature has to find a way of resolving close attachments between parents and children when this attachment no longer serves a protective function and in order to allow the development of a procreative bond. We call the period of this resolution adolescence and recent findings (Rutter et al., 1976) that approximately one-half of 14-year-olds display symptoms of emotional turmoil, raise the question of whether the biological process of disruption of bonding is the cause.

There are at least three seemingly different phenomena which result from the disruption of attachment bonds; the separation anxiety of children, the turmoil of adolescents and the pangs of grief after bereavement. Now there are some questions raised by that statement. Does the resolution of attachment bonds always mean loss; can loss occur in the absence of previous attachment? Is loss only about human bonds? Can you lose what you do not possess? Can you possess people as opposed to things? Since in my view we cannot speak of loss of people in the same way as loss of toys, houses or dreams, what is it we lose when someone we love dies? The work of Parkes may help us to answer these questions. He has suggested that at times of psycho-social transition,

the internalised model of our world (the 'assumptive world') is
rendered redundant, and we must make changes in our model
(Parkes, 1971 and 1977b). The changes we make may be incomplete
so that we retain two incompatible views side by side. For example,
a woman may know her husband is dead but goes on behaving as
if he were alive.

   The replacement of a redundant world model by a more appropriate
one can be encouraged by certain techniques, discussed later, and
the process of mourning can be seen as an adaptive way of relinquishing a redundant model and restructuring one's internal world.
The work that needs to be done to move from, say, the status of
single person to married person, is just as great as the amount of
work needed to be done to move from married person to widow.
The differences lie in the willingness with which the work is done.
The resistance to doing the work of restructuring is what the pain
of grief is about. There are also changes which are ambiguous –
like the marriage of a daughter where the bride's mother may behave
as if she is grief-stricken, on a day most people regard as a joyful
one. So in these cases of bereavement, what is lost is our image or
model of our world – one which contains a husband or child or
parent with all the relationships that implies. In the case of a
husband a woman loses his love and companionship and someone to
love and care for, the model of herself as a 'wife' and 'housewife'
and a host of other roles and relationships which go with him. When
an adolescent leaves home, what is lost is similar and the feelings,
though usually not so intense or painful, are also similar.

THE EFFECTS OF LOSS

> The pain of grief is just as much a part of life
> as the joy of love; it is, perhaps, the price
> we pay for love, the cost of commitment.
>
>   (Parkes, 1972)

Grief is a process; whenever we lose someone (or something) to
whom we are attached, certain phenomena occur in a more or less
orderly manner. These are well described by Freud (1917),
Lindemann (1944), Parkes (1972) and others and consist of a
short period of numbness and shock, which normally gives way to
a period of protest or alarm – loud wailing, agitated hand-wringing,
anger and restless searching. This, in turn, gives way to the
quieter keening of the period of despair – accompanied by withdrawal, sleeplessness, anorexia and feelings of guilt and self-
reproach. Eventually in normal grief, a period of recovery ensues
and the individual emerges with a new identity. These phases of
grief are identical of course to the phases of separation anxiety
observed by Robertson (1968) with hospitalised toddlers. They
are universal phenomena, and have been described in people who
have had a limb amputated (Parkes, 1975), in people who move
house (Fried, 1962) and can be observed in children who lose a
favourite toy.

If a human experience is so universal, it must serve an adaptive purpose, to aid our survival. How can such a series of painful experiences be adaptive? One can see that the protest phase would serve to reunite attached couples if the person were not dead but merely strayed. However, under the impact of reality-testing, when loud calling and crying does not bring him back, the realisation of loss impinges and protest gives way to despair. The features of this stage of grief are identical to a depressive illness except that we know the cause. The features of depression which are adaptive are the repetitious rumination and the withdrawal which aids the restructuring of one's internal assumptive world. Those people who avoid the depression of bereavement by ceaseless activity indeed 'come to grief' later on in both senses of the phrase.

PATHOLOGICAL GRIEF

> I have no respect for you
> For you would not tell the truth about your grief
> But laughed at it
> When the first pang was past
> And made it a thing of nothing.
> You said
> That what had been
> Had never been
> That what was
> Was not:
> You have a light mind
> And a coward's soul.
>   (Stevie Smith)

Grief in adults can be absent, delayed, prolonged or distorted (Parkes, 1972). What happens to bereaved children? Pathological variants of grief are common in children (Bowlby, 1963; Rutter, 1966). Is this because children are developmentally incapable of mourning (Wolfenstein, 1966) or because of the associated changes in their world which are even greater than in the bereaved adult's world? Children, of course, have limitations on their understanding of concepts such as death, heaven, etc. (Anthony, 1941; Koocher, 1974) but it is rarely that they are given much opportunity to grieve. People avoid talking to children about a dead parent, misconceptions persist and the child gets little chance of accurately restructuring his world. The child needs to have the experience of the numerous small losses inevitable in childhood, made sense of for him by a caring adult who can help him to mourn. It is the necessary rehearsal for the larger losses which will come later on. But of course these experiences are often neglected by parents who themselves may have been reared in families which view the attachment behaviour of the child unsympathetically, as something to be grown out of as soon as possible (Bowlby and Parkes, 1970). These standards will be adopted by the child and when he suffers

a serious loss in adult life, he will suppress his feelings instead
of expressing them. In this he is encouraged by his network of
relatives who are products of the same family culture. Maddison and
Walker (1967) found that widows who developed pathological responses
to loss were likely to lack a supportive network of people who
encouraged the expression of grief, and Paul and Grosser (1965)
suggest that incompleted mourning may produce defences against
further losses which are transmitted to other family members and
produce a rigid family system. Coping strategies are learned in
the family and it is to the family we must turn for the remedies
for loss. Indeed, Pattison (1976) suggests that children can cope
with death but not with the family myths and mystifications about
death.

WORKING WITH ACUTE GRIEF

> Give sorrow words – the grief that does not speak
> Whispers the o'er fraught heart and bids it break.
>   (Shakespeare, 'Macbeth')

Much of human life is spent in avoiding death yet it is a taboo
subject. Many family myths and secrets centre round death and the
avoidance of grief and mourning typifies many dysfunctional
families. As fewer people experience the death of someone close,
the community and the family becomes less competent to support
and help the bereaved and avoidance and denial become more common.
Euphemisms are used and distress signals go unrecognised. What
can others (lay and professional) do to help at the time of bereavement, and can intervention then prevent some of the later pathological sequelae? For centuries we have known that we must 'give
sorrow words' and recent research has confirmed this observation.
Two controlled studies (Raphael and Maddison, 1976; Parkes 1977a)
using various short-term techniques aimed at encouraging communication about the dead person and promoting grief have shown that
those bereaved people given such help have significantly fewer
disturbances on follow-up compared with the untreated control
group. The aim is to make them temporarily more unhappy and this
is a procedure that requires some confidence. It is more akin to
the boldness of a surgical incision than the cautiousness of a
wait-and-see therapy. As Parkes says (1977b), 'The bereaved
person has to be taught to look boldly at what has been lost in
order that the demarcation between the world that is and the world
that was becomes clearer.' *Boldly*, is the word that needs emphasising here. All people in psycho-social transition strive to maintain
a status quo, to avoid learning the skills appropriate to a new
unwanted world. People who are in a position to give support and
guidance to the bereaved must be prepared to assist them to
examine their assumptions, to clarify their previous world model,
and their present situation in order to discover which aspects of
it must be changed. This work is painful, time-consuming but

extremely rewarding, especially if done in a family setting.

How can we best help children who have lost a parent? Counselling the surviving parent, and working direct with children to help them to understand the finality of death and then express their grief can be done on an individual basis. The problem is that children are only brought for treatment if they are symptomatic, and as Rutter (1966) has shown, this may be many years later or even in adult life (Birtchnell, 1972). Perhaps we should be intervening earlier, to prevent later pathology? If the poorer outcome for children is a result of their greater propensity to respond to loss by pathological forms of mourning (Bowlby, 1963) can we encourage healthier outcomes by promoting mourning in children? The most economical and effective way of helping children to understand what has happened, and to promote mourning (the one must always precede the other - one cannot mourn until one understands the finality of death) is to meet the children with the surviving parent and, using the techniques of family therapy to help the family to share their understanding and then their grief. In this way, the parent learns about the child's misconceptions and misperceptions and can feel herself to be an effective parent in helping to correct them, with the encouragement of the therapist. The therapist can elicit, too, the feelings of anger and guilt which may otherwise isolate individuals in the family, and which by being shared, will diminish. Children's communications can be tentative, non-verbal, indirect and confused. They may need interpretation to a parent who is, herself grief-stricken. A parent's grief may alarm a child by its vehemence and unfamiliarity and the therapist can help the child to cope with it and to accept reassurance that his mother is not ill or dying and will gradually return to normal. The therapist's task is to clarify and promote communication, to help the parent understand the child's fantasies and anxieties which are based on his limited cognitive understanding of abstract concepts and to encourage the parent not to mystify, or mythologise about death to the child and not to resist the expression and eventual resolution of her own grief. Bowen (1976) has noted the 'emotional shock-wave' that runs through families after an important death such as a grandparent who was the head of the clan. That is a series of major life events such as physical or mental illness, academic or business failures, illegitimate births and accidents occur in the extended family and may not be at first connected with the significant death. Bowen advocates the use of family therapy around the time of dying and bereavement to open up communication. He uses direct words - 'death, die, bury' rather than 'passed on, deceased, expired'. He lays emphasis on the role-model provided by the professional person in helping survivors to achieve a better level of emotional functioning by calmly facing the anxiety of death.

The following cases taken from clinical practice and from a current research project by CRUSE which is evaluating family intervention at the time of childhood bereavement, illustrate the problems and the techniques used. (CRUSE is the national

organisation offering a counselling service for the widowed and
their dependants, 126 Sheen Road, Richmond, Surrey.)

THE HANNAN FAMILY

The two teenage boys in this family of four children where mother
had recently been diagnosed as having terminal cancer, were
truanting from school and were referred to the child guidance
clinic. The local authority social worker involved and I met with
the general practitioner and the teachers, and we decided that the
social worker and I would meet the family at home. The general
practitioner was adamant that mother must not be told her prognosis as 'she was not strong enough to take it.' The social worker
had observed the 4-year-old playing 'dying games' when she
visited and suspected that the truanting had to do with unexpressed
and avoided anxiety and fear about mother's illness. Father was
unemployed and often drunk and there had been long-standing
financial and marital problems.
  We found a chaotic house. When we got the family together,
mother chose to sit in a chair outside the family circle – she had
started to move out of the family and this made me suspect that
she already knew she was dying. My task then was to find some
way of being bold yet steering a way over the thin ice of the
general practitioner's prohibition and the frightened look on the
oldest boy's face. We started by asking about Mummy's illness,
and led them on to think about illnesses that did not get better.
What would they do if that happened? That enabled them to talk
about what Mummies do (the world that was). 'What could their
Mummy do now? What would happen if she could do less?' And so,
by slow degrees we started to talk about the Mummy who could not
get better. At that point Mrs Hannan said: 'I'm not going to get
better' and she spoke to the children for the first time about her
future – which I think they knew but it had never been talked
about. And then because of the 4-year-old's dying games, the
idea of death came up and fear froze the older boy. Mother
talked about her fear for the children if she died. She turned to
father and they started to talk together about how he would cope.
She moved her chair back into the family – she found she was of
use still to them in helping her husband to think about their future.
The children began to relax as they saw their parents take charge
again. It was an emotional session but we felt we had enabled the
family to communicate honestly about painful feelings. The children
returned to school the next day and there were no more attendance
problems. Mother took ten months to die and the social worker was
involved with them for the whole time. Father stopped drinking
too much and with mother's help made plans to move to a new town
and get work. His letter to the social worker, a few months after
mother's death told of the oldest boy's strength and helpfulness
with the younger children, his new job, and expressed his gratitude
for what we had done for them all.

Comment

The techniques which helped this family were - the use of modelling, intensification of affect, and boundary-making. The therapist modelled for the family a way of talking about death which they could use. Mother was then able to emerge from the isolation of not being able to acknowledge that she was dying, and find that far from being helpless, she had an important task to do before she died. Intensifying the affect (Minuchin, forthcoming) was necessary (the 'boldness' of the surgeon) to break through the deafness which held the family frozen and helpless. The therapist's task was also to help the parents to resume their parental function-ing. The success of the family therapy was such that father 'grew up' - started to work - take decisions and leave off alcohol - all very unlikely to happen after bereavement (Parkes, 1977a).

THE BAKER FAMILY

Mr Baker, an articulate, well-built man in his early 40s, had been left with the care of his two sons, Mark, 11, and David, 8, after his wife's death. Two years earlier, his wife, Penelope, had been diagnosed as having inoperable cancer and from then until her death, he and the boys cared for her at home, their care alleviated by occasional periods in hospital.

Mr Baker's work made it possible for him to spend some time working from home both during his wife's illness and afterwards. Apart from the support this gave his wife, it became an important buffer for the boys as their father took over some of the mothering, nurturing roles. Two months after mother's death, the family were offered six family counselling sessions by CRUSE as part of their research study. When Mr Baker and the boys were approached by the CRUSE counsellor, they were most welcoming and the atmos-phere in the small, well-kept home was very comfortable. All three family members were willing to talk about Penny's illness and the sadness mixed with relief they had felt about her death. David said: 'I'm sorry she died but I'm glad she has no more pain.' Mr and Mrs Baker had strong religious beliefs which helped Mr Baker feel 'it was not really the end' and Mark had participated at his mother's memorial service by singing one of the hymns solo.

What was obviously more difficult to come to terms with was remembering and mourning Penny as she had been prior to her illness. Mr Baker found he had a block in his memory and could only listen in surprise when friends said how lively and active a person Penny had been. Mark and David quite spontaneously opened up this painful area by finding photographs of their mother, some when she looked very thin, ill and gaunt in a wheel-chair and a few others prior to illness looking pert and pretty with lovely green eyes. The therapist, feeling that there was some avoidance of the pain of grief, pushed the family to recollect Penny, and to cry that she was no longer there. By the following interview, Mr Baker had been able to look though old photograph albums and

letters and his recollections were coming back. Some of the feelings the family had were angry ones - Why had she deserted them?
Why had they not had a proper mother? But on the whole, considering she had been ill long before they knew she was ill, the marriage
had been a good one and the feelings left were positive.

Father is now beginning to have a social life which goes well
when Gingerbread (a social club for one-parent families) is involved
and where the children are automatically included, but when he
goes out with a potential girl-friend, the children feel unhappy and
refuse to go to her house. When they were intended to go to her
house, for instance, for Sunday lunch, David felt it would be very
disloyal to his dead mother to go, and challenged his father,
saying: 'Would you rather go to Lilly's or to mother's funeral?'

Although the family has further stages to go through until they
are emotionally stable, the outlook for them seems good and the
therapist feels that father's ability to facilitate the work of facing
mother's illness and death has been the most important factor in
their recovery.

Comment
The techniques used by the therapist here included intensification of affect and forced mourning. She was able to help father
give permission to the children to opt out for the present, from
accepting his new girl-friend, and to help the children to accept
that the new relationship did not imply that mother had been replaced or forgotten. Whether the therapist's optimistic prognostica-
tion is confirmed by the follow-up remains to be seen. The hope of
reunion, which their religion promises them may have produced
an avoidance of grief which might lead to a poorer outcome for
the children.

THE ROSSMAN FAMILY

This family were approached by a CRUSE counsellor about two
months after mother's sudden death from cancer after a short
illness which followed a house move. They had few neighbourhood
or family supports although they were well known to social services
because of periods of unemployment, poverty and poor housing.

The family consisted of father, Donna, 6½, and Neil, 4½. They
accepted the offer of six family counselling sessions. The counsellor, an experienced social worker and family therapist, found
her attempts to engage the children blocked by father's need to
have her all to himself. He alternately ignored the children or
appeared to compete with the counsellor for their approval - as
when he supplied them with toys identical to those she carried
with her for their use during sessions.

Father's use of the counsellor was as a dustbin for his feelings
of fury with doctors, social workers, and of course wives who
die and leave you holding the babies. During this session, Donna
played with the doll figures, setting them up rigidly in family

groups with a mother, father and two children. She got repeatedly angry and threw the parent dolls on the floor, responding hostilely too, to the comments made by the counsellor about her unhappiness and anger. The father would not permit the therapist to make the link between mother's death and Donna's expressed anger.

The counsellor left feeling worried that the children were being physically neglected and that she was impotent to change anything, but she stayed with the feelings of rage and hurt that all the family were clearly expressing and which belonged to the bereavement, and using the fact that they were coming to the end of their contracted family meetings, tried to help them to express some of their feelings about her departure. Donna proffered the only clear verbal communication she had yet made: 'You stupid old cow', but again the link with mother's death was refused. At the last session the children looked better cared for, and father reported that he had found a part-time job and felt 'more manly and less of a serf'. He commented that the counsellor looked tired. Here was perhaps the beginning of some expression of his guilt towards his wife, but the session was a warmer, happier one, with Donna drawing a picture for the counsellor to take with her.

Comment

The counsellor's efforts in this case to facilitate the mourning process had to be limited to promoting communication and supporting the parental functioning. Father, a hostile and paranoid man, was able to talk about his wife and his feelings about her death, especially his feelings of anger and helplessness. This seemed to free him to care for the children and to seek a job but he was unable to listen to the children's communications, even when the therapist tried to interpret them to him. She was able to model for the father ways of parenting the children more effectively.

The three case studies above are examples of the use of family sessions to open up communication about death which enables the bereaved families to function more healthily and to be less incapacitated by the death of an important family member. It remains to be seen when the follow-up study is complete, whether the unselected bereaved families who had the family sessions do better than the control families who are not being offered intervention.

THE TREATMENT OF MORBID GRIEF

So far we have been discussing work with families who are about to experience or have suffered a recent bereavement. The aim here is to facilitate the expression of grief, and communication within the family. However, individuals and families often present to psychiatric clinics with disorders which are seen to be associated with a previous bereavement, and may have been caused by it. Pincus (1976) and Paul (1967) describe the effect on marriages of unresolved mourning and treat the marriage by promoting

mourning. Paul and Grosser (1965) and Lieberman (1978) use
what the former calls operational mourning and the latter calls
forced mourning to treat individuals where a previous bereavement
appears to be causing present disorder. Both of them advocate
treating the whole family and Lieberman considers the method to
be contraindicated only if the patient has few social supports and
many social and financial problems.

Uncovering a grief that went wrong may also be helpful in children.
I have described elsewhere (Black, 1976) the case of Steven, age
6, whose brother's death two years earlier for which he felt
responsible had led to his failing at school. The cause of this
academic failure was a psychogenic deafness, which was due to
an identification with the dead brother who Steven thought had
fallen to his 'deaf' instead of to his death. One family therapy
session was sufficient to release him from his silent prison of
guilt and follow-up two years later confirmed that he was well.

A 6-year-old boy, with symptoms of separation anxiety, whose
father had died two years earlier explained that his father had died
of a heart attack. 'What's that?', I asked, and he replied: 'Well
you know when soldiers are in battle, one side attacks the other.'
It did not take long to establish that he feared that his dead
father would punish the boy for being presumptuous enough to
attack his heart; thus he dared not leave the safety of his mother's
side. Psychotherapy helped him to mourn his father and bury him
beyond danger.

PREVENTION

All that lives must die   ('Hamlet')

Evidence is accumulating from animal experiments (Seligman, 1975)
that the lack of a sense of mastery and control over one's life
predisposes to depression and even death.

Can it be that the cause of the increased morbidity and mortality
following bereavement is associated with feelings of helplessness?
If so, it seems important that those who have the care of children
help them to acquire coping skills to deal with bereavement. Small
losses are the rehearsal for larger ones and must be given due
importance and mourned appropriately, not dismissed. Children
must be included in the mourning rituals of adults and be taken
to the funerals of acquaintances or distant relatives. The first
death they come close to should not have to be that of a parent or
a sibling. Death must be seen to be the inevitable end to life and
no longer a taboo subject, so that when death hits close to home,
the individual will have the strength drawn from his past experience to cope. It is in the family setting that coping is learned
and it is in that same setting that we can intervene and treat
acute or morbid grief to prevent later dysfunction. I suggest
that in all family situations where attachment pathology may occur,
e.g. separation anxiety, adolescent separation problems and bereavement, family therapy is indicated (Martin, 1977; Heard, 1978).

CONCLUSION

Family therapy is useful as a method of treating morbid grief, and as an intervention in acute grief to promote mourning and teach coping-strategies to children. The modelling role of the therapist is important as is the encouragement of the family to mourn the little loss of the therapist at the conclusion of the intervention.

Acknowledgments to R. Goldberg, J. Hildebrand and H. Jewitt, the social workers involved in the case studies, and to Stevie Smith's executor, James MacGibbon, for permission to re-print the poem, 'No Respect', from 'The Collected Poems of Stevie Smith' (Allen Lane).

REFERENCES

Anthony, S. (1941) 'The Child's Discovery of Death', Routledge & Kegan Paul, London.

Birtchnell, J. (1972) Early Parent Death and Psychiatric Diagnosis, 'Social Psychiat.', 7, 202-10.

Black, D. (1976) Intervention with Bereaved Families, 'J. Assn Workers Malad. Children', 4:1, 28-34.

Black, D. (1978) Annotation:- The Bereaved Child, 'J. Child Psychol. Psychiat.', 19:3, 287-92.

Bowen, M. (1976) Family Reaction to Death, in P.G. Guerin (ed.), 'Family Therapy, Theory and Practice', Gardner, New York, pp. 335-48.

Bowlby, J. (1963) Pathological Mourning and Childhood Mourning, 'J. Am. Psycho-Analyt. Ass.', 11, 500-41.

Bowlby, J. (1969 and 1973) 'Attachment & Loss, vols 1 and 2', Hogarth Press, London and Penguin, Harmondsworth.

Bowlby, J. and Parkes, C.M. (1970) Separation and Loss Within the Family, in C.J. Anthony and C. Koupernik (eds), 'The Child and his Family', John Wiley, New York.

Burton, L. (1974) Tolerating the Intolerable - the problems facing parents and children following diagnosis, in L. Burton (ed.), 'Care of the Child Facing Death', Routledge & Kegan Paul, London.

Freud, S. (1917) 'Mourning and Melancholia', Standard Edn, vol. 14.

Fried, M. (1962) Grieving for a Lost Home, in L.J. Duhl (ed.), 'The Environment of the Metropolis', Basic Books, New York.

Granville-Grossman, K.L. (1968) The Early Development in Affective Disorders, in A. Coppen and A. Walk (eds), RMPA, Headley, Ashford, Kent.

Heard, D. (1978) From Object Relations to Attachment Theory: a Basis for Family Therapy, 'Br. J. Med. Psychol.', 51, 67-76.

Koocher, G.P. (1974) Talking with Children about Death, 'Am. J. Orthopsychiat.', 44, 404-11.

Lewis, E. (1976) The Management of Stillbirth, 'Lancet', 2, 619-20.

Lieberman, S. (1978) Nineteen Cases of Morbid Grief, 'Brit. J. Psychiat.', 132, 159-63.

Lindemann, E. (1944) The Symptomatology and Management of Acute Grief, 'Amer. J. Psychiat.', 101, 141.

Maddison, D. and Walker, W.L. (1967) Factors affecting the

Outcome of Conjugal Bereavement, 'Brit. J. Psychiat.', 113, 1057.

Martin, F. (1977) Some Implications from the Theory and Practice of Family Therapy for Individual Therapy, 'Brit. J. Med. Psychol.', 50, 53–64.

Minuchin, S. (forthcoming) 'Training for Spontaneity', to be published.

Parkes, C.M. (1971) Psychosocial Transitions: a field for study, 'Soc. Sci. and Med.', 6.

Parkes, C.N. (1972) 'Bereavement: Studies of Grief in Adult Life', Tavistock, London.

Parkes, C.M. (1975) Psychosocial Transitions: comparison between reactions to loss of a limb and loss of a spouse, 'Brit. J. Psychiat.', 127, 204–10.

Parkes, C.M. (1977a) Evaluation of Family Care in Terminal Illness, in E.R. Pritchard et al. (eds), 'Social Work with the Dying Patient and the Family', Columbia University Press, New York.

Parkes, C.M. (1977b) What becomes of Redundant World Models?, 'Brit. J. Med. Psychol.', 48, 131–7.

Parkes, C.M., Benjamin, B. and Fitzgerald, R.G. (1969) Broken Heart: a statistical study of increased mortality among widowers, 'Brit. Med. J.', (1), 740.

Pattison, E.M. (1976) The Fatal Myth of Death in the Family, 'Amer. J. Psychiat.', 133:6, 674–8.

Paul, N.L. (1967) The Role of Mourning and Empathy in Conjoint Marital Therapy, in G.H. Zuk and I. Boszormenyi-Nagy (eds), 'Family Therapy and Disturbed Families', Science and Behaviour Books, Palo Alto.

Paul, N.L. and Grosser, G.H. (1965) Operational Mourning and its Role in Conjoint Family Therapy, 'Community Mental Health Journal', 1, 4.

Pincus, L. (1976) 'Death and the Family', Faber, London.

Raphael, B. and Maddison, D. (1976) The Care of Bereaved Adults, in O.W. Hill (ed.), 'Modern Trends in Psychosomatic Medicine', 3, Butterworths, London, pp. 491–506.

Rees, W.D. and Lutkins, S.G. (1967) Mortality of Bereavement, 'Brit. Med. J.', (4):13.

Robertson, J. (1968) 'Young Children in Hospital', Tavistock, London.

Rutter, M. (1966) 'Children of Sick Parents', Oxford University Press.

Rutter, M. (1972) 'Maternal Deprivation Re-assessed', Penguin, Harmondsworth.

Rutter, M., Graham, P., Chadwick, O. and Yule, W. (1976) Adolescent Turmoil: fact or fiction?, 'J. Child Psychol. Psychiat.', 17, 35–6.

Seligman, M.E.P. (1975) 'Helplessness – Depression, Development and Death', Freeman, San Francisco.

Wolfenstein, M. (1966) How is Mourning Possible? 'Psychoanalytic Study of the Child', Vol. 21 International Universities Press, New York, pp. 93–123.

Young, M., Benjamin, B. and Wallis, C. (1963) Mortality of Widowers, 'Lancet', 2, 454.

12 BRIEF FOCAL FAMILY THERAPY WHEN THE CHILD IS THE REFERRED PATIENT

Arnon Bentovim and
Warren Kinston

PART I CLINICAL

INTRODUCTION

Over the past two decades there has been considerable interest in
finding ways to shorten psychotherapeutic work, and generally
increase the efficiency of psychiatric professionals via brief intervention methods (Malan, 1963: Sifneos, 1967; Parad and Parad,
1968; Small, 1971). This trend has only relatively recently become evident in the field of child and adolescent psychiatry,
coincident with the development of theories and techniques which
recognize the parents, extended family, and social network both
as targets for change and agents of change (Skynner, 1969;
Rosenthal and Levine, 1970; Argles and Mackenzie, 1970; Leventhal
and Weinberger, 1975; Minuchin et al., 1975).

Within the broad rubric of 'family therapy', many treatment
approaches have been used. Most of the shorter methods require
an active technique with the therapist engaging directly with the
family members, setting family tasks, openly acting as a model of
healthy functioning, providing videotape feedback of interactions,
interfering with dysfunctional behaviour patterns, advising, or
consciously double-binding (Alger and Hogan, 1969; Beels and
Ferber, 1969; Zuk, 1968; Haley, 1971; Crowe, 1973; Minuchin, 1974).
Even those techniques more directly emerging from psychoanalytic
theory, as described by Ackerman (1958), Dicks (1967), Zinner
and Shapiro (1974) and Boszormenyi-Nagy and Spark (1973), involve considerably more therapist activity and direction than is
customary in individual psychoanalytic therapy.

In our own growing experience of working with families con-
jointly over the past ten years in the Department of Psychological
Medicine at the Hospital for Sick Children, London, we have become
impressed by the value of family intervention whatever the orientation of the therapist. Diagnostic work usually takes place in a
family setting and wherever possible treatment aims are rapidly
clarified so as to harness the charge of potential associated with the
first meeting between a disturbed family and the professional (Haley,
1970). The problem then arises to determine an appropriate treatment technique to maintain and foster alterations in family function-

ing. Without a clear purpose or technique it is easy to allow work to become diffuse, commonly followed by various family members opting out. A particular problem is the emergence during family work of hidden problems and demands, most commonly in our experience in relation to long-standing, but carefully avoided, severe marital disturbance.

The success in shortening individual psychoanalytic therapy by using a focal approach (Malan, 1963; Balint et al., 1972) suggested the application of a similar model to family work. A work-shop was set up to enable staff to develop a 'family focus'. An experienced staff member of the Tavistock Clinic's Brief Psychotherapy Workshop agreed to act as consultant and group leader during the first year (1973-4) and cases were brought, family sessions written up, and the treatment process followed. This paper exemplifies the clinical work done with this 'brief focal' model. The results are set out in a second paper (Kinson and Bentovim, 1978). (See pp. 216-45).

THE WORKSHOP PROCEDURE

Following the department's full diagnostic procedure, the case was brought by the therapist(s) who provided the workshop members with details of the referral, a brief description of the family, and the salient pathological factors with elaboration as necessary. The workshop developed a hypothesis to explain the symptom in terms of the salient factors and a minimum of psychodynamic understanding. This 'focal hypothesis' then became a reference point for therapeutic progress, and a source of predictions for assessment of success or failure of the treatment. The actual treatment is determined by the 'focal plan' which suggests how the desired change is to be brought about. This plan varied from straightforward direction to the therapist, e.g. 'interpret the dynamics, i.e. the focal hypothesis', or 'get father to go out more with mother', to more subtle demands, e.g. 'clarify communication' or 'increase sharing of feelings'. The values of the workshop were psychodynamic in so far as there was emphasis on the importance of developmental factors, the needs of the family members to feel understood, and the necessity for a working alliance. As the treatment unfolded, new phenomena or information sometimes came to light which demanded a revision of the focal hypothesis or focal plan. To illustrate the process of developing a focal hypothesis and arriving at and implementing a focal plan, two cases will be described. In the first a focal plan could be formulated early and worked with consistently to termination, while in the other it could only be arrived at over a period of time as the therapists worked to create a 'shape' in the diffuseness of the pathology.

CASE 1: MARGARET AND HER FAMILY

Family
Margaret's family consisted of her father (43) and mother (37),
both secondary school teachers, and two sisters. Margaret at 10
was the youngest, Alice was 13 and June 15.

Referral
Although Margaret had suffered from complex tics since the age
of 4, these had become increasingly frequent and severe. The
abnormal movements included sniffing, coughing, snorting, sudden
teeth clenching, flapping of the elbow, slapping her chest or
thighs with both hands, and sudden stamping on the floor.

Salient facts from the history
Family history of illness: Maternal grandmother – chronic arthritis.
Three paternal uncles – all with moderately severe depression.
    1964: Mother suffers a depression (Margaret is 6 months).
    1967: The family moves from the north of England to London,
Margaret (4) commences school and her symptoms appear. Mother
starts at a teachers' training college.
    1970: Father becomes redundant, but appears unconcerned.
June (12) has tension headaches followed by eye-blinking. Mother
has a recurrence of her depression.
    1971: Father then takes up teachers' training. June's symptoms
remit.
    1973 (time of referral): Margaret's symptoms worsen. Father
is in his first year as a teacher at a school with high academic
standards but pupils of mediocre ability, and mother is also teaching.
Both parents are extremely conscientious about their jobs and work
hard to be successful. This attitude extends to home life, with
father doing chores which could be done by other family members
and mother doing a great deal for the children and effectively
treating them as if they were much younger than they are.

Observations of family interaction
    (a) There was a marked restriction of verbal and non-verbal
expression of feelings, and communication generally was marked
by inhibition of activity.
    (b) Feelings of anger, depression and areas of conflict were
avoided by all family members. Father, particularly, was not able
to tolerate and respond supportively to his wife's depression.
    (c) The family as a group depreciated itself, and members
failed to express appreciation of each other.
    (d) Each family member had excessively high standards of per-
formance for himself and for the others, resulting in a sense of
failure in the family atmosphere. This extended to the parent's
sexual relationship.

Dynamic hypotheses
After combining the salient facts with the observations at interview,
two focal hypotheses were determined.

1.   Margaret's tics were a way for her to deal with feelings
which could not be communicated within the family atmosphere of
inhibition, and with a desire for activity which had to be suppressed
in accord with the same family rule.

2.   The excessively high standards together with the lack of
mutual support and appreciation within the family meant that the
members' self-esteem and sense of well-being could not be maintained.

Focal plan
In this case, the plan follows from the hypotheses in that the
aim is to help the family appreciate the extent of the inhibition
they impose on themselves, to promote freer communication of
feelings, and to encourage expression of mutual appreciation
within the family. A series of ten interviews were suggested for
the carrying out of this plan . . . the interviews to be scheduled
at three weekly intervals approximately.

Developments in treatment
The ten interviews extended from November 1973 to June 1974.
Initially sharing of feelings and free communication between family
members was frustrated by June who routinely came between the
parents and overwhelmed mother at the expense of the other
children. This was observed in the sessions and reported by the
family. At home she monopolized mother, particularly late in the
evenings, and so prevented the parents from being together.
She was actively in competition with her younger siblings and
failed to appreciate their interests and capacities. The therapists
pointed out that the parents were allowing June to cross the
generational boundaries and prevent them having an adult relationship. They were also letting her prevent them from responding to the
other children and their needs. June's role in the family and the
family's collusion in its maintenance having been clarified and
challenged, mother's difficulties became apparent. She had a tendency to take over for the children and to speak for them. This
over-protectiveness was foiling their emancipation which she both
wanted and dreaded. Mother's dependency needs had not been
adequately met due to her own mother having suffered from an
arthritic condition. She took her needs to professional colleagues
rather than to her family. Father emerged as a family scapegoat in
spite of, or perhaps because of, his efforts to live up to family
expectations and meet his own ideals. His efforts left him and the
family frustrated.

An extract from the second interview will illustrate some of these
points.

After a period of limited spontaneous conversation, therapist B
asked June, who had been lively in the previous session, why she
was less lively on this occasion. The family informed the therapist
that June was writing examinations. Mother added that June had
got up early, panicked and did not seem to realize that panic would
not help. June was at the stage where she did not have enough

confidence - her parents had, her teachers had, but June did not.
Therapist A commented that the family as a whole seemed frightened
of trying anything new. He observed that although it was only June
who had the exam, no one else seemed lively either. There then
followed a spirited discussion as to how they had gone half a mile
west of the hospital and had walked back from the tube station
because they were early, and father had taken them the wrong way.
Alice retorted that 'he always did'. June said: 'I told him before
we started but he wouldn't listen.' Father then explained that he
had done this to check whether cheap seats were available at the
theatre for him to take the family after the interview. He did
not tell them because he was afraid that they would be disappointed
if his plan was not possible. He was also half afraid that June might
say she wanted to go to a different show and he wanted to avoid
challenging her over this. The family said that he tended to be
secretive like this and wanted to make decisions silently, expecting
others to read his mind without telling them what or why. Therapist
B suggested that perhaps father wanted to keep the plan secret
to avoid arguments since he always wanted to be right. He agreed
and the rest of the family laughed. June said Margaret was like
that as well.

This extract illustrates the inhibition of communication, the fear
of confrontation, the lack of appreciation, and the failed attempt
to be ideal with consequent frustration. It also shows the style of
therapist intervention and the family response. A subsequent interview with the parents alone clarified the patterns further. June had
been conceived too soon after the marriage, at which time father
became increasingly concerned about financial security and the need
to work more and mother became depressed. This set the stage for
distance between the parents, June's monopoly of mother and
conflict with father, and subsequent dysfunction. The parents were
poorly synchronized with each other in various areas of living,
e.g. when one was sleepy, the other was wakeful. Their difficulty
in achieving pleasure, emotional and sexual, within the family
relationship was reflected in their over-emphasis on the importance
of work, and cast a shadow on family life. When the family was more
relaxed during holiday periods, Margaret's tics were very much
less in evidence.

The family attended from a considerable distance and could accept
that Margaret's tics were only a part of the problem and everybody
and the family as a whole were in need of help. The inhibition of
talking and involvement was particularly marked in the two younger
girls. Alice behaved as a rather amused onlooker, while Margaret
was quite passive apart from her tics which became more directly
related to family stress during the course of therapy. Haloperidol
was tried with some benefit at one stage, but was discontinued
due to its side effects. The problem of inhibition within the family
was raised by the therapists and worked on repeatedly, especially
in relation to pleasure. There was a shared fear, most marked in
mother, that airing of such wishes might prove catastrophic, with
the wish for pleasure taking over and stopping any work at all.

Inhibition of anger was not dealt with in as much depth, except in relation to June's controlling ways with mother. Father's fear of depression was also barely touched. The problems of self-esteem were worked on in various ways. Father was able to admit his anxieties over his performance at work. At home he was set the task of getting the children to do household chores and get round on their own. Both parents were encouraged to appreciate their children and vice versa. Previously efforts had been unnoticed, e.g. the children's achievements at work and music, or taken for granted, e.g. father's organization of outings.

The workshop consensus was that the focal plan had been adhered to. Issues unrelated to the focal plan had emerged and been by-passed, e.g. sexual problems between the parents and sexual anxieties in the relationship between father and June. The focal plan had been clearly understood by the family and they had changed in response to the therapeutic effort.

Short-term follow-up
The method we have employed lends itself to meaningful follow-up assessments, as the focal hypotheses by their nature provide criteria by which assessment of change may be evaluated (Malan, 1959). In the case of Margaret's family the criteria would be as follows: each member should have access to the whole range of emotions and be able to communicate freely within the family; intra-family criticism should be low and mutual support and appreciation should be evident; the atmosphere generally should be pleasant with no member suffering undue depression; the tics should be absent.

A follow-up interview three months later confirmed the impression of real change in the family and its members. At this interview the girls were more relaxed and interacted more freely. The family began by describing a recent incident when June was out with Margaret. Margaret had tried to take over the parental role, telling June not to eat chewing gum just before dinner. In order to change the subject June got Margaret to race her home, but June slipped in the mud and got quite plastered in mess - so much so that she felt quite unable to cope. This was recounted with much amusement. Margaret at this point stopped fidgeting and pointed out that she had helped June by picking up the shopping and making her a cup of tea. Therapist A suggested that it was as if June really felt knocked out of her grown-up role and thrown in a baby one, and half-expected Margaret to pick her up. The family laughed at the incongruity. Both June and Alice then talked about their grown-up activities. June described her recent boy-friend and Alice her drama classes. Margaret had also shown she was more grown-up: once her parents had forgotten to collect her from her girl's club and instead of just sitting down and crying as she would have done previously she telephoned to remind them. The interview contained much less mutual criticism although mother felt that Margaret was more provocative and sometimes more babyish. The tics were much reduced. The family did not wish further help but wanted to keep a line open to the therapists if necessary.

Conclusion
In this family the focal plan was aimed at promoting freer communication, increasing mutual appreciation, and loosening inhibition of
feelings. It was adhered to and succeeded in considerably alleviating
the presenting symptom (tics), releasing the maturation processes
in the 'well' siblings, and permitting the parents a closer relationship with each other and a more realistic and gratifying relationship
with their children, particularly with respect to fostering their
emotional growth and development. Limitations are clearly apparent:
the symptom is not totally removed, marital difficulties are still
present, and individual members are still struggling with significant
emotional problems. This family was given a rating of 'some improvement' - on our scale of 'no improvement', 'some improvement' and
'much improvement', and Margaret was rated as 'much improved'.

CASE 2: RACHEL AND HER PARENTS

Family
Rachel was a 5-year-old girl with a sister, Beth, 2 years younger.
The parents are in their early 30s and work professionally, having
been brought up and trained abroad.

Referral
Rachel was referred with temper outbursts and excessive fearfulness and anxiety. Initially the case was dealt with by providing
individual therapy for Rachel. Over six months a social worker
saw mother or father (depending on who brought Rachel up for
her session). However, while Rachel made good progress, the
parents became increasingly disturbed. Both parents formed intense and somewhat sexualized relationships with the social worker
and the mother became increasingly dependent. It was felt that
such strong feelings might be appropriately directed towards each
other rather than to the social worker who was not seeing them
in a therapeutic setting which permitted resolution. Conjoint meetings including both parents, the social worker and a psychiatrist
were arranged specifically to work on these problems after individual
therapy with Rachel ceased. Beth's development and psychiatric
status were within normal limits and as the focus was a marital one
it was decided not to involve her in specific treatment.

Salient facts from the history
Both parents had major difficulties in their families of origin.
Father's father, a school headmaster, was often absent during his
childhood, and his mother was depressed and suicidal for many
years. Mother in her family, had always felt pushed out by a
younger sibling, and her father had been absent also while being
idolized by her mother. She denigrated her mother but felt identified with her. Both Rachel's parents found a solution (partially)
in their work, and used their work role as a source of identity
and a means of valuation as individuals. Even after marriage they

had continued to use people, work and situations outside the
marriage to obtain satisfaction for their needs, and did not turn to
each other. Both worked very long hours, father especially leaving
mother at home alone and depressed. They led separate lives.

Observations of marital interaction
Neither parent perceived the needs of the other and both avoided
communicating about their own needs and pain. They expressed
intense anger about their parents, their marriage and the therapists
in a messy way, scattering cigarette ash around the room and
using sexual talk similarly. Simultaneously they were frightened of
the damage they might cause. They were unable to help each other;
each emphasized his own vulnerability while being patronizing and
critical of the other.

Dynamic hypothesis
Both parents have been unable to find their own identity and have
obtained security via self-idealization. Each is frightened of intense
primitive rage and neither is able to see the other in a real and
caring way.

Focal plan
It took a number of sessions to formulate the above hypotheses
and develop a workable focal plan. It was decided that the therapists
should aim at making the therapeutic situation a containing environment where better communication could be established with consequent reduction of primitive fears, opportunity for contact with
each other's personal reality, and the possibility of sharing and
mutuality. Contact with their own capacity to care would both
enable them to support each other and permit greater responsiveness
to the children. It was decided that meetings should be held weekly
for six months.

Developments in treatment
Not surprisingly, the focal plan was not easy to implement. Both
parents wanted to be therapists: father was critical and mother
patronizing, and the sessions were initially vague, messy and
permeated with hostility. Mother was particularly angry about
having to share the sessions and give up her idealized relationship.
She had affairs which upset the marriage as well as disrupting the
basis of the focal plan. Father was no less disturbed. Both showed
defensive play-acting in the sessions with little openness or change
in their behaviour and ways of relating. They initially pretended
to meet the focus while looking for magical solutions outside the
marriage as they had always done. Mother was pushed by father
into the 'sick role' and used it to gain attention.

   An extract from an early session exemplifies the issues: Father
reported his absolute fury and anger at finding that his wife was
having an affair with a man whom he sees as being in a position of
responsibility. He stated that he was so furious that he thought
of leaving his wife, writing to the man (her boss) and 'bashing

him up'. By the time of the session he just wanted to get rid of such awful feelings. He described his idea of marriage: an ordinary ideal everyday middle-class existence with extra stimuli from intellectual things and with each partner making the other stronger and cutting out weaknesses and failings. Therapist C queried the possibility of strength being built up by meeting each others needs rather than ignoring them. While father was saying that needs were not important, the therapist believed that weaknesses were just as important as strengths. Mother was distressed that therapist D did not share her view that there was nothing to apologize for over the whole affair. She suggested that forgetting was the best way of coping with anger and perhaps she just needed another man: father had been unfaithful and she was just testing him to see if he cared. She knew that what he wanted was what she did not want. She wanted to be herself. Therapist C suggested that perhaps she did not really want to be married at all, and that there had been a good deal of deception and falsity in the marriage – playing at being married. Mother agreed that she liked to seem close to her husband in public, whilst being very distant at home; and father said that he was not ready for marriage. Both felt that there were many skeletons in both their cupboards. The therapists emphasized that despite its hurtfulness, father's anger about the affair had not been destructive but rather evidence that he cared and provided attention for her. Mother claimed it was the attention that a naughty girl got from father and not the response she expected from a husband.

The next extract from a session about two months later shows the beginning of change which subsequently progressed further: Father stated that 'when we talk, we block about needs – we don't seem to get anywhere.' He then asked mother what her needs were. Mother replied 'Can't we talk about them later? . . . well I need tenderness.' Father said that he needed commitment. Mother then spoke about how unsatisfied she was with her mother, and therapist C referred to the difficulty she had in foregoing her individual sessions (with therapist D) and wondered about dependency. Mother reacted strongly: 'dependency!? a horrid word – surely we don't have to be dependent on each other?' Father asked what was wrong with dependency and mother replied that it meant being controlled – people who are dependent on her are so puny and they are demanding and she cannot bear demands. She preferred angry people and then she could respond. Therapist C then pointed out that she seemed to perceive dependency as controlling and being controlled, overwhelming and being overwhelmed, and involving total submission rather than a part of herself being dependent on her husband and part of her husband being dependent on her. Father then asked 'Why, if you are so afraid of dependence, why do you stay with me?' Mother broke down in tears and sobs, acknowledging she wants her husband, likes him, and really is dependent on him. Father moved his chair so he could comfort her and though mother said she liked it, she simultaneously shifted her position so that she was turned away from him. Her non-verbal contradiction

of her verbal acceptance was made explicit in the therapy, and
discussed.

Therapy was completed in six months as planned, and over this
time communication improved and became more real and direct.
The couple ceased attacking each other, and reduced their mutual
denigration, hence they could move closer together. Their capacity
to care for each other increased and at the end of the period,
mother became pregnant. Trust remained fragile and communication
at times was difficult. Both showed changes as individuals: father
becoming more open and mother less attention seeking.

Short-term follow-up
In the case of Rachel's family the criteria derived from the focal
hypotheses would be: the parents should obtain need gratification
within the family as indicated by spending time together with
pleasure; practical and emotional support should be evident; the
parents should be able to describe themselves and each other in
a realistic and sympathetic way; no member should be symptomatic.

At five months after the last session most of these criteria were
met. Rachel's symptoms were fully abated, Beth continued well,
mother was enjoying domestication, and father though angry and
authoritarian was good humoured. The parents remained able to
discuss problems and see each others point of view, sharing conflict
and giving in when necessary.

Conclusion
Following a period of individual treatment of the child, marital
problems became evident. Although a simple operational focus could
not be defined, a plan was devised which enabled the therapists to
sustain a therapeutic relationship and help the parents examine
the similar personal problems which led them to marry and inevitably
run into difficulties. The dynamic hypothesis guided the interventions which consistently aimed at confronting the idealized expectation of the other, and revealing each as a real person with needs
which could be meaningfully gratified within the marriage. In this
case both the family and the index patient received ratings of
'much improved'.

DISCUSSION

The two cases described above demonstrate the applicability of a
time-limited active focal approach. The first case described was
an integrated family with high motivation for change. The members
showed willingness to accede to therapist directions and had no
difficulty in accepting the authority of the therapist. The presenting
symptom could be easily linked to family stresses, and the nature
of the stress as experienced by individual members was in terms
of easily understandable emotions. The required changes in interaction were not difficult to define and once the family were in a
working alliance simply indicating problems led to alterations in

family functioning. In the second case the therapists were faced with a quite different situation. Both parents were suffering from severe characterological disturbances and the marital relationship had few positive qualities for the therapists to begin work with. A simple description of dysfunctional aspects was impossible and the setting up of a working alliance was not to be taken for granted. It took longer to formulate a meaningful dynamic hypothesis and focal plan. Each of the parents were seen as similar: ignorant and frightened of their own needs and infiltrating their interactions with primitive aggression. The treatment focused on helping them form a real relationship rather than altering a number of unhelpful interactions. Not surprisingly more intensive work was required: twenty-five weekly sessions.

Other cases seen in the workshop improved as much as, or more than, the cases presented here; but many did not. This paper aims at characterizing the approach which we are convinced is a worthwhile and important one. It is not possible to comment in detail on the technical aspects of the work. The therapists were psychoanalysts, psychiatrists, psychologists and social workers, and their backgrounds and styles varied considerably. Using the criteria of the GAP Report (1970) they were Position M therapists. They encouraged interaction between family members and took up verbal and non-verbal aspects of the interaction. The experiences and problems of individuals were not avoided but related to the family context and to other family members. The psychoanalytic method of connecting present feelings, thoughts, and behaviour patterns to past events and experiences in the family and to aspects of the families of origin was used and found to be helpful. The therapists aimed to foster integration for the individual members as well as for the family, and also to provide the opportunity for corrective experiences. They provided education about developmental and emotional factors in family life, set tasks, modelled parental roles, and used challenges to dysfunctional value systems. The most characteristic aspect of psychoanalytic therapy – vigorous and detailed examination of the transference – was not a feature of the work, although working with marital couples brought such issues more to the fore where they could not be ignored. The various specific techniques currently being developed by family therapists (e.g. sculpting, genograms, videotape feed-back) were not used, though they are clearly adaptable for the type of approach described here.

We agree with Rosenthal and Levine (1970) that the high therapist motivation for short-term work, the pressure due to the time-limit, the collaboration between family and therapist, the clear definition of goals, the clarification and use of family strengths, and the open invitation to the family to return if necessary are all major factors in the success of a brief approach. Goals, by themselves, are not enough to guide the therapist as it is commonly not apparent why the family members let themselves persist in interacting dysfunctionally. The perception of a 'workable/meaningful focus' is an important aid to the therapist enabling him to use his skills

and abilities without the diffusion of effort or inappropriate narrow-
ing of attention which can occur so easily in work with families.
Although our therapists have had considerable experience in many
forms of individual and group treatments of varying orientations,
none have had formal training in family therapy – for which, in
any case, no standard technique has emerged. The focused approach
became an easily assimilated 'technique'. A further factor in our
success in this venture requires mention: the workshop. Malan
(1963) indicated the power of the group to foster a particular
philosophy and way of working. Not only does the discipline of
having one's work scrutinized increase involvement and enthusiasm
for the work itself, but its supportive (and sometimes critical)
function enables the therapists to maintain role and not drift into
colluding with the family system or lose the focus. Sharing one's
knowledge of the family and reporting sessions enables transference
and counter-transference difficulties to be more rapidly recognized.
They need to be understood and dealt with, even though they will
usually not be interpreted to the family. At this stage we cannot
know how far being a workshop member increased the effectiveness
of the work, and whether the skill of recognizing and pursuing
a workable focus without support and lengthy discussion has been
retained.

CONCLUSION

This paper describes a style of family work which initially derived
from the brief individual psychoanalytic therapy developed at the
Tavistock Clinic by Malan and co-workers. The approach is highly
suitable for use in busy Child Guidance Clinics where the alternatives are no treatment at all, or occasional supportive interviews
with counselling. Even where resources are available, the method
may prove a treatment of choice offering an opportunity for the
improvement of the context of the individual's emotional life. The
approach emphasizes seeing the whole family or marital couple,
determining a few dynamic hypotheses which organize the salient
facts from the history with observations of family interaction, and
then constructing a focal plan. This plan links with the hypotheses
but is operational and serves as a guide and reference point for
the therapist in his work with the family. The frequency of sessions
varies from once- to six-weekly, and period of contact is between
three and nine months. The therapeutic technique is an active one
which does not rest on any rigid theoretical ideas. A contract and
working alliance are set up in the initial sessions which also provide
further opportunity for alteration of the hypotheses or plan. The
role of the workshop group in supporting the therapist and helping
the therapeutic work is emphasized. Two cases with very different
psychopathology and family pathology have been described as
examples of the clinical process.

REFERENCES

Ackerman, N.W. (1958) 'The Psychodynamics of Family Life. Diagnosis and Treatment of Family Relationships', Basic Books, New York.

Alger, I. and Hogan, P. (1969) Enduring Effects of Videotape Playback Experience on Family and Marital Relationships, 'Am. J. Orthopsychiat.', 39, 86–98.

Argles, P. and Mackenzie, M. (1970) Crisis Intervention with a Multi-problem Family - a Case Study, 'J. Child Psychol. Psychiat.', 11, 187–96.

Balint, M., Balint, E. and Ornstein, P.H. (1972) 'Focal Psychotherapy. An Example of Applied Psychoanalysis', Mind and Medicine Monographs, London.

Beels, C.C. and Ferber, A.S. (1969) Family Therapy: a View, 'Fam. Proc.', 8, 280–318.

Boszormenyi-Nagy, I. and Spark, G.M. (1973) 'Invisible Loyalties', Harper & Row, New York.

Crowe, M.J. (1973) Conjoint Marital Therapy: Advice or Interpretation, 'J. Psychosom. Res.', 17, 309–15.

Dicks, H.V. (1967) 'Marital Tensions', Basic Books, New York.

GAP (Group for the Advancement of Psychiatry) (1970) 'The Field of Family Therapy', vol. 7, Report no. 78.

Haley, J. (ed.) (1971) 'Changing Families', Grune & Stratton, New York.

Haley, J. (1970) Family Therapy, 'Int. J. Psychiat.', 9, 233–42.

Kinston, W. and Bentovim, A. (1978) Brief Focal Family Therapy when the Child is the Referred Patient - II. Methodology and Results. 'J. Child Psychol. Psychiat.', 19, 119–43 (see pp. 216–45, below).

Leventhal, T. and Weinberger, G. (1975) Evaluation of a large-scale brief therapy program for children, 'Am. J. Orthopsychiat.', 45, 119–33.

Malan, D.H. (1959) On assessing the results of psychotherapy, 'Br. J. Med. Psychol.', 32, 86–105.

Malan, D.H. (1963) 'A Study of Brief Psychotherapy', Tavistock, London.

Minuchin, S. (1974) 'Families and Family Therapy', Harvard University Press, Cambridge.

Minuchin, S., Baker, L., Rosman, B.L., Liebman, R., Milman, L. and Todd, T.C. (1975) A conceptual model of psychosomatic illness in children. Family organization and family therapy, 'Archs Gen. Psychiat.', 32, 1031–8.

Parad, H. and Parad, L. (1968) A study of crisis-oriented planned short-term treatment: Part 1, 'Soc. Casework', 49, 346–55.

Rosenthal, A. and Levine, S. (1970) Brief psychotherapy with children: a preliminary report, 'Am. J. Psychiat.', 127, 646–51.

Sifneos, P.E. (1967) Two different kinds of psychotherapy of short duration, 'Am. J. Psychiat.', 123, p. 9.

Skynner, A.C. (1969) Indications and contra-indications for conjoint family therapy, 'Int. J. Soc. Psychiat.', 15(4) 245–9.

Small, L. (1971) 'The Briefer Psychotherapies', Brunner-Mazel, New York.

Zinner, J. and Shapiro, R. (1974) The family group as a single psychic entity: implications for acting out in adolescence, 'Int. Rev. Psycho-anal.', 1, 179-86.

Zuk, G.H. (1968) Prompting change in family therapy, 'Archs Gen. Psychiat.', 19(6) 727-36.

PART II   METHODOLOGY AND RESULTS

INTRODUCTION

Over the past twenty years, consideration of the family as a target
for change in child psychiatry has become established (GAP Report,
1970; Sager and Kaplan, 1972). In our growing experience of
working with families in the Department of Psychological Medicine
at the Hospital for Sick Children, we have become convinced of
its usefulness in producing symptomatic remission in children.
However, despite this, and other positive impressionistic reports
of the value of the family approach, there have been relatively few
attempts to evaluate it. Wells et al. (1972) reviewed the literature
and found only two studies, both of adults and from the same
research programme, which could be considered methodologically
adequate. Measurement of outcome in these two studies was based
on rates of rehospitalization. From a family theory point of view,
knowledge of family change is as important. However, despite a
large number of attempts (Straus, 1969), few instruments exist
with adequate psychometric properties to measure such changes.
One widely used test (Ferreira and Winter, 1965) is a decision-
making task: although it distinguishes normal and abnormal families,
it showed no change after family therapy (Ferreira and Winter,
1966). Most studies (Wells et al., 1972) relied on clinical judgment
despite its drawbacks. More recently, the particular difficulties
in this field have been reviewed by Framo (1972) and Cromwell
et al., (1976).
    We have been concerned not only about the conflicting merits of
child vs family treatment (McDermott and Char, 1974) and the
implications for resource allocation, but also with the question as
to whether families were actually changing as a result of our therapy.
These concerns led us to develop a time-limited focused technique
for use with families and to organize our data collection to include
evidence of family change. We were stimulated by the successful
use of a focal approach to shorten individual psychoanalytic therapy,
introduced by Balint et al. (1972) and developed by Malan (1963,
1976) at the Tavistock Clinic. In association with this therapeutic
model, Malan has developed a methodology for the assessment of
improvement on an 'individualized' basis (1959).
    Fiske et al. (1970) in their recommendations to researchers plan-
ning studies of effectiveness of psychotherapy note: 'Little systematic consideration has been given to the design and analysis of
studies oriented towards testing whether therapy produces particular effects designated as desirable for the individual patient.'
We wished to apply this to families. Practical and clinical factors
precluded the organization of a controlled trial, but we aimed to be
specific in our therapy and in our evaluation.
    To this end a weekly workshop was set up for staff to develop
and work on a family focus and to record relevant data. An experienced staff member of the Tavistock Clinic's Brief Psychotherapy
Workshop agreed to act as a consultant and Group Leader during

the first year (1973-4). Cases were brought, focal hypotheses and
plans made, criteria for success laid down and family sessions
written up and circulated so that the treatment process could be
followed. The clinical aspects of the work are described in an
accompanying paper with two cases presented in detail (Bentovim
and Kinston, 1977). The present paper describes the assessment
methodology, the operation of the workshop and all families seen
in the first two and a half years. The implications of the data
and difficulties in evaluating families are discussed.

METHODOLOGY

Origins of the method
As developed for brief individual psychotherapy, the assessment
carried out by Malan (Malan, 1959; Malan et al., 1968, 1975)
included:
   A. Basic details (name, age, complaints and their duration).
   B. All known disturbances in the patient's life with evidence
(usually under two headings: relationships and symptoms).
   C. A minimum psychodynamic hypothesis required to explain B
(varying from a simple description of overt conflict, to more conventional psychodynamic unconscious motivation).
   D. Evidence required for an assessment of the results of therapy
as determined by C (usually divided into the 'ideal' result, and a
discussion of the value of partial results).
   At this point the brief therapy is instituted and subsequently
followed up.
   E. All disturbances listed under B are re-examined at interview
and changes noted.
   F. Tentative psychodynamic assessment of the results by comparing D with E.
   The principles of psychodynamic assessment required an identification of the patient's 'predisposition' as well as the 'specific stress'
to which he was vulnerable. The predisposition referred to those
aspects of the patient's constitution that rendered him vulnerable.
The stress was sometimes an event and sometimes a 'vicious circle'
which interacted with the predisposition.
   The requirements for improvement psychodynamically were
(a) that the patient should be better than he was before the breakdown, i.e. the predisposition must be altered (and any other
personality changes achieved are secondary). The proof of this
required that the patient had been exposed again to the specific
precipitating stress and had reacted in a new and better way.
Any vicious circles that were present must have been broken by
the patient's efforts. (b) Not only must disturbances (symptoms
and vicious circles) have disappeared, but they must be replaced
by something positive, i.e. withdrawal or avoidance responses
are not enough. This requirement was particularly important when
predisposition or stress could not be identified.
   Finally as an essential part of the presentation of the findings,

Malan claimed it was necessary to provide the case material and
assessment in reasonably complete detail so that the reader could
critically draw his own conclusions about the final ratings of
improvement.

Procedure in the workshop
Following the department team's full diagnostic procedure (typically
multi-disciplinary and family oriented) a case could be brought by
the team members to the weekly one and a quarter hour workshop.
The workshop accepted any out-patient case excluding psychotic
children and this meant that initially 'problem' cases were brought.
In the discussion, hypotheses were developed which could encompass
the reason for referral and presenting symptoms, salient facts from
the history and observations of family interaction - using a minimum
of psychodynamic theory. These focal hypotheses then became the
reference point for therapeutic progress and the source of predictions for evaluation of outcome. At times new information came to
hand which made it necessary to modify the original hypothesis.
The workshop then determined a 'focal plan' which aimed to provide
the therapist with guidance as to how the desired changes were to
be brought about. The duration and frequency of sessions for the
successful completion of the focal plan were also estimated. These
conclusions formed the basis of the contract to be offered to the
family. All families were seen by two therapists, a common department practice, and both were required to be workshop members.
Usually cotherapists were male and female. Sessions were written
up by one or both therapists in detail and pre-circulated. The
workshop then functioned as a 'supervisor' for the therapy.
   Constructing a focal plan is required because the hypothesis
does not imply any therapeutic method. Malan (1959) omitted this
step presumably because the individual psychoanalytic therapy
he used implied a standardized therapeutic attitude and technique.
More recently, however, he has included discussion of a 'therapeutic plan' (Malan, 1976).

Therapy
Members of the workshop included psychiatrists, psychoanalysts,
social workers and psychologists. They varied in expertise and
theoretical orientation and many had experience in other forms of
individual and group treatments of children and parents. Their
styles differed and none had had formal training in specific
techniques of family therapy. The treatments had very little more
in common than that they were influenced by a focal plan constructed by psychodynamic hypotheses. In contrast to individual
therapy with its few powerful schools that serve as reference
points, family therapy is a melange of tactics and techniques (Beels
and Ferber, 1969; Haley, 1971; Bloch, 1973). Using the criteria
of the GAP Report (1970) on the field of family therapy, our
therapists were encouraged to be 'Position M' therapists, i.e. to
regard both individual and family factors as important. The tech-

nical aspects of therapy are outlined in the clinical paper
(Bentovim and Kinston, 1977).

REVIEW OF THE CASES

Demographic data
In the thirty months under review a total of twenty-nine cases were
managed under the auspices of the workshop. As a child psychiatry
facility we treated families referred for disturbance in the child.
Table 12.1 summarizes the distribution of ages, social class and
family size of the cases.

The majority (63 per cent) of referrals were pre-pubertal,
school-age children and most of the rest were in early adolescence.
The absence of children (i.e. referred children) over 14 is a reflection of the population which is referred to the Hospital for Sick
Children. In comparison to the department population, the social
class distribution showed an upward trend. About half of our
cases were in classes II or III and the rest were evenly divided
amongst class I or classes IV and V. In all cases but one, both
parents were alive, together, and required to participate actively
in the treatment. The unusual case, the 'B family', consisted of
three sisters and a brother between 3 and 8, in care of the local
authority, living together and referred as a group. Treatment
involved the housemother and a female helper from the residential
home. Most of the families were small: only 14 per cent (4) contained more than three children.

Referral data
Excluding the B family, 75 per cent of the referrals were boys and
25 per cent were girls. Sixty-one per cent of referrals were for
neurotic disturbances, and this included three asthmatic children
involved in a trial assessing the use of family therapy in asthmatics
irrespective of psychiatric presentation. The children showed a
large range of presenting symptoms: school refusal, separation
anxiety, excessive fearfulness, temper tantrums, stealing, learning problems, depression, irrational or immature behaviour, isolation, excessive masturbation, encopresis, tics, psychosomatic
disorder (polymyositis, migraine), and others. All cases reflected
longstanding disturbance in the child (and usually the family)
and referral was instigated either by an exacerbation of the
symptoms, or by external agencies, e.g. in several, the school
was threatening expulsion. In a few cases, psychological precipi-
tants were apparent. In other cases, a symptom which was not
considered serious at a younger age was either worsening slowly or
was becoming more handicapping in relation to increasing demands
on the child. General practitioners played an important part in
coaxing some parents to seek psychiatric help.

Table 12.1   Demographic data

Number of children referred	32	
Number of families (cases)	29	
Age range of children in years		
Pre-school (2—4)	3	(9%)
School (5—10)	20	(63%)
Adolescent (11—14)	9	(28%)
Social class of families		
Class I	8	(28%)
Class II and III	14	(48%)
Class IV and V	7	(24%)
Family size		
1 child	4	(14%)
2 children	10	(34%)
3 children	11	(38%)
4 or 5 children	4	(14%)

Table 12.2   Referral data
        N = 28* (100%)

Sex of referred child		
Male	21	(75%)
Female	7	(25%)
Diagnosis		
Preschool behaviour problem	2	(7%)
Neurotic disorder (including psychosomatic)	17	(61%)
Conduct or mixed conduct — neurotic	9	(32%)
Duration of problem		
Acute	0	(0%)
Chronic	28	(100%)

*The 'B Family' is excluded.

Therapy process data

The data presented in this section were extracted from the circulated reports and summaries of the meetings and were not part of the Departments records (case files). All case numbers refer to Table 12.5.

Focal hypotheses were formulated in 27 of the 29 cases. They were lacking in two families which failed to engage after the initial interview, and Case 10, Beth. The formulation of the hypotheses, looked at in retrospect, appeared at times highly subjective and they varied in complexity and style. Commonly two or three were required for a family. Focal plans were developed in 25 of the 27 cases for which focal hypotheses were formulated. A focal plan

was not developed for two other families which failed to engage.
A plan could be made for Case 10 despite the lack of a focal
hypothesis. The focal plans also varied greatly. They might be
directly implied by the focal hypotheses or only indirectly linked
to them.

Twenty-four per cent (7) of the cases failed to engage. In one
case (No. 24) the failure to engage was spread out over four
months of missed and attended sessions till the family explicitly
rejected the offer of therapy: such an experience might well be
considered 'treatment'. The more usual pattern involved various
family members opting out and therapy discontinuing over a few
weeks after the first or second session. Four of the seven failures
to engage involved children with conduct disorders; the others
had neurotic disorders.

The commonest recommended treatment programme was for six
sessions at three or four weekly intervals. When a patient was seen
more frequently, a larger number of sessions was usually planned,
i.e. the duration of the therapy was usually five-nine months, but
the intensity varied. Although the contracted number was generally
adhered to, in many it was not possible and often not appropriate
to stick to the planned timing of the sessions: either the therapists
could not be regular or the families required alterations to be made.
Several of the families were offered second courses of brief therapy
with the focus on the marriage; this was only accepted in two cases
(Case 12 and Case 17). Therapeutic work could be maintained in
relation to the designated focal plan in 77 per cent (17) of the
engaged cases. The other five cases (Nos 6, 7, 9, 10, 14) showed
complex or severe marital or family pathology. Five cases did
not complete the course they had initially contracted for (Nos 1,
4, 6, 7, 8).

Outcome data: short-term results
Implementation of the focal plan took place under supervision from
the workshop and changes in plan or tactics were determined only
following discussion. At the conclusion of the therapy or on short-
term follow-up (three-six months), the family was judged for
improvement against the criteria developed from the focal hypotheses. Improvement for the index patient was a criterion for
each case. A simple three-point scale was used for both the index
patient and the family-as-a-whole: worse or no improvement, some
improvement, much improvement. Rating of improvement was by
workshop consensus using therapist reports.

Families fell into only five of the nine (i.e. 3 x 3) possible combinations of index patient and family improvement. Table 12.5 lists
all cases (pseudonyms provided) according to this schema: three
cases showed no improvement for the index patient or the family,
eight cases showed some improvement for the index patient but
none for the family, four cases showed some improvement for both
the index patient and the family, three cases showed much improvement for the index patient and some for the family and four cases
showed much improvement for both the index patient and the family.

Table 12.3   Workshop data

Number of families	29
Focal hypotheses formulated	27
Focal plans formulated	26
Engagement in therapy	22
TREATMENT PROVIDED	
1 course of therapy	20
2 courses of therapy	2
Total number of therapies	24
SYSTEM WORKED WITH	
Family only	16
Marital only	4
Family and marital	4
PLANNED NUMBER OF SESSIONS/COURSE	
4 sessions	1
6-8 sessions	14
10-20 sessions	8
Contract not established	1
FREQUENCY OF SESSIONS	
Weekly	6
Fortnightly	4
3-4 weekly	12
5-8 weekly	2
Completed courses	19
Uncompleted (includes drop-outs and missed final sessions)	5
THERAPEUTIC WORK IN RELATION TO THE FOCAL PLAN	
Yes	19
No	5

Table 12.4   Short-term outcome

Number of families	29 (100%)
Failed to engage	7 (24%)
Engaged	22 (76%)
Completed full course	19 (66%)
Subsequently seen long-term	4 (14%)

IMPROVEMENT RATINGS IN ENGAGED CASES $N = 22$

Improvement	Index patient	Family-as-a-whole
Nil (or worse)	3 (14%)	11* (50%)
Some	12† (55%)	7 (32%)
Much	7 (32%)	4 (18%)

   *In one case the family was assessed as functioning adequately, the child being the site of the pathology.
   † The B family children have been given a single rating.

The seven cases which failed to engage are also listed. We found
that the index patient's rating was never lower than the family
rating and that we had no cases of major symptomatic change in
the absence of family improvement. To allow statistical comparisons
an overall score of improvement was developed using a nine-point
ordinal scale as follows: failure to engage or no change for either
the index patient or the family scored 0 or 1 for minor changes.
The appearance of symptoms in a previously well sib nullified the
effect of symptomatic improvement in the index patient (e.g. Case
4). Some symptomatic change without family change scored 2 or 3.
Some family change scored 4 or 5 depending on how much improvement there was for the index patient. Much family change, always
associated with much symptomatic change, scored 6 or 7. Total
recovery according to all criteria scored 8. From a family therapy
point of view any case scoring less than 4 cannot be considered
a result of 'successful' therapy. On this criteria our success rate
is 50 per cent (11 families) excluding cases which failed to engage.
Using a 2 x 2 contingency table for success (11) vs failure (11)
and the Fisher Exact Probability Test (Lindgren and McElrath,
1966) psychiatric disturbance in the parents (four cases) was
significantly related to failure ($P < 0.05$). Unexpectedly, there
was no significant association between marital disturbance and
success (Fisher Exact Probability Test) or the ordinal ratings of
outcome [Mann-Whitney U-test (Lindgren and McElrath, 1966)].

Summary of cases
The cases are described in Table 12.5 to inform readers of our
hypotheses, therapy plans, outcome criteria and results. For
reasons of space we have not been able to provide the salient
factors from the history and observations of family interaction,
nor our reasoning. A full account of two cases (No. 16, Margaret,
and No. 22, Rachel) illustrating the derivation of the data presented in the table is given in the accompanying paper (Bentovim
and Kinston, 1977).

DISCUSSION

Evaluation of results
About two-thirds (66 per cent) of the children referred showed
some improvement from the treatment offered. The figure is conservative as it assumes no improvement in families that did not
engage. Sigal et al. (1976) found that families that refused contact after no more than two interviews did as well as those who
received treatment: their 'no treatment' group would correspond
to our failures to engage. For the purposes of considering the
effects of brief focal therapy, we may exclude this group in any
case on the grounds that they did not receive therapy. Eighty-
seven per cent of those accepting therapy improved. Such a
result could be described as 'typical' (Kaffman, 1963; Safer, 1966;
Sigal et al., 1967; Wells, 1971); it complements the finding in

Table 12.5

Case no.	Index patient and sibship	Presentation	Focal hypotheses	Focal plan
NO IMPROVEMENT FOR EITHER THE INDEX PATIENT OR THE FAMILY				
1	Patrick 8 yr Only child	Slowness of thought Poor co-ordination	Failure of integration of sexuality and aggression with isolation of family members Failure of communication of feelings preserves status quo	Help each member listen to the others, and bring out feelings that are attached to words and actions
2	Anna 6 yr Youngest of 3 sibs	Eccentric behaviour Learning problems	Parents' own deprivation makes it difficult for them to respond to the needs of their children	Helps parents meet each others' needs
3	Paul 4 yr Only child	Asthma	Excessive self-consciousness and need for control	Reflect to family what they are like Discover something lively
SOME IMPROVEMENT FOR THE INDEX PATIENT, BUT NONE FOR THE FAMILY				
4	Darren 10 yr Second of 3 sibs	Encopresis	Depression is not acknowledged by mother or rest of family Darren is being scapegoated	Tell the family to ignore the encopresis and let Darren manage it Help all members acknowledge depressive feelings in others
5	Henry 11 yr Oldest of 3 sibs	School phobia Migraine Obsessional traits	Henry carries father's denied fears Henry fears success in relation to father's absences and bears guilt over a previous stillbirth	Interpret dynamics to the family

Criteria to be met for successful outcome	Treatment	Outcome	Score
Emotional distance between family members to be reduced: manifested by their listening to each other and recognizing and responding to feelings, both positive and negative Patrick to assert himself more outside the family	Series of 6 fortnightly sessions was not completed. Focus was adhered to – family opted out after 4th session	Family acknowledged their problems Father's alcoholism worsened	0
Parents to turn to and be satisfied by each other, e.g. sexual relations to be re-established Parents to respond appropriately to the needs of the children Anna's behaviour to mature	After 5 family sessions, 20 weekly marital sessions given. Mother, Anna and one sib then entered individual therapy	Parents became aware of problems with a high motivation for continuing therapeutic work. Intra-familial criticism had diminished	1
Family to interact freely and more confidently Asthma to lessen	6 sessions (3-weekly) regularly attended	Family not pathogenic. Family behaviour within sessions became more relaxed Asthma lessened in association with medical management	1
Depression to be acknowledged and shared within the family with expression of mutual care to increase Darren to regain normal bowel habits	6 sessions (monthly) planned. Family missed an appointment after each attendance. Soiling stopped by fifth session and final session missed. Further therapy refused	Soiling ceased; sib's asthma returned; depression worsened but was not acknowledged. Family showed slightly more positive support	1
Father to acknowledge his fears and weakness, but to be relied on by Henry despite this Parental coalition to become more effective thus freeing children from sick roles Henry's symptoms to lessen	6 fortnightly sessions	No change in family apart from an improvement in Henry's relation to Father Henry returned to school prior to initial session. He remained a loner but had fewer headaches and obsessions. Sib developed mild phobic symptoms (2 years later both Henry and family showed much improvement)	2

Case no.	Index patient and sibship	Presentation	Focal hypotheses	Focal plan
6	Richard 12 yr Third of 5 sibs	Irrational and impulsive behaviour	'Normal' aggressive feelings are excessively inhibited	Help the family appreciate their inhibition and intolerance of criticism
7	George 10 yr Twin with a younger sib	School refusal Fears Depression	Inability of the family to cope with the unexpected	Relate George's symptoms to marriage and help parents recognize their marital problems
8	John 11 yr Youngest of 3 sibs	Separation anxiety Fearfulness	Overprotective mother, passive father and son with early separation experiences	Increase John's self-esteem Increase father's effectiveness Separate mother and son
9	Anthony 13 yr Middle of 3 sibs	Depression with suicidal ideation, secondary to polymyositis treated with steroids	Family expectations of perfection make them unable to tolerate a chronic illness 'Bad feelings damage' is a family belief	Promote open communication to enable sharing of feelings and acknowledgement of the distress of others
10	Beth 8 yr Oldest of 3 sibs	Excessive masturbation since infancy now occurring at school	(Connections made with parental sexuality and deprivation – but no hypothesis was fully satisfactory)	Reformulate the problem around unhappiness and deprivation; and explore the marital relationship
11	Barry 9 yr Only child	Behaviour problems Learning problems Asthma Tension in family School refusal	Parents are uncertain about parenting and their marital relationship Closeness is frightening	Work on positive aspects of the marital relationship

Criteria to be met for successful outcome	Treatment	Outcome	Score
Family to acknowledge and express assertiveness and mutual appropriate criticism to be possible Parents to expect and allow age appropriate behaviour, children to mature	After 3 of 6 planned monthly sessions family opted out of therapy using Richard's improvement as an excuse. Only 1 session attended by whole family. Focus poorly adhered to	Family agreed in principle to therapeutic formulations but did not wish to pursue the implications Richard's behaviour settled and he was less scapegoated	2
Family to recognize impossibility of total control of events and to respond adaptively to stresses George's symptoms to improve, including return to school	11 sessions at irregular intervals over 6 months with various combinations of family members, but work on focus could not get started	Serious marital disharmony uncovered; but parents had no wish to work on this George returned to school and was happier in himself	2
Change in marital pattern: with mother to be less overprotective, father to be more active and assertive John to be less obstructive, spoiling and provocative	8 sessions (3-weekly) mainly attended by parents plus John. Last appointment missed	John's behaviour improved at home and school but mother refused to perceive this and regarded him as 'deeply disturbed'. She spoiled father's attempt at assertion	2
Family to bear sadness and threats of loss directly Family, including Anthony, to accept Anthony's illness	8 family, individual and marital sessions over 6 months. Focus proved insufficient in context of severe family disturbance. Continued long-term individual therapy for Anthony with parents seen by social worker	Anthony became less depressed but remained unable to tolerate his parents Parents could not allow examination of their relationship	2
Unhappiness and deprivation to be expressed and met more satisfactorily by family Masturbation to reduce	7 sessions over 6 months with various combinations of family members. Father's absence prevented marital work	Mother less resentful towards Beth Reduction in public masturbation	3
Parent's confidence in their ability to increase and they should control Barry more Marital relationships to improve: parents to do things together with enjoyment Barry's symptoms to improve	Previously seen in long-term individual therapy. Focal therapy comprised 8 fortnightly sessions. Subsequently family seen long-term	Tension in the family reduced, Barry returned to school and was less of a problem at home Family's attitude to treatment improved	3

Case no.	Index patient and sibship	Presentation	Focal hypotheses	Focal plan

SOME IMPROVEMENT FOR BOTH THE INDEX PATIENT AND HIS FAMILY

12	Nigel 12 yr Older of 2 sibs	Obsessions Learning problems	The children in the family take over and express parental conflicts	Clarify children's fears that their needs will not be met, and deal with their fears of frail parental unity
13	David 13 yr Younger of 2 sibs	Abdominal pains and missing excessive school	Family has conflicts over dependency and assertiveness	Show the family that 'bad' parts of the self can be constructively used
14	Judith 13 yr Older of 2 sibs	Antisocial behaviour at school	Adolescence is stirring unresolved adolescent conflicts of parents who are simultaneously stimulating and trying to control Judith	Help parents with their adolescent conflicts
15	B Family 8 yr 7 yr 5 yr 3 yr	Referred by social services for preparation to meet father who is in prison for killing a half sib Various nervous symptoms, e.g. sleep-walking, enuresis, tantrums	Children still experience after-effects of killing of half-sib by father They are coping with separations and a new life in the children's home	Emphasize and openly discuss the reality situation (including preparation for visit to father)

Criteria to be met for successful outcome	Treatment	Outcome	Score
Parents to acknowledge conflicts Parental coalition to improve and children's needs to be more adequately met Symptoms to lessen	Family sessions at monthly intervals but after 3 interviews (of 6 planned) a crisis arose leading to weekly sessions. After 18 family sessions, 20 weekly marital sessions given. Nigel received concurrent remedial teaching	Parents become aware of their problems and the pressures on the children diminished. Their relations with families of origin improved Obsessions diminished and learning improved (2 years later parents were living apart; Nigel's symptoms were fluctuating at previous level)	4
Family members to demonstrate their need for each other and to do things together with pleasure Family members, especially David and father to assert themselves more positively David to attend school regularly with less abdominal trouble	6 sessions monthly Some difficulty in keeping to the focus	David's symptoms abated and all family members showed individuation Better relations between David and his father	4
Parents to treat daughter appropriately for her age School behaviour to improve	6 sessions (3-weekly) Further marital therapy was refused	Both children improved at home and Judith settled well in a new school During therapy focus moved to a severe hidden marital problem which was not helped	4
Children to openly refer to father and his imprisonment and to make a satisfactory visit to father Children to attach to house-staff and to reduce aggressive behaviour there Symptoms to lessen	10 sessions 2-4 weekly with children, housemother and female helper Focus adhered to with difficulty Subsequently seen 2-monthly	Some acknowledgment of past events Visits to father have been satisfactory 3 of 4 children showed symptomatic improvement	4

Case no.	Index patient and sibship	Presentation	Focal hypotheses	Focal plan
MUCH IMPROVEMENT FOR THE INDEX PATIENT AND SOME FOR THE FAMILY				
16	Margaret 10 yr Youngest of 3 sibs	Tics and mannerisms	Overprotection and excessive inhibition of aggression within the family Shared self-depreciation and unrealistically high expectations	Make the family aware of the extent of its inhibition Promote free communication with mutual appreciation and tolerance
17	Graham 2 yr Only child	Separation problems Excessive stranger anxiety	Very poor marital situation: marriage unconsolidated due to failure of expectations following previous marital failures on both sides	Explore failures and expectations in marriage Help couple talk through problems and create a future together
18	Lynette 9 yr Oldest of 3 sibs	Asthma	Fear of madness Guilt about the genetics (maternal grandmother was psychotic)	Modify sib's shrieking Discuss guilts and fears
MUCH IMPROVEMENT FOR BOTH THE INDEX PATIENT AND HIS FAMILY				
19	Kevin 9 yr Only child with older step-sister	School refusal Temper tantrums	Kevin has problems in separation and competition Family has problems with aggression Psychic pain has to be kept secret in the family	Help parents adopt a more realistic attitude to discipline and painful matters
20	Thomas 8 yr A twin (no other sibs)	Asthma Anxieties	Fears of death Parental denial of asthma	Explore fears openly and discuss the asthma
21	William 12 yr Oldest of 3 sibs	Excessive sibling rivalry Behaviour problems Moderately educationally subnormal Depressed mother	Despair (especially about handicap) is unacknowledged Family members make inappropriate demands on each other	Share painful feelings and clarify positive realities Realistic assessment of William's handicap

Criteria to be met for successful outcome	Treatment	Outcome	Score
Family to obtain whole range of emotions and to be able to communicate freely about them Family to diminish criticism and to increase mutual support and appreciation among its members Margaret's tics to disappear	10 sessions over 7 months (without the children at 2 of these)	Family atmosphere was less inhibited and parents developed a closer relationship Margaret's symptoms abated and all children became more relaxed (18 months later the family atmosphere and interaction had further improved)	5
Parent's expectations to become more realistic Parents to communicate and make family decisions jointly	Graham was referred to day centre to enable him to separate from parents. Parents given 2 series of 6 and 10 weekly sessions over 5 months	Parents become more involved in the marriage and with each other Graham's anxieties diminished	5
Family to accept and understand maternal grandmother's illness Lynette and mother to become more separate persons Lynette's asthma to improve and sib's shrieking to lessen	6 sessions 3-weekly, 2 family, and 4 marital but father did not attend 2 of the marital sessions	Shrieking stopped rapidly and asthma lessened Fears of madness persisted especially for mother, but guilt was less Marital relations stabilized freeing Lynette to be herself	5
Open acknowledgment of psychic pain within the family Parents to enforce discipline despite Kevin's protests Kevin to attend school regularly	4 sessions over 7 months	Parents expressed their own experience of pain Parental discipline improved Kevin was left with a tension cough but no school problems	6
Fear of death to decrease Realities of asthma to be openly discussed Severity of asthma to lessen	6 sessions (3-weekly)	Family co-operated and discussed the issues (Mother temporarily immobilised with slipped disc during therapy) Asthma improved and family tension diminished	6
Parents to make demands within William's capacities and vice versa Family to look positively towards the future Marital relationship to improve	6 sessions 4/6-weekly	Marriage became more mutually supportive Mother less depressed William's behaviour improved	7

Case no.	Index patient and sibship	Presentation	Focal hypotheses	Focal plan
22	Rachel 5 yr Older of 2 sibs	Temper outbursts	Parents' unresolved maturational problems are being projected on to the children Unable to find their own identity the parents have obtained security by self idealization They are frightened of rage inside and are unable to be caring	Provide a containing setting for the marital relationship to help parents cope with their needs, drives and rage Focus on fears preventing sharing and commitment within marriage
FAILURE TO ENGAGE				
23	Christine 6 yr Younger of 2 sibs	Temper tantrums Isolation	Fear of madness in family, with resulting problems in behavioural control	
24	Giles 9 yr Youngest of 4 sibs Adopted	Epilepsy Behavioural problems at school	(Preliminary observation: problems of communication and secrecy)	
25	Jake 8 yr Youngest of 4 sibs	Encopresis Immature and destructive behaviour Asthma	Lack of adequate parenting Jake identifies with father 'the failure' Marital conflict	Work on infantile needs and deprivation
26	Sam 14 yr Youngest of 3 sibs	Learning problems Behaviour problems at home and school	Father's chronic malignant illness dominates the household Excessive demands made on Sam conflict with his neediness	Decrease split between parents and children Discuss father's illness
27	Marlon 9 yr Older of 2 sibs	Panic states Temper tantrums	Marlon's dwarfism is associated with vulnerability to parental conflict Mother has not separated from maternal grandmother	(Preliminary plan: discuss whether to continue in family or marital format)
28	Joseph 10 yr Younger of 2 sibs	Obsessions and compulsions	Joseph used as container for mother and marriage Symptomatic behaviour enacts unconscious impulses and conflicts	Explore marital problems

Criteria to be met for successful outcome	Treatment	Outcome	Score
Parents' needs to be met within the family; they should provide each other with practical and emotional support Parents to describe themselves and each other in a realistic and sympathetic way Rachel to remain asymptomatic	20 marital sessions weekly (this followed 6 months of weekly individual therapy for Rachel and single parent casework)	Increased caring, communication and commitment in the marriage Parents settled in themselves and relations with children improved	7
	Contract not established 2 sessions with members absent Mother resistant to therapy	No improvement Comment: Mother's mother and aunt were psychotic Family dysfunctional in all major areas	0
	Refused family therapy at initial session but agreed to 6 marital sessions. Only 2 attended	No improvement Comment: Giles suspended from school. Parents contemptuous of psychiatric help	0
Marriage to stabilize and parenting to improve Mother to become less over-protective and father less harsh	Contact not established 1 session only	No improvement Comment: Mother became determined to leave family and divorce occurred subsequently	0
Family to free itself from father's illness and to express feelings about it Parenting to improve Sam's symptoms to diminish	After initial interview mother demanded individual therapy to protect father. This was provided, with parents only seen occasionally	Sam improved symptomatically, but a sib took on relinquished symptoms	0
	The family had been previously treated with 6 sessions of marital/family therapy when 1 cotherapist left Family did not return for course of therapy	No improvement assumed	0
Marital conflict to be openly dealt with Joseph's symptoms to lessen	1 session No alliance with mother achieved and family did not return	No improvement assumed	0

Case no.	Index patient and sibship	Presentation	Focal hypotheses	Focal plan
29	Charles 10 yr Fourth of 5 sibs	Temper tantrums Stealing at home Asthma (also in father and a sib)	Family myths: Men bear symptoms and are attacked by women. Men cannot hate Use of opting out as a family defence	

Criteria to be met for successful outcome	Treatment	Outcome	Score
Family to abandon stereotypes and to be more flexible in role allocation Charles' symptoms to lessen	1 session attended Contract not established	Charles improved slightly Family was resistant to therapy	0

psychotherapy research that a high percentage of patients receiving any psychotherapeutic treatment (including being assessed
and put on a waiting list) show improvement (Meltzoff and Kornreich, 1970; Luborsky et al., 1975). The common non-specific
factors of psychotherapy (Rosenzweig, 1936; Frank, 1965; Strupp,
1975) are present in family therapy.

Although therapy was specifically aimed at the family, only
eleven of the families, 38 per cent of the referrals and 50 per cent
of those engaged, were rated as having improved, i.e. scored 4
or more. It is difficult to know whether this is typical of family
therapy. Some workers (Weakland et al., 1974) are only concerned
with the presenting complaint in their evaluation of outcome, others
(Sigal et al., 1976) rely on parental reports of satisfaction with
family functioning, whilst others (Minuchin et al., 1967; Sigal
et al., 1967) rate the family comprehensively and lose specificity.
This study was concerned only with change in a specified way: a
particular area of family pathology was delineated and its resolution
was a requirement for a rating of improvement irrespective of how
well the family might be functioning in other respects - for example,
as a consequence of a reduction in stress following the symptomatic
improvement of the index patient.

  e.g. Case 4, Darren.
  The disappearance of Darren's soiling reduced stress within the
  family and they responded with increased support and positive
  feeling for him. However, the family's handling of depression
  remained unaltered.

The family might make helpful alterations which facilitate improvement in the index patient and terminate treatment without having
fully dealt with the underlying problem (as defined by the workshop).

  e.g. Case 14, Judith.
  Judith benefited when her parents arranged for her to attend
  a new school. However, the parent's handling of her adolescence
  was not fully satisfactory.

This may correspond to what Malan calls a 'valuable false solution'.
A valueless false solution occurs when the index patient's loss of
symptoms is rapid and this is used by (perhaps produced by) the
family to maintain their dysfunction or deny their problems (e.g.
Case 7, Richard). The paradox of the index patient routinely
improving more than the family is partially explained by such
manoeuvres. However, the main reason for it is simply that improvement on dynamic criteria is a far more stringent test of improvement
than target symptom improvement or global rating of improvement.
It is a requirement that the patient or family improve just in the
area where they have maximum problems and prove it. As we did
not rate the index patients for improvement on dynamic criteria,
they appear to have done 'better' than our families.

We present our findings as a preliminary attempt to assess
family therapy in an individualized way. In the absence of controls
we cannot say how specific our results are to our form of therapy

nor how much a factor of natural remission is contributing. Never-theless, this study provides indirect evidence that therapy related to improvement. Although all children had been suffering for long periods, the symptomatic child was regarded as a manifestation of a family problem; this problem was diagnosed and a treatment carried out on the basis of the diagnosis. Changes in the family which were predicted to occur if therapy was successful were always associated with improvement in the referred child, and the greater the improvement in the family the greater the improvement in the index patient ($P < 0.001$, Sign Test).

Malan's methodology and family therapy
Our short-term follow-up assessment as described uses a goal attainment procedure based on Malan's methodology. This method-ology was developed for the evaluation of dynamic (intrapsychic) change in individual adults. We found problems and limitations in its application to families and family therapy.

A full application would demand assessment and, if required, focal hypotheses about each individual (at least the index patient), the marital subsystem, and the family-as-a-whole. The complexity of such a procedure in a clinical situation is immediately apparent. We were mainly concerned with establishing a technique for brief family therapy and therefore constructed our hypotheses in terms of family functioning. In view of the type of referral, the index patient's symptomatic improvement was always a criterion of out-come; but psychodynamic hypotheses for individual members were not made. The result is an inversion of Malan's procedure where assessment of marriage and family life is kept at a 'symptomatic' level. From our experience, an individual's reports do not provide an accurate guide to the interactional status of his marriage or family. Many of Malan's cases were married at follow-up: in one 'untreated neurotic' patient with 'apparently genuine improvement' (1975), No. 16 – The Printer's Assistant, the patient simply re-fused to discuss his marital and sexual life.

We are raising the difficult problem of the assessment of the relation between intrapsychic states and external behaviour; it cannot be assumed that one is the direct correlate of the other. For instance, relationships may be used to externalize and relieve disturbed intrapsychic states (Dicks, 1967; Zinner and Shapiro, 1972, 1974). A spouse may be chosen on this basis [see Case 22, 'Rachel' described more fully in Bentovim and Kinston (1977)], and children may be used similarly (e.g. Case 8, John). Malan's basic assumption is that relationships improve when intrapsychic changes occur – the family therapy assumption is that intrapsychic changes occur when relationships improve. Clearly these formula-tions are interdependent; in the first case, relationships do not always improve (Malan gives examples), and in the second, intra-psychic change is not an inevitable concomitant of an improved environment (unfortunately our study did not permit this to be demonstrated). Relatively healthy individuals may become caught

in dysfunctional patterns of interaction from which they are unable
to extricate themselves. Family therapists are used to the striking
improvements in disturbed children following family intervention,
often when individual therapy appears to have failed (Skynner,
1969). Modification of the family may permit intrapsychic change
occurring during the individual therapy to show itself.

e.g. Case 11, Barry.

Individual therapy had continued over fifteen months without
appreciable effect. Following six family sessions at monthly
intervals, Barry was less symptomatic, happier and functioning
better at both home and school.

Psychoanalysts (Freud, 1966; Winnicott, 1971) have observed that
problems are not always internalized permanently by the child,
i.e. by implication needing psychoanalytic therapy. Even long-
standing situations can be unlocked. The question is: Why do
children take such a part in the family problem and how can they
respond so promptly? One explanation is that the child shows
symptoms in order to support 'to be loyal to' (Boszormenyi-Nagy,
1972) some aspect of family life, often a disturbed parent or a
bad marriage.

e.g. Case 12, Nigel.

Nigel's obsessional symptoms were related to his loyalty to his
mother and maternal grandfather. When father and mother acted
in concert and his symptoms were no longer necessary, they
reduced. They returned again when mother was isolated.

When both individual disturbance and family disturbance are
present, one would expect prognosis to be poor. Some evidence
for this comes from our poor results with families which had a
member with a history of psychiatric illness. Difficulties remain
in disentangling family and individual disturbance, e.g. Beiser
(1972) described a case in which, against all predictions, a woman
improved markedly rather than collapsed following the death of
her mother with whom she had lived in symbiotic dependency.

In Malan's work evidence for improvement is based upon alterations in the individual's 'predisposition', the breaking of 'vicious
circles' and the individual handling specific stresses in a new and
better way. This evidence comes from the individual's behaviour
in his outside life. For assessment of family change we must look
for evidence in the family's life, as well as the way the family and
its members relate to the outside community.

Vicious circles are characteristic of family pathology and can be
relatively easily recognized. Improvement requires that they disappear and be replaced by something positive.

More complex is the problem of specific stress. If this stress is
external to the system (as it not uncommonly is for the individual:
authority, social relations, sex) then repeated exposure is likely
and can be awaited. For example, if the stress centred purely
around a developmental phase of one child, then the handling of
the next child going through the same phase could provide evidence as to improvement. However, if the stress is internal, i.e.
an aspect of developmental change for an individual, such as

puberty, then repetition will be impossible. The corresponding
example in the family might be the youngest child starting school.
In cases where stress is not, or cannot be, repeated, then we
must have evidence that the predisposition has altered. 'Predisposition' in a family is a difficult concept. From the viewpoint
of systems theory and psychodynamic theory it would refer to the
family boundaries (rules, myths), family coalitions (alliances,
affective bonds), inter-member channels (the nature of communication, control and exchange) and the family's relation to the
community. Presumably accurate reliable clinical descriptions of
families along these lines are possible; however, the field of
family therapy is at a disadvantage here. The vocabulary for
describing family interaction is confused in the literature. The
field is comparatively young and although many terms and categories
do exist, clear definitions and consensus on them do not. For
reliability it is necessary to use terms which are generally accepted
and understood, even if the cost is a loss of discrimination. For
our research the cost was excessive. An accepted terminology is
a form of 'short-hand' description. Without it the amount of relevant data from an interview with a family increases enormously.
Reporting, particularly of non-verbal behaviour, becomes a complex
and problematic aspect of the whole procedure. Video-tape recording of interviews would have been a valuable addition to the
circulated reports. True intrapsychic change is stable but many
of the family parameters, though relatively stable, e.g. family
decision making (Ferreira and Winter, 1966), may be altered by
the natural life cycle of the family. This complicated evaluation of
change in the predisposition. Further research into the natural
history of the family from the interactional point of view is necessary.

Clinical findings
The workshop accepted all cases referred and it was hoped to
discover which families would respond favourably to a brief focal
approach. Severity of disturbance or chronicity of the problem had
no obvious bearing on outcome, but we failed to engage larger
family groups containing four or five children.
   Prognosis in individual and group therapy relies on introspec-
tiveness, curiosity and willingness to understand oneself, and
realistic expectations of therapy (Bentovim and Wooster, 1968;
Sifneos, 1968). These qualities do not seem so pertinent to family
work. This is probably because of the possibility of focusing on
behavioural and emotional interactions as they occur. It did seem
that an inability to recognize and accept that the presence of a
symptomatic child might be indicative of a family problem was a
poor prognostic sign.
   e.g. Case 6, Richard.
   The family accepted their problem 'in principle' (i.e. complied
   with the therapists), but discontinued therapy when he improved.
It is likely that when a whole family accepts and shares in the
responsibility for the problems of one of its members, this will
be a sign of strength. Older sibs clearly wished to be involved

despite practical difficulties in some families, e.g. Case 13, David; Case 16, Margaret. One specific factor emerged as possibly an important predictor for selection of families for our approach. If one or both parents has been (or could be) given a formal psychiatric diagnosis then the family is probably unable to work briefly and intensively, e.g. Case 1, Patrick (father: alcoholism); Case 2, Anna (mother: puerperal despression); Case 4, Darren (mother: depression); Case 8, John (mother: unspecified breakdown with psychiatric hospitalization in the past). This association was confirmed statistically. Two factors appear to be operating. First, the parents are vulnerable and threatened by psychotherapeutic approaches so time is required to involve them. Second, the psychopathology is complex. A child may be required to be a container for the sick aspect of the parent, e.g. John, Case 8; or if psychiatric illness is present in the family of origin the parent may need a relationship to a 'sick' person.

e.g. Case 23, Christine.

Christine's temper tantrums were regarded as evidence that she carried the family psychosis (maternal grandmother and maternal aunt suffered) and hence controls were not appropriately supplied. Despite this fear that another member of the family was showing signs of madness, there was resistance to attending, particularly on the mother's part.

The most important factor affecting the plan of intervention was the state of the marital relationship. The existence of marital disturbance when the child is the referred patient is not a new finding. Epidemiological studies (Rutter, 1971; Richman, personal communication) have shown that there is a high rate of marital disorder in children of all ages presenting with psychiatric disturbances. Satir (1964) wrote: 'The marital relationship is the axis around which all other family relationships are formed.' Outcome in cases with severe marital disturbance varied greatly: the family failed to engage (Case 25, Jake; Case 28, Joseph), or did not improve (Case 7, George; Case 10, Beth) or continued in long-term therapy of some form (Case 2, Anna; Case 11, Barry; Case 12, Nigel). Case 14, Judith, improved as a family but the marital subsystem remained disturbed and marital therapy was rejected. Improvements occurred in Case 17, Graham (two courses; 6 and 10 weekly sessions) and Case 22, Rachel (20 weekly sessions) where the marital disturbance was intensively taken up. Characteristically the disturbance was covert and had been missed during the initial diagnostic procedure. During therapy exposure became inevitable and the parents experienced this as a major emotional crisis to which they reacted by flight or request for help. Careful assessment of the marriage of any case considered for brief focal family therapy is necessary, and this may require separate interviews if it is suspected that long-standing denied or hidden problems exist. In other words, marital diagnosis must be a primary concern for treatment planning.

Evaluation of the workshop

The family therapy approach is becoming widely accepted as part of the therapeutic armamentarium in child psychiatry. In the absence of developed training facilities, it is worth examining the functioning of the workshop: its capacity to foster family work and the problems we encountered.

The particular therapeutic approach outlined here has considerable value for the beginning family therapist (Cleghorn and Levin, 1973). It provides a comprehensible and assimilable method in a complex field, encouraging a meaningful ordering of the data and demanding a determined therapeutic effort. One of the problems that our therapists had in their previous work with families was maintaining the impetus of change in family functioning which often commenced during the diagnostic interview. Therapeutic diffuseness leads to non-attendance of family members and loss of meaning in the therapy. The focal time-limited method placed a useful pressure on our therapists to recognize and describe family interactions and transactions, and then to face the families with their disturbance. It required a defined contract and specific goals.

The workshop was probably an important factor in the efficacy of treatment. It provided enthusiasm, discipline and supervision. It ensured the examination of transference and counter-transference difficulties and acted as a countervailing system to minimize the usual tendency of the therapist to become enmeshed in the interactions of families. Whether therapists can continue similar work creatively perceiving a significant focus via integration of the family history, presenting complaints and observations of family interaction, is uncertain at this stage.

The major problem of the workshop was the lack of a coherent generally accepted conceptual framework for family therapy. Neither developments from psychoanalytic theory (Boszormenyi-Nagy and Spark, 1973; Zinner and Shapiro, 1972, 1974), nor the precepts of system theories (Zuk, 1968; Minuchin, 1974; Fleck, 1976) were integrated effectively; and resistance to conceptualizing at a family level persisted (Jackson, 1966; Sluzki, 1974). Our members were able to work together on clinical problems but full discussion of families was seriously limited. Description of families qua families was crude and simplistic in comparison with the richness and complexity of description of the individuals. The GAP Report (1970) remarked on the absence of a common vocabulary for the family and urged that its formulation be given priority. Without a clear theoretical base indicating the data to be gathered, our research efforts were handicapped.

A moderately standardized semi-structured approach can be applied to the interview of a child or parent, and such interviews have been shown to have acceptable reliability and validity (Rutter and Graham, 1968; Graham and Rutter, 1968). Development of a technique for interviewing the whole family to assess current patterns of interaction, i.e. a 'family state' is now under way.

WORKSHOP PERSONNEL

Dr. A. Bentovim, Mrs. M. Boston, Mr. S. Dorner, Miss A. Elton,
Mrs. E. Gasper, Miss L. Gilmour, Dr. W. Grant, Dr. G. Hsu,
Dr. W. Kinston, Mrs. M. Kirk, Mr. R. Lansdown, Dr. B. Lask,
Mrs. R. Szur, Miss A. Tobias, Dr. S. Woollacott.
  Workshop Consultant: Mr. J. Boreham.

Acknowledgments
The authors would like to acknowledge the financial support of
the Sembal Trust and secretarial assistance of Miss Sue Service.

REFERENCES

Balint, M., Ornstein, P.H. and Balint, E. (1972) 'Focal Psycho-
  therapy. An Example of Applied Psychoanalysis', Tavistock,
  London.
Beels, C.C. and Ferber, A.S. (1969) Family Therapy: a View,
  'Fam. Proc.', 8, 280-318.
Beiser, M. (1972) The Lame Princess: a Study of the Remission of
  Psychiatric Symptoms without Treatment, 'Am. J. Psychiat.',
  129, 257-69.
Bentovim, A. and Wooster, E.G. (1968) Factors in Choice and
  Perseverance in Patients offered Group compared with Individual
  Psychotherapy, 'Proc. 4th Int. Cong. Group Psychotherapy',
  75-82.
Bentovim, A. and Kinston, W. (1977) Brief Focal Family Therapy
  when the Child is the referred patient - I. Clinical. 'J. Child
  Psychol. Psychiat.', 19, 1-12 (see pp. 202-15 above).
Bloch, D. (1973) 'Techniques of Family Psychotherapy: A Primer',
  Grune & Stratton, New York.
Boszormenyi-Nagy, I. (1972) Loyalty Implications of the Trans-
  ference Model in Psychotherapy, 'Archs Gen. Psychiat.', 27,
  374-80.
Boszormenyi-Nagy, I. and Spark, G.M. (1973) 'Invisible Loyalties',
  Harper & Row, New York.
Cleghorn, J. and Levin, S. (1973) Training Family Therapists by
  setting Learning Objectives, 'Am. J. Orthopsychiat.', 43, 439-46.
Cromwell, R.E., Olson, D.H. and Fournier, D.G. (1976) Tools and
  Techniques for Diagnosis and Evaluation in Family Therapy,
  'Fam. Proc.', 15, 1-49.
Dicks, H.V. (1967) 'Marital Tensions: Clinical Studies Towards
  a Psychological Theory of Interaction', Routledge & Kegan Paul,
  London.
Dicks, D.W., Hunt, H., Luborsky, L., Orne, M., Parloff, M.,
  Reiser, M. and Tuma, A. (1970) The Planning of Research on
  Effectiveness in Psychotherapy, 'Archs Gen. Psychiat.', 22,
  22-32.
Ferreira, A.J. and Winter, W.D. (1965) Family Interaction and

Decision-making, 'Archs Gen. Psychiat.', 13, 214-23.

Ferreira, A.J. and Winter, W.D. (1966) Stability of Interactional Variables in Family Decision-making, 'Archs Gen. Psychiat.', 14, 352-5.

Fleck, S. (1976) A General Systems Approach to Severe Family Pathology, 'Am. J. Psychiat.', 133, 669-73.

Framo, J.L. (ed.) (1972) 'Family Interaction: a Dialogue between Family Researchers and Family Therapists', Springer, New York.

Frank, J.D. (1965) 'Persuasion and Healing: A Comparative Study of Psychotherapy', Johns Hopkins Press, Baltimore.

Freud, A. (1966) 'Normality and Pathology in Childhood', Hogarth and the Institute of Psychoanalysis, London.

GAP (Group for the Advancement of Psychiatry) (1970) 'The Field of Family Therapy', vol. 7, Report no. 78.

Graham, P. and Rutter, M. (1968) The Reliability and Validity of the Psychiatric Assessment of the Child: II. Interview with the Parent, 'Br. J. Psychiat.', 514, 581-92.

Haley, J. (ed.) (1971) 'Changing Families', Grune & Stratton, New York.

Jackson, D.D. (1966) Family Practice: a Comprehensive Medical Approach, 'Compreh. Psychiat.', 7, 308-14.

Kaffman, M. (1963) Short Term Family Therapy, 'Fam. Proc.', 2, 216-34.

Lindgren, B. and McElrath, G. (1966) 'Introduction to Probability and Statistics', Macmillan, New York.

Luborsky, L., Singer, B. and Luborsky, L. (1975) Comparative Studies of Psychotherapies, 'Archs Gen. Psychiat.', 32, 995-1008.

Malan, D.H. (1959) On Assessing the Results of Psychotherapy, 'Br. J. Med. Psychol.', 32, 86-105.

Malan, D.H. (1963) 'A Study of Brief Psychotherapy', Tavistock, London.

Malan, D.H. (1976) 'The Frontier of Brief Psychotherapy', Plenum Press, New York.

Malan, D.H., Bacal, H.A., Heath, E.S. and Balfour, F.H.G. (1968) A Study of Psychodynamic Changes in Untreated Neurotic Patients. I. Improvements that are Questionable on Dynamic Criteria, 'Br. J. Psychiat.', 114, 525-51.

Malan, D.H., Heath, E.S., Bacal, H.A. and Balfour, F.H.G. (1975) Psychodynamic Changes in Untreated Neurotic Patients. II. Apparently Genuine Improvements, 'Archs Gen. Psychiat.', 32, 110-26.

McDermott, J.F. and Char, W.F. (1974) The Undeclared War between Child and Family Therapy, 'J. Am. Acad. Child Psychiat.', 13, 422-36.

Meltzoff, J. and Kornreich, M. (1970) 'Research into Psychotherapy', Atherton Press, New York.

Minuchin, S. (1974) 'Families and Family Therapy', Harvard University Press, Cambridge.

Minuchin, S., Montalvo, B., Guernery, B.G., Rosman, B.L. and

Schumer, F. (1967) 'Families of the Slums: An Exploration of their Structure and Treatment', Basic Books, New York.

Rosenzweig, S. (1936) Some Implicit Common Factors in Diverse Methods of Therapy, 'Am. J. Orthopsychiat.', 6, 412-15.

Rutter, M. (1971) Parent-child Separation: Psychological Effects on the Children, 'J. Child Psychol. Psychiat.', 12, 233-60.

Rutter, M. and Graham, P. (1968) The Reliability and Validity of the Psychiatric Assessment of the Child: I. Interview with the Child, 'Br. J. Psychiat.', 114, 563-79.

Safer, D.J. (1966) Family Therapy for Children with Behaviour Disorders, 'Fam. Proc.', 5, 243-55.

Sager, C. and Kaplan, H. (1972) 'Progress in Group and Family Therapy', Brunner-Mazel, New York.

Satir, V.M. (1964) 'Conjoint Family Therapy: a Guide to Theory and Technique', Science and Behaviour Books, Palo Alto.

Sifneos, P.E. (1968) The Motivational Process: a Selection and Prognostic Criterion for Psychotherapy of Short Duration, 'Psychiat. Q.', 42, 271-9.

Sigal, J., Rakoff, V. and Epstein, N. (1967) Indicators of Therapeutic Outcome in Conjoint Family Therapy, 'Fam. Proc.', 6, 215-26.

Sigal, J.J., Barrs, C.B. and Doubilet, A.L. (1976) Problems in Measuring the Success of Family Therapy in a Common Clinical Setting: Impasse and Solutions, 'Fam. Proc.' 15, 225-33.

Skynner, A.C.R. (1969) A Group Analytic Approach to Conjoint Family Therapy, 'J. Child Psychol. Psychiat.', 10, 81-106.

Sluzki, E.C. (1974) On Training to 'think interactionally', 'Soc. Sci. Med.', 8, 483-5.

Straus, M.A. (1969) 'Family Measurement Techniques', University of Minnesota Press, Minneapolis.

Strupp, H.H. (1975) Psychoanalysis, 'Focal Psychotherapy' and the Nature of the Therapeutic Influence, 'Archs Gen. Psychiat.', 32, 127-35.

Strupp, H.H. and Bergin, A.E. (1969) Some Empirical and Conceptual Bases for Coordinated Research in Psychotherapy. A Critical Review of Issues, Trends and Evidence, 'Int. J. Psychiat.', 7, 18-90.

Weakland, J.H., Fish, R., Watzlawick, P. and Bodin, A.M. (1974) Brief Therapy: Focused Problem Resolution, 'Fam. Proc.', 13, 141-68.

Wells, R.A. (1971) The Use of Joint Field Instructor-student Participation as a Teaching Method in Casework Treatment, 'Social Work Education Reporter', 19, 58-62.

Wells, R.A., Dilkes, I.C. and Trivelli, N. (1972) The Results of Family Therapy. A Critical Review of the Literature, 'Fam. Proc.', 11, 189-208.

Winnicott, D.W. (1971) 'Therapeutic Consultations in Child Psychiatry', Hogarth and the Institute of Psychoanalysis, London.

Zinner, J. and Shapiro, R. (1972) Projective Identification as a Mode of Perception and Behaviour in Families of Adolescents, 'Int. J. Psycho-Analysis', 43, 523-30.

Zinner, J. and Shapiro, R. (1974) The Family Group as a Single
   Psychic Entity: Implications for Acting out in Adolescence,
   'Int. Rev. Psycho-Analysis', 1, 179–86.
Zuk, G.H. (1968) Prompting Change in Family Therapy, 'Archs
   Gen. Psychiat.', 19, 727–36.

13 RECORDING CHANGE IN MARITAL THERAPY WITH THE RECONSTRUCTION GRID

Anthony Ryle and
Susan Lipshitz

Epidemiological evidence amply confirms what common observation suggests: that the marital relationship is of key importance in determining the mental health of the marriage partners and of their children (e.g. Ryle, 1967; Kreitman et al., 1970; Rutter et al., 1970; Dominian, 1972). Recently there has been more interest, in both psychiatry and social work, in couple-based treatments and in work with whole families (e.g. Ackerman, 1958; Skynner, 1969; Barnes, 1973). Evidence that an approach based upon the treatment of couples or upon group therapy of marital pairs can be more effective than individually focused treatment has been summarized by Gallant et al. (1970), Olsen (1971) and Lloyd and Paulson (1972); and it is likely that more resources will be committed to work with marital pairs in the future. In view of the large potential case-load, it becomes a matter of importance to evaluate how effective different forms of contact or intervention may be. This paper reports a method for recording changes in the course of joint marital therapy which is of potential value in this field.

The method described is a form of repertory grid technique. A major advantage of grid technique is that it uses the subject's own vocabulary to describe people or relationships, and enables them to demonstrate what they, personally, feel to be important - which may not necessarily coincide with what is held to be significant by the therapist. In the present case, the method was used to monitor the progress of a couple in brief joint therapy with one of the authors (A.R.).

METHOD

Following individual diagnostic interviews with the husband and wife, a joint session was held at which a dyad grid was constructed. In this form of grid, the elements are dyadic relationships rather than individuals (Ryle and Lunghi, 1970) and, as in the cases described by Ryle and Breen (1972), the elements included the relationships between the couple, their relationships with their parents, and the relationships between their parents. The analysis of this dyad grid is not reported here, but the constructs elicited in the construction of this grid were also used in the reconstruction grid described in this paper. These constructs consisted of eighteen describing behaviour towards the other, and fifteen describing feelings towards, or about, the other.

In the case of the reconstruction grid, the elements are the relationship of husband to wife and wife to husband rated on successive occasions. In all, the couple attended for sixteen sessions of joint therapy and completed a grid rating of their own relationship on eleven occasions preceding sessions. At each of these ratings, two elements - one of self-to-other and one of other-to-self - were rated, and therefore the total grid contained twenty-two elements rated against thirty-three constructs. This type of grid is analogous to Slater's use of successive self-descriptions as a grid (Slater, 1970). The grid was analysed on the INGRID program of the MRC unit for the processing of repertory grids. The 'occasion-elements' can be plotted on a two-component graph, the reciprocal dyad elements being joined by dyad lines, and the successive positions being numbered sequentially, thus tracing the change through time of the way the relationship was construed. Alternatively, self-to-other and other-to-self can be plotted serially against one principal component. Illustrations of both these methods of display are provided below. Changes in the construct relationships through time can be examined by comparing construct correlations in a grid made up of the early testing occasions with one made up of the later testing occasions.

CLINICAL HISTORY

The couple were in their mid-30s and were both university lecturers, visiting the country for one year from an overseas English-speaking culture. They were accompanied by their three children. Both were professionally competent, and neither had any history of psychiatric disorder. Marital unhappiness had been present for about five years, and three years previously, following some signs of emotional disturbance in their eldest child, they had had a brief, but unhelpful, experience of joint counselling. The request for help came from the husband, who felt increasingly rejected and unvalued, and who saw no point in continuing with the marriage if some change could not be achieved. After he had been seen on one occasion, the wife was invited to attend. Despite the fact that she felt considerably threatened, and felt that the husband, and perhaps she too, really needed individual help, she agreed that the immediate crisis was in the marriage and that joint attendance, despite their previous bad experience, was worth a trial. It was agreed to meet for four once-weekly sessions, and then to discuss whether the approach would prove fruitful or not, with the possibility of continuing for up to the six months that remained before their return home. In the event, treatment lasted for sixteen sessions before it was discontinued by mutual agreement.

COURSE OF TREATMENT AND OUTCOME (account by the therapist)

Phase 1
During the first five sessions the couple made increasing use of
the opportunity to give voice to negative feelings. The husband
described his sense of having undergone an increasing diminution
of his role in the family. He felt that he was regarded as a reasonably efficient odd-job man and domestic help, but was seen as un-
reliable as a father and was rejected as a husband. In return, the
wife began to express some of her resentment at the husband's
failure to be of support through her most depressed times, or to
be effective or consistent with the children. She felt contact between
them was like him draining her, but it also became apparent there
were ways in which she would not allow him to give anything to her.
This problem seemed linked with her own fear of becoming an
extinguished person, which was how she saw her mother to be.
She, therefore, had taken over both expressive and instrumental
roles in this family, which was what her father had done in her own
family of origin, while resenting her husband's failure. I felt that
her need to be strong had led to her projecting the dependent,
incapable part of herself into him. In return, he had put into her
the undermining, obsessional superego derived from his own
parents, and was always under a sense of obligation and of failure.
   During this phase the husband was a co-operative and helpful
patient, and the wife a somewhat threatened and covertly angry
one. She nearly withdrew before the fifth session, and when she
came expressed a lot of anger as she felt that her feelings were
not being heard. There seemed a shared sense of powerlessness
in the face of the other, linked paradoxically with the belief that
the other was too vulnerable to be able to withstand the full force
of negative feeling.
   During this first phase I felt able to contain the situation and
was hopeful of being able to help. I felt that each of them had
qualities which the other could not at the time appreciate, and
both seemed able to use interpretations to some degree.

Phase 2
This started with more optimism from the couple, both humour
and conflict becoming more possible in the sessions. On one occasion the wife telephoned between sessions and was very angry
that I brought this up at the next session, especially at my
suggestion that this represented a bid for an alliance with me,
excluding the husband. Husband and wife responded to this
suggestion by a joint attack upon me for putting all the pressure
on the wife. At the next session both were very mocking of an
interpretation offered as explanation for the wife's symptoms
when, on one occasion, she had been unable to eat when taken out
by the husband's parents. I had suggested, quite possibly wrongly,
that this might be related to her split feelings towards her own
mother. In a later session in this phase the wife demonstrated the
power of her passive anger by sitting in the corner of the room

throughout a session. She became anxious at the recognition of
how angry she felt towards her husband, and again telephoned me
after the session, but on this occasion was able to discuss with
her husband her anger and fear of hurting him, before their
next attendance.

Phase 3
A prepared statement from the couple accused me of stage-managing
sessions in such a way that the husband made an initial statement,
but was then left on the sidelines while the wife was attended to,
or attacked. This, I felt, highlighted their shared feeling of being
unable to determine the course of events in any way, and also
represented, to some extent, a recapitulation of the history of
the marriage. Understanding this seemed clarifying. Following this
session, there was a greater capacity to work at problems between
the sessions, and greater initiative during them, and an increasing
understanding was gained by each of the way in which self-
defeating or self-destructive aspects of the self had been projected
into the other. Problems of sex-role confusion were also touched
upon during this phase. Increasingly, the husband saw how his
experience of demanding parents meant that, even if he himself
chose to do something, it became a resented obligation; and the
wife began to see how her need to be seen as warm and effective
meant that her anger and negative feelings had, to a large degree,
been denied or projected. In the last session, both reported that
they felt things were very much more possible, and as they were
now able to talk constructively together about their problems,
they felt no need for further contact. At a follow-up session they
reported a continuing ability to use conflict constructively, and
to provide some mutual support. Both felt that they might, at
some time in the future, seek individual treatment, but they no
longer felt that the marriage was destructive or in danger.

RESULTS OF THE RECONSTRUCTION GRID

The INGRID analysis of the serial ratings of self-to-partner and
partner-to-self demonstrates the changing view of their relationship in the course of therapy. Figures 13.1 and 13.2 record this
progress in terms of the first two components, self-to-other and
other-to-self elements being plotted for every second testing
occasion (to avoid clutter), the dyad line on the two-component
graph joining the reciprocal elements on each occasion. In the
wife's reconstruction grid (Figure 13.1) it is seen that she-to-him
moved initially from being extremely, but ambivalently, negative
(bored, indifferent, scared of, but also reassuring and respecting)
to being rejected, rejection-provoking, dominating and hostile on
the third occasion. Thereafter she moved towards the seeking
comfort and reassurance and being contented and accepting area.
She saw less change in him-to-her than in herself-to-him, locating
him in the more accepting, helpful but confusing quadrant through-

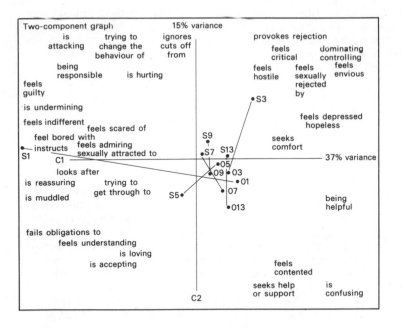

FIGURE 13.1 Wife's reconstruction grid displayed in terms of first two components. Every second occasion is recorded. S = self-to-other; O = other-to-self.

out. The husband's reconstruction grid followed a similar pattern in that he saw himself as moving from an ambivalently attacking and undermining position through being hostile, envious, depressed and critical to a final position in which self-to-other and other-to-self are both in the contented but also dominating quadrant. By the end of therapy, therefore, they agree in seeing their mutual relationship as much more similar than had been the case when they began treatment.

In Figures 13.3 and 13.4 the elements are displayed in relation to the second component only. The second component was selected as, in both instances, it represented an evaluative dimension, contrasting constructs to do with sexual rejection, hurt, confusion and hostility with those indicating acceptance, understanding and concern. This display is easier to follow, though obviously gives less information. The distances between self-to-other and other-to-self diminished for the husband as soon as treatment began. A large shift is apparent for both after the fourth session which, perhaps significantly, was the time at which they decided to continue in therapy. For both husband and wife, the final view of the relationship is much more positive than the initial one.

One problem of plotting change through serial ratings of the elements is that concurrent changes in construct relationships cannot be revealed in the analysis. Perceived changes in the

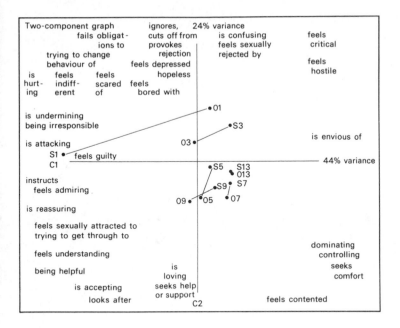

FIGURE 13.2 Husband's reconstruction grid. Every second occasion is recorded. S = self-to-other; O = other-to-self.

implications of certain feelings or behaviours may, of course, represent an important aspect of the reconstruction process. To investigate changes in construct relationships, the elements were divided into two groups: those referring to the first five and the last six testing occasions. These two groups were analysed separately, and the two grids were compared on the COIN program. Changes in the intercorrelations of ten selected construct correlations were investigated and the results are summarized in Tables 13.1 and 13.2. The COIN program gives construct correlations as correlation values and angular distances; an angular distance of 90° representing no correlation, lower values indicating positive, and higher values indicating negative correlations. In these tables, changes in correlations of an angular distance of 30° or more are recorded. (See statistical note at end of paper.) On the basis of this table, the main change for the husband can be summarized as follows: dominating behaviour is now seen as less confusing, less likely to provoke rejection and more likely to be consistent with feeling affectionate: being helpful is less likely to be seen as confusing to the other, more likely to provoke rejection from the other, and less likely to be associated with feelings of affection or sexual attraction: attacking behaviour is more likely to be seen to be associated with both affection and guilt: confusing behaviour is more likely to be seen as provoking rejection, and less likely to be associated with feeling sexually attracted: feeling sexually

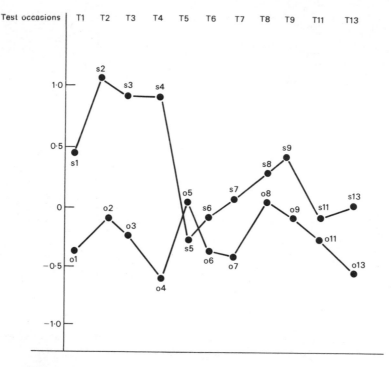

FIGURE 13.3 Wife's reconstruction grid: Comp. 2 (15 per cent var.). Highest and lowest five construct loadings: Provoking rejection from; critical, contemptuous; sexually rejected by; hurting; hostile (positive). Contented, accepting; affectionate, loving; accepting, acknowledging; seeking help or support; failing obligations (negative).

rejected by the other is seen as less likely to be associated with dominating, attacking behaviour, and more likely to be associated with being helpful and feeling guilty, but also more associated with feeling sexually attracted to the other. For the wife, not all these correlations could be examined as her use of two constructs did not distinguish between the elements on later testing occasions ('provokes rejection from' and 'sexually rejected by'). The meaning of the changes in the wife's construct correlations can be summarized as follows: seeking comfort from the other is less likely to be seen as associated with dominating behaviour, less likely to be seen as associated with being helpful to the other, and less likely to be seen as associated with affectionate feelings, while more likely to be associated with feelings of guilt: attacking behaviour is seen as less likely to be associated with feelings of guilt and more likely to be associated with feelings of affection.

In summary, both have come to see dominating and attacking behaviour as less dangerous and more positive, and both give evidence of according less value to being helpful and to comfort-seeking behaviour.

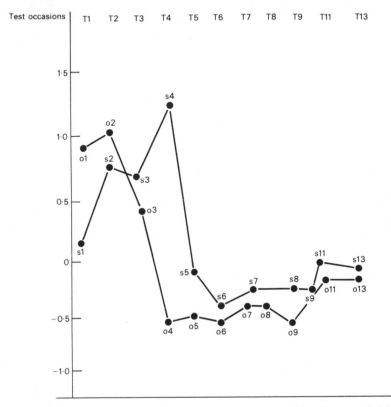

FIGURE 13.4 Husband's reconstruction grid; Comp. 2 (24 per cent var.). Highest and lowest five construct loadings: Provoking rejection from; ignoring, cutting off from; critical; hostile; bored with (positive). Affectionate, loving; contented, accepting of; accepting, acknowledging; looking after, caring (negative).

DISCUSSION

The main object of the present paper is to demonstrate the possibility of tracing the course of marital therapy using the serial ratings of the couple's view of their own relationship as elements in the reconstruction grid. In the brief intervention reported and investigated by this method, the reconstruction grid records a considerable amount of change. Clinically, it seemed that the intervention had enabled the couple to contain the crisis and to break an interlocking mutually destructive pattern of relating. Grid changes, notably in respect of feelings of hostility and in respect of behaviours which were probably placatory or based upon denied

Table 13.1   *Husband: changes in construct correlations between first and last halves of treatment*

	Being helpful	Attacking	Seeking comfort	Confusing	Provoking rejection	Feeling affectionate	Feeling guilty	Sexually attracted	Sexually rejected
Dominating				−*	−***	+**			−**
Being helpful				−***	+***	−**			+***
Attacking						+*		−*	−*
Seeking comfort							+*		
Confusing					+*			−**	
Provoking rejection									
Feeling affectionate									
Feeling guilty									+***
Sexually attracted									+***
Sexually rejected									

* ** and *** indicate differences in angular distances of $> 30°$ $< 40°$, $> 40°$ $< 50°$ and $> 50°$, respectively. See Statistical note. + = positive correlation; − = negative correlation.

negative feelings, seem in line with the clinical account. Change is likely to be related to the increasing ability of the couple to voice negative feelings, an ability which was apparent during the first and second phases of treatment, which is in accord with the grid evidence of the major change occurring around the time of the fourth or fifth session.

It is of interest to speculate what effect the research testing may have had on the course of treatment. Completing the serial ratings of their own relationship may have enabled, or forced, the couple to acknowledge denied feelings, and may have contributed to the relatively rapid change achieved. Mann and Starr (1971) have reported that filling in questionnaires about sexual behaviour and also about marital and family interactions has the effect of modifying the behaviours even when no other intervention takes place. There is certainly no reason to suppose that the testing had any adverse effect upon the course of treatment, although complaints about it did, at times, provide a means of expressing negative feelings towards the therapist.

In a long intervention, additional interest might lie in analysing separately grids based on the ratings of self-to-other and of other-to-self to see how far changes in the implications of feelings or behaviours are seen to apply to both self and other. The test results could also be used to demonstrate to the couple discrepancies in their mutual perceptions. The role of the therapist or therapists in joint therapy could be explored by including the couple's relationship with the therapist(s) on the reconstruction grid, and such a modification would be of interest in studying the course of transference.

Table 13.2   Wife: changes in construct correlations between first and last halves of treatment

	Being helpful	Attacking	Seeking comfort	Feeling affectionate	Feeling guilty	Sexually attracted
Dominating			–**			
Being helpful			+*		+**	
Attacking				+**	–**	
Seeking comfort				–**	+***	–**
Feeling affectionate						
Feeling guilty						
Sexually attracted						

*, ** and *** indicate differences in angular distances of $>30°$ $<40°$, $>40°$ $<50°$ and $>50°$, respectively. See Statistical note. + = positive correlation; – = negative correlation.

We believe, therefore, that the reconstruction grid as described, and as it could be developed, can play a part in both the process and the assessment of therapy.

ACKNOWLEDGMENTS

We are grateful to Dr Patrick Slatcr at the MRC Unit for the processing of repertory grids for the analyses reported in this paper. We are also grateful to the couple for their permission to publish and for their comments on this paper.

STATISTICAL NOTE

Since it was not expected that there would be *no* difference between construct correlations before and after the middle of treatment, comparison using a null hypothesis was abandoned in favour of two cumulatively exhaustive hypotheses to decide whether more or less important change had occurred. These hypotheses were:

H_1: all density of belief about the value of the distance between the angles is at $0°$, i.e. sine $\Theta = 1$ (which is equivalent to a correlation of 0.0).

H_2: indifference to any value of sine Θ except that of sine $\Theta = 1$.

These hypotheses had equal weight initially, i.e. prior odds of 1 to 1. On a larger sample, Jeffrey's test can be used to compute posterior odds given sine Θ of an obtained value, and these odds can be read off from a table compiled by Dr Larry Phillips (see Phillips, 1975). Here, observed angular change was converted to correlation coefficients, and then z scores, and a credibility interval for these scores was calculated to give confidence limits on angular change. It was only possible to say with 95 per cent confidence that change *had* occurred when this credibility interval did not include $0°$. This was not true of a $30°$ change. But differences of $40°$ and $50°$ between occasions *did* show change. The relations between constructs for which this is true can be seen in Tables 14.1 and 14.2.

The authors are indebted to Dr Patrick Humphreys and Dr Larry Phillips of Brunel University for their advice on Bayesian statistics (see Phillips, 1973).

REFERENCES

Ackerman, N.W. (1958) 'The Psychodynamics of Family Life', New York: Basic Books.

Barnes, G.G. (1973) Working with the Family Group: some Problems of Practice, 'Soc. Wk Today', 4, no. 3, 65-70.

Dominian, J. (1972) Marital Pathology: a Review, 'Postgrad. Med. J.' 48, 517.

Gallant, O.M., Rich, A., Bey, E. and Terranova, L. (1970) Group Psychotherapy with Married Couples: a Successful Technique in a New Orleans Alcoholism Clinic, 'J. Louisiana State Med. Soc.', 122, 41.

Kreitman, N., Collins, J., Nelson, B. and Troop, J. (1970) Neurosis and Marital Interaction: Personality and Symptoms, 'Br. J. Psychiat.', 117, 33-46.

Lloyd, R.A. and Paulson, I. (1972) Projective Identification in the Marital Relationship as a Resistance in Psychotherapy, 'Archs Gen. Psychiat.', 27, 410-13.

Mann, J. and Starr, S. (1971) The Self-report Questionnaire, as a Change Agent in Family Therapy (paper read to the Western Psychological Association, San Francisco).

Olsen, E.H. (1971) The Marriage: a Basic Unit for Psychotherapy, 'Am. J. Psychiat.', 127, 945-8.

Phillips, L.D. (1973) 'Bayesian Statistics for Social Scientists', London: Nelson.

Phillips, L.D. (1975) 'Psychol. Rev.' (in the press).

Rutter, M., Tizard, J. and Whitmore, K. (1970) 'Education, Health and Behaviour', London: Longmans.

Ryle, A. (1967) 'Neurosis in the Ordinary Family', London: Tavistock.

Ryle, A. and Breen, D. (1972) A Comparison of Adjusted and Maladjusted Couples using the Double Dyad Grid, 'Br. J. Med. Psychol.', 45, 375-82.

Ryle, A. and Lunghi, M. (1970) The Dyad Grid: a Modification of Repertory Grid Technique, 'Br. J. Psychiat.', 117, 323-7.

Skynner, A.C.R. (1969) A Group-analytic Approach to Conjoint Family Therapy, 'J. Child Psychol. Psychiat.', 10, 81-106.

Slater, P. (1970) Personal Questionnaire Data Treated as Forming a Repertory Grid, 'Br. J. Soc. Clin. Psychol.', 9, 357-70.

14 A BEHAVIORAL INTERACTIONAL MODEL FOR ASSESSING FAMILY RELATIONSHIPS*

John R. Lickorish

THE FAMILY MODEL

Every investigation into family relationships requires a theoretical model of the family that will facilitate the organization of concepts and empirical data. The model should enable the description of the family's behavior to be economically summarized and handled statistically. It should also facilitate the planning of treatment and the provision of base lines against which changes in behavior may be assessed. In addition, the model should be sufficiently flexible to apply to all types of families and should be able to show the relationship between the family and the community in which it lives.

Types of models
Many of the theoretical models of the family that have already been described have been reviewed by Gurman (9) and Wertheim (27). But as Wells and Rabiner (26) point out, these models for the most part are either 'too molecular and unwieldy to be of broad clinical usefulness' or they are 'insufficiently explicit or systematic to provide the kind of informational comparability that is desirable.' Moreover, current models of the family make little use of formal logical structures and even less use of linguistic concepts in their analysis of intra-family communication. It seems therefore that there is room for the sort of model described in this paper, which has a formal, logical, and geometrical structure and which makes use of current linguistic concepts in analyzing intra-family communication and behavior.

The present model is similar to the interactional concept of the family described by Wells and Rabiner (26) and to the more behavioristic views of Balentine (3) and Liberman (19). Its geometrical structure elaborates that used by Fogarty (6) and Howells (11), but so far as the present author can discover, the model breaks new ground in its use of linguistic concepts and its methods of coding and statistical analysis. The coding system is, however, similar to some of the methods reviewed by Guttman, Spector, Sigal, Epstein and Rakoff (10). The model describes the family in terms of discrete items of behavior that are linked together into a formal, logical system.

THE LOGICAL ANALYSIS OF INTERPERSONAL BEHAVIOR

The behavior of any two people may be represented geometrically
as shown in Figure 14.1. The two circles represent the two people
x and y, and the straight uni-directional arrows represent the
activities that take place between them. Each arrow represents a
transitive, asymmetrical action, which is also represented by the
logical symbol R (16, p. 54). A diagram consisting of two circles
x and y, connected by a single uni-directional arrow, is therefore the geometrical equivalent of the logical expression xRy.
Expressed in words, this reads, 'A one-way relationship R exists
between 2 people x and y.' In Figure 14.1, the upper arrow
represents the relationship yRx between y and x. It is simply a
matter of convenience whether the right- or left-hand circle is
labeled x or y. Similarly, the upper or lower arrow may point in
either direction and be labeled xRy or yRx accordingly. The
symbol R may take any value, provided it is transitive and asymmetrical. In the present model, R represents some form of mental,
verbal, or physical activity. The activity is always directed from x
to y, or vice versa. Thus R may be replaced by verbal phrases like
'looks at,' 'cares for,' 'dislikes,' 'thinks about,' and so on.

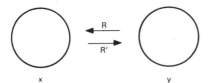

FIGURE 14.1 Diagrammatic representation of the interaction within
a dyad. The circles x and y represent people (or objects). R and
R´ represent the uni-directional, logical relationships between x
and y as shown by the formulae x R´ y and y R x.

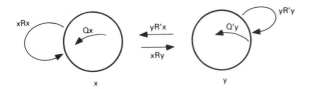

FIGURE 14.2 Geometrical and logical representation of the three
basic relational properties of a dyad. R and R´ represent uni-
directional relationships; Q and Q´ represent properties, or
characteristics, of x and y, respectively; x and y represent people
(and/or objects); y R´ y and x R x are reflective activities of
y and x.

The curved arrow within each circle in Figure 14.2, labeled
Qx or Q´y, represents qualities, or properties, attributed to x and

y, respectively. These properties are logically represented by Q
(16, p. 49). They are intransitive and frequently form the complement to the phrase 'x is ___.' Thus Q may stand for properties like,
'happy,' 'tall,' 'intelligent,' 'seems sad,' and so on.

The curved arrows outside the circles in Figure 14.2 labeled
xRx and $yR'y$, respectively, represent reflexive activities of x
and y. Thus xRx might represent a statement like, 'He is feeling
sorry for himself,' 'She is looking at herself,' 'The boy is pleased
with himself,' etc.

A reciprocal action between x and y is formally expressed by
$([xRy] + [xR'x])$. The value of R need not be the same in each
expression within the brackets. If the verbal phrase 'looks at' is
substituted for R (where $R = R'$) and boy is substituted for x and
girl for y, then the expression within the brackets reads, 'Boy
looks at girl and girl looks at boy.' That is, 'Boy and girl look
at each other.'

Any statement about x or y, or the relationship between them, or
any description of their activities may therefore be logically represented by one or other of the formulae just described. The formulae
may also be used as a means of recording the activities that take
place within dyads. A sequence of activities is represented by an
additive series of the relevant formulae. Thus a simple conversation
between x and y would be formally expressed as $(xR_1y + yR_2x + xR_3y + . . . + yR_nx)$. In this series $R_1 R_2 . . . R_n$ represent the
words that one says to the other.

Since any relationship may be represented by R and any personal
quality by Q, the total complex of behavior and personal characteristics within a dyad during any given interval is formally represented by the sum of the relevant values of xRy, yRx, xRx, yRy,
Qx and Qy.

ANALYSIS OF THE FAMILY GROUP

The use of these logical formulae may be extended to describe
the complex of activities and properties within a family group.
Whatever views may be held about the family 'as a whole,' it is
logically permissible to regard it as consisting of a series of interacting dyads as shown in Figure 14.3. (Some objections to doing
this are considered later.) It thus comprises a 'system' according
to the definition given by Bertalanffy (4, p. 55). The analysis
of the family's behavior by means of the symbols already described
may at first sight seem to do less than justice to the patterns of
behavior which are observable in family life. But such an analysis
is a preliminary step toward a clearer understanding of the family's
behavior patterns. It is rather like analyzing an 'utterance' into
words and sounds in order to understand more clearly the patterns
of speech and the meaning of a sentence (8).

It is convenient to consider a four-person family for the purpose
of formal analysis, since the interactions between four people can
be easily represented geometrically. A three-person family over-

simplifies the dyadic analysis, while a family of more than four
is difficult to represent clearly in a diagram. However, the same
principles apply to all sizes of family, and the dyadic system of
analysis can be extended to a group of any size.

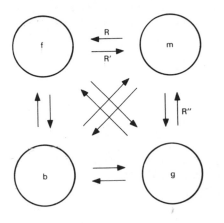

FIGURE 14.3 Geometrical representation of the interrelationships
within a family of four people. Each arrow represents a uni-
directional relationship, R, R´, R´´, etc.; f = father; m = mother;
b = boy; g = girl.

The number of dyads to be found in a group of 'n' people is
given by the formula $nC_2 = n!/2(n-2)!$, where (!) stands for
the expression 'factorial.' A four-person family therefore contains
six dyads, as given by the formula $4C_2 = 4x\,3x\,2x1/2x1\,(2x1) = 6$.
Each of the six dyads contains two uni-directional arrows represented by (xRy) + (yR´x) as shown in Figure 14.3. Each dyad
also contains the curved arrows (see Figure 14.2) represented by
xRx and yR´y, as well as the personal qualities denoted by Qx
and Qy. The values of x and y correspond to the members of the
family, and so they may be replaced by f (father), m (mother),
b (boy), or g (girl), as required (Figure 14.3).
An analysis of family interaction necessarily implies that the
family's behavior has been observed and reported. A skilled
observer may code behavior as it occurs, or alternatively, as
it is observed in the play-back of a film or videotape. A fully
comprehensive coding system would record not only the words
and actions of the family but also their facial expressions and
gestures, as well as the tone of voice, the feeling, and the stress
with which their utterances were made (20). All these items of
behavior take place either between two or more members of the
family or as a result of one individual's activity. If it is further
agreed that Qx or xRx may represent covert, or intra-psychic
behavior, as well as overt activity, then the present model may
be used to describe any kind of reported family behavior in terms
of the formulae Q_x and xRy.

However, most analyses of family behavior probably still make use of a verbal description of what has taken place within the family. Such a description may be obtained from a family interview, from observations of family life, or by means of a projective technique or a one-to-one conversation. The report of the behavior forms the protocol, and in the analysis that follows it is assumed that each protocol consists of only one person's views of the family situation.

METHOD OF ANALYZING THE PROTOCOL

Material and subject
The sample analysis that follows uses as its primary data the verbatim transcript of a set of responses made by one speaker to cards taken from the Family Relations Indicator, a projective technique devised by Howells and Lickorish (12). The transcript is given in full in Appendix A. The analysis is carried out in three stages, and the results of each stage are entered on the analysis sheet shown in Table 14.1.

Stage 1. Classification of sentences
Having recorded the projective responses and transcribed them, the next step was to edit the protocol by taking out the exclamations, interjections, and various 'noises' that were in the verbatim transcript. These items were removed because this method of analysis makes use of semantically acceptable sentences and semi-sentences only (8, p. 13). These two types of sentences were used as raw data because they contained the information provided by the speaker about the topic under discussion, i.e., his family situation. It is important to emphasize, however, that the features that have been eliminated for the purpose of this analysis would have to be taken into account if the speaker's total reaction to the stimulus situation were being analyzed (15). Moreover, these eliminated features of the protocol might provide valuable indirect information about the speaker. They might also be used as 'unobtrusive measures' (Webb, Campbell, Schwartz and Sechrest [25, p. 127]), of fluency, anxiety, defensive tactics, and so on. A much more complex analysis would be required, however, in order to assess the full significance of these features.

The next step was to mark the boundary of each simple sentence by means of a 'slash' (/) and then to divide all compound sentences into their constituent clauses in the same way. Thus the protocol was divided into a series of simple sentences, which were then numbered seriatim, and the numbers were entered in Column 1 of the Analysis Sheet shown in Table 14.1. (It is true that by dividing up compound sentences in this way, subordinate clauses are treated as if they were independent sentences and thereby some information may be lost. For although this procedure does allow the information within the clauses to be extracted, it does not take into account the causal, conditional, or consecutive relationships between the clauses and the main sentences in which they occur. Hence the

Table 14.1 Analysis Sheet. Constituent and Logical Analysis of Father's Responses Shown in Appendix A

1	2	3	4	5	6	7	8
						Rating	
No	SQ S'R	Q	x	R	y	Q	R
1	Ss						
2	S						
3	S						
4	Ss						
5a	R	—	f	talks to	b		v
6	R	—	b	talks to	f		v
6	Q	domineering	f			at—	
7	R	—	f	(—) understand	b		at—
8	R	—	f	reprimands	b		v—
9	Ss						
10	Q	alarmed	b			ft—	
11	S						
12a	Ss						
b	Ss						
13	Q	(—) bad minded	b			at+	
14	Q	have tempers	b			ft—	
15	Ss						
16	Q	dismayed	b			ft—	
17	Q	done damage	b			a—	
18	Q	apologetic	b			v+	
19a	R		b	sees	f		a
b	R		b	sees	m		a
20a	R		b	reports to	f		v
b	R		b	reports to	m		v
21a	Q	right attitude	f			at+	
b	Q	right attitude	m			at+	
22	Ss						
23a	Q	relaxed	f			ft+	
b	Q	reads paper	f			a	
24	Q	experiments	b			a+	
25	Q	thinks	b			at—	
26	R		f	looks at	b		a
27	R		f	(—) rejects	b		a+
28	R		f	interested in	b		at+
29	R		f	helpful to	b		a+
30	Ss						
31	R		f	helps	b		a+
32	Ss						
33	S						
34	Ss						

Table 14.1   cont'd

1	2	3	4	5	6	7	8
						Rating	
No	*SQ* *S'R*	*Q*	*x*	*R*	*y*	*Q*	*R*
35	S						
36	Ss						
37	Q	brings report	b			a	
38	Ss						
39	Q	(--) agitated	b			ft+	
40a	Ss						
b	Q	no fear	b			ft+	

reasons for, and the consequences of, some actions may not be included in this analysis.)

Next each of the numbered statements (St.) was assigned to one of the following four categories:

Category 1. A simple descriptive statement about the stimulus situation denoted by S (e.g., 'This room is hot,' 'There are 4 people in this picture.').

Category 2. An opinion denoted by S´ (e.g. 'I like that picture.').

Category 3. A statement describing a property or quality of a person denoted by Q (e.g., 'That boy is happy.').

Category 4. A relationship between two or more people denoted by R. The statements in the sample protocol are classified in this way and the appropriate category code letters (S, S´, Q or R) are shown in Column 2 of Table 14.1. The statements classified as S and S´ are not analyzed further, as they did not provide information about the family's relationships. This completed Stage 1 of the analysis.

Stage 2. Immediate constituent analysis
Each statement classified as 'Q' in Table 14.1, has the logical form Qx, where x stands for a person or object and Q represents some property or characteristic of the object or person. The value of Q is usually denoted by an adjective or a verbal complement, or by an adjectival or adverbial clause or phrase, or its equivalent. This word, phrase, or clause is entered in the appropriate row of Column 3 in Table 14.1. The person represented by x is denoted by an appropriate letter placed in Column 4 in the same row as the corresponding value of Q. Since this particular analysis is concerned with family relationships only, x is denoted either by a proper name or by f for father, m for mother, b for boy, and g for girl, etc.

The analysis of the statements classified as R is a little more complex. These statements are of the logical form xRy and correspond to the syntactical form $NP_1 + VP + NP_2$, where NP stands for a noun, or a noun clause or phrase and VP stands for a simple or compound verb or a verbal phrase. Each R-type statement may therefore be analyzed into the three main constituents NP_1, VP, and NP_2. This analysis is similar to the traditional analysis of sentences into subject (NP_1), verb (VB), and object (NP_2). But this method of 'constituent analysis' is more convenient for the present purpose and forms part of the modern theory of transformational grammar (Slobin [23, pp, 8-20] and Lester [17, p. 127]).

Complex sentences contain one or more noun phrases, NP, or even whole sentences embedded within the NP of the main sentence. Such embedded sentences or phrases may be analyzed as separate sentences in their own right. Thus the sentence, 'The man who saw the boy called after the girl,' is analyzed as follows:
$$NP_1 + S' + VP + NP_2$$
The man / who saw the boy / called after / the girl.
Then NP_1 contains within it S´, i.e. 'who saw the boy.' So S´ may be analyzed as:
$$NP_1 \quad VP \quad NP_2$$
S´ → the man / saw / the boy.
Since 'who' clearly refers to 'the man,' the noun is substituted for the relative in the analysis.

The phrases and clauses NP_1, NP_2, VP are called 'constituent phrases,' and any sentence may be analyzed into its constituents by the use of 'slashes' (/) as shown in statements 6, 8, 26, and 27 in Appendix A.

Stage 3.   Coding the information
Each NP necessarily contains a noun, pronoun, or its equivalent as the 'subject' in NP_1 and the 'object' in NP_2. The former corresponds to x and the latter to y in the formula xRy. The value of x in each analyzed statement is entered in Column 4 of Table 14.1 and the corresponding value of y (= NP_2) is entered in Column 6. The value of R (i.e., the verbal phrase VP) is entered in the appropriate row in Column 5. The values of y are denoted by proper names or the letters f, m, b, g, etc., as previously explained for the recording of x.

The recording of the noun phrases seldom presents any difficulty, but the verbal phrase (VP) does sometimes require careful consideration before it is entered in Table 14.1. If the verb is a simple transitive verb like 'is reprimanding' in St.8 or 'would see' in St.19, then the verb is entered just as it stands in Column 5. If, however, the verbal phrase is complex, as in St.7, then a paraphrase is necessary, or the entries may be too clumsy or extensive to record easily. In St.7 the VP is 'is not getting down to the level of understanding.' This may be paraphrased as 'is not understanding' and is recorded as '(-) understand,' where (-) is a neat method of recording a negative. Paraphrasing a long VP in this way may occasionally omit some of the information the VP contains, but it retains the essential nature of the relationship R and makes recording reasonably accurate without being unwieldy.

Reciprocal relationships require two separate entries to be made. Thus St.5, which obviously refers to father and son, must be

recorded as 'f discusses with b' and 'b discusses with f.' Words
that have a dual meaning like 'parents' also require two entries,
e.g., 'His parents admire the boy' must be recorded as 'f admires
b' and 'm admires b,' (see statements 19, 21, 40 of Appendix Λ).

The values of R recorded in Column 5 of Table 14.1 are next
classified as verbalizations (v), actions (a), feeling-tones (ft),
or attitudes (at). In addition each v, a, ft, and at is rated on a
three-point scale according to the following code: verbalization,
v + v v -; action, a + a a -; feeling-tone, ft + ft ft -; attitude,
at + at at -. The items carrying a (+) sign are helpful, friendly,
benign etc., and those with a (-) are of course, opposite in nature.
The items v, a, ft, at, with no sign are 'neutral.' They may also
be used when there is doubt about the quality of the item. These
ratings are entered in Column 8.

A similar rating is carried out for the values of Q using the same
code and the same three-point rating. The Q ratings are recorded
in Column 7 of Table 14.1. The analysis of the speaker's responses
is now completed. The Analysis Sheet, Table 14.1, contains a
summary of the protocol given in Appendix A. It also contains a
coded summary of this information in Columns 6, 7 and 8. This
coded information may readily be handled statistically, as explained
below.

Uses of the Analysis Sheet
The Analysis Sheet may be used to compare the frequencies with
which the four types of statements (S, S´, Q, R) are made. If
used in conjunction with other independent sources of information,
it might be possible to show that the ratios between these frequencies
are indicative of certain types of behavior. Thus a relatively high
value of S´ might indicate self-centredness. Defensive reactions
might be reflected in the S or S + S´ scores, while the ratio of Q
to R frequencies might indicate the existence of individual prefer-
ences or prejudices within the family group.

Summarizing the data
The information provided by one speaker (Father), which is analyzed
in Table 14.1, may be conveniently summarized by using the matrix
shown in Table 14.2. The values of F, M, and B at the heads of
the columns correspond to the value of 'x' in the formulae Qx
and xRy. The values of 'y' are given in the rows at the left hand
side, while the value of R is inserted in the cell at the junction of
the appropriate row and column. The relevant values of Q are
recorded in the cells of the bottom row of the table where the row
Q intersects the appropriate column. The reflexive values of R
(i.e., xRx) are recorded in the diagonal cells of the matrix. (There
are comparatively few entries in this matrix, because only a short
transcript has been analyzed for demonstration purposes.) One
column and one row is required for each person mentioned in the
R-type statements in the protocol. Since this analysis is concerned
with a family group, the values of x and y may be written f (father),
m (mother), b (boy), g (girl). Other values like gf (grandfather)

might be required with other protocols. The number of values of x and y depends simply upon the persons that the speaker mentions. Once the table has been set up with the necessary values of 'x' and 'y' in rows and columns, the only entries to be made are the values of Q and R. The coded values of R have been given in Column 8 of Table 14.1.

Each of these coded values is entered in Table 14.2 in the cell lying at the intersection of the appropriate row y with the corresponding column x. The values of Q are given in Column 7 of Table 14.1 and entered in the row Q at the bottom of the matrix in Table 14.2. Once the investigator is familiar with the method of analysis, it is possible to dispense with Table 14.1 and proceed directly to the recording matrix of Table 14.2, which summarizes the views of one respondent. The protocol is analyzed as already explained and the values of x y R and Q may be noted upon it before they are transferred to table 14.2. A separate matrix is required for each subject's responses. If a large number of different people are mentioned in the protocol, the analysis requires a correspondingly large matrix. This may be slightly inconvenient to handle, but the method of analyzing and recording the statements is not affected.

Table 14.2   Summary of father's responses

	F		*M*		*B*	
F					talks to	v
					sees	a
					tells	v
M					sees	a
					tells	v
B	talks to	v				
	(—) understands	at—				
	reprimands	v—				
	looks at	a				
	(—) rebuffs	a+				
	interested in	at+				
	helps	a+				
	helps	a+				
Q	domineering	at—	right attitude	at+	alarmed	ft—
					not bad	at+
					tempers	ft—
	right attitude	at+			dismayed	ft—
	relaxed	ft+			damage	a—
	reads paper	a			apologetic	v+
					experiment	a+
					thoughtful	at+
					modern ideas	at+
					brings report	a
					(—) agitated	ft

STATISTICAL ANALYSIS

Constructs and elements

The coded data in Table 14.2 is suitable for statistical analysis, and the analysis here described is based on the 'Ingrid 72' program devised by Slater (22). But of course other types of analysis may be carried out.

Table 14.3   *The frequencies with which the elements (= R) of father's responses are characterized by the constructs shown in the left-hand column (The responses from Appendix A are analyzed in Tables 14.1 and 14.2)*

Constructs	Elements					
	f − m	*f − b*	*m − f*	*m − b*	*b − f*	*b − m*
1 v+	0	0	0	0	1	0
2 v	0	0	0	0	1	0
3 v−	2	1	2	0	0	0
4 a+	0	1	0	0	1	0
5 a	0	0	0	0	0	0
6 a−	0	0	0	0	0	1
7 at+	1	2	2	1	0	0
8 at	0	1	0	0	0	0
9 at−	0	4	0	3	1	1
10 ft+	0	0	0	0	0	0
11 ft	0	0	0	0	0	0
12 ft−	0	0	0	0	1	1

The data were analyzed as follows. There are six possible dyadic asymmetric relationships in a three-person family. They are: f - m, f - b, m - f, m - b, b - f, b - m. These are termed the elements and are placed at the head of the columns in Table 14.3. The ratings (v +, v, v-., etc. = R) are termed the constructs and are placed in the left-hand side column of the table. The cells of the table contain the frequencies with which each construct is ascribed to each element. Owing to the small amount of material analyzed for demonstration purposes, many cells contain no entry, and the frequency in any cell does not exceed four. However the 'Ingrid 72' program accepts a dichotomous rating as well as a graded, or ranked set of frequencies. So although this particular set of data was rather slight, it could be processed because any frequency in a cell was graded 1, while 0 was accorded to all other cells. If a quality a, v, ft, etc. is ascribed to a dyadic relationship at least once, it does not follow that it would be more intense if it were ascribed with greater frequency to the same dyad. So it seems reasonable to use a dichotomous grading. It follows, therefore, that this analysis is based upon a qualitative rather than a quantitative view of dyadic relationships. The resulting grid was analysed to give a set of three principal components, as described by Slater (22, p. 10). The results of the analysis of both father's and mother's views are shown for comparison on the same graph, in Figure 14.4.

Characteristics of relationship
The print-out of the 'Ingrid 72' program provides sets of inter-correlations between the constructs and between the elements. It also provides correlations between constructs and elements that are expressed in degrees. A small angle between an element and a construct may be interpreted as indicating that the construct is characteristic of that particular element. Thus, in Table 14.4 the angle between construct No. 3, (v-) and element 1 (f - m) is zero according to father's information. This may be interpreted as meaning that, in father's view, he is verbally hostile toward his wife. That is to say that the 'one-way' dyadic relationship (f - m) is characterized by 'negatively loaded,' (i.e., hostile) verbal activity. An angle of 90° between an element and a construct indicates that there is no consistent relation between them. An angle of 180° means the construct is un-characteristic of the element. So the angle between element m - f and construct at-means that a negative attitude is not characteristic of the relationship of m to f. However, it cannot be assumed that the attitude of m to f is therefore good, simply because a 'bad' attitude has a negative correlation with it. The characteristics of other asymmetrical, dyadic relationships may be tentatively deduced from the angular distances shown in Table 14.4.

DISCUSSION

Some features of the BIM
The behavioral interactional model (BIM) of the nuclear family may be regarded as a 'system' within the terms of Bertalanffy's definition (4). It is, however, highly unlikely that there would be any need to apply to this simple family model the sophisticated mathematics of 'general system analysis.' The model does, however, form a useful basis for organizing and analyzing data about the family, and it is capable of being extended to large family groups and networks.

The BIM may also be used as a simple communication model for messages and activities that are transmitted within the family, since any pathway through the family can be indicated by the unidirectional arrows in accordance with the elementary theory of graphs (28). Generally speaking, there is an insufficient number of 'pathways' or 'channels of communications' within an ordinary

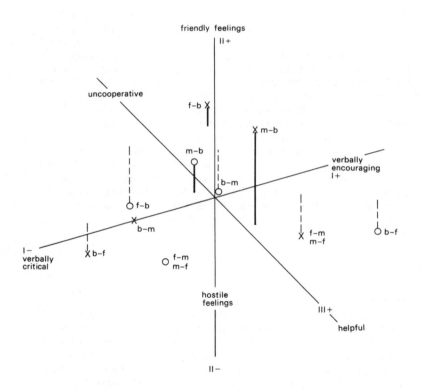

FIGURE 14.4 Geometrical representation of father's and mother's
views of the relationships between themselves and their 13-year-old
son. O = father's views; X = mother's views. The results of the
factor analysis have been plotted on 'perspective paper' with
respect to the three principal factors extracted by the analysis.
Dotted lines indicate the plots below the horizontal axes, full
lines indicate those above them. f – m indicates general attitudinal
relationship of father toward mother, m – f that of mother toward
father, and so on.

(N.B. The plotted values of father's views of f-m and m-f
coincide and so do mother's views of the same relationships.)

Table 14.4   The relation between elements and constructs shown in terms of degrees.
Father's responses as analyzed in Tables 14.1 and 14.2

Constructs	Elements					
	1 f − m	2 f − b	3 m − f	4 m − b	5 b − f	6 b − m
1 v+	147	107	147	102	0	77
2 v	147	107	147	102	0	77
3 v−	0	61	0	120	162	135
4 a+	135	70	135	110	40	89
5 a−	118	102	118	102	80	30
6 at+	0	66	0	70	180	150
7 at	93	43	93	102	103	102
8 at−	180	86	180	69	35	54

family to make the application of mathematical analyses worthwhile.
But when family networks (2, 24) are being investigated, the
behavioral interactional model may facilitate an investigation into
the properties of a large group.

The analysis of family interactions based on this model makes use
of statements that are made about the family either by other people
or by the family members themselves. The original data may therefore consist of observations made by an observer or of statements
made in response to a projective technique or statements made
during an interview or conversation. Whatever the source, the
data for analysis consist of a recorded version of the speaker's
utterances.

The use of the BIM in behavioral analysis
The behavioral interactional model of the family may be used as a
basis for behavioral analysis (7, 14) as applied to family groups
and individuals. These analytical methods identify and catalogue
specific items of behavior corresponding to the values of R and Q
already described. One possible form for such a catalogue of
behavior is given in Table 14.5. The behavioral items are classified
as acceptable or unacceptable. The former are to be encouraged
and the latter to be discouraged by the means specified in Column 7.
The class of behavior, whether Q or R, is shown in Column 1. The
actual items are specified in Column 2, their frequency is recorded
in Column 3, and their severity or intensity is rated on a three-
point scale in Column 4. The length of time the behavior has been
continuing is noted in Column 5, and the person against whom it
is directed is shown in Column 6. Such a catalogue of behavior is
composed of items precisely similar to those of the analyzed protocol
given in Table 14.1. By identifying specific behavioral items in
this way, the therapist can formulate specific aims for his treatment program. He also obtains a base-line against which subsequent
change may be assessed. Since individual behavioral items can be
scored for duration, frequency, and intensity, this type of

assessment is more sensitive to change than the traditional method of rating on a five-point scale, so frequently employed in the past (9).

Table 14.5　Behavioral analysis sheet

1	2	3	4	5	6	7
Q or R	*Item of Behavior*	*f*	1 2 3	*t*	*y*	*Method of Modification*

Section A
Acceptable behavior
Section B
Unacceptable behavior
Section C
Potential behavior
Section D
Skills, interests

Logical basis of the model

There is a specifically logical basis for this model of the family, and the logical formulae used to describe its interactions may be indefinitely extended to cover as large a family as required. By substituting specific properties and people for the symbols in the formulae xRy and Qx, a very wide variety of relations and characteristics can be summarized and coded. Since these formulae are applicable to a system of any size, they may be used to describe a family or social network (24) as well as the relationships within a single family. The values that are substituted in the formulae readily lend themselves to being recorded in matrix form and may then be handled statistically (see Tables 14.2 and 14.3).

The use of behavioral ratings instead of global or nosological categories enables family problems to be defined with greater precision. The inter-rater reliability for category type classification is notoriously low (18), and category type assessments are of little use in making therapeutic plans. On the other hand, an itemization of behavior enables the therapist to aim at modifying specific and detailed behavioral activity. By selecting specific individual items for behavior modification, it is sometimes possible to bring about small changes in the family's behavior, when it would not be possible to change the family 'as a whole.' The isolation of specific behavioral disorders also enables a variety of techniques to be used, so that the family therapist is not dependent upon an 'all or nothing' approach to family problems.

The behavioral interactional model, because of its emphasis upon discrete items of behavior, is admirably suited to the detailed study of the single case. Although the single case method has usually been applied to individual clients (21, 29), it is applicable to the study of an individual family. The constitution and the environmental conditions of families vary so enormously that there is much to be said for treating each family as an 'individual' in its own right and to refrain from attempting to push it into a nosological category.

Some objections to a dyadic analysis of the family
Objections are sometimes raised against regarding the family as a series of dyadic interactions on the grounds that the family group is a 'unity' and should be treated as such. One reason for adopting a unitary view of the family is the way we think and talk about 'the family.' The word 'family' is obviously a singular noun that per-forms the same grammatical function in a sentence as other discrete singular nouns. So by a process of association the word 'family' tends to be regarded as indicating a simple, discrete entity. More-over, it is usual in ordinary conversation to speak of 'the family' as if it were a well-defined, compact, and cohesive structure. Hence common usage also encourages the view that the family is a unitary concept.

This linguistic concept of the family has been reinforced by attempting to classify families in nosological terms as nuclear, extended, cohesive, uni-parent, happy, and so on. Such classifica-tion has a very limited value. Families differ so widely that it is almost impossible to find a sufficient number of common features with which to form satisfactory categories. Moreover, as Agnew and Bannister (1) have shown, even traditional psychiatric dis-orders can be adequately described in everyday language. A detailed description of the individual activities of the family in ordinary language would therefore seem to be in keeping with the current therapeutic practice and would favor an analytic, rather than a unitary view of the family.

A further argument against an analytic description of the family is that the family forms a Gestalt and should therefore be con-sidered as a 'whole.' If, it is argued, the family group is analyzed into its constituent parts, some of its vital properties will in-evitably be lost. It is true that at any one moment the set of relationships within a family may be regarded as forming a Gestalt. But the family Gestalt changes, sometimes very quickly as a result of the processes of growth and decay and the impact of its environ-ment. It follows, therefore, that the family group can be analyzed, at least to the extent of detecting changes within it. Although a Gestalt is perceived as a 'whole,' that does not prevent it from being analyzed, as any 'scanning' process demonstrates.

There is also an element of mystique still associated with the family that is derived from tradition and folklore and that regards the family as an inviolable whole. This mystique is given a pseudo-rational expression by invoking the principle that 'the whole exceeds the sum of its parts.' It is true that a family as a group possesses properties that cannot be possessed by its members as isolated individuals. But as Bertalanffy has pointed out, 'If . . . we know the total of parts contained in a system and the relations between them, the behavior of the system may be derived from the behavior of its parts' (4, p. 54). It is therefore difficult to accept the view

that there is still 'something left out' if the family is analyzed
and described as a system of interacting dyads. To do so would
savor more of animism than of science.

Another still popular view of the family is the biological analogy,
which regards the family 'as if' it were a living organism. But
family groups, like other social groups, can be dismembered and
reconstituted in a manner that no organism could possibly tolerate.
Moreover, the 'units' of which families are composed exist in their
own right and interact with each other in a manner quite different
from the highly specialized, functional parts of the organism. The
comparison of social groups with organisms is of little use as a
method of scientific description, since it rests upon the logically
dubious method of analogy. It leads to a metaphorical explanation
of the family in terms of something that is quite different from it.
The scientific approach analyzes the family in terms of its own
structure, so that the units of analysis are found within the group
itself and not borrowed from an outside source.

The complexity of family interactions
One very practical objection to the BIM of the family arises from
the sheer amount of data that may have to be handled. For example,
in a relatively unstructured interview, the range of topics may be
quite large. Hence there will be many more values of 'x' and 'y'
than are obtained when a small family situation is being discussed.
The actual number of persons and objects represented by 'x' and
'y' does not of course alter the method of analysis, but it may make
the number of rows and columns in Table 14.2 uncomfortably large.
If a matrix requires a large number of rows and columns, it encounters the criticism that Wells and Rabiner (26) made about
other models of the family, namely that it may prove somewhat
'unwieldy' in practice. If so, the 'unwieldyness' is inherent in the
data being handled. There are a large number of possible interactions within even a four-person family, as the structure of the
present model makes plain (see Figure 14.3). This model enables
four different kinds of interactions to be recorded in each of
three grades so the total number of recorded behavior items may be
very large. The alternative to such a detailed recording of behavioral elements is the use of more inclusive categories of behavior
like those described in the review by Gurman (9). The fact that
a family's behavior is made up of a large number of individual
items is one of the intrinsic difficulties encountered when attempting to give an adequate description of a family group. It does,
however, seem worthwhile to attempt to devise a method of
cataloguing specific behavioral items instead of relying upon the
use of broad categories of behavior. The use of such categories
often leads to a lack of clarity about what actually happens within
the family. It may also obscure important, individual items of
behavior, which are difficult to categorise, but which may be of
crucial importance to the functioning of the family. Broad classification thus becomes in the words of Wells and Rabiner (26) 'insufficiently explicit.'

It should also be remembered that large numbers of items are now easily handled by computer analysis. The 'Ingrid 72' program accepts a 25 x 25 grid for analysis, while some programs can accept grids as large as 50 x 50, or even larger. The BIM can easily be extended to analyze information about twenty or thirty people in one protocol, even if a rather large sheet of paper would be required! Fortunately, interviews and therapeutic conversations rarely include such a wide range of significant objects within their fields of discourse. If they do, it is a salutary reminder that inter- personal behavior is extremely complex, and we do our clients and ourselves a disservice if we try to oversimplify it.

APPENDIX A

Father's responses to cards F2, B2, F3, M3 of the Family Relations Indicator. The responses have been edited, leaving only acceptable sentences and semi-sentences in the protocol. The constituent analysis of the statements is shown by means of 'slashes' (/). (NP = noun phrase; VP = verbal phrase; Adv = adverbial expression; NEG = negative; S´ indicates that this constituent implies another sentence within the deep structure of the main sentence.) These abbreviations are placed within brackets () after the relevant phrases in the following analyzed statements numbered 6, 8, 26, 27 and 40.

Card F2. Father and son standing looking at each other.
1) I am puzzled by this picture / because 2) Father and son are both standing / . 3) Had they been sitting / 4) I would have thought that / 5) they are having a discussion / . 6) Father (NP) / is being rather (Adv) domineering (VP). He is not getting down to the level of understanding of the boy / . 8) He (NP$_1$) / is reprimand- ing VP / the lad (NP$_2$). 9) I don't really feel that / this suggests anything else to me. /

Card B2. Boy with broken vase on the floor.
10) The lad is expressing alarm / and 11) a vase has been broken. / 12) I like to think / it was an accident. / 13) Boys are not intentionally bad-minded. / 14) They get into tempers. / 15) But here is a typical accident. / 16) The boy is showing dismay / 17) because he has unfortunately broken something. / 18) The boy would be most apologetic. / 19) He would see his parents / 20) and tell them / what he has done. 21) The parents' reactions to an accident would be the right one. /

Card F3. Father in chair and boy playing on floor.
22) This is what I like. / 23) Father relaxed in his chair / and is reading the paper. 24) The lad is experimenting with modern life. / 25) His thinking is modern. / 26) Because Father (NP$_1$) / has turned (VP) / his head (NP$_2$) / to look (S´), / 27) he (NP$_1$) / is not (Neg) pushing (VP) / the boy (NP$_2$) / off (Adv). 28) He is

interested in / what the lad is doing. / 29) He's quite prepared
to make suggestions. / 30) I like to think / 31) he'll even get
down on his hands and knees on the floor with the lad. / 32) This
is a happy picture. /

Card M 3. Mother standing on the doorstep, boy looking up at her.
   33) A typical situation is this. / 34) It does not convey really
anything to me. / 35) It could be a person coming from their
house. / 36) There is certainly no emotional expression in this
picture. / 37) He's bringing his school report. / 38) I'd be pleased
to think that / it was his school report / 39) because his appearance
gives no indication of any agitation. / 40) Children (NP$_1$) / should
not (NEG) have a fear of (VP) / showing their reports (NP$_2$) / to
their parents (S´). /

NOTE

* Grateful acknowledgment is made to Dr Patrick Slater of the
Maudsley Hospital and to the MRC Unit for providing the service
for analyzing data by means of the 'Ingrid 72' program. I am
indebted, too, to Dr John G. Howells, Director of the Institute
of Family Psychiatry, for the data provided by two of his patients.
Thanks are also owed to the Data Processing Manager of the East
Anglian Regional Hospital Board for carrying out the analysis.

REFERENCES

1 Agnew, J. and Bannister, D., Psychiatric Diagnosis As a Pseudo-
     Specialist Language, 'Brit. J. Med. Psychol.', 46: 1973, 69–73.
2 Attneave, C. L., Therapy in Tribal Settings and Urban Network
     Intervention, 'Fam. Proc.', 8: 1969, 192–210.
3 Balentine, R.W. The Family Therapist as a Behavioural Systems
     Engineer, in J.O. Bradt and C.J. Moyniham (eds), 'Systems
     Therapy', Washington DC, Groome CG Center, 1972, pp. 96–102.
4 Bertalanffy, L. von, 'General System Theory: Foundations Develop-
     ment Applications', London, Allen Lane the Penguin Press, 1971.
5 Chomsky, N., 'Aspects of the Theory of Syntax', Cambridge,
     Mass., MIT Press, 1965.
6 Fogarty, T.F., Family Structure in Terms of Triangles in J.O. Bradt
     and C.J. Moyniham (eds), op cit. (ref. 3), pp. 43–9, 19[7]
7 Franks, C.M., 'Behavior Therapy, Appraisal and Status' .ew
     York, McGraw-Hill, 1969.
8 Gleason, H.A., 'An Introduction to Descriptive Linguistics' (re-
     vised edition), New York, Holt, Rinehart & Winston, 1969.
9 Gurman, A.S., The Effects and Effectiveness of Marital Therapy:
     A Review of Outcome Research, 'Fam. Proc.', 12: 1973, 145–170.
10 Guttman, H.A., and Spector, R.M., Sigal, J.J., Epstein, N.B.,
     Rakoff, V., Coding of Affective Expression in Conjoint Family
     Therapy, 'Amer. J. Psychother.', 26: 1972, 185–94.

11 Howells, J.G., 'Theory and Practice of Family Psychiatry', Edinburgh, Oliver & Boyd, 1968.
12 Howells, J.G., and Lickorish, J.R., 'The Family Relations Indicator,' New York, Brunner/Mazell, 1973.
13 Katz, J.J., Semi-Sentences in J.A. Fodor and J.J. Katz (eds), 'The Structure of Language: Readings in the Philosophy of Language,' Englewood Cliffs, New Jersey, Prentice-Hall, 1964.
14 Krasner, L. and Ullman, L.P., 'Research in Behavior Modification. New Developments and Implications,' New York, Holt, Rinehart & Winston, 1965.
15 Laffal, J., An Approach to the Total Content Analysis of Speech in Psychotherapy, in J.M. Shlien (ed.), 'Research in Psychotherapy. Proceedings of the Third Conference Chicago 1966, Washington, DC,' American Psychological Association, 1968.
16 Lee, H.N., 'Symbolic Logic: An Introductory Textbook for Non-Mathematicians,' London, Routledge & Kegan Paul, 1962.
17 Lester, M., 'Introductory Transformational Grammar of English,' New York, Holt, Rinehart & Winston, 1971.
18 Ley, P. Acute Psychiatric Patients, in P. Mittler (ed.), 'The Psychological Assessment of Mental and Physical Handicaps,' London, Methuen, 1970.
19 Liberman, R., Behavioral Approaches to Family and Couple Therapy, 'Am. J. Orthopsychiat.,' 40: 1970, 106-18.
20 Mahl, G.F., Gestures and Body Movements in Interviews, in J.M. Shlien (ed.), 'Research in Psychotherapy,' vol. III. Washington DC, American Psychological Association, 1966.
21 Shapiro, M.B., The Single Case in Fundamental Clinical Psychological Research, 'Brit. J. Med. Psychol.,' 34: 1961, 255-62.
22 Slater, P., 'Notes on Ingrid 72,' Institute of Psychiatry, de Crespigny Park, Denmark Hill, London, SE5, 1972.
23 Slobin, D.I., 'Psycholinguistics,' London, Scott Foresman, 1971.
24 Speck, R.V. and Rueveni, U., Network Therapy - A Developing Concept, 'Fam Proc.,' 8: 1969, 182-91.
25 Webb, E.J., Campbell, D.T., Schwartz, R.D. and Sechrest, L., 'Unobtrusive Measures. Nonreactive Research in the Social Sciences,' Chicago, Rand McNally, 1966.
26 Wells, C.F. and Rabiner, E.L., The Conjoint Family Diagnostic Interview and the Family Index of Tension, 'Fam. Proc.,' 12: 1973, 127-44.
27 Wertheim, E.S., Family Unit Therapy and the Science and Typology of Family Systems, 'Fam. Proc.,' 12: 1973, 361-76.
28 Wilson, R.J., 'Introduction to Graph Theory,' Edinburgh, Oliver & Boyd, 1972.
29 Yates, A.J., 'Behavior Therapy,' New York, Wiley, 1970.

Part 3

DIFFERENTIAL APPROACHES

15 PSYCHOANALYSIS AND FAMILY THERAPY

Christopher Dare

INTRODUCTION

There is, as yet, no authoritative history of family therapy, although Skynner (1969), Bell (1975) and Zuk (1971) have summarised aspects of the subject from their own different points of view. History requires a distance from its subject that is great enough for foreground to be discerned from background and chance features distinguished from central phenomena and it can be argued that the therapeutic practice of family interventions is of too short a duration to gain such a historical perspective. This makes it difficult to put family therapy and psychoanalysis into relationship with each other without entering into polemic.

Some writers (e.g. Haley, 1973, 1976 and Watzlawick et al., 1974) have argued that the points of view of psychoanalysis and family therapy are contradictory, whilst others (e.g. Boszormenyi-Nagy and Spark, 1973 and Stierlin, 1977) show the strong indebtedness of their versions of the theory and practice of whole family therapy to psychoanalysis.

The most important theories of psychoanalysis are to do with the development and functioning of a hypothetical entity, within the individual person, which is the 'mind'. The theory of family therapy is at its most distinctive when it is addressed to a quite different hypothetical entity which is the family as a system. The characteristic activities of the psychoanalyst as a practitioner are in a one-to-one therapy in which the task of the therapist is his close observation of his patients' mental processes. Interventions with therapeutic intent, interpretations, are aimed at increasing the patients' self-understanding. This is considered to have an effect in bringing about changes in the psychological structures - that is, in the mind. Structural mental change is thought to be facilitated by the length and regularity of the treatment which enables multiple repetitions of interpretations of different form and with different contents, to be made. This is known as working through. The setting of the therapy is itself thought to have therapeutic qualities but this 'real' contingency is thought to be less powerful than 'transference' interpretations. The nature of this class of intervention will be discussed later in the chapter, at length, because it is of central importance.

The family therapist, on the other hand, may be considered to

281

have a wider range of activities than is encompassed by that of the interpretative mode of psychoanalysis. He is like the analyst in so far as he has to make hypotheses about the structure of the processes underlying the phenomena presented to him by his subject. His communication of that understanding as an insight provoking interpretation is not his principal therapeutic intervention. Would-be therapeutic activities are directed at attempting to get the family members to interact with each other and then to change the sequence and patterns of their interactions. If insights are offered the purpose would be the furtherance of change in family interaction, rather than in the promotion of self-understanding as an end in itself. As the emphasis is upon the formation and practice of new patterns of relationship within the family, the dependence and associated length of treatment of psychoanalysis is not sought by family therapists who tend to favour short-term or crisis intervention. None the less, many family therapists have a theory of change which puts the aim of therapy as being the securement of enduring change in the structure of the family system.

In this introduction I have commented upon the differences in subject matter, the contrasting features of the duration, persons present and therapeutic activities of psychoanalysis and family therapy. The style of presentation is intended to give hints of the direction of the line of argument of the chapter which is that there are analogic connections between psychoanalytic therapy of the individual and the dominant classes of family therapy of the systems theory and structural schools. The next section gives a paradigm to make further links and distinctions between family therapy and psychoanalysis. (Freud (1916–17) pointed out that psychoanalysis as a word was used to describe both a theory of the mind and a therapy. In this chapter the phrase family therapy is taken to imply both a therapy and a theory of the family.)

THE LOCATION OF TREATMENT INTERVENTIONS IN FAMILY THERAPY AND PSYCHOANALYSIS

This section of the chapter will show that there are similarities and distinctions between the site described by family therapists and psychoanalysts to locate their distinctive therapeutic activities.

Three British psychoanalysts (Bentovim, 1979: Cooklin 1979 and Dare, 1979) have shown a convergence of views as to certain connections between the theories of family therapy and of psychoanalysis. They all three argue from the standpoint of psychoanalysts who also use whole family therapies, strongly influenced by Minuchin's (1974) particular form of systems theory of the family. The convergence consists of a particular way of using a broadly agreed object relations theory of psychoanalysis. This view emphasises the role of internalised experiences within the family of origin of the person as being crucial in determining the nature of the adult personality. The structure of the mind is seen as bearing the imprint of interactions, over time, between the person and members of the family

of origin as individuals; as showing internalisations of perceived
and fantasised interactions between the various dydadic, triadic
and quadratic groupings contained within the family and of the
efforts of the person to adapt to the demands and seeking both ad-
herence to and distinction from, the family as a whole system. Such
thinking gives rise to a 'model' of the mind of a family participant
such as that displayed in Figure 15.1. The person draws upon the
experiences of life in their family of origin whilst growing up, which
lead to patterns of tendencies and which contribute to the 'negotiations' between family members. These help to create the actual
systemic structure of the individual's new family.

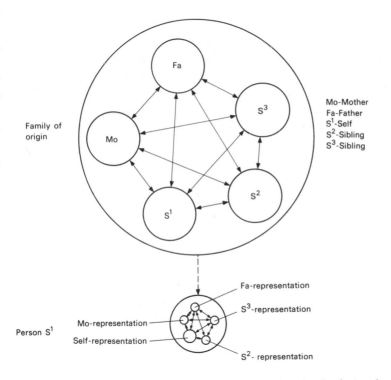

FIGURE 15.1 The process of 'internalisation' of the family of origin
in the person S^1

Notes

1   The arrows joining family members and internalised representa-
    tions of family members identify multiple transactions, over time.
2   The internalised representations and their interactions are
    analogically reproduced from the family of origin to the mental
    structure of the individual members of the family. The mental
    structures called upon during family interaction draw upon
    derivatives of experiences within the family of origin as well

as those within the family of creation.
3   The mother and father (Mo and Fa) have mental structures
    derived from their own families of origin, which are drawn upon
    for the creation and maintenance of their own family interaction
    activities.

Figure 15.1 shows that each member of the family of a person S[1]
is recorded within his memory and that patterns of interaction between himself and the persons of his family of origin are represented
as potential for interactions when he himself is making a family. The
relationship between the past family experiences lead to the formation within the person of what Boszormenyi-Nagy (Boszormenyi-
Nagy and Spark, 1973) has named 'relationship needs templates'.

The site of action of psychoanalytic psychotherapy
In the early days of psychoanalytic therapies, the work of the therapist was considered to be that of attempting to discern the underlying pattern of meaning that lay behind the utterances of the
patient during the course of so-called 'free association'. When such
a pattern was observed it was related to the patient as an interpretation as to the workings of his mind. The theory of therapy relied
heavily upon the notion of insight, defined in terms of making unconscious aspects of mental life more conscious. However, in the
early years of this century (Freud, 1912, 1915) the process of
psychotherapy began to be understood in a different light. Freud
realised that the apparent wish of the patient to get better, and
hence to co-operate in treatment was obstructed not simply by the
mental forces of repression limiting the patient's ability to gain
knowledge of his unconscious mental life, but also by the nature
of the relationship that tended to develop between patient and psychoanalyst. Initially the patient's tendencies to become deeply, although ambivalently, attached to the psychotherapist were seen
merely as a nuisance impeding therapeutic progress. As experience
of the process led to its understanding, the attachment of patient
to analyst came to be seen as arising not only out of actual qualities
and features of the patient-therapist dyad, but also from factors
which were entirely to do with the patient's past life, especially his
past life of intense and crucial family experiences. For many years
psychoanalysts were mainly interested in the repetitions of positive
loving feelings of the past (especially those of an oedipal nature)
that occurred in therapy. For example, if a female patient developed
intense shame over loving and erotic fantasies about the male therapist, these would be seen as containing elements of past feelings towards the father of the patient.

In the last thirty years, analysts have been increasingly interested
in the repetitions of early infant-to-mother types of feelings and
expectations with both intensely positive and negative qualities that
regularly develop in the course of intense psychotherapy.

Over time, the understanding of these processes, which are those
of transference, have come to dominate the psychoanalytic concepts
of therapy and therapeutic change. Psychoanalysis as a treatment although continuing to be thought of as directed towards the bringing

about of 'structural mental change', became, in practice, directed
towards helping the patient move away from patterns of feelings
about the self and others, dominated by past family relationships.
This move has been exemplified in the work of Strachey (1969) who
designated the effective psychoanalytic interventions as 'mutative
interpretation'. Essentially, he used this term to apply to interpretations which pointed out the way in which expectations about com-
mands, rules or prohibitions derived from the actual (or fantasy
distorted) parents, were shaping the manner of the patient towards
the psychoanalyst. Malan, in a series of publications (summarised
in Malan, 1963, 1976a and 1976b) has gone some way towards sub-
stantiating Strachey's propositions. He has shown that efficacious
short-term psychoanalytic psychotherapy can be carried out if the
therapist directs attention towards understanding the relationship
in the patient's mind, of attitudes towards the therapist (transferences), the figures of the family life of the patient as a child
(the original objects) and the important people of the patient's
current world.

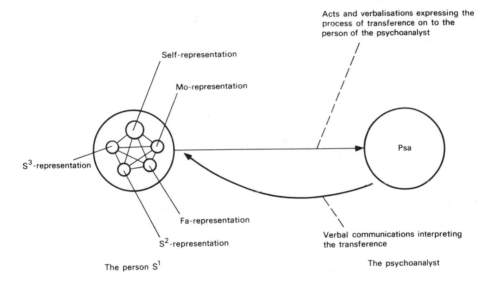

FIGURE 15.2 The process of psychoanalytic psychotherapy involving the person (S^1) and the psychoanalyst (Psa)

Notes

1   It is not assumed that all the communications of the patient to
     the psychoanalyst are transference derivatives, nor that the
     therapist's communications to the patient are solely verbal and
     consist only of transference interpretations.
2   The figure represents the process whereby the patient experi-
     ences the psychoanalyst, symbolically, as a member of the

family of origin. This is commented upon by the psychoanalyst and such interpretations are deemed 'mutative' if they link past family relationship tendencies, to present thoughts, feelings, attitudes and expectations towards the analyst and to patterns of behaviour and feelings about people in the patient's current world (cf. Strachey, 1969; Malan, 1976a, 1976b).

In Figure 15.2 an attempt at displaying the location of psychoanalytic therapeutic interventions, pictures the internal world of past (and of course, to some extent, present) family relationships, affecting some of the patient's communications towards the therapist. The psychoanalytic psychotherapist is selectively interested in derivatives of such past relationship tendencies, as they are experienced in the present, in the psychotherapeutic set-up. Interpretations of the nature of the patient's communications to the analyst try to show the patient the rather fixed, perhaps inhibiting and restricting, nature of the patterns of feelings and their archaic origins.

In this process, the analyst does not see himself as an uninvolved outsider, but expects to find himself drawn into enacting aspects of the family figures of the patient's past life. These enactments ('countertransference acts') may consist of getting unreasonably irritated, or rejecting or excessively protective and smothering. The therapist hopes to detect them as feeling tendencies in himself, rather than to put them into actual practice. If 'caught in time' these feelings are important clues as to aspects of the patient's past experiences.

In summary, psychoanalytic psychotherapy has come to take as its subject matter, the derivatives of the patient's past family life, as expressed transferentially in the therapeutic setting. Interpretations are aimed at demonstrating the effects of the past, on the present, as the internal world of the family figures of the past, within the patient's mind, are externalised on to the person of the psychotherapist. By interpreting the externalisations, rather than by enacting a role towards the patient in repetition of the past relationship systems, the analyst hopes to facilitate the patient's abilities to change the disadvantageous features of his repetitive patterns. Because of the dyadic nature of the therapeutic situation, it is not surprising that psychoanalysis, with its increasing interest in transference phenomena, has come to concentrate particularly on the crucial dyad of development, that of the mother-infant pair.

The site of action of whole family therapy
In Figure 15.1 the family was portrayed as an interacting group of individuals whose pattern of transactions shaped the mental life of the children of the family. (This must not be taken to mean that the family processes are without effect upon the adult members of the family – the parental, marital couple.) The circle around the family members can be taken also to show that the sum of the parts constitutes a total which differs from the qualities of the individuals seen separately. The way that a family actually conducts its relationships cannot simply be predicted from a knowledge, however complete, of the family members' past experiences. The family as a

system uniquely yet unpredictably balances the needs, demands, fears, expectations and wishes of the family members, directed towards each other. Although unpredictable solely from a knowledge of the psychology of the family members, the patterns, when established, become extremely defined, and the identification from observing fixed sequences of interactions, of the transactional systems of the family, is the subject matter of the family therapist. The conceptual leap from observing underlying structures of the mental processes of the individual to observing sequences revealing the underlying structure of a family group, is one that has to be taken by all family therapists, whatever conceptual framework they may use.

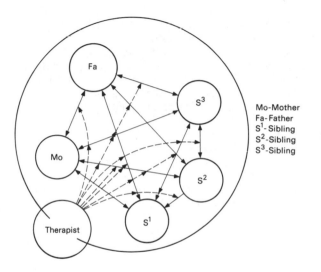

Mo-Mother
Fa-Father
S1-Sibling
S2-Sibling
S3-Sibling

FIGURE 15.3 The process of family therapy

Notes

1 Continuous lines, arrowed, between family members, indicate the patterns of interaction between them. The broken lines from the therapist to the interaction lines of the family members, indicate treatment interventions by the therapist.

2 The family therapist perceives regularities in the pattern and sequences of family interactions (the 'structure' of the family). By his interventions the therapist attempts to change these interactions and hence effects the processes being internalised by the family members which are going towards shaping the inner world of the mental life of the family.

3 The mother and father of a family are, as explained in Figure 15.1, note 3, influenced in their attitudes, beliefs and expectations about the sort of family patterns they create, and tend to certain types of interactive behaviour within the family, on

the basis of internalised patterns from their own families of origin. Some therapists use these historically comprehensible, intergenerational features to shape their therapeutic strategies and techniques (e.g. Boszormenyi-Nagy and Spark, 1973; Lieberman, 1979; Byng-Hall, 1979 and Dare, 1979).

Figure 15.3 depicts the process of family therapy in order to discuss the site of action of such therapies. The therapist is shown as relating to a five person family, and from a position on the boundary of the family directs interventions towards the interactions of the family. The circle around the family members is meant to show that the family system contains and describes the patterns of family life and the therapist is shown as being partly inside and partly outside of that system. By his interventive techniques he hopes that he will not be irrevocably drawn into the system, so that he can only act, like a family member, to perpetuate the dysfunction; instead he attempts to experience the processes of the family and, by his techniques, produces change in the patterns of interaction. The process of being drawn into the family system so as to play a role in perpetuating the equilibrium of the system is known as 'affiliation' (Minuchin, 1974). It is an identical process to the absorption into the individual's habitual interpersonal systems that constitute countertransferences. Both affiliation and countertransference enactments can block the therapeutic efficacy of the psychotherapist in individual and family work. At the same time the processes provide sources of understanding of the subject matter of the therapy.

By his therapeutic activities, the therapist will, if effective, change the interactive processes of the family, hopefully releasing family members from the constraints associated with bearing symptoms. At the same time it can be noted that processes whereby the external, real, world of family interactions, internalised into the inner world of the mental life of the individual family members, will be transmuted by family therapy. In summary, the family therapist intervenes on those external processes which are being internalised to become part of the crucial psychological make-up of the family members. The site of action of family therapy interventions is thus the same as that of psychoanalytic psychotherapy but whereas psychoanalytic psychotherapy is directed towards the point at which the internal world is being externalised, family therapy is directed towards the point at which the external world is becoming internalised.

This fact makes for certain great similarities between the psychoanalytic therapy of the individual and that of the whole family, but it also makes for certain essential differences. The nature of the processes within families is extremely familiar to the psychoanalyst, although psychoanalysts without experiences of meeting whole families may feel as bewildered and engulfed as a therapist of any other background by the power and subtlety of the family's power to absorb and incorporate the therapist. Moreover he has to learn that straightforward interpretations of the processes of the family, when he learns to observe them, are commonly ineffective, and frequently merely lead to the family using such insights to redouble their already high level of effort and ability to forestall change. Further, the psychoanalyst will find that although transference–like phenomena can be observed, and interpreted to the family, such comments produce little therapeutic change and are particularly in-effective in maintaining a continuing attendance and commitment to the therapy.

The author would argue that such a simple transportation of technique from one area of work to another could be predicted to be useless. The psychoanalyst in family therapy must use a wider range of therapeutic techniques than that of interpretation, and learns that although insight can sometimes effect change, that change is a powerful promoter of insight.

CLINICAL CONCEPTS OF PSYCHOANALYSIS

In order to schematise some aspects of the links between psycho-analytic psychotherapy and whole family therapy, the two activities are contrasted and compared in Tables 15.1 and 15.2.

Table 15.1   The distinctions between psychoanalytic psychotherapy of the individual and whole family therapy

	Individual therapy	*Whole family therapy*
Patients	Never more than one	Two upwards
Setting	Privacy and confidentiality ensured	Observational settings (e.g. one-way screen or video-recording) often used
Frequency	Usually one to five times a week	Usually once every one to three weeks
Duration	May be measured in years rather than months	Usually lasting a few weeks to a few months
Therapist	Never more than one Often will have had personal, individual therapy in training	One or two (co-therapy) Will not have had a 'didactic' therapy
Definition of pathology	Intrapsychic conflict or defect of psychological structure	Dysfunctional family structure
Technique	Verbal interventions, predominantly interpretative	Multiple in form, active, task setting, paradoxical instructions, etc.
Aim of therapy	Insight promotion	Change in family structure
Therapeutic stance	Tends to be passive and receptive, little conscious manipulation	Tends to be active, intrusive and controlling. Conscious manipulation regularly used

Table 15.1 shows that at a descriptive level, family therapy and psychoanalysis are clearly distinct. However, even at this level there is an immediate discrepancy for, in the last entry in the table, the contrasting therapeutic stances of the individual and family therapists are designated along an axis of activity, control and manipulation. Yet the psychoanalytic passivity has a strongly

controlling aspect. Just as 'no communication' IS 'communication',
then 'passive non-intrusiveness' IS 'activity'. The analyst's unre-
sponsiveness, refusal to answer questions (unless he wishes to do
so), his request to the patient to lie down on the couch, not to
expect advice about life or symptom-derived problems, to free
associate, and so on, are in fact controlling and active injunctions.
That they are made in an apparent context of permissiveness and
freedom, is part of the essentially paradoxical nature of psychoanalytic therapy.

The author would argue that the main differences that appear on
the list can be understood as an outcome of the constitution of the
therapeutic setting. In a dyadic therapy, the patient is obliged, if
he wishes for an audience, to address his remarks to the therapist.
If the therapist has a rather impervious attitude to the patient's
questions and tends to respond to certain topics rather than others,
then the patient is going to come under the influences of these
contingencies. The patient will tend to take notice of what the therapist says, even if the criteria of interest that the therapist displays
are different to those of the patient. Here again attention is being
drawn to elements of psychoanalytic treatment, not out of a wish to
disqualify the activity, but to point to some of its paradoxical
features.

The family therapist, however, cannot guarantee the interest of
his audience, for the family members have each other to talk to and
need take no notice of the therapist for guidance or entertainment
during the session. The psychoanalyst's inactivity can function as
an active intervention, because of his unique presence. The therapist's activities in family therapy have to be more obvious and insist-
ent, to gain his audience's attention. The family have to be encouraged to take notice of the family therapist in a way that is quite unlike the demands on the individual therapist. However there is a
limitation upon this statement when the therapist is treating children,
for a child's play and fantasy can be much more absorbing than the
therapist's verbalisation. Moreover, a child is often in therapy for
reasons that are nominated by people other than himself, and this
makes him less inclined to take notice of the psychotherapist's comments and presence.

Even the overt contrasts of individual therapy as conducted by a
psychoanalyst, and family therapy, show convergences. Table 15.2
uses the treatment concepts of psychoanalysis to show more obvious
similarities. The definitions in this section, are derived from one
source (Sandler, Holder and Dare, 1973) which drew on a large
range of psychoanalytic sources.

Setting
The clinical situation of psychoanalysis and family therapy appear
distinct, but in fact the therapist in both settings is attempting to
create a milieu within which the patient or family is able to express
itself, demonstrating its nature, so that the therapist can see
through the outward processes that occur in the treatment room.
At the same time as obtaining the essential data upon which to base

Table 15.2   *The parallels between psychoanalytic psychotherapy of the individual and whole family therapy*

	Individual therapy	*Whole family therapy*
Setting	Carefully structured to facilitate evolution of fantasies about the therapist out of the patient's past family life	Carefully structured to enable the therapist to engage and disengage in relation to the family system
Subject matter	The patient's subjective experiences revealing the underlying mental structures	The family's spontaneous interactions revealing the underlying systemic structure of the family
Attitude to symptoms	Viewed as surface manifestation of underlying psychic structures	Viewed as surface manifestation of underlying family structure
Therapeutic alliance	Requires patient to give up pressure for symptom cure, in pursuit of self-understanding through analysis of 'free associations'	Family encouraged to present the symptoms during 'free family interactions' and to accept structural interventions changing patterns of interactions
Resistance	Seen as obstructions to 'free associations', motivated so as to avoid psychic pain and change	Seen as obstruction to 'free family interaction' motivated so as to avoid disturbance of family homeostasis and change
Transference	Analysed as it evolves between the patient and therapist	Observed in interactions between spouses and between parents and children (most clearly seen in multi-generational approach or phase of treatment)
Counter-transference	Considered both as source of knowledge and as a potential obstruction to therapeutic efficacy (one reason for use of didactic analysis)	Seen as tendency for therapist to become enmeshed in family pattern, revealing such patterns but also tending to endanger therapeutic efficacy (one reason for training investigation of therapist's family of origin (e.g. family tree, sculpting, role play, family re-union)
Acting out	Verbalisation by the patient always encouraged, but enactment seen as informative. Children in therapy expected to enact in play	Both verbalisation and enactment encouraged
Working through	Multiple repetitions of related sequences and metaphors of central foci thought necessary for securing structural psychic change. Relapse and repetition expected throughout therapy	Family expected to show repetitive but modified versions of underlying family structures throughout treatment. Relapse of symptoms expected and sometimes advised before termination
Interpretations and other interventions	Instructions, questions, constructions (re-constructions) used as adjuncts and preliminary to interpretations	Instructions, questions, constructions, confrontations used therapeutically. Interpretation used sparingly

Table 15.2   cont'd

	Individual therapy	Whole family therapy
Insight	Always sought but acknowledged as having an unclear and variable relationship to therapeutic improvement	Not usually thought of as leading to therapeutic change with any predictability (but certainly may follow on change)
Aims of therapy	Accession to age appropriate developmental level (Freud, 1970)	Entry into appropriate phase of life cycle (Haley, 1973)

treatment interventions, the therapist must retain freedom for manoeuvre to mobilise therapeutic resources. The patient in psycho-analysis is encouraged to allow his thoughts to be expressed openly, in words, without consciously withholding anything. This is known as 'free association', although the analyst will use the absence of freedom shown by the patient's expressed thoughts, to lead him to an understanding of the way the patient's mind works. In the table, the family therapist is presumed to operate so as to encourage the family to interact freely around the everyday tasks which it presents as being problems. In the family's inability to demonstrate 'free family interaction', the therapist perceives the structures of the family interactional system. The concept of 'free expression' in both settings, is paradoxical and analogous, for the verbalisations in psychoanalysis and the interactions in family therapy are carried out under the therapist's instructions, and cannot be free.

Therapeutic Alliance
This is also known as the treatment or working alliance and refers to the covert or open agreement between the patient or family and their therapist concerning the aims, subject matter and processes of the treatment. This is necessary to enable sufficient co-operation to be mobilised for the task of the therapy to be undertaken. Neither psychoanalysts nor family therapists are inclined to tell their patients the full nature of the treatment being offered. Both classes of therapists are inclined to engage their subjects in the treatment, slowly revealing the expectations and strategies, as the treatment relationship progresses.

Resistance
When the style of the therapist's offerings to and expectations of the patient or family have been established, the therapist awaits the revelation that the patient or family is unable to carry out the tasks of the therapy that have been indicated to it. The patient in analysis finds that he is not fully disclosing his thoughts and the family find that they cannot undertake the activities prescribed for them. This disability is resistance, as usually defined, and is the starting point of the therapist's understanding of the psychic struc-ture of his patient or the systemic structure of the family. In both treatment modalities the inability to carry out the instructions of the therapist reveals the nature of the subject of therapy. Resistance

can only be inferred when the treatment tasks have been accepted, i.e. after a therapeutic alliance has been formed.

Transference
Within psychoanalysis, as the beginning section of this chapter has described, the phenomenon of transference has an especial importance. As a clinical concept, transference

can be regarded as a specific illusion which develops in regard to the other person, one which, unbeknown to the subject, represents, in some of its features, a relationship towards an important figure in the person's past. It should be emphasised that this is felt by the subject, not as a repetition of the past, but as strictly appropriate to the present and to the particular person involved (Sandler, Holder and Dare, 1973).

The entry in Table 15.2 emphasises that transference interpretations are not part of effective family therapeutics but that the phenomenon may be observed in the intra-familial relationship patterns. That is to say, the wife and husband can be seen relating to each other in ways that reveal expectations that the other is being, in part, a parent rather than a spouse. The type of parent that the partner is expected to replicate can be aspects of both mother or father, regardless of the actual gender of the spouse.

The task of the psychoanalytically oriented family therapist is to understand the intra-familial transference. The pattern of the relationship contributing to the overall structure of the family will be subject to therapeutic interventions to enable the family to be free to change in the present and be less fettered by the past.

Countertransference
This is a complex subject. Within psychoanalysis countertransference was first defined as the block to effective understanding that developed in a therapist when features of the patient's mental life or functioning had a particular impact on the therapist, impairing the acuity of perception of the patient's mental processes and thus depleting therapeutic resources. Later, analysts came to regard such idiosyncratic and specific responses to aspects of the patient, not only as potential blocks to the analyst's understanding, putting therapeutic efficacy at risk, but, if raised to consciousness, a valuable source of understanding of the patient.

Countertransference responses are recognised by the therapist's introspective observations of the feelings, reactions and attitudes towards the patient, but may not be realised until they have been present for some time or until an outsider, a supervisor, observes them. There are countertransferential aspects in the responses of all therapists to all patients. The sorts of reactions engendered by a patient in a therapist are specific to the nature of that relationship.

In family treatments, the therapist can be observed responding to aspects of the family in ways that are identical to those defined by countertransference. That is to say, the therapist tends to be put into a relationship with the family that represents not just the professional functioning of the therapist, nor the open wishes of the family to get help, but are the outcome of the family finding a role for the therapist which is in keeping with their habitual ways of functioning. This process is known as affiliation, and it both endangers the professional (and therapeutic) activities of the therapist, but, if identified, is a rich source of understanding of the nature of the family.

Interpretation and other verbal interventions
Verbal interpretations - communications to the patient from the psychoanalyst, having the intention of promoting insight - are the major therapeutic intervention described by analysts. The list in Table 15.2 is given to show that there is a wider range of descriptions of the psychoanalytic armamentarium and the setting itself must be considered to be a major intervention. For example it would seem likely that the privacy, long-term and intensive contact, and the stance of the psychoanalyst, all part of the setting, constitute a potentially significant intervention, in the patient's life. The entry in Table 15.2 is designed to point out the number of classes of spoken communications which can affect the patient and can have therapeutic valency. The most active family therapists will also find themselves using a wide range of verbal interventions in whole family treatments.

CONCLUSIONS

The central theme of this chapter is that there is a crucial similarity between the site of action of family therapy and of psychoanalysis. However, as psychoanalytic psychotherapy takes place in a dyadic situation the patient will tend to direct thoughts and attention to the only other person in the room, namely the therapist. He will tend also, in turning his thoughts to the therapist, who he hopes will be reliable and helpful, to develop some dependence and attachment. The contingencies of the situation, with the patient designated as being in need of help, and the psychoanalyst as being an ordered and professional person, apparently the expert and in charge of the situation, will lead the patient, naturally, to feel in some ways like a child. He therefore begins to experience aspects of past childhood, family, experiences and expresses them more or less disguised, in some of his communications towards the analyst. The most vivid and powerful aspects of the treatment setting are the feelings and communications of patient to analyst and vice versa. Contemporary psychoanalytic psychotherapy sensibly exploits these natural features, and has evolved techniques which focus upon these here-and-now feelings from which the patient and analyst can learn about the effect of the past on the present and as the past is manifest in the present can learn to change. The close contact between patient and analyst fosters the analyst's empathic identification with the patient and careful observation of the therapist's feelings and attitudes towards the patient will show evidence of the patient's tendencies to get important people in his life to act and feel in a certain pattern towards him. By the same token the analyst may find that this trend can distort his proper 'professional behaviour' (Balint, 1968) and to enact the role the patient would tend to thrust upon him and hence to perpetuate rather than to facilitate change of such patterns. The psychoanalytic activity is rich in paradoxical qualities as Jackson and Haley (1963), amongst others, have shown. The work of Balint (1968) and of Winnicott (1965) has shown psychoanalysts how much adaptation of technique they willy-nilly embark upon to meet the needs of different patient groups.

These innovations in conceptualising the paradoxical and the adaptational activities of the psychoanalyst, and above all the experiments, so long ago by Ferenczi (1950) and carried further by Balint (1968) into 'active' techniques, all carry the psychoanalyst into the technical needs of whole family therapy.

Whole family therapy requires that the elements of paradox in the psychoanalytic treatment situation (e.g. 'If you don't ask me to talk about your symptoms and learn not to think of them as the point of therapy, then you will lose your symptoms') are made more conscious and deliberate. The silence and non-interventive stance of the psychoanalyst must be seen for what it is - necessarily active and controlling - and then the psychoanalyst can see that his techniques can be adapted to the treatment of whole families.

Conversely, the non-psychoanalyst can find that many of the preoccupations of the family therapist are also central to psychoanalysis: the discernment of underlying fixed structures from a diffuse seemingly protean variety of interactions and manifestations; the problem that resistance to change poses for therapists; the need to find and maintain a working alliance when the treatment is painful and the patient/family and therapist seem against each other, and, perhaps above all, the tendency that both individuals and families have to incorporate their therapist into pre-existing patterns of behaviour, rather than to use the therapeutic encounter for change.

Summary
This chapter has not discussed the richness of the psychoanalytic understanding of families as the author has, in part, fulfilled this task elsewhere (Pincus and Dare, 1978; Dare, 1979). It has addressed itself instead to the task of showing how psychoanalytic treatment concepts (Sandler, Holder and Dare, 1973) can be used to describe the process of family therapy. Further, the chapter points out some similarities between the site of activity of individual and whole family therapist. The relationship of the psychoanalytic concept of countertransference and the family therapy idea of 'affiliation' (Minuchin, 1974) is given especial importance. The discussion of the role of paradox in psychoanalysis and of activity in family therapy, relates the two areas of therapy. Psychoanalysts do not fully appreciate the deeply paradoxical nature of their activity and therefore cannot, usually, employ it deliberately. Further, psychoanalysts do not extend the activity and control implicit in their apparently permissive and non-interventive stance, into consciously determined areas.

The author believes that family therapists are remiss if they do not learn what they can from psychoanalysis. Similarly, family therapy is a rich and fruitful source of relevant knowledge for psychoanalysts and as a treatment technique it meets patients' needs in situations where psychoanalysis has been unavailing, especially for the poorly motivated, for younger children and in economically deprived areas.

REFERENCES

Balint, M. (1968) 'The Basic Fault', London, Tavistock.

Bell, J.E. (1975) 'Family Therapy', New York, Jason Aronson.

Bentovim, A. (1979) Theories of Family Interaction and Techniques of Intervention, 'Journal of Family Therapy', 1, 321–45.

Boszormenyi-Nagy, I. and Spark, G. (1973) 'Invisible Loyalties', New York, Harper & Row.

Byng-Hall, J. (1979) Re-editing Family Myths during Family Therapy, 'Journal of Family Therapy', 1, 103–16.

Cooklin, A. (1979) A Psychoanalytic Framework for a Systemic Approach to Family Therapy, 'Journal of Family Therapy', 1, 153–76.

Dare, C. (1979) Psychoanalysis and Systems in Family Therapy, 'Journal of Family Therapy', 1, 137–51.

Ferenczi, S. (1950) 'Further Contributions', London, Hogarth Press.

Freud, A. (1970) Problems of Termination in Child Analysis, in A. Freud, 'Problems of Psychoanalytic Technique and Therapy', London, Hogarth Press, 1972.

Freud, S. (1912) 'The Dynamics of Transference', Standard Edition, 12.

Freud, S. (1915) 'Observations on Transference-love', Standard Edition, 12.

Freud, S. (1916–17) 'Introductory Lectures on Psycho-Analysis', Standard Edition, 15–16.

Haley, J. (1973) 'Uncommon Therapy: The Psychiatric Techniques of Milton H. Erickson', New York, W.W. Norton.

Haley, J. (1976) 'Problem-Solving Therapy', New York, Harper & Row.

Jackson, D.D. and Haley, J. (1963) Transference Revisited, 'Journal of Nervous and Mental Diseases', 131, 365.

Lieberman, S. (1979) Transgenerational Analysis: the Geneogram as a Technique in Family Therapy, 'Journal of Family Therapy', 1, 51–64.

Malan, D.H. (1963) 'A Study of Brief Psychotherapy', London, Tavistock.

Malan, D.H. (1976a) 'The Frontier of Brief Psychotherapy', New York, Plenum Press.

Malan, D.H. (1976b) 'Towards the Validation of Dynamic Psycho-therapy', New York, Plenum, Press.

Minuchin, S. (1974) 'Families and Family Therapy', Cambridge, Mass., Harvard University Press.

Pincus, L. and Dare, C. (1978) 'Secrets in the Family', London,
    Faber & Faber.
Sandler, J., Holder, A. and Dare, C. (1973) 'The Patient and the
    Analyst', London, Allen & Unwin.
Skynner, A.C.R. (1969) A Group-analytic Approach to Conjoint
    Family Therapy, 'Journal of Child Psychology and Psychiatry',
    10, 81-106 (Reprinted as chapter 4 in this volume).
Stierlin, H. (1977) 'Psychoanalysis and Family Therapy', New York,
    Jason Aronson.
Strachey, J. (1969) The Nature of the Therapeutic Action of Psycho-
    analysis, 'International Journal of Psycho-Analysis', 50, 275-92.
Watzlawick, P., Weakland, J. and Fisch, R. (1974) 'Change:
    Principles of Problem Formation and Problem Resolution', New
    York, W.W. Norton.
Winnicott, D.W. (1965) 'The Maturational Process and the Facilitating
    Environment', London, Hogarth Press.
Zuk, G.H. (1971) 'Family Therapy: A Triadic Approach', New York,
    Human Sciences Press.

16 FAMILY BITS AND PIECES:
framing a workable reality

Gill Gorell Barnes

INTRODUCTION

Any account of structural family therapy written from an English
viewpoint will repeat ideas that have already been clearly and force-
fully stated by clinicians at the Philadelphia Child Guidance Clinic,
principally by Salvador Minuchin whose book 'Families and Family
Therapy' (1977) stands as a classic text on this approach to work
with the family. In the family therapy programme, a part of the
Department for Children and Parents in the Tavistock Clinic,
London, we are also indebted to Harry Aponte, now director of the
Philadelphia Child Guidance Clinic, and to Marianne Walters,
Director of Training, both of whom have spent time working with us
during 1978 and 1979. Dr Minuchin also spent some months in
London in the spring of 1979 and was generous in his teaching time.
My first direct experience of his work was in 1972 when I visited
Philadelphia having read 'Families of the Slums' (1967). I saw how
much sense the approach outlined there made for many of the families
we were seeing at Woodberry Down Child Guidance Clinic where,
working with Robin Skynner, the team were developing a family
group approach. I made a point of visiting Philadelphia and seeing
as many of the training films as they could show me as well as doing
some observations behind a one-way screen. This chapter then
marks for me another step in the long process of integrating a structural approach into a psychodynamic orientation, some of the dilemmas
of which I first outlined in an article published in 'Social Work Today'
in 1973 (included in this book, chapter 5).
  In this chapter the emphasis is on how the use of this approach
affects the therapist's overall conceptualization, his chronicling of
the process of the session and his style in therapeutic intervention.

STRUCTURAL FAMILY THERAPY

Vignettes 1972
A family are sitting in a room, two daughters, a mother and father,
and Salvador Minuchin. The symptom the family present is a father
who is vomiting. The parents do not like to admit to arguing. (The
eldest daughter is quiet like her father, but her sister screams.)

298

The therapist asks the children to describe the row, which happens downstairs while they are upstairs. He elicits details of the escalation. He notes differences in the ways the two children organize themselves around the parents' interaction. The eldest daughter says she has got used to it, she does not think she can change them, she stays out, she's sad but not upset. 'I don't dwell on it that much.' The therapist asks who starts the fight, the eldest daughter says it is a combination of them both. The therapist asks, 'Who do you think is right? For whom do you feel?' The eldest daughter replies, 'I feel for my mother.' The therapist comments, 'That's why you're sitting together.' Everybody laughs and the daughter nods. The therapist adds, 'It's difficult for you being put on the spot, but you are feeling your mother's pain.' Then he turns to the little daughter and asks her what happens when mother and father argue? The little daughter says she does not know much about it as she usually goes to her room. However, she goes on to give a number of details. Minuchin points out that she has her ears stretched to hear their quarrelling in spite of her denial.

A few moments later in the session Minuchin stops the discussion and argument between mother and father, saying that the confrontation does not belong to both the kids only to the eldest daughter. He moves her between the two parents because that is where she is in the family quarrels at home. He asks her why she thinks that she needs to defend her mother, then invites them both to stand up, and requests them to look at each other and decide who is the bigger. Mother is the bigger by several inches. He asks the eldest daughter if she thinks that mother needs her protection.

Later on the therapist dismisses the younger child from the room, 'She is young, she can be protected by separation. But you [to the eldest daughter] are there.' The mother is longing to continue the row. He says to father, 'You are an accommodator, can you change your style?' At this point as mother recommences her attack on father, he moves the daughter out of the middle of the two parents and says to her, 'Come here, I want to protect you.' He moves the daughter in next to him.

In these brief extracts we can see a number of features of structural family therapy as we have now come to practise it. The intensity of the emotional interactions between family members is pointed out in terms of their physical relationship in the room, and the validity of existing alliances is questioned by getting the members themselves to examine the way they are sitting or the way they are defending or protecting themselves. People are moved in order to make a point about the need for a boundary between two generations, parents and children. The children are questioned in turn about their perception of the interaction between parents and not only the comments that they make but the way they join with their eyes and their bodies is noted as part of the constellation and patterning, that both creates and sustains the family system, of which the symptom is a part. Where the children are able to stay out of the pathology they are left free and are not involved in the session. Where they are already enmeshed they remain with the problem under discussion,

until the parents are able to let them go, expressing a wish to discuss things without the children. Then there is a move from family
into marital discussion.

Later in the interview while the parents are arguing, the therapist
requires them to resolve it, 'continue this argument and come to an
agreement.' Turning to father he adds, 'You have shown me you are
able to be effective in an argument.' Mother says, 'We will never
finish it.' The therapist says, 'Do it now.' The mother says she is
not skilful enough to finish, and cries. The therapist moves to her
and points out that she is continuing in the same way, 'You are
parallel.' He insists that the argument is continued until they achieve
resolution in a different way. In the enactment and intensification
of the problem in this insistence on a resolution during the session,
another key element of the structural approach is shown: that a
change in behaviour should be achieved during the session, and the
experience of the possibility of relating in different ways be felt
before the couple or the family leave the clinic.

A further request to this couple was that they be specific in their
disagreement. They argued about a kiss. Father gave mother a kiss,
and her response was to say, 'That's not much of a kiss, it's a
cold unfeeling kiss.' He commented in despair that however he tried
to do it mother would complain. He itemized exactly how the event
had taken place. Mother tried to generalize, 'Over twenty years, we
have learnt to behave in such and such a way', and was told to go
back to the point at hand and to continue arguing specifically, about
how the particular piece of interaction was negotiated. The therapist
left the couple to argue by themselves and watched them from behind a screen. 'I will help you if you need it, don't help each other.'
He changed sides lending strength first to mother then to father.
He ended the session at the point where he felt some change had
been achieved.

In the context of the National Health Service, symptom bearers
are categorized by their age and the helping services available to
them, as well as by the professional specializations, developed
accordingly. A move from viewing the individual patient to scanning
the whole family requires shifts in the professional network as well
as in the patient family: a wider scanning of the declared symptom.
A mother is complaining of her daughter's temper tantrums and
childishness. Both daughters are restless and irritable, demanding
attention continually. Father sits back and speaks introspectively,
rarely taking action in controlling or responding directly to any of
the five children. The eldest daughter wants to get closer to her
father and resents her mother's anxious preoccupation and control
of her brother. Each member of the family is asked by the therapist
to contribute to a plan to get their wishes met so that the restless
energy begins to be channelled in ways that the family define and
can act upon. The children demand more time with their parents.
Father retreats as they grow noisy and mother comments that this
often happens. The therapist puts the focus on limiting demand to
something that is both concrete and manageable between father
and daughters. The eldest daughter asks her father to play a game

with her and is asked how often she thinks he will manage that.
'Every night', she replies. Negotiation takes place about a realistic
number of times a week this might happen. Father is encouraged to
teach the daughters how to play a particular game. Father is to be
in charge of the games taking place and the responsibility is to be
lifted from mother's shoulders. Whenever the eldest daughter tries
to talk about how her contact with father might be managed, the
second daughter interrupts. She is thanked for her help but told
she must let her elder sister manage her own negotiations with
father. There is emphasis on what is happening not why.
T.   (Trying to establish issues of reliable anticipation rather than
deal with mother's unproductive behaviour:) Do you have a regular
games day every week, Daisy?
D.   No, now and then.
T.   What would be a reasonable number of days a week when you
could do this (turning to include Kathleen)? Do you play the games
too (aiming at specificity), did you play them too last night?
K.   Yea, I kept winning.
T.   Did you (interested) and did Sian?
D.   No, Sian was watching telly.
T.   I see, so you set something up with your Mum and Dad, how
often do you think you could manage to do something with your Mum
and Dad like that? (Looks at Daisy who looks hopefully at Dad and
quickly drops her eyes.)
T.   (Repeats to Kathleen:) How often would you like to do something
with your Mum and Dad like that?
K.   Tonight and the next night, and the next night, and the day
after that.
T.   I don't think you'll manage three times a week (reducing it to
a concrete number).
D.   (hopefully) Two?
T.   Ask your parents (corrects self) ask your Dad, can he manage
it twice a week?
D.)   I just asked him.
K.)   (Simultaneously) Dad, do you think you could manage it . . .
four times a week?
T.   (Presses Daisy) You ask him. (To Kathleen) No not four times.
K.   (Irrepressible) Three times.
Dad: No.
D. and K. (together in a chant:) Two times?
Dad: Two, I'll have to think about that.
D.   Once?
K.   (Discouraged) We can't get anywhere can we.
T.   (Picking up Kathleen's discouragement:) Yea, let's try and
get an answer. If you want to get something in your family you
have to go on until the other person gives an answer. It's no good
just tossing something into the air (imitates Kathleen) and hoping
someone will hear you – you have to learn to make your Dad believe
you really want him to play a game with you.
D.   (Looks at the therapist and opens her mouth) –
T.   It's no good looking at me, you have to look at him.

D.   (Does so.)
Dad (Begins to answer:) Well, I think we should do something every
night between 6 and 7.30 (baby yells).
T.   (Sensing failure:) Well I don't think a man of your responsibilities can realistically manage that.
Mum Yes I think it's too hard to stick to a certain time.
T.   What is a reasonable number of times, taking into account all
the things you have to manage? How often is reasonable - once a
week?
Mum Yes we must find time once a week, you should be able to do
it a lot more but that depends.
T.   I think we can all agree you can't be expected to do it more -
the question is whether you can do it at all.

Working in the Present
In this approach to therapeutic work the structural therapist may
share the pain that the family are experiencing but he will make no
attempt to link past and present experience. His assumption is that
understanding is not in itself an agent of change. For therapists
such as myself, professionally trained in psychodynamic understanding and believing from personal experience that understanding
is an agent of change, the move from offering insight to creating a
different experience for the family through focusing on interaction
in the room is the most difficult move to achieve successfully. A
further piece of learning is in knowing when change has been suf-
ficently experienced by the family for them to maintain their different relatedness under further stress, an uncertain area in which
behavioural therapists should be able to lend their experience. The
psychodynamic therapist will be anxious that if family members have
no basic insight they will have nothing to draw on in a new crisis.
The structural therapist will argue that they have a different experience of each other's capacities and a wider and more flexible range
of family behaviours to resort to. At present the most frequently
expressed British position combines the psychoanalytic and the
systems view (Bentovim, 1979; Byng-Hall, 1979; Cooklin, 1979; Dare,
1979).

In structural family therapy the therapist works from the premise
that the energy of the family, and therefore the energy for change,
goes into the transactions between family members, that, repeated
day in day out over time, form the family system. Changes in the
transactions will lead to the possibility of change in the experience
of the individual. 'In family therapy transformation or the restructuring of the family system leads to change or the individual's new
experience . . . the change occurs in the synapses - the way in
which the same people relate to each other'. (Minuchin, 1977, p.111).
Change is therefore approached in small ways, the units of interaction in subsystems being the main focus of attention. A transaction transformed will ramify and affect other aspects of family
life. 'In systems containing many interconnected homeostatic loops
the changes brought about by an external impact may slowly spread
through the system' (Bateson, 1973, p. 416). Just as Blake could

see 'life in a grain of sand', so the therapist can see the essence of
the family system in the minutiae of one repeated behavioural sequence – 'Where are my wellington boots – where did I tell you to
put them last time?' Unless the philosophical premise of seeing the
whole in the detail is grasped, it is difficult to understand the technical emphasis on highlighting and interrupting the small sequences
that take place or that are created between members during family
sessions. In focusing on the relationship, 'the delicate balance between the organism and its surround', the structural therapist is
taking an ecological overview as propounded by Bateson whose
original thinking underlies so much of the subsequent systemic
family therapy approach. As Bronfenbrenner (1978) recently wrote
of research in child psychiatry, 'The defining core of an ecological
approach to human development is its focus upon the dynamic tensions between the organism and its surround with both the person
and the environment engaged in reciprocal tensions and activities.

In considering the differential effects of therapeutic impact, there
is divergence about how a professional can affect these tensions for
the better. Should he work to improve the organism on behalf of
its surround or vice versa? The psychodynamic family therapist
would not risk throwing the total system out of balance and would
move at the pace of the family in helping them discover and create
their own adjustment. Both the structural and the strategic therapist would risk upsetting the balance, by increasing tensions in the
existing system. The strategic therapist would try to change the
rules that govern the system overall, so that change is effected in
different parts of the system simultaneously. The structural therapist would aim at a new ecology by changing a piece at a time and
letting other adjustments develop.

A Family Model: Goals for the Therapist
The model of the family that an 'ideal' structural therapist holds recognizes two major sets of constraints for family life. The first set
is universal, that there must be a power structure in which parents
and children, and children of different ages, have different levels
and degrees of authority. There must be complementarity, different
members carrying different functions and capable of accepting some
interdependence, operating together on behalf of one another. There
must be nurturance, boundary maintenance and eventually the
attainment of separation (Lidz, 1964; Dare, 1979). The second set of
constraints is the idiosyncratic set peculiar to any one family, involving mutual expectations whose origins may be lost. It is in relation to this second idiosyncratic area of choice and constraint that
so much British family and marital therapy has been addressed,
based on object relations theory and the reasons why certain kinds
of 'fit' exist in marriages (Dicks, 1967; Pincus, 1960; Bannister and
Pincus, 1965; Byng-Hall, 1973, 1979).

The model, developed by Minuchin is a developmental one and fits
well with other developmental theories familiar to British psychotherapists (Dare, 1979). All families go through certain developmental stages and face these with greater or lesser degrees of

adaptation and flexibility. All families function in a social context and have to respond to inputs from outside. All these social requirements change over time.

In this sense the family is an open system which is continually changing, receiving and giving messages to the individuals within it and to the world outside it. Pragmatically, the therapist looks at whether the family is able to meet the requirements of its members at the time they come to him in relation to the life stages they are at, and the way in which the expectations each of them have about how this period of their lives are being met. He is looking not at the individual psychodynamic development of each family member but at how the family is carrying out the tasks of each particular developmental stage, since the requirements of one stage will differ from the requirements of another and these requirements may be conflicting, self-defeating or may require a shift the family is not prepared to make (Dare, 1979). 'What I aim at is a clear parental system, boundaries that are strong but permeable and a system of relationship that operates appropriate to the stages of development which the members of the family are in' (Marianne Walters, 1978, personal communication).

The family may also come for help with a social adaptation they do not feel equipped to make. The continued existence of the family as a system depends on having a sufficient range of patterns and the flexibility to mobilize them when necessary. As the family are required to respond to internal and external changes, it needs to be able to change its shape in ways that meet new circumstances without losing the continuity that provides a frame of reference for its members. Most families have a limited number of ways of approaching a problem and the fewer options they have in their repertoire, limited as it may be by poverty, lack of education, ill health or mental illness, the more likely they are to get stuck when an old solution fails to meet the requirements of a new situation. For example, Korzybski's powerful phrase, 'the map is not the territory', a statement about the necessary transformation between a thing and its symbolization, was made concrete in the psychiatric problems of many newly immigrant West Indian families referred for help in the early 1970s in inner London whose previous adaptations to rural life in the islands had left them conceptually ill equipped to code the symbol and transform it back into the world around them. Abstract adaptations such as relating an underground map or a road plan to the transport system on which they travelled, or the streets where they lived, were impossible. Minor failures of this kind multiply into major stress. Families facing consistent stress in the organizational requirements made of them, often develop great strengths in other ways of being together, which do not translate into, and may even be an adaptive response against, the requirements that are being made of them by social forces outside their boundary. Energy goes into patterns that become more rigid in the face of uncertainty. In such families a certain form of organization, well established and understood by them, may be seen as disorganization by authorities such as schools, courts, employers and therapists. The family structure is dysfunctional for the new tasks required by society and the therapist may be called in at this point. The problems this gives rise to in a child psychiatry setting were discussed by Minuchin et al. (1967) in their first book 'Families of the Slums', and have been discussed by me in a British context elsewhere (Gorell Barnes, 1973, 1975). Walters (1977, p. 190) states, 'I think change requires that families be presented with concrete alternatives to the impasse or dilemma which brings them into therapy, and that they try them on in the interview. I do not believe change can occur until people can feel some competency and I think that the leadership of the therapist in bringing about change is dependent on her being intrusive, directive and in control of the process. As soon as opportunity presents itself, I move people from content to process, from information to interaction, and in so doing I try to give the family a new perspective of the situation they are in. This business of giving the picture a new frame is as important for the therapist as for the family. I want to put the problem into a perspective for both of us, the family and myself, where I can begin to feel effective and transmit this feeling, this sense of hope to the family. I need to create a workable reality; to select and reframe a piece of the action where some change can be initiated.' Aponte (1977, 1978) has additionally emphasized the need for professional help to be firmly linked to the peculiarity of the family's own style of structural organization. The work may be slow, may not generalize, and may particularly require the involvement of family allies other than those immediately involved in the nuclear family group.

THE THERAPEUTIC PROCESS: GROUND RULES FOR THE THERAPIST

1 *Micro-observation*
Structural work is based on close observation and analysis of the process in the room. Any small transaction between any two members is taken as material for examination once the therapist is aware of the overall patterning. In an over-involved family a mother telling her teenage daughter to take off her coat, or a father brushing some fluff off his grown-up son's trousers, can be the material of the therapeutic intervention. Working on detail in this way is based on the premise that such interactions characterize the family style that underlies the presenting problem. Interventions are put in such a way that the family look at the complementarity in the system. For example:

Therapist: You are very helpful to your son.
Father: I don't like to see him looking sloppy.
Therapist: You look after him very well. Matthew, you are a good son to your father, letting him take care of your appearance. What else do you let him do for you?

Such intervention aims to make family members more conscious of themselves, their automatic functioning and the effect this has on one another. In order to move behaviour into the conscious realm

where it is more available to cognitive control and therefore choice
the therapist may heighten an incident in such a way that it can no
longer take place without awareness again.

For example, in a family where fights between the two boys are
presented as the main complaint, mother and granny are complaining
that a window pane has been broken and that mother is then expected to pay for it. This relates to her anxiety that the boys always
want more from her than she is able to give them (in every way).
She tells the therapist that she has taken the boys right through
the 'housekeeping' accounts to show them that at the end of the
month there is nothing left over, 'They were even wondering how
they get fed.' The therapist takes up the metaphor of the window
pane and uses it to push the family's consciousness of how much
'fighting' they can 'afford'.
T: You're going to have to think about whether you want to have
a one pane fight or a two pane fight.
Jim: Eh? I don't get you.
Granny: (Eagerly) Yes, how much you're going to break and how
much you can afford.
T: (To Jim) Do you get it?
Jim: I don't want to break anything.
T: Then you need to learn how to arrange things better. If you
set up a fight not wanting to break something, and you do, you
didn't get the fight organized properly.
Jim: What do you need to organize a fight for?
T: Well you fight anyway, you must learn to fight so you get what
you want out of it.

He pursues the theme of fighting in terms of 'managers' and 'rules',
which granny in particular helps him to develop. He also assures
the family that the fighting between the boys is very important for
all of them. In a later session in which the family report that there
has been no fighting that week, he recommends that it should continue between the boys so that the family know where to look after it.

2   *Family language*
There are many points at which family interactions can be analysed
in this way and it is important for the therapist to be certain that
he is choosing an issue and using language that goes with the style
of the family. Whereas an experienced structural therapist can begin work in this way within a few minutes of the session beginning,
those less familiar with family scenarios usually need more time to
gather the evidence from which to begin. Having spotted and
analysed such sequences, they will note that they recur frequently
and therefore worry less about using them, knowing the opportunity
will come again and that the sequence fits the family.

The therapist will also try to find words and metaphors that appeal
to family members and catch their imagination. So far as the therapist
exercises this skill in metaphor, links between the behavioural and
the psychodynamic aspects of structural work can be glimpsed.
Minuchin is masterly at this. He will say to an anorectic girl, 'When
you have your own voice you will have your own body', and expand

this image, commenting, 'When you have a voice you will have a brain, you will not be so intellectually thin and you will have a fuller life.' To turn images of physical thinness into mental images in this way is to use symbol to bring an awareness of the relationship of one process to another that makes a bridge with analytic psychotherapy, linking body to mind and the physical to the emotional life.

To use symbol in this way is not a central feature of structural family therapy as it is formally taught by its American exponents, many of whom do not discuss any concept of the unconscious. However, it is important to allude at this point to the recurrence of poetic images, symbol and the careful choice of metaphor in much structural work and to the connection of these to the processes of change within a systemic framework. Many British family therapists are interested in connecting the behavioural and symbolic potential in structural work. Bateson reminds us of the absurdity of choosing to assert only one 'bit' of the mind as representing the best it is capable of, when he reframes Freud's view of 'dreams' as the royal road to the unconscious to include the creativity of art, poetry and the best of religion. 'These are all activities in which the whole individual is involved.' The therapist working on one level only is depriving himself of wisdom, exchanging one partial view of self for another partial view. 'It seemed to me that pure dream like pure purpose was rather trivial. It was not the stuff of which we are made but only bits and pieces of that stuff. Our conscious purposes similarly are only bits and pieces. The systemic view is something else again.'

The relationship between language and change which has recently received attention in Watzlawick (1979) stems from many traditions that precede psychotherapy and place the work of therapists in frames that range from the court jester* to the mystic recluse. To be able to use words to effect a change with purpose and precision is a therapeutic skill that has always characterized much of the best in healing from the days of the Sphinx and the Delphic oracle; and elements of the same skills are constantly at work in the phrasing, timing and delivery of therapeutic inputs, whatever their orientation. Working structurally in no way precludes such work; it is simply a difference in the emphasis of language.

3 Confirmation and increasing competence

The therapist will always aim to confirm the existing competence within the family. Seeing the positive connotations of behaviour

---

*See for example an earlier structural family therapist c. 1600:
Lear: When were you wont to be so full of songs sirrah?
Fool: I have used it much e'er since thou madest thy daughters thy mothers for when thou gavest them the rod and putest down thine own breeches 'they for sudden joy did weep and I for sorrow sing: that such a king should play bo-peep and go the fools among.' ('King Lear'; 1.4 169)

that may also maintain a pathological system is a very important
feature of structural work and one that many people accustomed to
pointing out pathology in negative terms find extremely hard to
learn. Labelling positively (i.e. an over-protective father as very
caring) leads to the next step - a suggested change in the participant's perception of the interaction in a frame to which they can
respond: 'You know the more you brush his hair for him, the less
he will have to learn to do it for himself.' The enhancement of the
son's competence might then be brought in through other activities
in which he is known to succeed and the question put: 'How can
you help him to be competent in this area?' That aspect of the
parent that is motivated to increase the competence of the child is
heavily relied on in this approach.

4 Thinking small

This recognition of the importance of small transactions as the stuff
of family life and family problems has always been an important
feature of family work for me (Gorell Barnes, 1978). By focusing
the issues which cause heat within the daily lives of the family pro-
tagonists, the emotions, quarrels, tensions that actually render a
shift in the family system difficult are brought into the room and
can there be argued through as they would have to be in the home.
This enactment of the struggle between two or more people is one
of the features of structural family therapy that is most powerful.
In therapy the enactment is accompanied by intensification; that is,
the therapist selects and focuses issues on which a resolution must
be reached and a change achieved in a new way during the session.
He decides between whom the discussion will take place and directs
the discussion beyond the normal point of no resolution when it
appears to be flagging, with participants wanting to return to their
old steady state rather than move onto a new resolution.

In the following example, a husband and wife have been directed
to discuss her retreat into brooding silence which drives him to
explosive anger. She has given up. They turn to the therapist and
shrug. The therapist indicates they should continue.

W.   I usually can't compete with you in an argument (husband
turns to therapist who re-directs him to the wife).
H.   I think you should try.
W.   You shout longer and louder than I do.
H.   Wait five minutes and try - (going off on another tack), but
you don't try with Penny either.
T.   Just stick to you two for the minute, try again.
H.   Wait two mins and try again.
T.   (to wife) You don't know how to go about the next bit do you?
W.   No.
T.   Which is how to win him back to your side.
W.   No I don't know that one.
H.   In our house the most difficult thing is to say sorry - like
extracting a tooth it would be like admitting you're wrong to start
talking.
T.   We need to think about some possibilities of how to get across.

W.   My brain goes numb.
H.   It can't stay numb for that number of days (five days is the length of the angry silence under discussion). If it went numb 'cos someone shouted, when they stop it's got to start again.
W.   I often stop thinking for a bit.
H.   It's not a bit – it's days.
T.   Right now she's saying she feels stuck – what are you going to do to help her now.
H.   (evasively) Many things have been tried.
T.   Talk to her about what's been tried and why it doesn't work.
H.   Talking.
T.   She's already said talking doesn't help. (Therapist has got into the trap of 'talking' for mother and defusing rather than 'heightening' the enactment of the silence.)
W.   No he stops me being able to think – I can't think now, I'm sure he's right.
H.   What you've just said is a classic example of you, your mother, your mother's mother and probably her mother before that.
W.   (reacts astonished – he has caught her attention)
T.   I think now you're doing very well together. You don't need me for the next bit. Go on with this and if you get stuck you can call me in. (The therapist moves away and sits on the desk in a corner of the room.)
W.   (to husband) What do you mean?
H.   (emboldened, he begins to instruct his wife with a good deal of humour about the effects of her silence and similar silences observed in her mother's family. They engage in working together on the problem without the therapist.)

MEETING THE FAMILY

When the therapist first meets the family there are certain things he has to achieve before he can begin to work with them. He has to get to know them and the issues they are presenting, he has to understand the way they interact, side with one another, and under-mine one another; he has to get some feel of their flexibility and responsiveness to inputs from outside their own system. He also has to make them feel that he is someone they can trust, that he knows more or less what he is doing and that he respects them the way they are while wanting to show them that the problems they are bringing are something he intends to get them to do some work on with him. The beginning emphasis on joining with the family and knowing them experientially is familiar in psychotherapy but carries a range of differing implications in terms of subsequent therapeutic procedure in structural work. For better or worse a range of expressions defining this process has been developed within the literature, joining, accommodating and tracking being those most important to understand in terms of clinical process since they are all essential in forming the therapeutic system from which the therapist can begin to structure change. The pace and style of

managing the offered therapeutic experience are radically different
to psychodynamic psychotherapy in that there is far more emphasis
on the work to be done by the therapist in successfully engaging
a family and getting them to begin work.

As outlined in the previous section the therapist in joining the
family will bear in mind the need to confirm family members' sense
of identity; he will respect family hierarchy and values and will
highlight existing positives. He will pay attention to increasing
competence and observe how it may be extended. He will begin to
clock up family language and expressions so that his ideas can be
put back in appropriate metaphors. He will track, without intervention at first, the content the family brings. He will bear in mind
Marianne Walters' pithy phrase, 'Have you exchanged pleasantries
sufficient that you can begin to say no' (1978, personal communication); and will not therefore challenge the system until he has been
adequately accepted by the family.

Tracking is an accommodation technique familiar to all non-directive
therapists. It means, at its simplest, following the content and behaviour the family brings, encouraging family members to continue,
asking clarifying questions, amplifying a point and not challenging
what is said. Tracking can be of behaviour or of content and is extended from one person to two and three person behaviour. A
daughter's observation to the therapist is turned into a discussion
about the same issue with her brother. Their views are checked
out against the parents' views. A father's observation about his son
not liking the dark is followed through to his daughter's sleeplessness, his wife's nightmares and his own fear of dying. The issue
or theme is followed along all the family pathways and explored in
detail. In this process the therapist confirms the family as experts
in relation to their own situation. They know more about themselves than anyone else. The therapist simply elicits and clarifies
what they know and in the process they discover things they did
not know.

The therapist may also accommodate by altering his style and behaviour to suit the family. He may slow down his speed or speed it
up; he may adopt a mournful air or laugh a lot. He may smoke because the family are smoking. Some therapists make conscious use
of aspects of their own family life that are similar to the family's,
where they think this will strengthen an alliance.

When working structurally the process in the interview at any
one moment appears one-sided. The therapist looks not only as if
he is ignoring individual dynamics but as though he may be insensitive to the needs of family members not engaged in a current transaction. This is why it is important to have built up trust so that
family members will follow him even when he is felt to be unfair.
As Mr Stevens (company director) said after a hard working marital
session, 'You take us down many roads and some of them are right
and some of them are wrong, and I'm prepared to follow you because
in this area you have more experience than I have, but right now
I don't see the relevance of this to the fact that I don't get on with
my daughter.' The experience of the therapist as supportive is

obviously essential even when he seems to be pushing hard for change in some aspect of personality that conflicts with a crucial family need. It is also essential that the family feels able to challenge the therapist on the road he is taking. Mr Kelly (machine operator and shop steward) said, 'It's like going down a corridor and unlocking the doors on rooms you don't want to go into. I don't want to go in sometimes and I know I can say so, but if that's wrong and I know it is, we can go back later.' It is likely that unless the family pick up from the therapist a real commitment to them and a respect for them in spite of the pushes he is making, that they will leave therapy.

CHANGING THE PUNCTUATION

In the process of moving from one state of equilibrium towards a new one, the family will experience stress and at the point where the therapist joins with one family member, lending his strength to achieve a small shift, the family's overall sense of the therapist's fairness may be threatened. In structural work, as opposed to many forms of strategic and paradoxical work, the therapist does not stay in an outside position for long. He works from within the system, trying to maintain links with each member even while focusing on a part of the system. The delicate and speedy mental footwork this involves is what has led to Minuchin's favourite metaphor of the 'dance'. The speed of the dancer, the intricacy of his steps and the range of his variations, add up to his style. A different metaphor introduced by Bateson (1973) is that of punctuation, which links the inner notion of the 'stream of experience' in the material of the therapeutic encounter to the family in its existential environment, 'The cybernetic circularities of the self and the external world' (p. 420). In our work with families we can be seen as helping them to punctuate their experience, to stop and look at small aspects of it from a different angle so that it takes on another sort of coherence and sense. Translating this into the length of a therapeutic intervention, Minuchin asks his trainees to consider what is the length of space they wish to occupy, a semi-colon; or a full stop? Both thinkers are emphasizing the arbitrary nature and scale of the therapist's imposition of form upon experience, and the need to consider the choice of forms within an awareness of the total experience of a family and of the range of possibilities for attention 'delimitation . . . must always depend on what phenomena we wish to understand or explain' (Bateson, p. 433). (Bateson's constant concern for the whole leads him to suggest rather too densely that, 'The way to delineate the system is to draw the limiting line in such a way that you do not cut any of these pathways in ways which leave things inexplicable' (1973, p. 434).)

DIAGNOSIS

A structural family diagnosis involves the therapist in making use
of the information he has gathered in the process outlined above,
relating it to the problem as the family present it, and broadening
the conceptualization of the problem to include their interactions.
Minuchin (1977) has outlined six major areas of diagnosis.

First – the family structure, its preferred ways of interacting
that the therapist sees as being available at that point. Second –
the system's flexibility; the range of problem solving skills different
members possess and the capacity for adaptation that they show.
Third – the family's sensitivity to individual members' action. If
they are too enmeshed, very small moves will be seen as major
threats and restraints will automatically be activated. If they are
too disengaged individual inputs will be insufficiently noticed so
that, for example, distress signals may not be picked up. Fourth –
the therapist looks at the family network and at sources of support
and stress. Fifth – he will consider the families' developmental stage
and its performance of the tasks appropriate to that stage. Sixth –
he must examine the ways in which the identified patient's symptoms
are used to maintain those ways of being together that suit his
family best.

PHILOSOPHY OF ACHIEVING CHANGE

Theory in Action
The therapist's right to restructure the family takes us to the core
of the philosophical attack on structural family therapy. 'The therapist must be intrusive, directive and in control of the process'
(Walters, 1977). 'The therapist functions like a director as well as
an actor. He creates scenarios, choreographs, highlights themes
and leads family members to improvise within the constraints of the
family drama' (Minuchin, 1977). 'The family takes charge of itself
through the therapist taking charge of the therapy' (Goren, 1979,
personal communication). The message is clear. The therapist does
not sit back and wait for the family to pace itself. If he is to work
structurally he has to drop the operational model of psychodynamic
psychotherapy whether or not he abandons the theoretical construct
of an inner self. His attention is focused on the family in interaction
rather than on the individual self and the way in which the goals
of therapy are followed become physically as well as mentally and
emotionally active in that the therapist feeds back his understanding
and professional skill in the form of redirected transactions between
members rather than in offered understanding either to individuals
or to the family as a group; since the offering of understanding
alone is not seen as leading to the required microsystemic changes
in the interactions of the family in relation to the problem they are
bringing. Families come into therapy because they are in pain
and need help and where they are in pain through existing
chronic dysfunctional patterns the structural therapist

addresses himself to these, to the multiple sequences between people that generate aspects of self. The process of habit formation, as Bateson pointed out long before he began to apply himself to the problems of dysfunctional families, 'is a linking of knowledge down to less conscious and more archaic levels . . . a major economy of conscious thought . . . we can afford to sink those sorts of knowledge which continue to be true regardless of changes in the environment, but we must maintain in an accessible place all those controls of behaviour which must be modified for every instance'. As has been extensively discussed in family therapy literature, the origins of such dysfunctional behaviours in families may be buried in previous generations (Byng-Hall, 1973) and I have discussed this more particularly as it relates to a two generation family system (Gorell Barnes, 1978). The process of bringing the latent meaning of habitual dysfunctional transactions out into the open can often be done most effectively as they are enacted between members in the room. Resistance to change is then experienced in action, 'If you want to understand the relationship between the developing person and some aspect of his environment, take a good look; try to budge one and see what happens to the other' (Bronfenbrenner, 1978).

By making conscious the meaning involved in the smallest transactions, family members begin to think about the effect of their habits on one another and 'acquire the habit of looking for contexts and sequences of one type rather than another in their interactions, a habit of punctuating the stream of events to give repetitions of a certain type of meaningful sequence' (Bateson, 1973, p. 140). Painful transactions and the rules that govern them can then shift from the less conscious level to the conscious and are available for change.

RESTRUCTURING OPERATIONS

1 *Enactment*
It is only possible to comment briefly on some of the more important structural techniques so I have selected those which have had most impact on my own work.

Enactment involves a request from the therapist to the family to move from description to transaction in the room, thus supplying the therapist with direct information on the ways in which family members normally fight, support one another or undermine each other's positions. Working in this way decentralizes the therapist and helps family members experience themselves in a heightened way as the therapist focuses in on their exchange. Specific comments like, 'Will you talk with your wife about that', or, 'If you want to talk to father you must look at him, not at me and convince him you want his help', move the family in the direction of taking responsibility for working with each other on their problem. Minuchin points out (1979, personal communication) that it is essential for the therapist to have a number of ways of removing himself as a channel of

communication in order to throw the family back on talking to each
other and unblocking blocked channels at the point where they
habitually get stuck. Looking at your shoes, moving the chair back,
moving out of the chair onto a seat away from the family, are all
useful methods. Once families are engaged and have accepted that
talking to each other directly is a rule of therapy, a brief indication
without words that they talk with each other may be enough, for
example, pointing to the relevant person or drawing two chairs in a
few inches. Some families may need the specific instruction, 'Talk
with your son/father/wife and I will help you if you get stuck.'

2   *Changing space*
It was scathingly said at one time that the move from individual to
family therapy was marked by the therapist learning to request
family members to change their seating arrangement at regular intervals. 'Bodies' rather than 'internal objects' were moved as the
mark of a professional shift from individual to family therapy. While
it has always been recognized by those struggling towards transactional change that movement in itself achieves little without a clear
therapeutic purpose; moving bodies to intensify an interaction or
create boundaries remains a regular practice in structural work because of its power to shift a system that is stuck. If a daughter
complains in a general way about her mother's behaviour, directing
the two to move close to discuss this face to face while the rest of
the family temporarily sit back and bear witness, carries considerable power and, by intensifying the mother/daughter interaction
attention is clearly focused on issues within that subsystem that
need to be resolved. If a mother and father never confront one another directly, but always involve the children or a particular child,
as a channel of communication, blocking that triangulation by removing the child from between the parents, makes what is happening clear to both parents and the child and clears the way for the
parents to face each other directly.

3   *Creating boundaries*
As I have discussed more fully elsewhere (Gorell Barnes, 1978),
individual boundaries within the family are marked by very simple
things which may nevertheless carry large emotional overtones. Not
sitting in a particular chair, or drinking from a particular glass,
not opening mother's handbag or tidying away a child's game before it is complete, are daily 'life and death' struggles between individuals competing for personal space. In therapy these minutiae
of family life can be observed in the tiny impingements that carry
implications of age inappropriate handling, of enmeshment, of the
fusion of bodies to a degree that may be confusing to the children.
In the third session with the Meyer family, mother tells her daughter,
aged 15, 'It's warm in here, take off your coat.' The therapist,
choosing this as the boundary impingement issue remarks how for-
tunate Lizzie is to have a mother who cares for her so much that she
thinks constantly on her behalf about her comfort, her body tem-
perature and her physical needs. He pursues this line with mother

and daughter, exploring who chose the coat and the other clothes
Lizzie is wearing; who decides on their composition, fabric, colour-
ing and their suitability for Lizzie's daily life, and in so doing he
ensures that mother and daughter begin to realize the absurdity of
their behaviour and the power of mother's over-protectiveness.
Such evidence examined in the session is irrefutable, and is in the
room for all members to discuss. It opens up larger issues of who
controls whom in other areas of family life and whether such control
and care is appropriately offered. It is often these very small but
intensely felt impingements of autonomy that make individuals feel
powerless in families and that provoke tremendous rage and anger
in family life. Because of the intimacy of family life and the continual
rubbing against one another physically and emotionally that family
members experience, they often do feel one another's habits and
bodies as if they were their own. One little boy with persistent tics
was finally able to say to his mother who was complaining that she
was intensely worried in a non-specific way about him, 'I cry because I see your anxious face. Your worry makes me worry.' In
another family in which each member had a different somatic complaint, the daughter who was the main family symptom bearer and
spokesman asked the therapist: 'There are different sorts of pain.
Do you mean pain in the body or pain in the heart? We don't know
who's got that one.'

4 Subsystem boundaries
Within the family, particular subsystem boundaries may need reinforcing in order that the involvement in other subsystems may
diminish. For example, in a single-parent family a brother and
sister are required by the therapist to discuss their mother's right
to have a boy friend. The therapist helps the brother use his 'extra
two years' to enable his sister to understand the inappropriateness
of her over-involvement with her mother's social and sexual life.
The therapist congratulates the boy on his maturity and supports
him when embarrassment threatens the precarious 'maturity'. The
boy is successful in making his point. In another family a question
to Marie, the 14-year-old identified patient, 'You need a backer to
say what you want to say; who's your ally?' draws the support of
her younger brother in confronting the father with his lack of concern for mother. Such defining of a subsystem boundary can transform a scapegoated family member into a concerned person with a
responsible point of view about family issues. When a one person
problem is redefined as an issue between two people in a family, a
third family member can be brought in to help solve the transactional problems of the other two. This work on one dyad is succeeded by work on another, the problem 'couple' becoming the allies
and joining the therapist on work with another transactional problem elsewhere in the family.

5 Escalating stress
The more skilled the family at avoiding the issues they bring for
the therapist to 'solve', the more likely he is to need to heighten

intensity between members in the room. Families who are skilled
at conflict avoidance may involve the therapist in the same game,
diffusing points that he makes, agreeing smilingly to his propositions and leaving him feeling he is the only one doing any work on
change. 'Well, thank you very much for doing so much on our behalf and giving us so much of your valuable time.' The point of
escalating stress between people in the family is to create and
emphasize difference; to seek and find resolutions for these differences in the session and to highlight the fact that they can be
separate but survive together. The manner in which the therapist
chooses to do this will vary depending on his courage, his belief
that his job is not just about making things easy for people and his
moral perception of whether he has a right to increase stress in
order to create change.

In systems theory Ps is taken as that point at which the maximum
number of functions essential to the existence of the system con-
verge. If this point is modified it effects maximum change with the
minimal amount of energy. The negotiation involved in such a change
is bound to create anticipatory stress. In the emotions surrounding
the interactions that Ps symbolizes, the family investment against
change will be at its highest since those elements of self that are
generated by the sequences in charge are threatened. Such key
points of stress need proper anticipation before they are approached.
As Bateson pointed out, biological change is conservative and learning is aversive (Bateson, 1973, p. 417). Consciousness and self
are closely related ideas and the consciousness of family members
seeking help on behalf of one of their members is likely to contain
systematic distortions of view which at the point where an impending change is sensed will threaten each person's central self as
hitherto construed. (The reader may be interested in referring to
chapter 19 where Procter examines a different approach to this
issue.)

It is in relation to the management of this change that important
differences in style between structural family therapy and strategic
family therapy can be found. The structural therapist as outlined
above, will work on the minutiae of interaction and on changing
these on the premise that within a system transformation can be
achieved through small subsystem changes. He is working on Bateson's second level of learning in which 'those characteristics of the
self generated by experience in multiple sequences are punctuated
in a different way by the introduction of new meaning to the sequences' (Bateson, 1973, p. 276). The strategic therapist addresses
himself to the third level of learning making an intervention that
changes the frame of the rules governing the second level behaviours, a change in the 'context of those contexts' (Bateson,
1973, p. 275). This is brilliantly demonstrated by the work of Mara
Selvini Palazzoli and her colleagues in Milan who are concerned with
changing the rules of the family game (Palazzoli et al. 1978) and as
an approach has been extensively documented by Haley (1963, 1973),
Watzlawick et al. (1967, 1974) and in Britain by Cade (1978, 1979).

For the structural family therapist the unit of intervention will be

a subsystem. An individual, a pair, a threesome or a nuclear family
are all subsystems. 'In the therapist's formulation will be a recognition of the family's connections with the extended family and its
spatial and social relationship to society . . . the time unit of intervention . . . i.e. holistic. It is the individual in the web of significant relationships in which people interact' (Minuchin et al. 1978).
As proposed throughout this chapter the structural therapist works
in the belief that in systems containing many interconnected homoeo-
static loops, changes brought about by an external impact in one
part will slowly spread through the system. Bateson (1973, p. 277)
in discussing the relationship of the part to the whole, has said,
'The resolution of contraries reveals a world in which personal identity merges into all the processes of relationship in some past ecology
of aesthetics of cosmic interaction. That any of these can survive
seems almost miraculous but some are perhaps saved from being
swept away on oceanic feeling by their ability to focus on the minutiae of life. Every detail of the universe is seen as proposing a
view of the whole.' With such complex awareness the structural
family therapist creates a delicate but clearly defined series of inter-
laced spaces within which small issues can be resolved.

6 *Tasks*
It should be established by this stage in the chapter that it is in
the minutiae of life that the structural therapist develops his professional skills. Some will find it exciting and some merely irritating
that wellington boots, pocket money and eating meals together are
details of the family's world that propose a view of the whole and as
such occupy so much of the therapist's attention. Finding tasks for
families to do at home is a valuable therapeutic strategy, as well as
using the kind of task enactment in the room that has already been
discussed. Whether the task is done or not provides clues about the
families' flexibility and capacity for change. It is better for the
family to find their own task and make their own contract, than for
the therapist to find one for them, although he will want to help
find a task most relevant to the complaints they are bringing. In
the extract that follows the therapist is helping the family in the
negotiation stage, lending support to different members in turn,
and finally swinging the family together against her by the use of
a little therapeutic pessimism which mobilizes father to take charge.
The extract also shows the way in which a symptom is brought
into play to try and maintain the family homoeostasis. As Joanne
attacks father and the conflict continues in the open, Peter produces
one of the pains that has taken him round many hospitals in search
of a cure over the last five years. Later on when the therapist's
pessimism has made father determined to succeed in the plan and
mobilized the authority which he usually displays in business but
not at home, Peter, anxious about impending change, produces a
hand washing symptom, another of the many habits that the family
are anxious about yet need in order to stay the same.
Therapist (to Joanne)?: Why don't you turn round and talk to him -
try turning your chair like this and talk to him.

Mother: (on sidelines) Yes go on.
Joanne (embarrassed, giggles)
Therapist (to Peter): Do you agree with what Joanne is saying?
Peter: Yes.
Therapist: So you both want to talk to Dad about it?
Peter: Yea.
Joanne: (continues) . . . and then they both have dinner.
Therapist: Well join with her and see if you can both talk with Dad about what you would both like to do with him - you obviously both have an idea.
Joanne: Yes, well it would just be nice if we could sit down and spend a bit more time talking as a family - we never just sit down and talk about things - anything - it's always, 'You two get out of the room' (trails away), we don't get any time.
Therapist: Can you think of a time that you can have with Dad - maybe he needs some help in thinking how to do something with a 13-year-old girl and a 10-year-old boy.
Joanne (continues to complain)
Peter pulls a face.
Mother (to Peter): Have you got a pain?
Peter develops a pain.
Peter: Yea it's in my ribs.
Mother (concerned): Well sit up straight.
(Dad moves in for the come back.)
Dad: Hang on people . . . when I come home what's the first thing that happens. . . .
Peter: You come and kiss us.
Therapist: May I make a suggestion?
Dad: Please do.
Therapist: Whatever the rights or wrongs of it are, I suggest you don't talk about it.
Dad: I'm trying to find out what I'm not doing/should be doing.
Therapist: I know you are but I would still like Joanne to make one positive suggestion that she (to Joanne), that you can put to your Dad about what you can do with him, because it's much easier for someone to respond to a positive suggestion. (Silence.)
Joanne and Peter: (Talk together - laugh.)
Joanne: Well, maybe just two evenings a week if we could have supper and sit and talk: even if we go out to eat somewhere Dad talks to Mum about business, that's all we ever hear, business isn't it (to Peter).
Peter: No.
Joanne: And football.
Peter: Yes (Joanne makes a face).
Therapist repeats Joanne's suggestion and asks Peter: What would you like?
Peter: Well I'd just like to sit down and talk a bit and talk about problems, it doesn't really matter what we talk about, it would be just nice to see Mum and Dad more times during the day.
. . . . . .
Mother: We don't spend enough time, we don't sit quietly.

Therapist (encouraging): You said this earlier in the evening that you set the table and one by one they slip away.
Mother: Yes and very often I'm left sitting by myself.
Therapist: Any one person who tries doesn't manage it: they've got to find a backer.
Father: I would rephrase it as not being a time that they (indicating Joanne and Peter) have chosen.
Therapist: OK then, you've got to negotiate. Your daughter has made a very positive request which is . . .
Father: (enthused): OK let's negotiate - come on, move your chair.
Therapist: (encourages Joanne) Come forward, why don't you two negotiate a time when you can talk.
Father: Well it seems to me in order to solve the problem we could have dinner in the kitchen every night.
Joanne: Not every night (Peter yawns).
Therapist: Twice a week she suggested (indicating Joanne).
Joanne: But you always talk about business.
Father: We won't talk about business, we'll just talk, OK? How's that.
Peter: In a couple of weeks we'll forget to do it.
Therapist (sighing pessimistically): It won't work of course.
Peter (agreeing): In a couple of weeks we'll forget to do it.
Father to Therapist: But why not? With respect, that's a very negative statement.
Therapist (looking doubtful): We'll have to see.
Father: You can't just say something like that and just let us go away.
Peter: We can't always miss our favourite programmes.
Therapist (indicating Peter's resistance): That's one of the reasons.
Father: Yea, but we all have different likes and dislikes.
Therapist to Father: You will have to make sure it works, Mr G.
Father: What we'll have to say is one week it's Monday and Wednesday and next week Tuesday and Thursday, etc. It will always happen. We're never going to satisfy everyone, so forget it - if you miss something, tough luck. (Children argue vigorously with their father. Mum proposes organizing the week around the television programmes.)
Father to Joanne (takes charge): Let me ask you a question. When do you think we ought to talk if it's not going to be then? (Children discuss the shape of the day - no other time seems to be available.)
Father: Right. Do you have an alternative. Well, do you? Tell you what, we'll do it every day from Monday till Friday. (Children resist.)
Joanne: Between the time Daddy comes in and the time 'Crossroads' starts.
Father: No that's no good 'cos I don't always know what time I'll be home - right?
Peter: In the morning we don't have any time, Dad, right?
Mother: So what else do you suggest?
Peter: Maybe after supper.
Joanne: And then someone wants to watch something on TV.
Father (pressing his head): So do you have an alternative?

Peter: Sunday is a good day, there's nothing on TV on Sunday and Thursdays - (Peter and Joanne agree).
Father: Tell you what we'll do - we'll do it Monday to Friday.
Peter: Pardon.
Father: Monday to Friday.
Peter and Joanne: What, every day?
Joanne: What time?
Father: Yes, why not?
Peter and Joanne: Not every single day.
Father: Why?
Joanne: I don't want to.
Father: Why?
Peter: We won't be able to watch a thing.
Joanne: No. If we see each other every day (quietly) we'll get sick of each other.
Peter: And anyway sometimes you go away - you go out to eat.
Therapist: The kids are saying a little will work.
Father: I'm discouraged because you said a little wouldn't work.
Therapist: No, I said I didn't think the plan would work. . . .
Joanne (interrupts): Why?
Therapist: Because as a family you are so good at allowing freedom of choice that you will undermine one another. . . .
Peter (producing another symptom): Excuse me, can I wash my hands please.
Therapist: Let's just finish, OK? . . . (Peter nods) . . . (continues:) . . . unless someone really takes charge of it.
Peter: I'll take charge of it.
Therapist (indicating Dad): Your father's already taken charge of it.

7 The use of the symptom in the session

The use of the symptom in therapy will depend on both the therapist and the family. With some families, the choice will be to focus on the symptom and its meaning as the key to the family's major dysfunctional preoccupations (Whiffen, 1979). With another family, the choice may be to exaggerate the symptom as we saw earlier in the chapter. In the extract above the emphasis has been taken away from the symptom into another area of family behaviour that the children, the symptom bearers, consider problematic. A range of other symptoms in family members have also been opened up. The choice to de-emphasize and move away from the symptom was in this case made because so much professional attention had previously been focused on the children to the exclusion of the family as a whole. The relabelling of the symptom within the context of the family as a whole is sometimes explicit and helpful to the family, sometimes only helpful for the therapist. It is often valuable to change the affect round a symptom so that it takes on a different meaning to the family in simple words; relabelling, for example, 'whoring around' as 'teenage necking' or 'fascist control' as father's 'protective love'. In so doing the therapist is flipping the coin for the family, helping them see the alternative or complementary side

to the behaviour of another; possibly redefining as a skill a behaviour others have labelled problematic.

A further example of the brief productive relabelling of a symptom
comes from a family where the son was referred for exposing himself
to the little girl next door and become liable for police prosecution.
When the family with great pain and anxiety brought themselves to
the clinic it was apparent that Irving, a very active West Indian
17-year-old, had to spend a lot of his time caring for his severely
handicapped brother Clifton in order to give his very devoted
church-going mother some relief. Both boys were being smothered
by her anxiety and over-protection. During this time he helped his
brother with his sexual fantasies by talking about his own sex life
and keeping that part of his brother alive and growing in imagination as well as actively taking him to clubs and discos. Both boys
were touchingly explicit about how Irving had to 'do it' for both of
them and on this occasion of exposure Clifton had been watching
through the window, to observe the effect of Irving's action. In two
sessions the family had literally relabelled Irving from 'potential
rapist' to 'good brother' as well as someone who needed freedom and
recognition appropriate to his age. Mother also faced up to Clifton's
need to develop a much wider social life of his own without her
constant presence.

In another family where a fat and rather immature little girl was
referred for pulling down her knickers in the playground and
telling rude stories in class, it was easy to discover that the first
action deflected gang bullying from older boys and the second was
seen as a skill by all her classmates, the maintenance of which ensured some popularity and further protection against the bullying
in the playground.

CONCLUSION

The placing of a symptom within its context is rarely simple and it
is probable that the longer the symptom has its own life the more
difficult it becomes for straightforward structural work to take
place, since a range of secondary behaviours grow up around the
symptom's management and internal meaning for different family
members. However, in my view the difficulty will be related primarily to the psychic investment the family has in those areas of
life symbolized by the symptom, and the level at which this preoccupation is carried, rather than to the duration of the behaviour
complained of. The more unconscious the family preoccupation is,
the more difficult I find it to work structurally because other areas
of my own professional interests then press for more space and
attention. The search for appropriate language with which to work
with any family remains for me the key, as it links less conscious
process with the necessary exploration of the behavioural transactions. However, at the level at which an unconscious preoccupation, fear or myth 'governs' the family transactions and keeps them
fixed, the interpretive style links to the prescriptive style and is

proving particularly valuable at that stage of adolescent development when separation from parents should be under way but is not occurring.

While I will remain committed to maintaining different approaches for different families since in my view working within a national health framework providing for the needs of all children and families referred, a range of approaches must properly be maintained. The structural approach adding, as it does, the developmental focus to a family systems view, has been of enormous theoretical and practical value in bringing together what I have learnt through working in child focused systems of care with the systemic approach to problem formation and problem solving that family therapy necessarily requires.

When a baby cries and an adult responds by picking him up, a system is in operation; when an adult raises his voice and a baby ceases to suck, a different part of the family system is being activated; but the variables at six days, and the issues around which these are focused are not the same as they will be at six months, six years or sixteen years. It is these developmental differences and the family behaviours that enact the meaning of the absence of proper difference, that structural family therapy insists the therapist attend to; and from which a proper theory relating to therapy with families containing developing and dependent beings, can itself be developed within the many different settings offered to children and their caregivers in this country.

ACKNOWLEDGMENTS

With sincere thanks to Harry Aponte, Marianne Walters and Salvador Minuchin who worked with us and taught us; to John Byng-Hall and Rosemary Whiffen for providing a learning and teaching setting; to David Campbell with whom some of this work was done and to Alec Clarke for a vignette from one of his sessions. My particular gratitude to Janice Uphill for her help in preparing the text.

REFERENCES

Aponte, H. (1977) The Anatomy of a Therapist, in P. Papp, (ed.), 'Full Length Case Studies', Gardner Press.
Aponte, H. (1978) The Family School Interview: An Ecostructural Approach, 'Family Process', 15, 3, 303-10.
Bannister, K. and Pincus, L. (1965) 'Shared Phantasy in Marital Problems', Institute of Marital Studies.
Bateson, G. (1973) 'Steps to an Ecology of Mind', Paladin.
Bentovim, A. (1979) Towards Creating a Focal Hypothesis for Brief Focal Family Therapy, 'Journal of Family Therapy', 1.2, 125-36, chapter 12, above.
Bronfenbrenner, U. (1978) Ecological Factors in Human Development in Retrospect and Prospect, in H. McGurk, (ed), 'Ecological Factors in Child Psychiatry', M. & H. Holland Publishing.
Byng-Hall, J. (1973) Family Myths used as a Defence in Conjoint Family Therapy, 'British Journal of Medical Psychology', 46, 239-49, chapter 6, above.

Byng-Hall, J. (1979) Re-editing Family Mythology during Family
  Therapy, 'Journal of Family Therapy', 1.2, 103-16.
Cade, B. (1979) The Use of Paradox in Therapy, in S. Walrond-
  Skinner, (ed.), 'Family and Marital Psychotherapy: A Critical
  Approach', Routledge & Kegan Paul.
Cade, B. and Southgate, P. (1979) Honesty is the Best Policy,
  'Journal of Family Therapy', 1.1, 23-31.
Cooklin, A. (1979) A Psychoanalytic Framework of a Systemic Approach
  to Family Therapy, 'Journal of Family Therapy', 1.1, 153-65.
Dare, C. (1979) Psychoanalysis and Systems in Family Therapy,
  'Journal of Family Therapy', 1.1, 137-51.
Dicks, H. (1967) 'Marital Tensions: Clinical Studies towards a
  psychological theory of intervention', Routledge & Kegan Paul.
Gorell Barnes, G. (1973) Working with the Family Group: some
  Problems of Practice, 'Social Work Today', 3, 65-70 (Reprinted
  as chapter 5 in this volume.)
Gorell Barnes, G. (1975) Seen but not Heard: Work with West Indian
  Families in Distress, 'Social Work Today', 5, 20, 606-9; 5.21,
  646-8; 5.22, 689-93.
Gorell Barnes, G. (1978) Infant Needs and Angry Responses. A
  Look at Violence in the Family, in S. Walrond-Skinner, (ed.),
  'Family and Marital Psychotherapy: A critical approach', Routledge
  & Kegan Paul.
Goren, S. (1979) Director Intra Mural Programme Philadelphia Child
  Guidance Clinic, personal communication, International Training
  Forum on Family Therapy Training; Tavistock Clinic.
Haley, J. (1963) 'Strategies of Psychotherapy', New York, Grune &
  Stratton.
Haley, J. (1973) 'Uncommon Therapy: The Psychiatric Techniques
  of Milton H. Erickson', New York, W.W. Norton.
Lidz, T. (1964) 'The Family and Human Adaptation', International
  Psychoanalytic Library.
Minuchin, S. (1977) 'Families and Family Therapy', Tavistock.
Minuchin, S. et al. (1967) 'Families of the Slums', New York, Basic
  Books.
Minuchin, S., Rosman, B. and Baker, L. (1978) 'Psychosomatic
  Families', Harvard University Press.
Palazzoli, M.S., Cecchin, G. Prata, G. and Boscolo, L. (1978)
  'Paradox and Counterparadox', New York, Jason, Aronson.
Pincus, L. (1960) 'Marriage: Studies in Emotional Conflict and
  Growth', Family Discussion Bureau.
Walters, M. (1977) On Becoming a Mystery, in P. Papp (ed.), 'Full
  Length Case Studies', Gardner Press.
Watzlawick, P. (1979) 'The Language of Change', Basic Books.
Watzlawick, P., Bevin, J. and Jackson, D. (1967) 'Pragmatics of
  Human Communication', New York, W.W. Norton.
Watzlawick, P., Weakland, J. and Fisch, R. (1974) 'Change:
  Principles of Problem Formation and Problem Resolution', New York,
  W.W. Norton.
Whiffen, R. (1979) 'Association for Family Therapy Newsletter',
  conference issue, spring.

17 EXPERIENTIAL FAMILY THERAPY

Erica De'Ath

If thought is father to the deed, then awareness is its mother and experience its ultimate source of wisdom. Walter Kempler, 'Principles of Gestalt Family Therapy', 1973, p. 60.

All therapy is experiential: to 'have experience of' something or someone is an acknowledgment of the past, an acceptance of the part it plays in our present, and an assumption that it will define our capacity or ability for future experience. Experiential awareness is that knowledge borne out of, or based on, actual experience: it is a form of learning. Since therapy, by definition, is an attempt to change, alter, or cure emotional or behavioural disorders other than by organic treatment methods, it must also be a form of learning. The idea of family therapy as a process of learning has been outlined by Ackerman (1966) as 're-education of the family through guidance, re-organisation through a change in the patterns of family communication, and resolution of pathogenic conflict and induction of change and growth by means of a dynamic, depth-approach to the affective currents of family life' (p. 405). Experiential family therapy encourages 'an experience that exposes to our awareness what we do to each other and how we do it. Briefly what and how of behaviour displaces why; experiences displace discussion' (Kempler, 1968, p. 90). The family provides the 'what' and the therapist looks at the 'how', highlighting the consequences and enabling family members to consider different ways of behaving.

The development of family therapy is an interesting example of creative eclecticism. Family therapy has not arisen from a unitary background but has drawn on theories and concepts from the analytical, behavioural and interactional schools, and from studies in the different disciplines of anthropology, sociology, education and management training that emphasise the importance of direct observations of the phenomenon under consideration and of participation in such situations: it is, in short, an experiential modality. In social anthropology and social psychology the rationale for observations of groups of individuals has been that there are some features of behaviour and patterns of interaction which would not be uncovered by the researcher, teacher, or therapist, if they had relied only on the spoken account and had not witnessed the action (Bott,

1957; Becker, 1961; Holt, 1967; Young and Willmott, 1957). Family therapy integrates various theoretical approaches and focuses on the family as a natural functioning unit, where the behaviour of any one member affects the behaviour of all other members. The disturbances in family life reflect the disturbances both of the individual and the family group. The focus of therapeutic attention is shifted towards discovering ways in which an apparent individual problem enables the entire family group to maintain its equilibrium. This chapter will consider ways in which the modality as a whole can be considered to be experiential; how different schools employ directly some specifically experiential approaches; and finally, some of the features which distinguish experiential family therapy as a school of family therapy in its own right.

The use of experiential techniques, or an experiential approach, in family therapy reflects the general shift away from a medical model, whereby a symptom is isolated and treated, to an educational approach where family members are encouraged to discover and resolve their dynamic entanglements and dysfunctional patterns of behaviour (Guerney, Stollak and Guerney, 1971). It highlights the shift from a linear and deterministic explanation of events to models of circular causation, from a concern with purposes and motivation, to models of self-corrective and rule governed systems. In many families, areas of experience are limited. Family themes are restricted and there is an emphasis on aggression, helplessness, abandonment and nurturance. Patterns of behaviour, of interpersonal responses, have been acquired and developed and a particular way of life formulated so that any new experience will be made to fit this pattern. In this situation, therapy or new learning is handicapped by previous experiential learning. By making family members aware of the way in which they function, the way in which certain transactions between family members have become automatic, behaviour occurring again and again in an automatically triggered sequence, the therapist can encourage family members to search for new solutions through interaction amongst themselves. It is important to acknowledge that in this form of experiential learning the behaviour of the therapist, which will reflect, communicate and model his own values, can influence the immediate learning and subsequent behaviour of the family group. Values become extremely important when generating alternative modes of behaviour. It must be remembered that if change in one individual member is inconsistent with the existing values of the family group, or of society at large, that individual must either accept the existing norms, become deviant in that situation, or leave. When you engage in experiential family therapy work you are exposing that family to the likelihood of change.

Family therapists from different schools use an experiential focus to obtain this goal and provide the context and encouragement for new individual and interpersonal experiences. For Minuchin (1965), 'The technique of task-oriented family therapy directs family members to participate in familiar tasks under conditions that are different from and sometimes the opposite of, their usual pattern of response'

(p. 280). For Satir (1967), 'a study of communication can help close
the gap between inference and observation as well as document the
relationship between patterns of communication and symptomatic
behaviour' (p. 63).Watzlawick (1974) describes reframing the client's
situation 'to change the conceptual and/or emotional setting or viewpoint in relation to which a situation is experienced and to place it
in another frame which fits the "facts" of the same concrete situation
equally well or even better, and thereby changes its entire meaning' (p. 95). Milton Erickson's theory of change is more complex and
is based upon the interpersonal impact of the therapist outside the
patient's awareness. In his early hypnotic work he brought into
awareness a past experience so that the past experience was recalled
or relived. His therapeutic approach now includes providing direc-
tives that cause changes of behaviour and emphasises communicating
in metaphor (see Haley, 1967; 1973).

Thus the experiential approach pervades the whole spectrum of
family therapy methods and can be employed in and attached to a
variety of strategies, techniques and interventions. It will always
relate to the influence of the personality and life experiences which
the therapist/s bring into the family encounter. What the therapist
learns about the family and what happens in any one session will
be related to his past experiences with this and similar families and
will be used as a point of reference in the future with this family
or other families with whom he works. It is as much a learning
experience for the therapist as the therapy is a learning process
for the family. The extent to which the therapist/s are prepared to
involve themselves overtly with a family, and to participate as
fully as they are able - showing pleasure, rage, sadness, despair,
able to feel and share their embarrassments, helplessness, frustration and confusion, will determine the extent of experiential learning for them as well as for the family. In describing a family therapy
training programme originated by Duhl and Kantor, Constantine
(1973) states: 'At Boston State Hospital we grow family therapists.
We do not make family therapists, nor, strictly speaking, do we
teach family therapy as a corpus of concepts, tools and techniques.
Like good gardeners, we strive to create an environment that is
conducive to growth and learning, one that blends spontaneous
caring within a carefully laid out plot, that balances sunshine and,
of course, a little rain.' Haley (1972) from his very different frame
of reference points out that in 1967 at the Philadelphia Child Guidance Clinic, staff could not learn family therapy in academia, they
had to learn it on the job with the result that 'most family therapists
have gone through a transitional process, sharing now a basic shift
in their ideas which comes about from the experience of working
with families. One can assume that the shift in ideas comes from
exposure to families, since often family therapists shift to a common
view even though they have not been exposed to the work of other
family therapists' (p. 156).

Family therapy is an action therapy, oriented towards the exploration of alternative ways of behaviour or modes of interaction.
Although the therapist's use of self offers a model for the family to

copy, the aim is not so much to provide behaviour for direct imitation but rather to illustrate alternative ways of handling difficult
incidents:

> when many needs seem to arise at once or when chaos seems to
> temporarily prevail . . . it behoves the experientially oriented
> family therapist to turn to his own needs first. Perhaps he will
> demand a moment's moratorium from bedlam in order to see in
> which direction he would arbitrarily wish to proceed. Possibly he
> will request some assistance from the working family in this
> matter. His own transient uncertainty is a welcome expression in
> a good experientially oriented therapeutic encounter. During the
> course of such encounters personal growth and family integration
> for each family member becomes explicitly possible. Even thera-
> pists grow in such an atmosphere (Kempler, 1968, p. 99).

In this situation, the therapist is able to conceptualise the confusion
and to teach the family not only that there are a variety of perceptions, opportunities, possibilities and alternative ways of responding
or reacting, but also to confirm that the family must assume responsibility for its own interactional difficulties. He may highlight
this process by getting one family member to take over the role of
the therapist: such a role reversal often introduces a number of
questions and issues of considerable import to the family which the
family has previously avoided or kept secret. It is the family who
must do the work: the therapist acts as instructor and guide,
whether by directing confrontation, redistributing roles, relations
and generational boundaries, or actively encouraging and directing
the integration of experiential awareness from the session into the
current interaction and family world.

The experientially oriented family therapist will present the
therapeutic session or task as a learning situation (whether change
is seen as a skill acquisition with a specific clear focus or as a
general process awareness):

- to allow the therapist to get to know the family - their names,
   ages, interests, who and how they decided to come;
- to let the family get to know the therapist - who s/he is, what
   family therapy means to him/her, how he will probably work
   with them (tasks, contracts, games, action, using video, drama,
   drawing posters and geneograms, etc.);
- to let family members get to know themselves better, as individuals and as a group, who each one is in the family, what is
   special about their family, how are they different from other
   families, what is the most important thing about their family;
- to elicit and clarify the expectations, hopes, fears and fantasies
   of family therapy, what do they expect to happen, what would
   they like to happen, what would they like to be different in
   their family;
- to begin to take an active, directive and instructive role in clarifying messages that come from each family member by: paraphrasing
   - repeating what family members say in different ways;
- adverb correction - check the details when a family generalise with
   'always', 'never'

   pronoun correction – one/us/you/we/she/he/they, exactly who
      referred to
   clarification of feelings and thoughts – check when feelings are
      expressed as thoughts or vice versa
   clarification of definitions – find out the implications and con-
      notations of a person's meaning for, and use of, words such
      as 'respect', 'duty', 'good behaviour';
to encourage and accept the possibility of diversity in a family –
   examine contradictory and complementary purposes, review past
   attempts to solve 'the problem';
to take the initiative in sharing own satisfactions and disappoint-
   ments, talking of appropriate and inappropriate action or consequences and of learning from our mistakes, rather than classi-
   fying events as successes or failures;
to demonstrate personal ownership of attitudes – 'I get angry
   when . . .' rather than 'He makes me angry . . .';
to decribe what you see without interpretation – distractions when
   particular family members talk together or to the therapist;
   body posture or behaviour at certain times or sequences in a
   session; interruptions generally; incongruent communication;
   general facial or bodily expressions in any or all family members
   (sad, lonely, angry, smiling, turned away, proximity, separateness).
The rationale for experiential sessions and techniques is that it
reinforces the nature of therapy as learning and change for both
the therapist and the family. The assumptions are: that experience
is an active and not a passive process; that each person has the
potential to learn and change; that learning is rooted in reality at
the experiential level; that change is difficult, frightening and
sometimes painful, and family members require help and practice
in changing; that the development of self-directed and significant
learning encourages insight; and, that these in turn develop self-
evaluation and self criticism and encourage self-awareness and
understanding of others. Such interventions, whether specifically
directed towards the presenting problem or to exploring alternatives
to the transactional patterns that have reinforced the problem syndrome, cannot be made from the 'outside'. The therapist must gain
experiential knowledge of the family interaction, of the controlling
power that the family system exerts, and of the range of thresholds
that the family system can tolerate. Minuchin (1978) explains his
use of the family lunch session in working with a family with an
anorexic girl:
   It seems to me that if we ask the parents and the girl to talk
   about the problem, what we get is their selective perception of
   the issues. And since they have been trapped in an impossible
   situation for a year, what they will present is the stereotype of
   that year's transaction. As much as possible, I want to participate, to experience what the family experiences. It's like asking
   people to dance instead of asking them to describe how they
   dance (p. 145).
The specific and habitual use of experiential tasks, exercises,

games and sessions, distinguishes the experiential approach. It has
its roots in other methods of family therapy and in developments
such as T groups, encounter groups, gestalt therapy and psychodrama. T groups (or human relations training groups) began in
1946 when Kurt Lewin and a team of social psychologists recorded
and coded behavioural interactions and sequences observed in small
groups. While they used role-play techniques and structured
exercises to diagnose behavioural and interactional aspects of 'back
home' problems and to practice alternative problem solving techniques, these experiential groups were considered as an instrument
of education and not therapy.

The encounter movement, encounter groups and the human potential movement (Carl Rogers, 1961; 1970) also provide important
source material for experiential family therapy. These groups combine cognitive and experiential learning and stress certain departures from established therapeutic practice within the therapist-
patient relationship: a move from talk to action; an emphasis on
group sharing and leader participation rather than individual
patient/therapist interaction; the facilitation of actual intense
experiences rather than discussion and interpretation of thoughts.
Rogers (1969) defines the elements of experiential learning in these
groups as follows:

It has a quality of personal involvement - the whole person in
both his feeling and cognitive aspects being in the learning event.
It is self-initiated. Even when the impetus or stimulus comes from
the outside, the sense of discovery, of reaching out, of grasping
and comprehending, comes from within. It is pervasive. It makes
a difference in the behaviour, the attitudes, perhaps even the
personality of the learner. It is evaluated by the learner. He
knows whether it is meeting his need, whether it leads toward
what he wants to know, whether it illuminates the dark area of
ignorance he is experiencing. The locus of evaluation, we might
say, resides definitely with the learner. Its essence is meaning.
When such learning takes place, the element of meaning to the
learner is built into the whole experience (p. 5).

Whilst the experiential family therapy group might share many of
the properties and concerns (self-awareness, fulfilment of potential,
being in touch with self) and employ techniques of the encounter
group, there is an important difference in the orientation to learning
and desire or capacity to change in the individual members of the
two different groups. Argyris (1968) differentiates the two extremes
as a 'competence orientation', a search for personal growth, improving the quality of personal interaction, being open to learning,
questioning, confronting. An assumption of encounter group members would be acquisition of interpersonal competence, self-
awareness and self-acceptance and a willingness to experiment with
new attitudes and behaviour which may replace older, less appropriate and less successful modes of behaviour. On the other hand,
a family with an identified member as a 'patient' generally has a
lower self-esteem and self-awareness and the identified member is
likely to be more concerned with protecting himself in order to sur-

vive, searching not for growth but for safety; a 'survival orientation', through which he withdraws, distorts or attacks the environment. The simple encounter group mandate 'to be open, honest
and trusting' is not a viable position for an individual or family
who are experiencing profound feelings of suspicion, rejection,
fear, anger, distrust, failure or self-hatred.

Gestalt therapy, developed by Perls (1951) and applied to family
treatment by Kempler, also concentrates awareness on current
feelings and implies that if the past needs attention, it must be
brought out into the present actively, not talked about. In his
book 'Principles of Gestalt Family Therapy' Kempler explains:
'Experience is the key to growth, regrowth and to the therapeutic
process. . . . Gestalt therapy directs its attention to experiences
that stimulate awareness – to new experiences that remind' (p.
60-1). Gestalt family therapy concentrates on the current interactions in the family as being the pivotal point, the 'here and now'
for all awareness and interventions, not by the exclusion of past
or future, but by encouraging occasional detours which are then
integrated into the present. An experiential technique might be
used to create a dialogue between the self and some other, either
because that other cannot be present in the session (he is dead,
or geographically distant); or because, although present in the
session, he is emotionally blocked and unable to participate in
the necessary interaction. A mother, father and daughter em-
broiled in a discussion about the daughter's behaviour can understand each other more clearly when they can integrate the mother's
childhood experiences into their current family world. The mother
is encouraged to think back, return to her childhood for a moment,
to close her eyes and speak to her mother in fantasy, to talk
about a particular incident that pained her. The therapist then
suggests she responds, now as the mother. When the client plays
the role of both parts, the self and the other, it is a dialogue
of one talking aloud in a witnessed and supervised way, both
parts negotiating, contesting, attempting to separate, distinguish
and unblock the enmeshed behaviour, moving from an experience
of confusion and helplessness to a position of recognition of
choice and responsibility for own behaviour. It provides an
opportunity for the whole family to re-experience and re-integrate
aspects that have been isolated, lost or repressed by one of its
members. The Gestalt therapist stresses the importance of each
family member achieving greater self-awareness, greater clarity
of experience and greater self-direction. S/he actively facilitates
each family member to be aware of what they are currently experiencing in its most concrete and direct expression: to attend
to bodily experience and emotional experience in the context of the
current therapeutic interaction. For example, a husband may be
listening to his wife with a smile indicating his agreement, whilst
at the same time sitting with his legs crossed against her, leaning
away from her, indicating disagreement and a desire to disassociate
himself completely from her; or a child may turn around completely
in its chair and stare out of the window when the parents begin to

talk to one another, thus excluding himself from the group and the conversation. The primary goals of gestalt family therapy are related to expanding awareness, 'growing', discovering resources, allowing individual members a new experience in the family, rather than a change at a behavioural level.

Psychodrama, created by Moreno (1946) allows for a different kind of enactment in dramatic terms. The therapist acts as director and the family as actors; the identified family member may be the protagonist and the other family members the auxiliaries. A family problem is given concrete shape by the enactment of an actual or potential scene exemplifying the parameters.

the manner in which we live in reality, in our relationships with the significant people in our lives, may be defective or inadequate, and we may wish to change – to attempt new ways of living. But change can be both threatening and extremely difficult, to such an extent, that we stay in our familiar ruts rather than risk a calamity which we cannot handle. Thus a therapeutic situation is needed in which reality can be simulated, so that people can learn to develop new techniques of living without risking serious consequences or disaster, as they might in life itself (Moreno, 1969, p. 15).

For example, a family was helped to come to terms with the death of one of six children in the family, a year previously from leukaemia, by re-enacting the death-scene around the child's bed. It was an Irish family who had brought the child home from the hospital in preparation for the funeral. In the psychodrama each family member was able to speak to the dead child in fantasy, to say goodbye and to respond as the dead child. The aim of this technique is to clarify the emotional components in this situation, especially those which affect the interpersonal perception, to improve empathy between family members, and to defuse anxiety, fear and guilt. In the re-enactment of the death scene, individual family members were able to express their own feelings of guilt at remaining alive, of taking over treasured toys and possessions, of confirming their loss and re-affirming to him and to themselves that they would not forget him (one child was having hallucinations and feared to go into his old bedroom). Psychodrama can also be used to work through the loss felt by children from a separated parent, perhaps to experience again the demands, anger, coldness of a parent and to experience it now from the standpoint of that other, as well as for oneself. It allows each family member to approach and redefine the situation from a number of different angles, until they achieve a sense of mastery or understanding of it.

The goal of all therapy is change and before such change can take place it has to be confronted and actively entertained by the individual and by the whole family system. The family needs to experience change within the therapy session if entrenched family patterns are to be disrupted and family members free to re-integrate relationships around altered experiences of self and of one another. By allowing each family we encounter the opportunity for practising new skills, for thinking in terms of new options of behaviour, we

offer the opportunity for new experiential learning to replace old
habits, rigid rules, inflexible roles, unrealistic expectations and
dysfunctional communication patterns. By creating a setting in
which the family are given a task (either engendered by the family's
current life experience or artifically injected by the therapist) new
behaviours, communication patterns and emotional experiences become possible for the family.

The experiential model is an inductive rather than deductive process, family members discover for themselves the learning offered
by the experiential process. Any individual's experience is unique
to himself; no one can tell him what he is to learn, or gain, from
any activity. The term 'structured experience', the implementation
of the experiential model, emphasises the two prime aspects of that
intervention: the existence of some boundaries (focus on individual
or particular behaviour, constructive feedback, processing, psychological and emotional integration) and the process of learning
through doing. It is essential in experiential family therapy that
there is a clear contract between the therapist and the family, that
the goals and the learning method be specified beforehand in
language that all the family members can understand. It is important that the sequencing and timing of particular structured experiences are adequately considered and allowed for to provide enough
time for the family to complete the task or exercise and still allow
plenty of time to process adequately the information generated.
Structured exercises are infinitely varied and variable, and the
skill lies in:

  making the goals on the experiential work explicit and specific;
  learning how to anticipate how particular family members are
  likely to respond to the various learning activities;
  combining and sequencing particular exercises in a meaningful
  way; developing the ability to redirect the learning experience
  while it is in progress;
  processing the activity itself, talking through the behavioural
  and feeling data that emerge and ensuring integration in a functional way.

The actual framework, format or setting of the therapeutic work
can in itself become the salient experiential factor. This is the case
with, for example, the clinical home visit (Bloch, 1973) whereby
the therapist gains a first-hand impression of the physical, psychological and social space available for family members and works
with this data as it becomes available. He becomes part of the daily
routine, experiencing the structure or lack of structure for the
day - food preparation, meal-times, household duties, school and
work routines, conversations and contact between family members,
the tasks, rules and roles in the household and the patterns of
activity between different family members (active, passive, placat-
ing, nurturing, controlling, dominating, distracting). A more
specific experiential session, already mentioned, is the family lunch
(Minuchin, 1978) when one member of the family is anorexic. This
allows the therapist to observe the actual transactions around eating and to make on-the-spot interventions to change the patterning

of these transactions, maybe increasing parental effectiveness or increasing distance between parents and child. The therapist would
also aim to neutralise the negative affect with which the eating
is surrounded, altering the concept of the identified patient within
the family by transforming the eating problem into an interpersonal
problem.

A different kind of experiential focus is achieved by inviting
several families to attend and working with them concurrently as in
Multiple Family Therapy (Lacquer, 1973) or enlisting those from the
family network, Family Network Therapy (Speck and Atteneave, 1973).
A multiple family session involves bringing several families together
in the same therapeutic session. This enables family members to
explore, experience and gain a better understanding, as well as
learning alternative ways of functioning, as sub-groups within the
family system: to learn about paternal/maternal/filial behaviour by
observing other fathers/mothers/children in action. This can be
particularly important for groups such as eldest children, youngest
children, adolescent boys, adolescent girls, grandparents, all of
whom tend to feel they have a 'special' or 'different' role in the
family. In family network sessions, the aim is to attempt a resolution
of the crisis or dysfunctional behaviour by enlisting family, relatives, friends and neighbours. This allows the therapist to gain an
impression of the common experiential background of the network
group (the social, educational, financial factors), to consider the
part played by the social network in the perpetuation of the presenting pathology in a family (pressures of peers, of crime and delin-
quency, social drinking, material success and social mobility) and
to attempt to use the resources available to shake up a rigid
system in order to allow changes to occur.

The experiential family therapist needs to select and build up a
repertoire of intervention techniques to suit his personality, value
system and cultural background - since these will influence his
style of working more significantly than the exact theoretical framework on which he draws. The therapist may create experiential
sessions (as above) or develop techniques within and/or between
sessions. The major experiential categories may be delineated as
drama, history, media and games, although there is considerable
overlap between them and all four might be used to implement and
process a particular strategy. Drama may be used, as we have seen,
for the re-enactment of an actual or projected scene. It is used in a
different way to sculpt a family (Duhl, Kantor and Duhl, 1973;
Jefferson, 1978) creating an image of family relationships non-
verbally through action in space, either past, present or future,
showing changes over time through the family life-cycle, the consequences of each new addition to the married couple's system and
to the family, the consequences of departures from the family (by
death, divorce, children leaving). It can also be used to create
images of 'ideal' family life and the consequences of change, by realignment or redistribution of family members within the family
(Papp, Silverstein and Carter, 1973). Role play encourages participants to learn by viewing and performing an event from a different

standpoint, by reversing roles (child and parent, male and female, therapist and family member) or by responding in different ways. This gives an opportunity for increased awareness of the effects of actions on others and the pressures felt, the possibility of assimilating information, attitudes and power that may accompany particular roles, and developing a sense of flexibility or interaction and an ability to anticipate and control the outcome of certain situations. Story-telling is another powerful form of family drama, whether using puppets (Irwin and Malloy, 1975) or play people in creating family stories, or asking family members to tell family myths, jokes or stories that have been passed down through the generations (Byng-Hall, 1979).

Family history in its broadest sense encompasses the transmission of those patterns, styles, customs, ceremonies, secrets, myths and dysfunctions that make each family unique. Transgenerational analysis (Lieberman, 1979) provides a visual diagram of family structure in the form of a geneogram which can include not only family events such as births, marriages, divorces and deaths, but also professional and family roles, emotional bonds and family patterns. Family mythology and family rituals unite family members in a powerful collective experience (Palazzoli, Boscolo, Cecchin and Prata, 1977), which can provide a therapeutic resource for both family and therapist.

The uses of media are many and various: from paper and pencil games and tasks to audio-video tapes and one way screens. Paper and pencil serve both to implement other techniques, such as geneograms, and in their own right: to see how a family communicates, negotiates and interacts during an active project, especially a non-verbal one. Asking a family to draw a house together, and resisting answering questions such as 'What kind of house?' 'Does it have to be our house?' by pointing out that a pre-drawing agreement would negate the process of non-verbal communication. Individual tasks can be given either within or between sessions: draw up a personal poster of achievements; list ten things you enjoy doing; two things you like about each member of your family; two specific things you would like to do (i) with the family as a group (ii) with each family member. Tape recorders may be used to record interactions for later analysis, to instruct a family in a task, to encourage a family member to speak to another member or to the family group indirectly. One way screens may be utilised to distance the therapists from the family, or a family member from the family - this might involve inviting a controlling, dominating or distracting family member to see how the family functions without them and to elicit their reactions and needs to the new arrangement, which is often a re-drawing of generation boundaries.

Video-tape recorders have numerous applications and effects (Alger, 1973): the instant playback allows family members to 're-experience' or 're-live' an interaction and to gain a 'second-chance' which Alger describes where 'a person has a second chance to express the feelings that originally were present, but which were unknowingly hidden during the actual incident' (p. 70). The possi-

bility of focused replay (Stoller, 1968) in an analysis post-session
or during a session, highlights repeating patterns of behaviour or
repeating sequences within a session, on a task, or during a structured exercise. Such analysis can lead to the generation of alternative modes of behaviour, the possibility of practising such alternatives and of viewing the results of new patterns of interactions.
Walter (1978) describes feedback, modelling and the interactive
effects of these two, as the most important utilisation of video tape
in enabling individual change. His conclusion is that feedback in
the form of self-confrontation and in the reappraisal of old ways of
doing things is the chief power in the use of video tape in therapy,
seeing oneself as others see you. Video is particularly valuable in
pointing out the incongruency of communication in family members -
the difference between what is said and how it is said; what is
expressed and what is intended. Watching the video monitor with
the sound turned off, family members are asked to guess what is
being said in a particular interaction (writing up the expressed
message on a large poster) the tape is then replayed with the spoken
words and the verbal message is revealed. In one family session, a
daughter under pressure from her mother clenched her fist, pounded
on her knee and shouted, 'I do love you, I do, I do!' Without the
words, the scene appeared to be one of aggression and confrontation. Family members are quite amazed when shown such incidents
in their own interactions.

Games, structured experiences and exercises, serve many functions in family therapy sessions. At their most basic level, they
give a common experience to all family members and therapist. They
can be used to identify, examine, implement, simulate and alter
particular themes in the family; such as decision making (Plan a
Three Course Meal for all the family), self-esteem (Draw up a Personal Success Shield), problem-solving (Brainstorming), acceptance
of individual differences (Draw a House together), negotiating skills
(How would you spend £50,000 as a family?), roles in the family
(Role Card Game), successful patterns (Draw a Life Graph), different levels and means of communication (Yes/No Game, Give it to Me
Game), commitment to past, present, future (Sharing Wallets). (For
references to instructions for implementation and processing
of these and other structures experiences see list following
the references.) Playing games which encourage a variety of responses, viewpoints and perspectives allows individual family members to experience the concept of multiple truths, multiple perceptions, multiple realities in the family without being overwhelmed or
intimidated. By relating the experiences of games, tasks and exercises in family therapy sessions to other experiences in other learning, or other therapy sessions, and then to experiences in other
situations in their lives, at home, at school, at work, the areas of
experience are expanded and alternative ways of behaving are
increased.

The ability to use experiential techniques successfully seems to
be a function, not so much of one's theoretical background, but of
being comfortable in a family group, being prepared to respond

actively within that group, enabling the family rather than the therapist 'do the work'. I use the analogy of an architect who might make suggestions as to what kind of house the family would like to live in, draw pictures of alternative designs, build models in space as in sculpting, advise on the advantages and disadvantages of more or less space for each family member, of the variety of uses and purposes for different rooms by different people. The therapist and the architect have the theoretical training together with their own personal knowledge and experience. The decision on the actual construction of the house has to be made by the family. It is their house, their family. Is it the way they want to live? How could it be different? What do they want to change? Do they have the skills to build it or must they start to learn them? Wynne (1973) says that one reason family therapists need to be more active than other psychotherapists is 'because the family has existed as a long-enduring system that tends to resist entry or absorb and dissolve those who enter' (p. 220). The use of experiential techniques makes family members more immediately aware of the part they play in sustaining the dysfunctional patterns of behaviour and makes the therapist more effective in helping the family to change.

REFERENCES

Ackerman, N. (1966) Family Psychotherapy - Theory and Practice, 'American Journal of Psychotherapy', 20: 405-14.
Alger, I. (1973) Audio visual techniques in family therapy, in D. Bloch (ed.), 'Techniques of Family Psychotherapy', Grune and Stratton.
Argyris, C. (1968) Conditions for Competence Acquisition and Therapy, 'Journal of Applied Behavioural Science', 4: 147-79.
Becker, H.S. (1961) 'Boys in White', University of Chicago Press.
Bloch, D. (1973) The Clinical Home Visit, 'Techniques of Family Psychotherapy: A Primer', Grune & Stratton.
Bott, E. (1957) 'Family and Social Network', Tavistock.
Byng-Hall, J. (1979) Re-editing Family Mythology during Family Therapy, 'Journal of Family Therapy', vol. 1, no. 2.
Constantine, L. (1976) Designed Experience: A Multiple Goal Directed Training Program in Family Therapy, 'Family Process', vol. 15, no. 4.
Duhl, F., Kantor, D. and Duhl, B. (1973) Learning, Space and Action in Family Therapy, A Primer of Sculpture, in D. Bloch (ed.), 'Techniques of Family Psychotherapy', Grune & Stratton.
Guerney, B., Stollack, G. and Guerney, L.F. (1971) The Practising Psychologist as Educator - An Alternative to the Medical Practitioner Model, 'Professional Psychology', vol. 3.
Haley, J. (1967) 'Advanced Techniques of Hypnosis and Therapy: The Selected Papers of Milton H. Erickson', Grune & Stratton.
Haley, J. (1972) Beginning and Experienced Family Therapists, in 'The Book of Family Therapy' (ed. A. Ferber, M. Mendelssohn, and A. Napier) Jason Aronson, New York.

Haley, J. (1973) 'Uncommon Therapy: The Psychiatric Techniques of Milton H. Erickson', Norton, New York.

Holt, J. (1967) 'How Children Learn', Pitman.

Irwin, E.C. and Malloy, E.S. (1975) Family Puppet Interview, 'Family Process', vol. 14, no. 2.

Jefferson, C. (1978) Some Notes on the Use of Family Sculpture in Therapy, 'Family Process', vol. 17, no. 1.

Kempler, Walter (1973) 'Principles of Gestalt Family Therapy, A Gestalt-Experiential Handbook', A.S. Jon Nordahls, Trykkeri, Oslo.

Kempler, Walter (1968) Experiential Psychotherapy with Families, 'Family Process', vol. 7, no. 1.

Lacquer, P. (1973) Multiple Family Therapy: Questions and Answers, in D. Bloch (ed.), 'Techniques of Family Psychotherapy', Grune & Stratton.

Lieberman, S. (1979) Transgenerational Analysis: the Geneogram as a Technique in Family Therapy, 'Journal of Family Therapy', vol. 1, no. 1.

Minuchin, S. (1965) Conflict-Resolution Family Therapy, 'Psychiatry', vol. 28, pp. 278-86.

Minuchin, S. (1978) 'Psychosomatic Families, Anorexia Nervosa in Context', Harvard University Press.

Moreno, J.L. (1946) (1959) (1969) 'Psychodrama', vols I, II and III, Beacon House, New York.

Palazzoli, M. Boscolo, L., Cecchin, G. and Prata, G. (1977) Family Rituals: A Powerful Tool in Family Therapy, 'Family Process', vol. 16, no. 4.

Papp, P., Silverstein, O. and Carter, E. (1973) Family Sculpting in Preventive Work with 'Well Families', 'Family Process', vol. 12, no. 2.

Perls, F. (1951) 'Gestalt Therapy: Excitement and Growth in the Human Personality', Dell, New York (Penguin 1973).

Rogers, Carl (1961) 'On Becoming a Person', Constable.

Rogers, Carl (1969) 'Freedom to Learn', Charles Merrill, Ohio.

Rogers, Carl (1970) 'Encounter Groups', Penguin.

Satir, V. (1967) 'Conjoint Family Therapy', Science & Behaviour Books, Palo Alto.

Speck, R. and Attneave, C. (1973) 'Family Networks', Pantheon.

Stoller, F.H. (1968) Use of Videotape (focused feedback) in Group Counselling and Group Therapy, 'Journal of Research and Development in Education', 1 (2), pp. 30-44.

Watzlawick, P., Weakland, J. and Fisch, R. (1974) 'Change'. Norton, New York.

Walter, G. (1978) Experiencing Video Tape, in 'Advances in Experiential Social Processes', Volume I (ed. C. Cooper and Alderfer), Hutchinson.

Wynne, Lyman (1973) What Family Therapists Do, Comments, 'The Book of Family Therapy' (ed. A. Ferber, M. Mendelsohn and A. Napier), Jason Aronson, New York.

Young, M. and Willmott, P. (1957) 'Family and Kinship in East London', Penguin.

STRUCTURED EXERCISES – EXAMPLES AND INSTRUCTIONS

Brandes, D. and Phillips, H., 'Gamester's Handbook', Hutchinson, 1978.
Butler, L. and Allison, L., 'Games, Games', Playspace, 18 Park Square East, London NW1, 1979.
De'Ath, E. Action Models – Learning by Doing, 'Journal of Family Therapy', vol. 1, no. 2 (1979).
Lewis, H. and Streitfeld, H., 'Growth Games', Abacus paperback, New York, 1973.
Ogden, G. and Zevin, A., 'When a Family Needs Therapy', Beacon Press, 1976.
Pfeiffer, P. and Jones, J., 'A Handbook of Structured Experiences for Human Relations Training', volumes I to VII, University Associates, California, 1969–79.
Priestley, P., McGuire, J. Flegg, D., Hemsley, V. and Welham, D., 'Social Skills and Personal Problem Solving, A Handbook of Methods', Tavistock, 1978.

18 THE 'EXTENDED FAMILY' SCHOOL OF FAMILY THERAPY

Stuart Lieberman

In a recent supervision session in our family therapy workshop a family was discussed in which the 10-year-old son, Christopher, was referred to the child psychiatry department as being totally uncontrollable. Cotherapy in conjoint family sessions was undertaken in which mother, father, 14-year-old brother and Christopher participated. Slow but steady progress occurred on a backdrop of increasing awareness by the therapists that father's sullen depressive stance had much to do with Christopher's lack of control. Finally, the therapists discovered that the family were living with another member, mother's mother. She was almost blind and had not spoken to her son-in-law for years. During a home visit by the therapist, grandmother claimed that Christopher was perfectly behaved when she was present. An extended family member living with the referred nuclear family profoundly influenced the quandary which that family faced. But extended family members need not live in intimate contact with a family unit in order to influence them. Indeed, transgenerational influences may continue long after the death of the older generation.

Amongst family therapists there are those whose theories and therapeutic strategies particularly emphasise the importance of the extended family, three-generational models, and transgenerational influences. This emphasis is sufficiently distinctive to be explored as a school within the field of family therapy.

It is interesting to note that many family therapists who worked initially and primarily with adult patients have tended to gravitate to a family therapy view which emphasises the extended family. Perhaps it is a necessary condition for family work with adults who are independent and forming families of their own while maintaining emotional attachments to parents, grandparents and other relatives.

In this chapter, I will attempt a review of the main features of the theory and practice of family therapists who have shown particular interest in the extended family.

MURRAY BOWEN

Bowen began his work in the field of family therapy in 1950 at the Menninger Clinic in Topeka, Kansas. He started by exploring the

role of mother/child symbiosis in the development of schizophrenia.
He pioneered the admission of nuclear families of schizophrenics,
between 1954 and 1956 during a family research project at the
National Institute of Mental Health in Bethesda (Guerin, 1976). He
was one of the original small group of family-oriented schizophrenia
researchers who took part in the March 1957 American Orthopsychiatry Association Panel on Family Research and the June 1957
American Psychiatric Association Panel on the Family (Bowen, 1975)
which created the initial explosion of enthusiasm for family therapy.
In 1959 the first of his theoretical concepts (triangulation or the
interdependent triad) was published as 'Intensive Family Therapy',
a paper based on his NIMH research (Guerin, 1976). Bowen later
published 'The Use of Family Therapy in Clinical Practice', his first
major family systems paper (Bowen, 1966). 'Towards the Differentiation of a Self in One's Family of Origin' (Bowen, 1972) was a seminal
paper originally published anonymously in which he describes his
work with his family of origin. It highlights the effects of the family
therapists' family on the course of family therapy.

Bowen is one of the most original family theorists in the field. He
developed a family systems theory based on his early research. He
has also added useful techniques to the repertoire of family therapists.

The Bowen theory currently consists of eight major interlocking
concepts aimed at an explanation of the interrelations between
individuals, their nuclear families, their extended families and
their transgenerational influences. These concepts can be divided
logically using the general system concept of hierarchial levels.

On the individual or whole person level, he has described two
concepts, sibling position and differentiation. These concepts refer
to the internal properties of each individual.

The sibling position and its relation to the family constellation
originated with Adler (Adler, 1927) and was later developed into
a 'family constellation' theory (Toman, 1961). Bowen's use of this
concept is based on his belief that certain characterologic traits
are determined by the ordinal birth position. Oldest sons differ
from youngest sons, oldest daughters differ from oldest sons and
only children differ from children with many siblings. These expected traits are ordered into specific sibling profiles which provide
an idealised representation of each sibling's personality.

The concept of differentiation is defined rather tortuously by
Bowen. Those individuals with high levels of differentiation of self
are emotionally and intellectually integrated with intellectual control
maintained. Individuals with low levels of differentiation of self are
said to have emotional and intellectual fusion. Here, the control of
the self is muddled so that the individual's reactions are liable to
be determined by the relationship (family) system and develop a
pseudo-self, a concept similar to Winnicott's false self (Winnicott,
1965).

The solid self is the part of the individual which is not influenced
by relationships. The level of differentiation is based on the solid
self rather than the pseudo-self. For this reason, highly differentiated individuals can withstand high levels and long periods of

anxiety with little change while poorly differentiated individuals change considerably as their pseudo-selves shift and change. The level of differentiation in an individual is fixed within them and is very resistant to change. Bowen has developed descriptive profiles of individuals who are at different levels of differentiation.

The concept of triangles and triads describes a phenomenon on the general relationship level. The smallest stable relationship system is a triangular one, involving three persons who are attached to each other. Two-person systems can only exist when anxiety levels are low and tension is minimal. The increase in anxiety or tension causes the most available and vulnerable third person to be triangulated in to form a stable relationship system. Any one of the individuals may feel anxious and tense but the system itself is maintained. Families consist of many interlocking triangles which can shift depending on the number of members in the family.

The nuclear family exists as a unit composed of various subsystems. Bowen has developed three concepts which apply to its various subsystems.

The nuclear family emotional system relates primarily to the marital subsystem. The relationship between husband and wife sets the pattern for the rest of the nuclear family. This concept was originally described as 'the undifferentiated ego mass'. Bowen assumes that spouses usually choose each other by recognising and being attracted to individuals of the same level of differentiation. The pseudo-self of each spouse interacts. This interaction may be sufficiently disturbed to cause one of three pathological family states: open conflict between partners, internalisation of the pathological interaction within one of the partners or internalisation of the pathological interactions within one or more of the children. In some families all three pathological emotional systems are acting at once.

The family projection process is the internalisation of pathological interactions within one or more children as previously mentioned. It relates specifically to the child-parent subsystem and is a concept of family pathology since it is concerned with the projection of problems from parents into the children. Bowen believes that the projection process can begin during the first mother-baby contact and that the interactions between mother and child result in a less differentiated child. The existence of a family projection process is used to explain the impairment of one particular child in a family of many siblings.

Emotional cutoff is another concept applying to the parent-child subsystem. It is a pathological way of handling the emotional separation and maturation which a child encounters when growing up. If the children cannot resolve their dependent attachments to their parents geographic distance or an internal (false self) separation may be used. These manoeuvres are considered by Bowen to be pathological and are termed emotional cutoff. Emotional cutoff is a pathologic method of separating from past influences in order to establish a life in the present.

The next concept to be described operates through succeeding

generations and so applies to the extended family. The multigenerational transmission process describes the transmission of
levels of differentiation from one generation to the next and so on.
It is an extension of the family projection process which explains
how a particular child in a family can be triangled into a lower level
of differentiation than the parents with the process continuing
through succeeding family generations until a child arrives whose
level of differentiation is so low that it is pathological. He does not
specifically state that the process also applies to children developing higher levels of differentiation than their parents but this
possibility would seem to follow logically from his reasoning.

The eighth and last of Bowen's concepts is that of societal regression. This is Bowen's first and only foray into the hierarchical
organisational level of the community and rules governing groups
of families. He believes that chronic anxiety in a society is met by
increasingly emotionally determined decisions until eventually the
society reaches a lower level of differentiation.

Bowen has introduced a number of interesting techniques for
working with families which derive from his theory. Detriangling,
reversing emotional cutoff and increasing differentiation of a self
are the three most prominent of these techniques. The first of these,
detriangling, involves work with a family subsystem, often the
parents of a labelled patient.

In detriangling, the therapist investigates a particular family
triad. He excludes the most vulnerable individual, whether child
or parent, from further sessions and arranges to meet with the
remaining family members. The therapist then sits back and awaits
triangling moves. When they come they are resisted and explored
by the therapist. The end result is, hopefully, an alteration in the
needs for triangulation by the family members which will generalise
to the family environment.

Reversal of emotional cutoff requires only one family member in
therapeutic sessions. Bowen coaches individual family members, not
necessarily the identified patient, to re-establish relationships with
relatives who were emotionally cutoff so as to reverse the process.
Once in contact he coaches them to establish a new type of relationship based on solid selves rather than pseudo-selves.

Increasing the differentiation of a self describes the method by
which Bowen attempts to raise the level of differentiation for his
patients. He asks individual patients to work with their family of
origin so as to continually detriangle themselves from the family.
The result of this manoeuvre is meant to be an increased level of
self differentiation. This technique is especially useful when faced
with adults emotionally arrested in their adolescent stage of development. While differentiating a self, the individual establishes a new
responsibility for himself as he is coached to make his own therapeutic manoeuvres. Bowen, after beginning therapy with adults
individually or in marital or family therapy, sends his adult patients
home to visit their family of origin, supervising them in their differentiating struggles.

ADHERENTS TO BOWEN THEORY CONCEPTS

Bowen's theory and practice of family therapy has been adopted in
either unmodified or modified form by many family therapists.

Dr T. Fogarty accepts the Bowen theory (Fogarty, 1975) but has
added to it the concept of the four dimensional man (Fogarty, 1974).
His theory divides the self into four dimensions: the depth dimension, object-relations dimension, interpersonal dimension and dimension of time. The self is therefore ever-changing, balanced within
its four dimensions as well as within the family setting. The balance
of the self may be wholly internal or, more usually, dependent on
the balance of the relationship system. Fogarty defines the self as
changeable depending on its context - there is no 'real self' (Fogarty,
1976a). His description of work with marital couples (Fogarty, 1976b)
consolidates his position as one in which the extended family are
considered of crucial significance.

Dr T. Hatfield occupies a unique position as a British general
practitioner whose interest in family therapy has led him to explore
a family psychiatry for general practice based mainly on Bowen's
theories (Hatfield, 1978). He considers family therapy to be part of
the third of three levels of intervention in the pathology generally
seen by general practioners, the relationship level. The first two
levels are biochemical and whole person medicine respectively. As
well as accepting Bowenian concepts such as fusion, triangulation
and differentiation, Hatfield develops the simile of a molecular
model of family interaction. One interesting concept which he
develops is that of power, a non-verbal emotional force which he
feels is possessed by all to varying degrees. Although he closely
relates power to the ethologic concepts of dominance and submission,
Hatfield feels that power is inborn and that families and society are
structured partially by this trait. 'The person who represents the
greatest threat to an individual's identity is the person who has the
most power over him.' Hatfield also acknowledges and values
Fogarty's concept of the four-dimensional man.

His therapeutic interventions in general practice involve him in
short family interviews in which differentiation and detriangling
moves are especially prominent. He takes a three-generational view
in many of his cases.

Guerin has edited a respected text on family therapy (Guerin,
1976). In it he describes the use of geneograms (family trees) as
a means of evaluating the family systems and indicated his interest
in a multigenerational model of family therapy which is more broadly
based than Bowen's concept of multigenerational transmission. He
uses fusion and triangulation as key concepts in understanding the
pathology of a family system. His text includes many other authors
who share some allegiance to the Bowen theory, as well as others
whose interest in the extended family is more directly linked to their
own clinical practice.

Dr J. Framo stands out as one of those whose family therapy practice acknowledges Bowen's work without necessarily adhering to
his theory. He has particularly emphasised the valuable contribution

that an adult family member's family of origin can make to conjoint family sessions (Framo, 1976).

NORMAN PAUL

Dr Paul is a Boston psychiatrist and family therapist whose clinical work is well respected in the USA. He became interested in family therapy in the 1950s after a pilot study on the rehabilitation of schizophrenics convinced him of the power of family influences. His training included individual, group and child analysis. He quickly established a reputation as a sensitive and skilled family therapist whose particular interest involved the impact of family losses on subsequent pathology in the family system.

Paul illustrates his transition from a traditional to a family-orientated psychiatrist (Paul and Paul, 1975) with a case study. He begins in 1960 with an individual adult schizophrenic patient, Joseph Y, and proceeds to unravel the threads of past family influences over a three-year period, determined to find the cause of the current distress. He includes first one, then another of Joseph's family members in conjoint sessions. During this voyage of discovery he uncovers family secrets related to Joseph's birth and his father's mental illness. His experience in healing this family led him to develop new techniques for exploring and healing other families in distress.

He published his first paper dealing with family therapy in 1964, a paper about the family's resistance to change (Paul and Grosser, 1965). In August 1964, Paul described his work on operational mourning in conjoint family therapy to the First International Congress of Social Psychiatry and the Sixth International Congress of Psychotherapy in London. In a classic paper he described the effects of uncompleted mourning on seventy-five families. His conclusions are summarised as follows:

> One derivative of incompleted mourning is a pervasive defense against further losses and disappointments. This reaction is often transmitted unwittingly to other family members, especially offspring. The resulting interaction patterns promote a fixated family equilibrium. Operational mourning is designed to involve the family in a belated mourning experience with extensive grief reactions. This shared affective experience can provide for empathy and understanding of the origins of current relational difficulties. The resulting effect is a weakening of the maladaptive family equilibrium with a gradual emergence of individuation and sense of personal identity (Paul and Grosser, 1965).

From 1964 to 1975 Paul developed his private practice based on unique techniques and coined the phrase 'Transgenerational Analysis' to describe the unravelling of the different family life-styles derived from the family of origin and transmitted through each marital partner to their children.

During this period of time he first worked at Boston State Hospital as a Consultant in Family Psychiatry; he became Assistant

Clinical Professor at Tufts Medical School and then moved to Harvard
University as Associate Professor of Psychiatry at Boston City
Hospital. In 1970 he chaired the Family Committee of GAP which
published the monograph 'The Field of Family Therapy' (GAP, 1970).
Unique amongst family therapists, he is now appointed as Lecturer
in Neurology at Boston University School of Medicine.

Although no theoretical system has been constructed by Paul, his
papers and clinical work provide a model of family therapy which is
discernible. The untangling of the influences of extended family
members through the use of conjoint marital and family interviews
was definitively described in his book 'A Marital Puzzle' (Paul and
Paul, 1975). Faced with a marital problem, Paul views his clients as
the end product of a long history of subtly complex collisions in
family life styles from generation to generation. He pieces together
the marital puzzle through a search into the past and present family
life of the couple rather than concentrating on their present interactions. 'Until there is evidence that family members feel more comfortable about their lives and their interrelationships, some important information is still missing that could make the family scene
more understandable' (Paul and Paul, 1975, p. 22).

His interest in family secrets (Paul, 1970) coupled with his ideas
on mourning and loss led him to conclude that often family members
must 'exorcise the ghosts of the past' from a position of dominance
within them before their current interactions improve.

Paul uses a bewildering battery of techniques to decode the transmission of family culture. He has been particularly aware of the
usefulness of audio and videotape playback (Paul, 1966; Paul and
Paul, 1975) and uses it to enable family members to gain self-
knowledge which is otherwise unavailable to them. He has also
developed a technique, cross-confrontation, which he uses during
his therapy sessions. Cross-confrontation is used to assist people
to perceive and understand that all feelings are normal and that
there are no abnormal fantasies, only abnormal behaviours (Paul,
1976). Letters, poems, audiotapes, videotapes, or films derived
from one set of family members are exposed to the views of a second
set of family members in order to stimulate an empathic emotional
response. The rationale of cross-confrontation is partly behavioural.
Paul uses it to destroy avoidances of painful emotions such as anger
and grief. Sexual material is also used to release the emotional
fears of family members of their own sexual fantasies.

Paul also assigns tasks to family members which involve tracing
past history or lost relatives. He sends individual family members
on a quest for the discovery of their roots and he will invite extended family members back to join in therapy sessions during
which shared information and feelings are used to help decode the
marital and family puzzle. His clinical emphasis on cathartic interventions often results in swift and profound shifts in the emotional
climate of a family during these sessions. Paul has also developed
the use of the multi-family group as a resource for some of his
families (Paul and Bloom, 1970). Family members from four to eight
different families are seen together weekly. Videotape playback of

individual family sessions is used in a cross-confrontation with many families present. Families share their problems; they can often generate solutions out of experience which have not previously occurred to members of a particular family. The multi-family group decreases the sense of isolation and despair within families and creates an extended family network which is often used outside the sessions.

Paul has consistently placed great emphasis on the transgenerational transmission of family culture. He does not restrict his view of this process to levels of differentiation as does Bowen. He includes patterns of behaviour and communication as well as memories, customs and emotional reactions to sexuality and death. Much of his work involves the use of the extended family and especially the family of origin as a resource.

TRANSGENERATIONAL OBSERVATIONS FROM MY CLINICAL PRACTICE

My psychiatric training was influenced by the work of Norman Paul. Through watching him I became interested in family therapy and the transgenerational influences which seemed so ubiquitous in the life of my patients, colleagues and myself. I developed my own style of working with families of adult patients, relying heavily on information gleaned from geneograms (Lieberman, 1978a). My interest in loss and morbid grief (Lieberman, 1978b) also originates in Paul's emphasis on operational mourning as a method of dealing with pathological homeostasis in families.

My recent concern has been to examine the assumptions upon which my clinical work has been based in order to facilitate their application to research questions and teaching. During this analysis I was struck with the applicability of General System Theory (von Bertalanffy, 1968) to the spatiotemporal model of a family. This led me to consider what a transgenerational theory might consist of. The following material is a summary of some of my speculations.

A transgenerational theory should detail and describe the rules governing the communication of acquired family culture, rather than inherited tendencies which are more the province of genetics. Acquired family culture is moulded into a child as its receptive, growing brain structure is fixed during critical periods of development. Alternatively it can be conveyed through association learning during the remaining life of the individual.

Defining transgenerational passage as the transmission of family tradition, custom, beliefs and behaviours, the mechanisms of passage would include the moulding of children and association learning in adults. Passage of acquired features would occur directly from living relatives or indirectly from absent or deceased relatives. A child could be moulded by the relationship field around him so that constitutive features in the parental relationship might become acquired characteristics within the child. (Constitutive features are traits which are only activated within a relationship.) In this way family conflicts would be moulded into an individual.

The family constellation theory (Toman, 1961) emphasises the importance of interlocking sibling positions as a determinant in the natural variation in acquiring family culture. It is an intriguing hypothesis which has been subjected to some scientific research with mixed results. Nevertheless, clinically the parents' sibling position does give clues to the strength of their bonds to particular children and between various members of the extended family.

Our strongest emotions are often generated by the formation, maintenance, renewal and disruption of emotional attachments (Bowlby, 1969). It is difficult to avoid using the simile of chemical bonds when describing these attachments. Bonds are constitutive in that they only exist in a relationship field. Our original need for others in close relationships stems from genetic evolutionary pressures. The primordial bonding of an infant and mother serves a protective life-giving function. But bonds distinguish family members from 'outsiders'. This function has an acquired, as well as a biologic, meaning.

Family losses occur and replacements of these losses are necessary occurrences if a family is to survive. Bonds are disrupted and the complex family molecule is permanently altered. Our individual reaction to loss is mourning, but often families react by replacing members. Replacements through marriage or birth may follow closely on the death of an important family member. The individual replacing the deceased family member often acquires the deceased member's function, traits and character or even their name. A family which is an open system can only survive as a unit if its members are continually replaced.

Families are living open systems in time and space. They must therefore consist of subsystems of differing functions with boundaries between them. One of the most common means of maintaining a boundary is to restrict the flow of information across it. Family secrets are such restrictions. Secrets may begin as feelings, fantasies or actions in one family member or may be shared between various family members. The older generation may share secrets that the younger generation never learn. The nuclear family may share a secret from extended family members. Family secrets are necessary to family life but the balance of information restriction is a changing one as family members change and mature and as families change as time passes.

Family evolution occurs with a rapidity which puts genetic evolution to shame. The changes in family culture from one generation to the next can be accomplished through many mechanisms. For family evolution to occur there must exist variations between family cultures in contact with each other, a means of passing on new cultural rules (to produce a variant moulded individual) and a difference in the fitness of such variants. New cultural practices may be equated with mutations which are then moulded into the next generation to receive some solidity and permanence. The idiosyncratic religious belief of a father may be passed on as a new religious family rule. 'Inbreeding' of various cultural elements may occur from chance, geographical or cultural isolation or may be encouraged as part of a larger cultural taboo. Hybridisation in which spouses from different cultures produce a unique family culture of their own which is moulded into the next generation is a common occurrence.

The collision of two family cultures which arises out of marital choice is an important area of interest to me. Many clinical family problems otherwise inexplicable can be traced to unresolved conflicts arising from family cultural collision. The parenting practices of spouses are particularly relevant in problems of children since the family collision is only made obvious when children are born. When family cultures collide, the resulting conflicts may become moulded within the children and later reappear in the following generations.

I have explored these concepts in greater depth elsewhere (Lieberman, 1979) but my clinical experiences have led me to view family problems from a broad cultural perspective. Those of us who share an interest in the extended family and its relationship to the problems of individual family members are bound together by our broader view of families in which the growth and maturity of younger generations is seen only as a part of a larger spatiotemporal family system.

REFERENCES

Adler, A. (1927) 'Understanding Human Nature', pp. 149–57.

Bowen, M. (1966) The Use of Family Therapy in Clinical Practice, 'Comprehensive Psychiatry', 7, 345–74.

Bowen, M. (1972) Toward the Differentiation of a Self in One's Own Family, in J. Frame (ed.), 'Family Interaction', Springer, New York.

Bowen, M. (1975) Family Therapy After Twenty Years, in J. Dyrud and D. Freeman (eds), 'American Handbook of Psychiatry', vol. V, Basic Books, New York.

Bowlby, J. (1969) Affectional Bonds: Their Nature and Origin, in H. Freeman (ed.), 'Progress in Mental Health', Churchill.

Fogarty, T. (1974) Four Dimensional Man, 'The Family', vol. 1, no. 1, 1–20.

Fogarty, T. (1976a) System Concepts and the Dimensions of Self, in P. Guerin, (ed.), 'Family Therapy', Gardner Press, New York, p. 144.

Fogarty, T. (1976b) Marital Crisis in P. Guerin, (ed.), 'Family Therapy', Gardner Press, New York, p. 332.

Fogarty, T. (1975) Triangles, 'The Family', vol. 2, no. 2, pp. 11–19.

Framo, J. (1976) Family of Origin as a Therapeutic Resource for Adults in Marital and Family Therapy, 'Family Process' 15: 2, p. 193.

GAP (Group for the Advancement of Psychiatry) (1970) The Field of Family Therapy, vol. VII, report no. 78, March.

Guerin, P. (1976) Family Therapy: The First Twenty-Five Years, in P. Guerin (ed.), 'Family Therapy', Gardner Press New York, pp. 2–23.

Hatfield, T. (1978) 'Understanding the Family and its Illnesses', monograph privately published, available from author.

Lieberman, S. (1978a) 'Transgenerational Family Therapy', Croom-Helm.

Lieberman, S. (1978b) 19 Cases of Morbid Grief, 'British Journal of Psychiatry', February, 159-63.

Lieberman, S. (1979) Transgenerational Analysis: The Geneogram as a Technique in Family Therapy, 'Journal of Family Therapy', vol. 1, no. 1, pp. 51-64.

Paul, N. (1966) Effects of Playback on Family Members of Their Own Previously Recorded Conjoint Therapy Material, 'Psychiatric Research Report No. 20', American Psychiatric Association, Washington DC.

Paul, N. (1970) The Role of a Secret in Schizophrenia, in N. Ackerman, (ed.), 'Family Therapy in Transition' Little, Brown, Boston.

Paul, N. (1976) Cross-Confrontation, in P. Guerin, (ed.) 'Family Therapy', Gardner Press, New York, p. 520.

Paul, N. and Bloom, J. (1970) Multifamily Therapy: Secrets and Scapegoating in Family Crisis, 'International Journal of Group Psychotherapy', vol. XX, no. 1, January, p. 37.

Paul, N. and Grosser, G. (1974) Family Resistance to Change in Schizophrenic Patients, 'Family Process', 3: 377-401.

Paul, N. and Grosser, G. (1965) Operational Mourning and its Role in Conjoint Family Therapy, 'Community Mental Health Journal', 1: 339-45.

Paul, N. and Paul, B. (1975) 'A Marital Puzzle', W.W. Norton, New York.

Toman, W. (1961) 'Family Constellation', Springer, New York.

von Bertalanffy, Ludwig, (1968) 'General System Theory', Penguin Books, Harmondsworth.

Winnicott, D. (1965) 'The Family and Individual Development', Tavistock.

19 FAMILY CONSTRUCT PSYCHOLOGY:
an approach to understanding and
treating families

Harry Procter

INTRODUCTION

Over the past decade, personal construct theory has come increasingly into prominence. It has found adherents among workers concerned with psychotherapy and clinical research as well as among
those concerned with purely theoretical issues. The purpose of this
paper is to examine whether construct theory has anything to contribute to our understanding of what goes on in families and to the
practice of family therapy.

This has particular relevance for this book, since strangely, construct theory in spite of being an American invention has achieved
its widest popularity among British practitioners. The theory and
its methodological offshoots are now taught in training courses designed for the whole range of helping professionals as well as to
students of psychology and sociology. In spite of being quite a
complex and elaborate theory it seems to have immediate appeal to
students who are otherwise disenchanted by the irrelevance of
much of the material with which they are presented.

Construct theory was originated by the late George Kelly, who
published his massive two-volume work in 1955. This remains by
far the most important contribution to the field. In spite of its size
and the new terminology that it introduces it is extremely readable
and Kelly can perhaps be ranked with Freud as having the
clarity of style that characterizes the writings of genuine
innovators.

Construct theory and family therapy appeared at about the same
time. It is interesting to speculate whether this was mere coincidence.
It seems unlikely. They are both expressions of American pragma-
tism. They share the optimism that things can be changed and the
belief that action that leads to change is of the most fundamental
importance. Even though they seem to have developed largely unaware of each other, I would argue that both disciplines can greatly
benefit from being cross-fertilized. This paper is designed to show
that the language of construct theory can add immeasurably to the
richness of our understanding of family processes.

My practice as a family therapist has been most influenced by
Minuchin and Haley. It remains my belief that a conception of the
family as an interacting system that tends to maintain its structure

through homeostatic processes is fundamental for effective family therapy. But personal construct theory as originally conceived is largely concerned with intrapsychic phenomena or at the most with dyadic relationships. It is clear therefore that a substantial extension of the theory into the area of multi-person relationships needs to be made if it is to serve our purpose. I hope to show that this is possible and that this makes available to the family therapist most of Kelly's theoretical and technical contributions.

It is common for those in the family therapy field either to restrict themselves to one school (and hence join its leader in his contemptuous derision of all the other schools) or to find themselves up to their necks in a confusing eclectic mixture of theories and techniques derived from a number of different approaches. Haley is surely right in his assertion that there is a discontinuous change between the various alternatives and that any kind of direct synthesis of them is therefore logically impossible. What we need is to be able to subsume all the different approaches in a theoretical framework that at the moment lies outside and at a greater level of abstraction to the various present alternatives. I hope to show that the extensions to personal construct theory outlined in this chapter (family construct psychology) provide such an overarching framework. Its theoretical 'openness' both in form and content allows a synthesis without any compromise of theoretical rigour and precision.

But it is not just theoretical approaches which must be subsumed. Even more important, we must have a framework for construing our interventions and strategies. This will lead to a much clearer idea of what to do when and increased predictability as to what the effects of each particular intervention might be. Construct theory itself has a whole range of therapeutic techniques to offer (to be found particularly in Kelly (1955) vol. 2) but it may also have things to say about what is happening when for example structural or strategic interventions are made. The task is ambitious and the brevity of this paper precludes an exhaustive treatment of the issues. A forthcoming book will take up the arguments in full (Procter, in preparation) and only the main theoretical and therapeutic issues will be dealt with here. Unfortunately, Kelly's contributions to research methodology, particularly the repertory grid, cannot be dealt with here even though the grid is probably one of the most promising tools for studying families and changes in family therapy. Readers interested in this aspect can consult Procter (1978) whilst Ryle (1975) outlines many creative uses of the grid both for research and therapy itself, particularly in the area of marital therapy. (See also chapter 13.)

THEORETICAL ASPECTS OF FAMILY CONSTRUCT PSYCHOLOGY

A brief outline of personal construct theory
Before introducing family construct psychology, a brief outline will be given, in this section, of the main theoretical premises of Kelly's psychology.

Kelly starts by outlining his basic epistemological position. He takes the materialist position that the world really exists and further, that people's thoughts really exist. However there is an infinite variety of ways in which the world can be construed and there is always a way of revising these constructions. Every person has a unique way of construing and people are similar to each other to the extent that they construe events in a similar way.

Kelly tries to illustrate how people operate by using the model of a scientist. Thus the task in which people are fundamentally engaged is the anticipation of events and their actions are taken in accordance with these anticipations. Acts can be viewed as hypotheses which are continuously validated or invalidated by experience. Ideally if they are invalidated they are abandoned and an alternative is found. Kelly is concerned to argue that any psychology should be reflexive, in other words, any assertion made about people should apply equally to the activities of psychologists themselves. What emerges is a theory that views the ordinary person compassionately. This means that the ordinary family member is in the same business as the family therapist - trying to make sense of situations and wrestling with the same sort of constraints. Construct theory's basic assumptions and its 'open' concern with process rather than content makes it epistemologically compatible with systems theory.

The central idea in the theory is the construct. This was originally defined as 'a way in which some things are construed as alike and yet different from others' (Kelly, 1955, vol. 1, p. 105). The construct is a bipolar dimension; for example, happy-sad, warm-cold, or north-south. To get closer to what Kelly meant, however, it is essential to understand a construct as a decision between a pair of alternative acts. This is made clear in Kelly's choice corollary:

A person chooses for himself that alternative in a dichotomised construct through which he anticipates the greater possibility for extension and definition of his (construct) system (Kelly, 1955, vol. 1, p. 64).

The construct is thus not just a pair of attributes or perceptions. Nor is it a continuous dimension or a scale. Kelly (1969) gives north-south as the clearest example to illustrate this point. Objects themselves cannot be 'north' or 'south' because it depends on where you are standing when you apply the description. There are no partial norths or souths between north and south. The construct is applied to objects in order to make a decision about which is further north or south when compared with another object. When one is defined as north the other is implicitly defined as south.

It is also important to underline that choices are not necessarily conscious or verbalized. Babies use constructs to make decisions and so do animals. This is important in family therapy because it underlies the theory of therapeutic change. The majority of social acts and choices are made quite unconsciously and furthermore therapeutic change does not necessarily involve insight and awareness.

Hypotheses are made by the linking of two constructs. Thus smiling-frowning might be linked to happy-sad: the hypothesis that some-one who is smiling is happy may or may not be validated. Over time a whole system of constructs evolves which the person uses to anticipate events and in particular to anticipate the behaviour of other people. So any choice becomes soaked with implications and anticipated reactions (again not necessarily at a conscious level). The system of constructs is seen as being arranged in a hierarchy with the more superordinate constructs governing the subordinates. A superordinate may be 'when I am smoking' versus 'run out of cigarettes'. A whole set of implications for social behaviour may be subordinated to these two alternative poles. The subordinated systems of constructs need not necessarily be compatible with each other, leading to apparent inconsistencies of behaviour.

Using this basic psychology Kelly has derived the most radical intrapsychic system of diagnosis since Kraepelin's. Psychological disorders are classified along dimensions of construction (for example a construct system excessively restricted in the events which it can anticipate) and dimensions of transition. Examples of the latter are anxiety (the awareness that events lie largely out-side the range of convenience of the system) and threat (the awareness of imminent comprehensive change in one's core struc-tures), the emotions being defined phenomenologically, from the inside, rather than being based on external criteria. These defini-tions supplement and elaborate our understanding of symptoms as functioning to maintain the family system.

The above example of smoking may be continued in order to elaborate these points. It may be observed that the smoker may notice that he offers a cigarette or smokes one himself whenever the conversation strays on to certain topics. The smoking functions in a homeostatic way in order to maintain the relationship in a certain pattern. From the construct theory viewpoint the smoker has a well elaborated subsystem of constructs subsumed under the 'when I am smoking' pole. He has become an expert at relating and at pre-dicting others' reactions when smoking. When he has run out of cigarettes he experiences anxiety because there is very little struc-ture subsumed under this pole. Certain constructs such as 'manly', 'me as giver', 'me as sharer' may have become linked to 'when I am smoking'. If the conversation strays to topics which he sees as invalidating these views of himself, he experiences threat when he is not smoking because he has no way of avoiding the invalidation. It therefore becomes difficult to give up and relapse becomes ex-tremely tempting when he does manage to give up.

If psychological problems are understood as occurring when the construct system is not generating hypotheses which successfully anticipate events, then psychotherapy is understood as the process of helping people to do this more effectively. Kelly sees the thera-peutic relationship as analogous to that between a research student and his supervisor. The student must do the front line work but the supervisor guides him and arranges the situation so that the student can make choices in the most elaborative way. Construct theorists have up to now restricted themselves largely to individual and group therapy formats and avoided conjoint family work. An extension of the theory is therefore necessary before it can become useful to the family therapist. Family construct psychology, the extension of Kelly's theory outlined in this paper, is discussed in the next section.

Readers interested in following up the basic tenets of personal construct theory will do best to consult Kelly (1955) a large but readable classic work. Kelly's collected papers (1969) are also worth reading. Bannister and Fransella (1971) provide a useful introduction to the field while further theoretical writings by various authors may be found in Bannister (1970; 1977) and Stringer and Bannister (1979). Fransella and Bannister (1977) contains a complete bibliography of writings in the area up to that year.

An outline of family construct psychology
Many writers in the field of family therapy have attempted to utilize intrapsychic psychologies, particularly psychoanalysis, for conceptualizing family processes. Laing, for example, proposed that each family member carried a fantasy of the entire system of family relationships, the 'family', in his head (Laing, 1969). Problems were seen to arise when 'inaccuracies', misunderstandings or disagreements occurred between the different member's fantasies. The logical conclusion is the idea of an infinite spiral of metaperspectives (I think that you think that I know . . .'), a position which can be conceptually tortuous and therapeutically unusable.

We need not fall into the same trap when extending construct theory because, as we have argued, it is epistemologically compatible with a wider, systems view. Kelly's theory is not restricted to the intrapsychic; it has simply not yet been elaborated in the area of multiperson relationships.

In his sociality corollary, Kelly (1963, p.95) states that, 'To the extent that one person construes the construction processes of another, he may play a role in a social process involving the other person.' In other words a person makes choices or behaves in accordance with how he anticipates that the other will respond. There is no question of 'accuracy' of perception here - going back to the fundamental philosophical position, there are many ways of construing the world and one is not necessarily more valid than another. The sociality corollary shows how Kelly's theory is ideally suited to the understanding of the complementary aspects of dyadic relationships. This is what the theory was designed for - individual psychotherapy.

The problem arises when we introduce more people and further when we examine groups of people who live together over an extended period of time - families. Two new corollaries were designed for this purpose by the writer (Procter, 1978):
The Group Corollary: To the extent that a person can construe the relationships between members of a group, he may take part in a group process with them.
The Family Corollary: For a group of people to remain together

over an extended period of time, each must make a choice, within the limitations of his system, to maintain a common construction of the relationships in the group.

What occurs in families is the negotiation of a common family reality or what we have called the family construct system (FCS). The FCS is understood to be exactly analogous to Kelly's notion, in other words a hierarchically organized set of family constructs, used by the family members to make choices and anticipations.

The family constructs provide the members with alternative 'slots' so they do not necessarily have to be in agreement. They do, however, share a finite set of avenues of movement. The FCS governs the sequences of contingent choices that constitute the interaction patterns of the family members. Over the years family members become highly sensitive to each other's reactions and behave together as in a 'dance' of mutual anticipation. Any change in the others' habitually anticipated choices will be experienced as anxiety provoking and threatening. An attempt will therefore be made to change the person back into predictable modes of behaviour. We can thus see how homeostasis will operate amongst any group of people living together over a period of time.

The finite number of alternatives in the FCS and their contingent nature explain the phenomena commonly observed by the systems theorists: the transfer of illness phenomenon, where another member of the family becomes ill when the identified patient improves, or where severe strain is put on the marriage when a child loses his symptoms or leaves the family. Another clear example is the 'see-saw' shift where for example one spouse is depressed and the other the care giver. From the systems point of view, it does not matter which of the pair occupies which slot. What is maintained is a certain sort of complementary relationship. This is the family's reality; they know of no other way of being together.

The concept of the FCS covers the same theoretical ground as a number of other concepts that have been proposed, particularly the family myth (Ferreira, 1963; 1965). However there is a basic philosophical difference between the theorizing underlying the family myth concept and that outlined in the present paper. The idea of myth implies an inaccurate or deceptive construction which needs correcting. For example Byng-Hall (1979) opposes 'false beliefs' to 'profound truths' and 'reality' to 'fantasy'. The FCS is understood rather as the family's total reality and it will include alternatives corresponding to the myth and its contrasting 'repudiated images' (Byng-Hall, 1973). The FCS is a construction held in the present and the family will select material from the past in order to validate it. The difference is subtle but is likely to have implications for theory and therapy. The aim of therapy is to help the family make a new construction in the present. This will lead to new understandings about what occurred in the past. The reframing of the past may well of course be a useful way to help the family negotiate a new construction.

Ideally the family has negotiated an FCS that allows each member to make choices that are consistently elaborative. Kelly uses the term propositional to describe constructs which carry no implications regarding the other realm membership of their elements. The constructs in the FCS of a well functioning family will tend to be propositional. In other words each member's actions and choices will be relatively uncontaminated by the opinions and actions of the other members.

Minuchin (1974) argues that for a family to function well there must be clear boundaries separating it from the wider social network and, within the family, separating various subsystems (for example marital, executive, sibling subsystems). In family construct terms the clarity of a boundary depends on there being a set of constructs which discriminate between the systems or sub-systems (including individuals) on each side of it. Family constructs can be classified as discriminating across the main family boundary, distinguishing the family member from people outside it or they may discriminate within the main boundary. The latter constructs govern the alternative choices that the family members make or the different role 'slots' that each tends to occupy. Kelly uses the term permeability to describe how easily new elements are admitted into the range of convenience of a construct. In a well functioning family the constructs in the FCS will be relatively permeable allowing the development and elaboration of new behaviour both in the family members and in members of the external social network and governing how easily the family allows new members to join the network.

It is important to view the family and its FCS in the context of the family life cycle. In ideal circumstances the family continuously negotiates an FCS around behaviour which is appropriate to the ages of each member. If this does not occur, if the FCS becomes fixated at an earlier developmental stage the family will experience difficulty when the time comes in making a transition in the life cycle (for example birth, a child leaving home, a child marrying). At this point, symptomatology will often develop, bringing the family to crisis point and leading them to seek help. Family therapy can be seen therefore as a process whereby the family is helped to negotiate an FCS that is appropriate to the ages of the members. When this has been achieved, transition will occur spontaneously. For example an adolescent may finally manage to escape from the family by using an across-boundary construct which is sufficiently propositional, so that the remaining members can function as a relatively autonomous unit.

Disorders of negotiation
In dysfunctional families the FCSs can be classified as evidencing various different forms of what might be termed disorders of negotiation. For example the FCS might have become excessively constricted in the range of events which it can anticipate. Thus the FCS may not be at all elaborated in the area of marital conflict. This will be observed in a family where the adolescent identified patient intervenes whenever the two parents are about to disagree, detouring the conflict on to himself. Alternatively the family may be defining themselves against contrasting figures outside the

family boundary so that whenever disagreement becomes an issue
they start discussing some bad neighbour or psychiatrist who did
not help them. These examples show how the psychoanalytic concepts of repression and projection can be subsumed within the
family construct approach.

The family constructs may on the other hand be related in an
excessively 'loose' way; in other words they lead to varying predictions. A family with a loose FCS will be characterized by chaotic
and unpredictable interaction. This is to be seen commonly in
families presenting with schizophrenic identified patients.

This method of analysis lends precision to Minuchin's rather
vague notions of enmeshment and disengagement (1974). Enmeshment may be understood in at least three separate ways. It may
imply that the family constructs are constellatory, in other words
the family constructs fix the other realm membership of their
elements. This is the opposite of propositionality and means that
any members' choice has immediate implications for other members
behaviour and vice versa. For example a family member cannot
remember an event and another member intervenes and acts as a
memory bank for him. Enmeshment may be the result of a lack of
within-boundary constructs. This form would be akin to Bowen's
'undifferentiated ego mass' (1978). Finally enmeshment may be
more simply the result of the FCS being appropriate to an earlier
developmental age level, for example in a family where the 19-year-
old anorexic patient functions with her parents as if she were 12.
Disengagement may be understood as excessive impermeability of
within-boundary constructs. New behaviour, for example parenting
in a disengaged father, is not admitted into the realm of certain
family constructs. Alternatively it may be understood as a fragmentation of the FCS, a situation in which different family construct
subsystems lead to incompatible predictions. The father here may
be understood as incapable of looking after his children because
whenever he tries, things go badly wrong.

The FCS is a genuinely interpersonal construction existing at a
systemic level of analysis. In addition it enables us to subsume
various intrapsychic concepts which in isolation have only partial
validity in family therapy. In particular many of the concepts from
object relations theory take on a fresh significance as the above
examples of repression and projection show. The projection or
introjection of good and bad objects can be understood as contingent
occupation of alternative slots in the FCS, as for example when promiscuous behaviour in an adolescent daughter is covertly encouraged
by parents who are not deriving excitement from their own sex life.
Family construct psychology has the advantage of not being restricted to either natural systems or extrafamiliar relationships. People
carry their family-negotiated realities around with them and use
them to construe individuals and relationships between people with
whom they come into contact. This adds richness to our understanding of the process of transference. Kelly's original theory can also
now be understood as a partial truth within a wider framework.

Theory of change in family therapy

The process of change that occurs during family therapy is not essentially different from that which occurs quite 'naturally' in the day-by-day and year-by-year experiences of a well functioning family. Kelly understood therapeutic change to be a process of reconstruction. This involves a change in the linkages between constructs, the addition of new constructs, the elaboration of sub-systems or a change in the range of convenience which the construct system covers. All these concepts can be extended to changes occurring in the family construct system during the process of negotiation. The family therapist deliberately aims to help the family negotiate changes in the FCS which it has failed to do naturally and spontaneously. Family therapy consists therefore in giving the family members experiences which enable them to elaborate and revise the family construct system.

Family construct psychology provides a way of overcoming and passing beyond the arguments between behaviourists and systems theorists on the one hand and the psychoanalytic and insight oriented theorists on the other. Theorists from these schools, claim that what is essential is a change in either behaviour and family structure on the one hand or for the family to gain insight into its own functioning before changed behaviour can occur. Neither is regarded by the present writer as an adequate account of the change process, having at best only partial validity. What is fundamental is that a change occurs in the negotiated family construct system. To clarify this in relation to the issues of behaviour change and insight it is necessary to return to the idea that the FCS is hierarchically organized. Constructs at the bottom of the hierarchy govern highly concrete and specific choices and interaction sequences at the level of 'microprocess'. These constructs are in turn governed by constructs at an increasing level of superordinacy. Superordinate constructs will tend to remain more stable over time and will be evidenced by redundancies in the interaction process and by themes which crop up again and again. The relationship between superordinate and subordinate constructs is dialectical. The superordinate constructs guide and govern the subordinates. The subordinates validate and maintain the superordinates.

A change in the FCS is likely to be accompanied by a change in behaviour and family structure. However this is not necessarily the case. One possibility is for the family to continue behaving as before but for this behaviour to be construed or framed in a new way. Similarly reconstruction is likely to be accompanied by the family gaining new conscious insights but this is again not necessarily the case. It is a frequent experience in strategic family therapy for massive changes to occur with the family having little or no realization that a change has occurred, let alone why it may have occurred. Cognitive awareness of the change depends on the existence of a set of superordinate psychological constructs which may or may not be present in the family members' construct systems. This will also depend on their developmental level - young children are likely to experience change at the level of feeling only. Adults are more likely to be able to provide a verbal construction as well.

Perhaps more important than how a change occurs is the question of how the change is maintained and the way in which the new configuration is stabilized. It is possible to help a family to behave in different ways but unless this is accompanied by change in superordinate construction a relapse will occur (homeostasis). For example it might be possible to get a father with a drink problem to stop drinking for a while (subordinate change). But until a revision occurs in the superordinate family construct, discriminating him (for example, cold, not part of the family) from his wife and children (as opposed to warm, part of the family), stabilization will not occur. Thus a change in family therapy will only be long lasting when the revision has permeated right through the FCS so that every opinion, every act and every memory has been reconstrued. Much of this process will happen quite spontaneously of course once the family is open to negotiation again. But the key to effective family therapy is to be cognizant that this process must occur. I suspect that the behaviourists have focused on subordinates and the analysts on superordinates. The partiality of the theories of each has led them to neglect the crucial processes occurring between the two.

The goal of family therapy is to help people to live in a system in which their habitual choices are consistently elaborative and the negotiation process flows on in accordance with the demands of everyday life. This must be viewed in the context of the family life cycle and the societal expectations of age and gender appropriate behaviour. It must also be looked at in the context of the social network (including society itself) surrounding the family. For example no amount of family therapy will be a substitute for a good school for the children. Finally the therapist must not forget that he himself is a crucial part of the social network. The therapist must disengage from the family leaving a stable and developing new system. This means that the construct of 'help' or 'therapy' must lie inside the family boundary. If it is left outside the family will soon seek out a doctor or therapist again.

Summary
Family construct psychology provides us with a broadly embracing theoretical framework which looks at the family's unique reality as structured by the family construct system. This is not merely a passive, perceived reality, but is a dynamic, active one, consisting of a system of hierarchally organized constructs or choices. The alternatives are linked together by implication and this allows each member to make anticipations which may or may not be validated in practice. This mutual anticipation and validation process may be termed negotiation. This ideally takes place continuously and in ways which can be characterized as well-functioning or disordered. Change is understood both in natural negotiation and therapy to involve reconstruction of the FCS. This view overcomes the conflict between behavioural and psychodynamic family therapists about the relative importance of behaviour change and insight.

The second part of this paper will examine some of the techniques which flow from the theory. Examples of how the theory throws light on the mechanisms involved in techniques derived from various schools of family therapy will also be given.

IMPLICATIONS FOR THERAPEUTIC PRACTICE

Family therapy is about encouraging the family to negotiate and revise its conception of reality and the way it habitually acts in accordance with this reality. The family is invited to see and act upon the world in novel ways. The family is put into situations in which negotiation can take place and through various techniques the process of change is stimulated and encouraged. Before discussing these techniques, however, the basic stance that is taken towards the family and the general method of investigating the FCS will be outlined.

Kelly attached great importance to the initial therapeutic stance to be taken with clients. He was discussing individual therapy but what he says applies just as much to family therapy. Fundamental is the acceptance of the client. Kelly defines acceptance as the therapist's attempt to employ the client's own construct system.

It involves the readiness to utilize the client's own modes of approach. . . . The therapist should attempt to anticipate events in the way the client anticipates them. He should try to employ the client's vocabulary. . . . He should give words the meanings the client gives them (Kelly, 1955, vol. 2, p. 587)

We may give as an example a medical construction of a symptom. Rarely should the therapist avoid or argue with the family about this. Full acceptance has the effect of reducing anxiety and creating the opportunity for the members to start entertaining alternative constructs, a process Kelly calls circumspection. These ideas elaborate what is occurring during the process of joining (Minuchin, 1974). Whereas Kelly was referring to the acceptance of personal constructs, we are of course discussing the acceptance of the family construct system. This involves flowing with, encouraging and utilizing the sequences and contingencies of the interaction process. For example if a child repetitively interrupts the parents' dialogue, this will be encouraged and utilized rather than blocked.

Kelly goes on to discuss two 'palliative' techniques that may be necessary initially and during particular phases of the therapy. Reassurance involves providing a simplified superordinate construction so that the client's behaviour and ideas will temporarily appear to him to be consistent, acceptable and organized. To illustrate, Kelly provides as an example what amounts to an interesting early use of paradox. He gave a girl's symptom back to her and said that 'she should not go too fast in getting rid of her limp, that "such things" were hard to get rid of all at once'. (Kelly, 1955, vol. 2 p. 656). Another technique is support which involves the validation of the client's anticipations so that he is permitted to experiment widely and successfully. Kelly lists the occasions when and when not to use these strategies.

The concept of the FCS can be used as a guide in the therapeutic interview. The process of investigating the family's alternatives, the across and within boundary constructs and the way the family constructs are linked together is not merely diagnostic. The process itself tends to stimulate interaction and negotiation.

The method itself is conceptually quite straightforward. One is basically looking for similarity and contrast and how the members of the family and social network cluster together on certain dimensions. These same methods have been used by other family therapists. Laing for example (chapter 2 in this volume) asks who in the family the boy takes after. Palazzoli et al. (1978) will ask who in the family is the most happy, the next most happy, the least happy and so on. The dialectical basis of constructs is crucial here. Thus the similarity between people implies their contrast and vice versa. This can be used by the therapist for therapeutic ends. If one wants to emphasize a difference or a boundary one connects the construct poles. If one wants to emphasize the similarity one looks for differences. Thus if one wants to intervene constructively with a marital problem it is often much more effective to emphasize the strengths in the marriage than to probe for pathology.

Having established some of the basic alternatives and boundaries, the therapist goes on to investigate the linkages in the FCS. Who lets daughter go out in the evening and who lets her back in? What does the other parent do? One is looking for how propositional, constellatory, permeable and loose the construct relationships are and searching for areas in which the FCS is functional and where it is dysfunctional.

One is, of course, particularly interested in the process but the content of family constructions is very indicative as well. The content must be continuously linked to the observable interaction process and checked for match or mismatch. But in itself the content will give important clues about fixation in the family life cycle and the age-appropriateness of the family's constructions.

Having made some hypotheses about how the FCS functions a range of therapeutic techniques are available to deal with the various disorders of negotiation. For example if the problem with the FCS is considered to be an excessive looseness, attempts will be made to tighten the system. In a chaotic family where the FCS is so loose that nothing seems to be predictable, the therapist will focus on highly concrete and specific issues and give the family very crisp and highly organized (but very brief) tasks to perform between sessions. An attempt will be made to link and tighten up the family's fragmented acts and to help them to recognize their looseness as being part of their creativity.

Another example might be a family with very few within-boundary constructs - everyone in the family is kind and considerate and helps each other. The problem is that this identity is maintained through its contrast - people outside the family boundary are inconsiderate, selfish and mean. So when 15-year-old Julie starts going out with boys and wanting to step across the boundary she has to adopt the family's contrast pole. Therapy will consist of elaborating the main construct, differentiating the people in the family and in the external social network.

It is possible to work in this manner directly sharing the therapeutic process with the family. It may however be better to work indirectly, helping the family to elaborate its reality through tasks, stories, metaphor and so on. Milton Erickson (Erickson and Rossi, 1979; Haley, 1973) is the master of indirect therapy.

Finally a few examples of therapeutic techniques from various schools of family therapy will be given in order to show how they can be subsumed within family construct psychology.

An important family therapy technique is reframing, providing an alternative way of construing a symptom or a piece of interaction. This clearly lies firmly in line with Kelly's view of therapeutic change. Kelly's techniques consist essentially in a whole series of methods of encouraging the client to reframe. The family therapist must above all be a good constructive alternativist and have the creative ability to generate an infinite variety of ways of looking at issues.

A good example of reframing, or providing a new construct, is Kelly's role-playing technique, fixed role therapy. The client is literally given a new construct and asked to try it for a period of time. In one of my own cases a client diagnosed as a paranoid schizophrenic was treated with this approach. First an assessment was made of his characteristic way of relating to others. He would scrutinize others in an attempt to assess if they were against him. He was operating with a basic construct: 'people are against me or not against me.' An alternative construct ('people are interesting versus not interesting') was chosen as being orthogonal to his own but covering the same ground. A character sketch was written around this idea. For ten days he agreed to role-play a character called John who regarded himself as an amateur psychologist. He was keen on observing others because of his interest in what makes them tick. He watched people on buses carefully and tried to work out what their interests were. A few additional items were provided, for example an interest in science fiction (he was given a novel to read over this period). The client was able to begin a fundamental process of change and started seeing all kinds of situations in a different light. This example is given because it provides a clear example of how therapeutic change is regarded as taking place. The new construct is accepted if it can be subsumed into a superordinate structure. It becomes a more enduring part of the system if a subordinate structure is elaborated under it. In family therapy new constructions can be given to each family member such as to enable them, by experimenting with new role extensions, to create a new jointly negotiated FCS.

The reframes provided will usually be positive. However, this is not the fundamental prerequisite. The important thing is that the reframe can be subsumed by the client's superordinate structure and that it elaborates it. Kelly's definitions of the various disorders

of transition are elaborative reframes. For example, hostility is defined as the 'continued effort to extort validational evidence in
favour of a type of social prediction which has already been recognised as a failure' (Kelly, 1955, vol. 2, chapter 17). Laziness may
be defined as the 'perception of things as being unchangeable'.
These are reframes which avoid the trap of moralism into which
everyday commonsense constructions often fall. A negative reframe
which is elaborative is exemplified in a paradoxical treatment of
depression (Cade and Southgate, 1979). The therapist took the
client's complaints even more seriously than the client and suggested
she was in fact not being pessimistic enough. This freed the client
to get over the block on elaborating her constructions and to discover that being optimistic was in fact more elaborative.

Reframing is also fundamental in the supervision of therapists.
Perhaps the bulk of the work of a family therapy support group
will involve helping the therapist to find elaborate reframes of the
family.

The techniques of the structural family therapist help the family
by encouraging the members to negotiate in ways regarded as
productive by the therapist. Minuchin's enactment, for example,
consists of the therapist encouraging the members to actively elaborate the family reality. Through re-enactment the therapist can
help the family validate new alternatives. For example a husband
may never share his sadness because he has learned to anticipate
anger from his wife or symptoms from his son when he starts to become sad. The structural therapist will prolong the couple's interaction, blocking interruption from the child, allowing them to have
some success in dealing with the issues associated with the sadness.
Similarly unbalancing involves forcing a member to occupy another
'slot' in order to elaborate it. Boundary marking encourages the
development of new within-boundary constructs.

In line with his view of man as being like a scientist, Kelly lays
great stress on providing tasks and designing experiments as the
example of fixed-role therapy shows. A task works by providing an
implicit reframe, changes the family's modes of relating and thus
generates new evidence for validating and invalidating constructions.
The same process occurs in the therapist's testing out and probing
the family system. A probe is a hypothesis which will elicit validating feedback. It is not a question of getting a task 'right' so much
as designing one which will provide responses from the family which
allows the therapist to discriminate between his hypotheses. One
type of task is the paradoxical task (Haley, 1963; Palozzoli et al.,
1978). This works in two ways simultaneously. It prevents the members from using certain habitual choices but at the same time vali-
dates their reality. This stimulates them to search for new alternatives. For example if a couple with a sexual problem are told to
avoid physical contact it prevents them from making the usual un-
successful attempts at rectifying the problem. Not relating sexually
has become validated by the therapist and this creates the safety
that allows them to try out new ways of relating.

Erickson and Haley's use of metaphor (Haley, 1976) can also be understood in this framework. The same patterns will emerge when a couple are eating, making love or cleaning out the garage. What is common between the situations is superordinate structure. The superordinate structure can be changed by working on innocuous topics and never arousing the resistance that for example a discussion of their sex life may engender. In one example, a couple's construct of their happy marriage was validated by saying their problem was like a tiny grain of sand in a gear box. They were able to accept that they had a problem by it being framed as minute. Further constructs could be built in using the almost infinite possibilities the metaphor generates - oil changes, syncromesh, reverse gears and so on.

Many of the techniques of the object relations theorists and analytically oriented family therapists can be understood as ways of helping the family reconstruct and dilate the FCS. Material can be used from the family's own past to invalidate its constructs and validate new and more functional realities. Interpretation consists in encouraging new construction, usually at a fairly superordinate level. Sculpting and children's play material can be used to validate the potential new structure, as it is rich in metaphorical implications.

Fragmentation is said to occur when two incompatible subordinate constructions of the same object are held. This process is akin to Klein's splitting mechanism whereby good and bad aspects of the same object cannot be entertained simultaneously. We can understand the strategies of the Kleinian therapist who may encourage the client to consider the incompatible alternatives first successively and then to encourage a consideration of the good aspect with a few elements of the bad aspect introduced. The client is encouraged to revise his system by forming a superordinate construct which can properly subsume the previously conflicting poles. Typically in a family a member will see himself as bad and another member as perfect or vice versa and this family construct comes to be maintained homeostatically. The above technique can be used in this situation. For example a couple in which the wife sees herself as totally bad and her husband as idealized may be encouraged to continue giving examples of this distinction. Some of her husband's actions can be labelled as better and some worse although all are clearly very good. Likewise some of her attributes are bad, some downright appalling. Gradually the construct is elaborated and extended and the rigid dichotomy is broken down and softened.

Finally some of the techniques from the experiential schools of therapy can be mentioned. The gestalt and bioenergetic techniques of focusing on bodily feelings and construing the body as autonomous can provide a rich set of within-boundary constructs. Massage may be used as an indirect metaphorical technique in couples who have difficulty with physical closeness.

The aim of this section has been to demonstrate how construct theory can integrate a wide variety of apparently unrelated family therapy techniques. More important, it can generate an apparently infinite variety of further techniques once the framework has been understood. Once the method has been grasped, content looks after itself and the therapist is freed to act in a spontaneous and natural manner.

CONCLUSION

It may well be argued that the language of the theoretical framework proposed here is complicated. However I believe that the underlying ideas once they have been grasped have an appealing simplicity. The advantage is having a single and all-embracing theoretical framework which at the same time allows an extremely wide ranging set of approaches and techniques to be understood and utilized.

REFERENCES

Bannister, D. (1970) (ed.), 'Perspectives in Personal Construct Theory', Academic Press, London.
Bannister, D. (1977) (ed.), 'New Perspectives in Personal Construct Theory', Academic Press, London.
Bannister, D. and Fransella, F. (1971) 'Inquiring Man', Penguin Books, Harmondsworth.
Bowen, M. (1978) 'Family Therapy in Clinical Practice', Jason Aronson, New York.
Byng-Hall, J. (1973) Family Myths used as Defence in Conjoint Family Therapy, Brit. Jnl Med. Psychol.', 46, 3, reprinted in this volume, chapter 6.
Byng-Hall, J. (1979) Re-editing Family Mythology during Family Therapy, 'Jnl Fam. Ther.', 1, 2, 103-16.
Cade, B. and Southgate, P. (1979) Honesty is the Best Policy, 'Jnl Fam. Ther.', 1, 23-32.
Erickson, M.H. and Rossi, E.L. (1979) 'Hypnotherapy: and Exploratory Casebook', Irvington, New York.
Ferreira, A.J. (1963) Family Myth and Homeostasis, 'Arch. Gen. Psychiat.', 9, 457-63.
Ferreira, A.J. (1965) Family Myths: the Covert Rules of the Relationship, 'Confin. Psychiat.', 8, 15-20.
Fransella, F. and Bannister, D. (1977) 'A Manual for Repertory Grid Technique', Academic Press, London.
Haley, J. (1963) 'Strategies of Psychotherapy', Grune & Stratton, New York.
Haley, J. (1973) 'Uncommon Therapy: the Psychiatric Techniques of Milton H. Erickson', Norton, New York.
Haley, J. (1976) 'Problem Solving Therapy', Jossey-Bass, San Francisco.
Kelly, G.A. (1955) 'The Psychology of Personal Constructs, 2 vols, Norton, New York.
Kelly, G.A. (1963) 'A Theory of Personality', Norton, New York.
Kelly, G.A. (1969) 'Clinical Psychology and Personality: the Selected Writings of George Kelly', ed. B.A. Maher, Wiley, New York.

Laing, R.D. (1967) Family and Individual Structure, in P. Lomas, (ed.), 'The Predicament of the Family', Hogarth Press, London.

Laing, R.D. (1969) Intervention in Social Situations, reprinted in this volume, chapter 2.

Minuchin, S. (1974) 'Families and Family Therapy', Tavistock, London.

Minuchin, S. Montalvo, B. Guerney, B.G. Jr, Rosman, B.L. and Shumer, F. (1967) 'Families of the Slums', Basic Books, New York.

Minuchin, S. Rosman, B.L. and Baker, L. (1978) 'Psychosomatic Families: Anorexia Nervosa in Context', Havard University Press, Cambridge, Mass.

Palazzoli, M.S. Cecchin, G. Prata, G. and Boscolo, G. (1978) 'Paradox and Counterparadox', Jason Aronson, New York.

Procter, H.G. (1978) Personal Construct Theory and the Family: a Theoretical and Methodological Study, unpubl. PhD thesis, University of Bristol.

Procter, H.G. (in preparation) 'Family Realities: An Outline of Family Construct Psychology', Routledge & Kegan Paul, London.

Ryle, A. (1975) 'Frames and Cages', Sussex University Press.

Stringer, P. and Bannister, D. (1979) 'Constructs of Sociality and Individuality', Academic Press, London.

NAME INDEX

Ackerman, N.W., 60, 62, 64, 125, 202, 246, 324
Adler, A., 340
Agnew, J. and Bannister, D., 273
Alger, I., 334
Alger, I. and Hogan, P., 202
Amerongen, S., 60
Anthony, E.J., 131
Anthony, S., 192
Apley, J., 168
Aponte, H., 298, 305, 322
Argyles, P. and Mackenzie, M., 202
Argyris, C., 329
Attneave, C., 000

Balint, M., 168, 203, 216, 295
Balentine, R.W., 258
Baldwin, J.A., 131
Bannister, D., 354
Bannister, D. and Fransella, F., 354
Bannister, K. and Pincus, L., 303
Bateson, G., 24, 61, 302, 303, 307, 311, 313, 316, 317
Becker, H.S., 325
Bentovim, A., 282, 302
Bentovim, A. and Kinston, W., 202-45, 217, 219, 223, 237
Bentovim, A. and Wooster, E.G., 239
Beels, C. and Ferber, A., 118, 136, 202, 218
Beisner, M., 238
Bell, J.E., 1, 61, 62, 68, 72, 281
Bell, N. and Vogel, E.F., 109
Berger, M.M., 141
Bernstein, B., 92
Bertallanfy, L. von, 134, 260, 273, 346
Bion, W., 63, 136
Birtchnell, J., 189, 194
Blake, W., 302
Black, D., 189, 199, 189-200
Blinder, M.G., 62
Bloch, D., 218, 332
Boszormenyi-Nagy, I. and Spark, G., 202, 238, 241, 281, 284, 288
Bott, E., 324
Bowen, M., 61, 138, 194, 339-44, 357

Bowlby, J., 1, 9-15, 60, 72, 132, 190, 192, 194, 347
Bowlby, J. and Parkes, M., 192
Brandon, D., 155
Braginski, B.M. et al., 51
Brodey, W., 62
Bronfenbrenner, U., 303, 312
Bruggen, P., 139, 143
Bruggen, P. et al., 106, 134, 142, 143, 144, 165
Bruggen, P. and Davies, G., 131-53
Burton, L., 189
Bychowski, G., 136
Byng-Hall, J., 3, 138, 288, 302, 303, 312, 322, 324, 355
Byng-Hall, J. and Bruggen, P., 154-66, 125, 144, 150
Byng-Hall, J. and Miller, M., 138

Cade, G., 316
Cade, B. and Southgate, P., 363
Caplan, G., 156
Cautella, J., 169
Chandler et al., 1
Cleghorn, J. and Levin, S., 241
Cobb, C.W., 136
Cobb et al., 175
Cohen, I.M., 61
Cooklin, A., 138, 282, 302
Cromwell et al., 216
Crowe, M., 202
Curry, A.E., 62

Dare, C., 3, 138, 281-97, 282, 288, 295, 302, 303, 304
Davies et al., 142
De'Ath, E., 3, 324-38
Deutsch, M., 92
Dicks, H.V., 107, 202, 237, 303
Dominian, J., 246
Donnelly, J., 71
Duhl et al., 326, 333
Durrell, V.G., 62
Elles, G., 1
Erikson, K.T., 33
Erikson, M.H. and Rossi, E.L., 362
Ezriel, H., 62

Fairbairn, W.R.D., 107

SUBJECT INDEX